CONTEMPORARY ISSUES IN HUMAN FACTORS
AND AVIATION SAFETY

Contemporary Issues in Human Factors and Aviation Safety

Edited by
DON HARRIS
HELEN C. MUIR
Cranfield University

LONDON AND NEW YORK

First published 2005 by Ashgate Publishing

Published 2016 by Routledge
2 Park Square, Milton Park, Abingdon, Oxon OX14 4RN
711 Third Avenue, New York, NY 10017, USA

Routledge is an imprint of the Taylor & Francis Group, an informa business

British Library Cataloguing in Publication Data
Contemporary issues in Human factors and aviation safety
 1. Aeronautics - Human factors 2. Aeronautics - Safety
 measures 3. Airplanes - Design and construction - Human
 factors 4. Flight crews - Training of 5. Air traffic control
 I. Harris, Don, 1961- II. Muir, H. C.

Library of Congress Cataloguing in Publication Data
Contemporary issues in Human factors and aviation safety / edited by Don Harris and Helen Muir.
     p. cm.
Collection of articles previously published in Human factors and aerospace safety.
Includes bibliographical references and index.
 ISBN 978-0-7546-4549-8
1. Aeronautics–Human factors. 2. Aeronautics–Safety measures. I. Harris, Don,
1961- II. Muir, Helen C.

 TL553.6.C654 2005
 629.132'52'0289–dc22

                                                              2005008921

ISBN 13: 978-0-7546-4549-8 (hbk)

MIX
Paper from
responsible sources
FSC
www.fsc.org   FSC® C013985

Printed in the United Kingdom
by Henry Ling Limited

Contents

Contributors

René Amalberti is a doctor of Medicine (Marseille, 1977), Professor of Physiology and Ergonomics (Paris, 1995), and holds a PhD in Cognitive Psychology (Paris, 1992). He entered the Air Force in 1977, graduated in aerospace medicine, and is presently head of the Cognitive Science Department at IMASSA (Air Force Aerospace Medical Research Institute). From 1980 to 1992, he was involved in four major research programmes: (i) to develop the French Electronic co-pilot for fighter aircraft; (ii) to develop an Intelligent-Training support system at Airbus; (iii) as a team member of the EC Research project MOHAWC (Model of Human Activity at Work) leaded by Jens Rasmussen; and (iv) as a co-developer of the first Air-France Crew Resource Management course. In late 1992, René was detached half-time from the military to the French ministry of transportation to take the lead of human factors for Civil Aviation in France. Soon after, in 1993, became the first chairman of JAA human factors steering committee. He held this position until late 1999. Since the he has continued to work as a specialist consultant for civil aviation authorities and has developed a great deal of research in the field of safety. He has published over 100 papers, chapters, and books, mostly on the emerging theory of Ecological Safety.

John D. Applegate is an Associate Technical Fellow in Systems Engineering/Functional Integration at Boeing Commercial Airplanes in Seattle. He leads the 7E7 Airplane Validation and Verification team developing the overall VandV plan for this new airplane model. In a previous assignment he was deputy to the Airplane Level Functional Integration Team for 767-400ER where he managed requirements and led teams working on complex integration problems. This team included airplane safety, certification, aerodynamics, weights, noise and reliability. Previously, John was Manager of Systems Engineering at PT. IPTN in Bandung, Indonesia for three years. John has chaired the Functional Integration Process Management Team where he was responsible for overall systems engineering process improvements for Boeing Commercial Airplanes. He also led the Airplane Level Engineering Strategy Team, preparing recommendations to senior management for product development improvements. John holds a MS EE from the University of New Mexico, a BS EE from Northwestern University and is a member of Eta Kappa Nu, Phi Eta Sigma and Tau Beta Pi honorary societies. He resides in Snohomish, Washington. He is an instrument rated pilot with 400 hours of flight time.

Peter Brooker has been the Civil Aviation Authority (CAA) Professor of Air Traffic Management and Environmental Policy at Cranfield University since 2001. He holds BSc, MPhil and DPhil degrees. His expertise is in air traffic control (ATC) systems and the environmental aspects of aviation, both as an individual researcher and as a manager of RandD programmes. His major current research area is the application of operational research and mathematical modelling techniques to aviation problems. His recent research work has covered safety, ATC capacity, noise and aviation cost benefit analysis. He has also worked on aviation strategic/corporate planning, and organisational and regulatory policy studies. While at Cranfield, he has published about 30 papers. His previous posts include: Head of ATC Systems Research in DERA; Chief Scientist and Strategy and Development Director in National Air Traffic Services; and as CAA's Planning and Corporate Director.

C. Shawn Burke is a Research Scientist at the University of Central Florida, Institute for Simulation and Training. Her expertise includes teams and their leadership, team adaptability, team training, measurement, evaluation, and team effectiveness. Dr. Burke has presented at 62 peer-reviewed conferences, published 31 articles in scientific journals and books related to the above topics, and has assisted organizations in evaluating aviation-related team training programs and reducing medical errors. She is currently investigating team adaptability and its corresponding measurement, issues related to multi-cultural team performance, leadership, and training of such teams, and the impact of stress on team process and performance. Dr. Burke earned her doctorate in Industrial/Organizational Psychology from George Mason University and is a member of the American Psychological Association, the Society for Industrial and Organizational Psychologists, and Academy of Management. Dr. Burke serves as an ad-hoc reviewer for *Human Factors* and *Quality and Safety in Healthcare*.

Sidney W.A. Dekker is Professor of Human Factors at the Lund University, Sweden. He received an M.A. in Organisational Psychology from the University of Nijmegen and an M.A. in Experimental Psychology from Leiden University, both in the Netherlands. He gained his Ph.D. in Cognitive Systems Engineering from The Ohio State University, USA. He has previously worked for the Public Transport Cooperation in Melbourne, Australia; the Massey University School of Aviation, New Zealand; and British Aerospace, UK. His specialties and research interests are human error, reactions to failure and criminalisation, organizational resilience and system safety. He has some experience as a pilot, type trained on the DC-9 and Airbus A340. His books include *The Field Guide to Human Error Investigations* (2002) and the forthcoming *Ten Questions About Human Error: A New View of Human Factors and System Safety*.

Francis T. Durso is Professor of Psychology and Director of the Cognitive Ergonomics Lab at Texas Tech University in Lubbock, Texas. Frank is senior editor of Wiley's upcoming *Handbook of Applied Cognition (2nd Edition)* and is on the editorial boards of the *Journal of Experimental Psychology (Applied)*; *Human Factors*, and *Air Traffic Control Quarterly*. Frank's research interests centre on cognitive processes in dynamic environments. Much of his work has been under a cooperative agreement with the United States Federal Aviation Administration.

Graham D. Edkins was appointed to the position of Director Public Transport Safety in May 2003 and has overall responsibility for the safety accreditation and regulation of rail, tram and bus services within the Australian State of Victoria. Graham leads the Public Transport Safety Group in implementing a more contemporary approach to transport safety regulation in Victoria and adding value to national policy matters on public transport safety regulation. Graham has extensive experience in safety management, accident investigation and human factors within both the aviation and rail industries with previous roles with Qantas Airways, the Bureau of Air Safety Investigation and within the rail industry. He has provided expert safety and human factors advice to safety regulators, public inquiries and private sector organisations and is co-author of a book on system safety and human factors called *Innovation and Consolidation in Aviation* published by Ashgate in 2003. Graham is the current President of the Australian Aviation Psychology Association (AAvPA) and past Vice Chairman of IATA's Human Factors Working Group. His qualifications include a Bachelor of Science (BSc), a Masters Degree in Organisational Psychology (MPsych) from Curtin University and a PhD from the University of Otago, which involved the development and evaluation of an airline safety management programme called INDICATE.

Rhona Flin is Professor of Applied Psychology in the School of Psychology at the University of Aberdeen. She is a Chartered Psychologist, a Fellow of the British Psychological Society and a Fellow of the Royal Society of Edinburgh. She directs a team of psychologists (Industrial Psychology Research Centre, www.abdn.ac.uk/iprc) working with high reliability industries on projects concerned with the management of safety and emergency response. The group has worked on projects relating to aviation safety (funded by EC and CAA), leadership and safety in offshore management (HSE and oil industry), team skills and emergency management (nuclear industry) and anaesthetists' and surgeons' non-technical skills (NES, RCSE).

Klaus-Martin Goeters is Head of Department of Aviation and Space Psychology at DLR-German Aerospace Center in Hamburg, Germany. He started his scientific career at DLR back in 1970. A special interest in scientific diving led to a mission as aquanaut in the underwater laboratory 'Helgoland' in 1973 and several studies concerning the environmental influences of the underwater habitat on performance and social life. He earned his Ph.D. in 1980 from the University of Hamburg where he is also teaching. His main work is in differential and diagnostic psychology and its application to the aerospace environment (mainly selection of science astronauts, pilots and air traffic controllers). Dr. Goeters is Board Member of the European Association for Aviation Psychology (EAAP). Besides numerous articles and technical reports he is the editor of *Aviation Psychology: A science and a Profession* (1998) and *Aviation Psychology: Practice and Research* (2004), also published by Ashgate.

R. Curtis Graeber is Chief Engineer for Human Factors at Boeing Commercial Airplanes. Previously he served Manager of Flight Deck Research and as Chief, Crew Operations, for the 737-600/700/800 Airplane Programme with design responsibility for flight crew, maintenance, and cabin human factors. He holds Ph.D. in Neuropsychology and was a research scientist at the Walter Reed Army Institute of Research and at NASA's Ames Research Center where he led the flight crew fatigue research program and served as Chief of the Flight Human Factors. He has authored over 80 scientific-technical articles and chapters and is a Fellow of the Royal Aeronautical Society and the Aerospace Medical Association. He also served as the Human Factors Specialist for the Presidential Commission on the Space Shuttle Challenger Accident. He has received numerous awards including the Guild of Air Pilots and Air Navigators' 'Cumberbatch Trophy', the Aerospace Medical Association's Boothby-Edwards Award, an *Aviation Week and Space Technology* 'Laurel' (1999) for his efforts to reduce crew error, and the International Federation of Airworthiness 'Whittle Safety Award' for co-developing the Maintenance Error Decision Aid. Dr. Graeber is a Visiting Professor at the College of Aeronautics, Cranfield University, UK, and in 2003 was selected as a Senior Technical Fellow of The Boeing Company. He chairs the Flight Safety Foundation's ICARUS committee, and co-chairs the Ultra Long-Range Crew Alertness Initiative and the FAA/EASA Part 25 Harmonisation Working Group on human error in flight deck design.

Don Harris is Reader in Human Factors Engineering in the Human Factors Group at Cranfield University. Since completing his PhD in 1988 on the subject of Human Factors in road traffic accidents, his principal teaching and research interests have been in the design and evaluation of flight deck control and display systems. Until recently he was also an aircraft accident investigator (specialising in Human Factors) on call to the British Army Division of Army Aviation. He is the Chairman of the International Conferences series on Engineering Psychology and Cognitive Ergonomics. Don sits on the UK National Advisory Committee of Human Factors for Aerospace and Defence and the FAA/JAA Human Factors Harmonisation Working Group. Don was editor of the volume *Human Factors for Flight Deck Design* and is also co-editor in chief of the academic journal, *Human Factors and Aerospace Safety* (also published by Ashgate). He sits on the editorial boards of the *International Journal of Applied Aviation Studies* and the *International Journal of Cognition, Technology and Work.*

Hans-Jürgen Hörmann is currently the Safety and Human Factors Manager at Boeing Research and Technology Europe where he is leading research activities on safety assessment and human performance enhancement. In 1987, he received his PhD in applied psychology from the Free University in Berlin. He then worked for 17 years as aviation psychologist for the German Aerospace Centre (DLR). At DLR he had been involved in pilot and air-traffic controller selection, cross-cultural research, and CRM training development for the aviation industry. Most recently, he participated in European research projects on designing and evaluating new human factors training programs for flight-deck crews. He also represents the European Association of Aviation Psychology on the Editorial Board of the *International Journal of Aviation Psychology.*

Barry Kirwan was born in Farnborough, England, gained degrees in Psychology, Ergonomics, and Human Reliability Assessment. He worked for several years as a consultant in offshore oil and gas, nuclear power, and chemical industries, on safety and human factors projects. He moved to British Nuclear Fuels and became responsible for human reliability in the design of their new plants. He recruited and ran a team of human factors professionals dealing with many aspects of safety and human error. He then moved to Birmingham University and lectured Human Factors and Engineering students for five and a half years. He then became Head of Human Factors for National Air Traffic Services, managing a team of Human Factors staff and contractors. He extended the traditional HF work in NATS to consider human error and various safety aspects of new and existing projects and systems, as well as feeding more human factors into the design of new systems. For the past four years he has been with Eurocontrol, working on Human Factors and Safety projects, and now runs the Safety Research Team, who aim to develop ways of making European ATM safer.

Carol A. Manning is supervisor of the Training and Organizational Research Lab in the Aerospace Human Factors Research Division at the FAA's Civil Aerospace Medical Institute, where she has worked since 1983. Carol has conducted research in the areas of air traffic controller selection and training and ATC performance measurement. She participated in a number of studies that investigated the use of paper flight progress strips in en route and tower air traffic control and methods for replacing them with electronic flight progress data. She also participated in the development and evaluation of objective measures of controller taskload based on routinely recorded ATC data.

Lynne Martin has worked in aeronautical human factors at NASA Ames Research Center, California, for seven years. In addition to research into CRM and NOTECHS, her work has included researching Air Traffic Management tools, controller-pilot data link communications, and decision-making training. She has a doctorate in Applied Social Psychology.

Ken I. McAnally is a Senior Research Scientist in human factors in the Air Operations Division of the Defence Science and Technology Organisation, Australia. He received a PhD in physiology and pharmacology from the University of Queensland in 1990 and has worked in the Department of Otolaryngology of Melbourne University, the laboratory of psychoacoustics of the University of Bordeaux and the University Laboratory of Physiology at Oxford before joining DSTO in 1996. His research interests include sensory neuroscience and experimental psychology.

James W. Meehan is a Senior Research Scientist in the Air Operations Division of the Defence Science and Technology Organisation. He holds a PhD in experimental psychology from Monash University, and was a French Government Scientific Fellow at the Centre d'Etudes et de Recherches de Médecine Aérospatiale. He has a special interest in human perception and cognition, and organizational psychology, particularly applications in aeronautical and medical systems.

Helen C. Muir is Professor of Aerospace Psychology at Cranfield University, Head of Department of Human Factors and Air Transport and Director of the Cranfield Institute for Safety, Risk and Reliability. She is a Chartered Psychologist and a Fellow of the Royal Aeronautical Society and Director of the Cranfield Institute for Safety, Risk and Reliability. Her personal research activity included the development of a unique methodology for conducting research into factors influencing survival in accidents. The research conducted by her team has led to the UK becoming recognised as world leaders in the field of safety and air accidents. Her department's activities include postgraduate teaching in the fields of aviation human factors, occupational psychology, ergonomics and human factors and health and safety. The academic and commercial research activities include passenger safety, human factors and air transport operations, defence psychology, road and rail safety, human factors and accident investigation, and confidential incident reporting programmes.

Herman Nijhuis is currently Human Factors Expert at EUROCONTROL Headquarters in Brussels. After studying psychology at the University of Amsterdam and Ergonomics at University College London, he became a Consultant in Aviation Human Factors at the National Aerospace Laboratory (NLR) in Amsterdam, the Netherlands. In 1997 he moved to the post of Head of Human Factors in Air Traffic Control, also in NLR. During his career he has covered a broad spectrum of the human factors and usability field. He was involved in all aspects of system design, like organising brain storming sessions, defining user requirements, writing human machine interface specifications, doing task analyses, carrying out experiments, simulations and validations, doing expert reviews, designing and carrying out of training programmes, designing questionnaires, doing work load measurements and applying many other techniques and methods. In his current position he is developing a long-term strategy for research and development in human factors, human resources and training in air traffic management.

Amy R. Pritchett is an Associate Professor in the School of Aerospace Engineering and a joint associate professor in the School of Industrial and Systems Engineering at the Georgia Institute of Technology. Her research encompasses cockpit design, including advanced decision aids; procedure design as a mechanism to define and test the operation of complex, multiagent systems such as air traffic control systems; and simulation of complex systems to assess changes in emergent system behavior in response to implementation of new information technology. Dr. Pritchett is the editor of Simulation: Transactions of the Society for Modeling and Simulation for the air traffic area; associate editor of the AIAA Journal of Aerospace Computing, Information, and Communication; technical programme chair for the aerospace technical group of the Human Factors and Ergonomics Society; and co-chair of the 2004 International Conference in Human-Computer Interaction in Aerospace (HCI-Aero).

Eduardo Salas is a Professor of Psychology at the University of Central Florida where he was selected as a Trustee Chair Professor and holds an appointment as Programme Director for Human Systems Integration Research Department at the Institute for Simulation and Training. He is the Director of UCF's Ph.D. Applied Experimental and Human Factors Program. Dr. Salas has co-authored over 200 journal articles and book chapters and has co-edited 11 books. His expertise includes assisting organizations in how to foster teamwork, design and implement team training strategies, facilitate training effectiveness, manage decision making under stress, and develop performance measurement tools. He is currently working on designing tools and techniques to minimize human errors in aviation and medical environments. Dr. Salas is a Fellow of the American Psychological Association, the Human Factors and Ergonomics Society, and a recipient of the Meritorious Civil Service Award from the Department of the Navy. He received his Ph.D. degree in industrial and organizational psychology from Old Dominion University.

Gideon Singer is an Experimental Test Pilot in the Flight Operations Department of Saab Aircraft AB in Sweden. Gideon started his career as a fighter pilot in the Israeli Air Force where he served until moving to Sweden. Since graduating from the Royal Technical Institute in Stockholm and Test Pilots School in the UK, he has worked on developing and certifying commercial aircraft in Europe. His work included participating in new products such as the Saab 2000, new Saab 340 derivatives and the Fairchild-Dornier 728. In recent years Gideon has been performing research in the field of Human factors in the cockpit environment and had also completed his PhD in this area. He has been involved in several committees addressing human factors in aviation in particularly regarding cockpit design aspects. Gideon lives in Linköping with his wife Anna and son Adam and daughter Mira. When not flying he enjoys motorcycling, wine tasting and just reading a good book in the sun.

Geoffrey W. Stuart is a Principal Research Fellow at the University of Melbourne. He received a Ph.D. in experimental psychology from Monash University in 1986, and was a Research Fellow in the Centre for Visual Sciences at the Australian National University from 1989 to 1991. He has worked as a consultant at the Defence Science and Technology Organisation since 1998. His research interests include visual perception and attention and their application to aviation human factors.

Lauren Thomas holds a BA in Psychology from the University of Liverpool and an MSc in Applied Psychology from Cranfield University. A chartered occupational psychologist, she is a lecturer in the Human Factors Group at Cranfield University. She is currently the course director of the MSc in Applied Psychology, and she also teaches on the MSc in Human Factors and Safety Assessment in Aeronautics and the MSc in Safety and Accident Investigation. Lauren's teaching areas include aircraft cabin safety, passenger behaviour in the aviation and rail industries, and human factors for accident investigation. Lauren's research and consultancy interests are in passenger safety, and recruitment and training in safety critical industries. Recent activities have included include the conduct of experimental aircraft cabin evacuations, evaluations of emergency signage for aircraft and railway passengers, validation of psychometric tests used in military recruitment and selection, and designing interview skills training for accident investigators.

Claude Valot is a Senior Research Psychologist, employed in the Cognitive Sciences department of the Aerospace Medical Research Institute (IMASSA) where he has been since 1980. He received his PhD in ergonomics from Toulouse

University. He has been involved in numerous human factors application areas in both military and civilian aeronautics including maintenance, development of human factors courses, human error research, violations and human centred design. Claude is a consultant to the CRM programmes in the French Air Force, the Navy and Army aviation. He is also involved in the Human Factors certification team and is a consultant for French Civil Aviation Authority. His current research interests include: automation in the cockpit; reasoning, decision making and temporal constraints; and metacognition.

Katherine A. Wilson is a Doctoral Candidate in the Applied Experimental and Human Factors Psychology program at the University of Central Florida (UCF). She earned a B.S. in Aerospace Studies from Embry-Riddle Aeronautical University in 1998 and a M.S. degree in Modelling and Simulation from UCF in 2002. In 2002, she was awarded the I/ITSEC Graduate Student Scholarship for her academic achievements and research conducted as a research assistant at the Institute for Simulation and Training. Katherine is the lead graduate student on a project funded by the Army Research Laboratory focusing on improving multicultural team adaptability. She is also working on several other projects which are examining teams in the aviation and healthcare communities. Finally, she has co-authored nine articles, six book chapters and has represented UCF at several national conferences.

Rebecca Wilson obtained her first degree from University College Northampton, and her MSc in Applied Psychology was awarded by Cranfield University. Rebecca is currently a Teaching Fellow within the Human Factors Group and contributes towards the MSc in Applied Psychology and the MSc in Human Factors and Safety Assessment in Aeronautics. Her research interests are cabin safety, aircraft passenger evacuations and aviation psychology. Rebecca is completing a PhD in passenger safety in very large transport aircraft and holds a BPS Level A certificate of competence in occupational testing.

Acknowledgements

We must express my deepest thanks to all those people who have contributed their works initially to the journal *Human Factors and Aerospace Safety* and subsequently to this volume. Their efforts are most appreciated.

We also need to thank Guy Loft of Ashgate, whose help and advice in the preparation and marketing of this book was most welcome, and Pauline Beavers also of Ashgate, for her help in turning the manuscripts into papers and the papers into a book worthy of publishing.

If we have omitted anyone from this list, can we apologise now, however, they can rest assured that their efforts were most appreciated.

Don Harris and Helen C. Muir
Cranfield University

Preface

The International Journal *Human Factors and Aerospace Safety* has recently completed its fourth year of publication. In most issues of the Journal an Internationally-respected researcher is invited to contribute a position paper, reviewing and criticising an aspect of safety-related Human Factors. In the first four years of publication, position papers have addressed safety issues in the broad areas of human factors and aircraft design, aviation operations and training, and air traffic management. This volume collates these papers and other selected manuscripts from the Journal into a single volume. The objective in doing so is to allow a wider audience access to these critical extended essays.

When the papers are assembled together it is also noticeable that no longer can the components in the aerospace system be considered in isolation. Safety can only be assured through the integration of its disparate component parts – design, operations, training, air traffic management and passenger safety. All must work together in harmony.

We hope that you find these papers stimulating and enjoyable.

Section One
Design

1 Integrated safety systems design and human factors considerations for jet transport aeroplanes

John D. Applegate and R. Curtis Graeber

Introduction

Improving flight safety is a goal expected by the flying public and shared by all aeroplane manufacturers and operators. The history of commercial aviation demonstrates the industry's success in achieving this goal with each new generation of aircraft. This progress is reflected in the hull loss accident rates for the world-wide commercial jet fleet as shown in figure 1.

The accident rate for recent designs, such as the B757, B767 and A310, are considerably better than the first generation jet aeroplanes, such as the B707 and DC-8. Recently certified designs, such as the B777, A330 and A340, have not experienced hull losses as of this writing, but are expected to demonstrate improved safety as a result of improvements in the systems safety design processes and more robust implementations of the designs.

A major factor in this expected improvement is the commitment of the aeroplane manufacturers to improved safety, together with improved certification regulations and continuing airworthiness programmes from the regulatory authorities, including the United States Federal Aviation Agency (FAA) and the European Joint Airworthiness Authority (JAA). The potential contribution of new flight deck technology to improved safety is an integral part of this process.

This paper was first published in Human Factors and Aerospace Safety 1(3), 2001, pp. 201-221

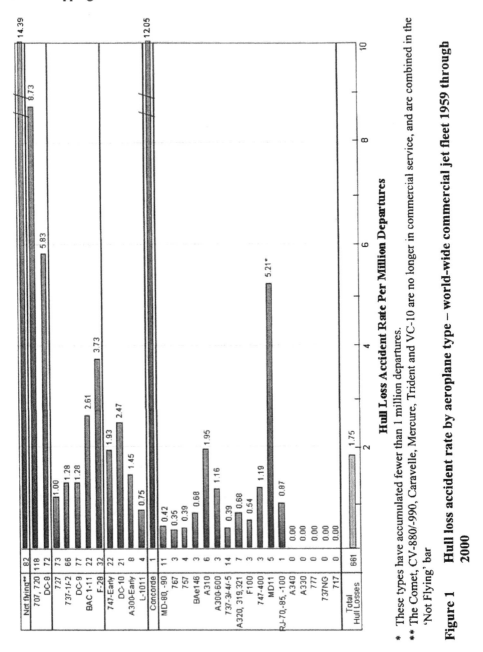

Figure 1 Hull loss accident rate by aeroplane type – world-wide commercial jet fleet 1959 through 2000

* These types have accumulated fewer than 1 million departures.
** The Comet, CV-880/-990, Caravelle, Mercure, Trident and VC-10 are no longer in commercial service, and are combined in the 'Not Flying' bar

As shown in figure 2, air travel on large commercial jet aircraft is expected to continue to expand in the years ahead. Annual departures are predicted to increase from the current level of approximately 17,000,000 to 30,000,000 in 2015. This will be accomplished by an expected increase in the number of transport aeroplanes in service from 15,800 today to over 23,000 by the end of this time period. If the accident rate were to be held constant at the level of the last five years, about one per million departures, this could result in a serious accident every one or two weeks in 2015. Unfortunately, the perception of safety in air travel by the flying public is based to a large extent on the frequency of news reports rather than the accident rate statistics, the legitimate basis for risk assessment. Allowing this perception to develop is considered unacceptable by the transport aviation industry. Further reductions in the accident rate are required to prevent this situation from occurring. As a minimum, a two-fold improvement is required but the goal should be greater, perhaps a reduction of as much as a factor of five, to ensure that the achieved results are acceptable.

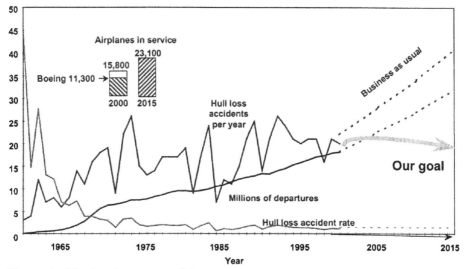

Figure 2   Need to improve safety

There are many areas that offer potential for safety improvements in large commercial aeroplane operations. These include improved safety in flight operations, maintenance and air traffic management, improved infrastructure and changes in design of the aeroplanes themselves as a result of applying lessons learned, new design and integration methods, new safety-related features and improved regulatory oversight.

Most of this overall improvement will result from improvements in flight operations safety. Accident trends indicate that future safety gains will depend more and more on our ability to reduce the number of accidents involving human error, especially for the flight crew. While flight crew error is one of the factors in a substantial portion of the accidents, the aeroplane and its systems have a strong influence on crew performance. For instance, controlled flight into terrain, a leading cause of fatalities, could be reduced by providing better situation awareness through the use of global positioning satellite navigation systems, enhanced ground proximity warning systems, and vertical situation displays now being implemented.

Analysis of the historical accident data collected by Boeing shows that about ten percent of the accidents involve aeroplane system failures. This type of failure includes loss of availability, functional errors, requirements errors and design errors. A proportional improvement in the safety of the aeroplane systems is required if the overall goals of achieving a lower accident rate are to be accomplished.

This paper will discuss improved safety methods used in the design of aeroplanes and their systems that implement the functions of those aeroplanes. The overall goal of Boeing's safety philosophy is to help prevent accidents and to ensure that the aeroplane's design neither causes nor contributes to an accident. Continuous improvement in the system safety design process and methods is an essential part of this commitment. Included in this effort is a renewed attempt to better address human factors concerns in the design process, particularly with regard to new flight deck technology, and to work closely with Airworthiness authorities to achieve this goal. Much of this effort is currently being directed towards the development of state-of-the-art certification processes through support of the FAA-JAA Harmonisation Working Group on Flight Crew Error and Flight Crew Performance Considerations in the Flight Deck Certification Process (Human Factors HWG). Success will largely depend on developing reliable and usable methods and tools to take human behaviour into account as new flight deck technology is developed and integrated into current or future flight deck designs. The evolving system safety design processes described below offer a fertile opportunity to incorporate such methods into the aeroplane design process. Improving our ability to address flight crew user issues will also depend on developing valid cross-cultural user requirements that can provide significant safety benefits.

Safety design process evolution

System safety design processes have been subject to conflicting pressures in the past two decades as technology changes allowed greater use of digital implementations, as shown in table 1. First generation aeroplanes, such as the B707/B727, were designed with relatively independent systems with only minor requirements for integration across systems. The management of many aeroplane functions was handled by the flight engineer. The B737 was implemented with simplified systems but still used analogue approaches. The elimination of the flight engineer added to the requirements for functionality, especially for fuel and engine management and for the electrical system.

The B757/B767 aeroplanes were the first Boeing models to make use of digital implementations. The system architecture for this generation of aeroplane was based on 'digitising' the former analogue designs. Moderate integration in design was required. The real departure toward digital implementation occurred with the B777. It utilised a new architecture for the systems, with much greater use of microprocessors. Consequently, the B777 functions are implemented through highly integrated systems compared to those of previous models. This level of integration expands the use of global resources which provide input parameters to a wide variety of systems. Digital fly-by-wire technology also required more extensive integration than was required on previous Boeing aeroplane designs.

Table 1   Systems evolution at Boeing

B707/B727	Little integration, brick wall systems Flight engineer for real-time systems integration
B737-100/200	Simplified systems - brickwall, analogue systems 2-crew real-time systems integration
B757/B767	Digital systems, traditional architecture Moderate integration in design
B777	Digital systems, new architecture Interdependent systems, highly integrated design

This change in technology from the previous analogue or hard-wired design to the widespread use of microprocessors with embedded software to control the operation of the systems enabled large potential improvements in reliability by replacing electromechanical analogue or analogue hybrid systems with microprocessor designs. This also caused new systems to be defined that supplied common functions used by multiple traditional systems.

Increased system interdependence and integration

The latest generation of aeroplanes has also been subject to greater demands for functionality from customers. Complex integrated displays and airborne information systems, and demands for improved performance through the use of digital fly-by-wire flight controls are examples of expanded functionality which is possible with the use of microprocessors. The additional functionality has increased the degree of integration of the aeroplane as a whole accompanied by considerable reliability gains enabled through the use of digital implementations.

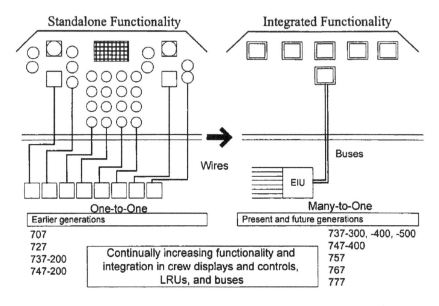

Figure 3 Trends in systems architecture

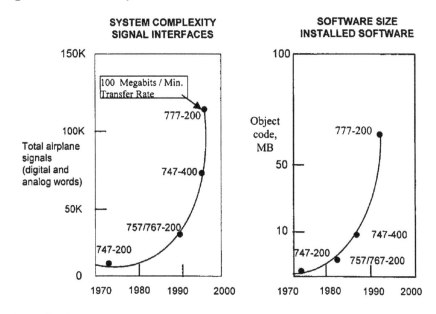

Figure 4 Growth in systems

8

The increased complexity and integration also impacted the system safety design as a result of greater interdependencies among the systems. Figure 3 summarises these trends, and figure 4 provides some specific examples of the growth in system signal interfaces and in the size of installed software for various aeroplane models. Recent aeroplanes, such as the B777, can be categorised as having systems that are more interdependent and highly integrated compared with earlier design implementations.

The increase in complexity of recent aeroplane systems together with the greater degree of integration of the systems to implement aeroplane level functions prompted the regulatory authorities to initiate several industry/government teams to prepare recommendations for ways to show compliance with the applicable safety requirements. Two teams produced new aerospace recommended practices (ARP) under the auspices of SAE International which will be referenced by the FAA/JAA as guideline material useful in demonstrating compliance with FAR/JAR Part 25.1309. These are ARP4754, 'Certification Considerations for Highly Integrated or Complex Airplane Systems,' and ARP4761, 'Guidelines and Methods for Conducting the Safety Assessment Process on Civil Airborne Systems.'

Together these two documents describe preferred processes for the development of complex aeroplane systems. The two documents should be viewed as companions with many cross references and connections. ARP4754 describes systems engineering processes, while ARP 4671 describes the closely related safety assessments. Together they recommend a structured, top down approach to the design and validation process for such highly integrated aeroplane systems. Figure 5 shows the high level relationship between these two processes, and the related hardware and software processes, such as RTCA DO-178B, 'Software Considerations in Airborne Systems and Equipment Certification.' Another committee sponsored by RTCA, SC-180, has developed the hardware standard.

Safety process improvements for the B777

First and second generation aeroplane designs were based on aeroplane architectures with relatively independent systems designs and a low level of integration, except for common electrical or hydraulic power sources. These designs did not utilise structured design approaches to achieve integration because of the simple interfaces between the systems. Each system had its own flight crew interfaces using analogue instruments and the controls and indicators found in the flight deck. FAA certification of this type of system implementation was accomplished with a certification process for each system, including a certification plan (analysis or testing) to show compliance with the regulations and a certification compliance summary. The safety aspects of these designs did not

9

require extensive consideration of the interfaces because most of the aeroplane level functions were implemented using a single system for each group of functions. This approach to certification has been referred to as the 'system by system' method whereby safety is achieved by ensuring that each system complies with the certification requirements.

Boeing recognised that this previous approach would have limitations for the highly interdependent B777 aeroplane architecture. Improved systems engineering methods and safety assessment procedures were implemented to ensure that the complex and highly integrated architecture would be safe, and that improved service readiness would be possible upon initial delivery of the B777 aeroplane.

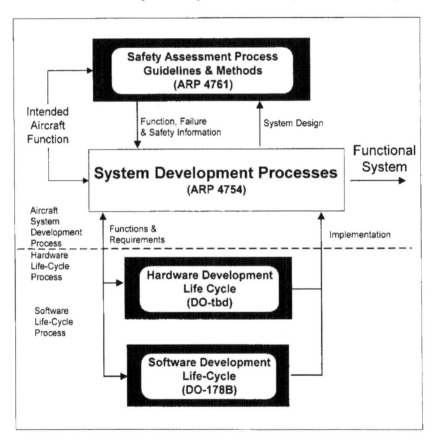

Reprinted with permission from SAE document ARP4754 ©1996 Society of Automotive Engineers, Inc.

Figure 5   Relationships between processes

The concept of a lifetime safety cycle (LSC), shown in figure 6, means that safety concerns are not limited to the engineering development phase of a programme, but also depend on the production and in-service safety programmes. This process provides a closed loop from the requirements stage of the programme, through the design implementation, into the manufacturing phase of the prototype aeroplanes, through the validation and certification and finally, throughout the entire service life of the aeroplane model.

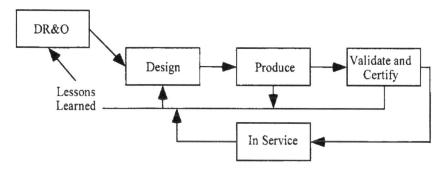

Figure 6   Lifetime safety cycle

The Boeing safety philosophy is based on a reliable process designed to capture more than 75 years of Boeing knowledge.   This philosophy includes an independent safety organisation to provide safety process management and an aeroplane-level perspective together with accident and incident data collection and analysis. It also ensures that the results of this data analysis are fed back into the design process, either for new model developments, or for safety-based design changes during production, or to aeroplane models in service. The following paragraphs describe this key process in more detail.

Requirements

Requirements are an essential first step in developing a safe aeroplane. Boeing has traditionally used Design Requirements and Objectives (DRandO) documents to clearly define the aeroplane level requirements for a new development programme. The DRandO contains all of the safety, performance, environmental, regulatory, new technology, operational and customer requirements for the new or derivative model. The DRandO also includes many lessons learned from previous programmes which resulted from manufacturing, certification and in-service field experiences. Each programme or major derivative aeroplane programme starts with the definition of the DRandO. The DRandO definition process includes extensive review and co-ordination by the entire development programme team.

The requirements process used on the B777 included the allocation of the aeroplane requirements into lower levels to define the system requirements. These requirements were documented in Systems Requirements and Objectives (SRandO) documents, one for each of the major aeroplane systems. Finally, the requirements for the system components, such as a controller, were captured in Specification Control Documents (SCDs). The tiered combination of the DRandO, SRandOs for each system and SCDs for each major component provided a structured set of requirements from the airplane level down to the components which represent the physical implementation of the systems.

This set of requirements documents is influenced strongly by the safety design prioritisation hierarchy at Boeing. This defines guidance for safety as follows:

1. Eliminate the hazard.
2. Minimise the effects of the hazard.
   a. Use of redundancy.
   b. Separation of systems, both physically and functionally.
   c. Use of robustness of the designs.
   d. Incorporation of safety devices.
3. Provide indications, procedures and training for coping with the hazards.

Design phase

Design reviews were carried out at the system level in a two-step process. The first review cycle, Preliminary Design Review (PDR), is intended to ensure that the requirements are fully understood and are correct and complete. The preliminary architecture of the system is included to show how the system design group intends to satisfy the requirements which apply. The design reviews are held with a wide representation of the engineering organisation from both within and outside the programme, including Safety and Systems Engineering. Action items usually result from the reviews and must be closed before the design group can consider that the design review was successfully completed.

A Critical Design Review (CDR) follows the PDR after the basic design work has been completed. This review compares the detailed system design against the requirements, again using a peer group team from a wide representation of engineering disciplines. Success in completing the CDR freezes the design and allows the component manufacturer to proceed with the building of the initial units to support laboratory and flight tests.

The design phase of the lifetime safety cycle includes many analyses to ensure that the designs will meet the performance and functionality requirements as shown in figure 7. Of greater importance to the safety community, however, are the safety analyses carried out as part of the system safety assessments. These analyses include the Functional Hazard Assessment (FHA), Fault Tree Analyses (FTA), Failure Modes and Effects Analyses (FMEA) and system separation and survivability analyses. Taken as a whole, this work represents a top-down, structured approach to ensuring that the requirements are correct, and that the implementations of the designs will comply with the safety requirements.

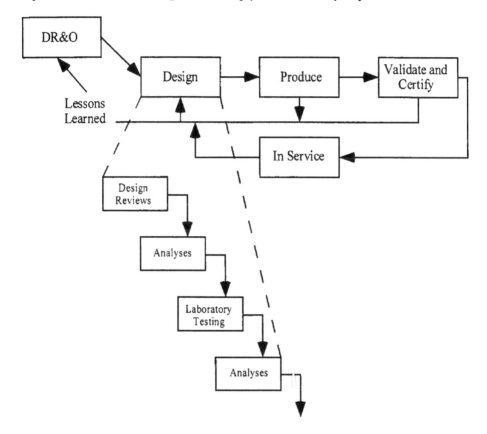

Figure 7   Design portion of aeroplane life safety cycle

The B777 programme utilised an improved safety assessment process to provide increased emphasis on the aeroplane level functions. This was necessary because of the high degree of complexity in the implementation of those functions. The complexity resulted partly from use of high speed, bi-directional digital data busses (ARINC 629) which allowed a far greater sharing of data between the systems than was possible on previous Boeing aeroplanes. Other factors involved new technologies and the increased number of global systems to support critical aeroplane functions.

A new process was implemented to ensure that any safety concerns were addressed during the design phase of the B777 programme. This was done by a multi-discipline team chartered by the Chief Project Engineer to review any concerns raised by any of the engineering organisations and then to take a lead in facilitating the study of these areas of concern and making recommendations for the solution and closure of the issue. Safety and Systems Engineering assumed leadership roles for this special team.

Interfaces are the central core of integration. Boeing utilised an interface control database (ICD) to capture and manage all electrical interfaces on the B777. This approach allowed early checks to be made of the interface definitions, made the detailed bus loading analyses more complete and also allowed many potential interface problems to surface before commitment to hardware and aeroplane wiring. The ICD was also used to define the characteristics of the inputs and outputs of the components so that the simulations used in the Systems Integration Laboratory (SIL) could be based on actual signal definitions. Finally, a robust interface change control process was implemented very early in the programme to ensure that interface changes initiated by one design group did not have an adverse and uncontrolled effect on other groups.

Of course, human interfaces are also a key factor in integration. An engineering simulator cab was developed much earlier than usual for the B777 as part of the SIL and was used for human error reduction and management by a team of human factors specialists and engineers combined with flight test and training pilots. Detailed flight scenarios were created based on various failure mode combinations and flight operations conditions. Customer airline pilots representing a wide range of experience and cultural backgrounds flew the simulated scenarios along with various Boeing pilots not directly involved in the aeroplane development process. Pilot interface features were modified or fine-tuned as a result of the performance observed during these rigorous simulations. Also, the maintenance crew interfaces and procedures were extensively validated to reduce the likelihood of maintenance errors.

Testing in the SIL was planned using the aeroplane level requirements as the starting point. The SIL was also used to test various failure scenarios defined by the safety organisation as an additional check against the redundancy management implementations in the hardware and software of the component implementations.

Produce phase

A broad spectrum of safety reviews were carried out during the produce phase of the B777 programme as shown in figure 8. These reviews were a part of the overall safety programme led by the B777 safety organisation and were performed on all B777 test aeroplanes. They were conducted in two phases: incremental tests conducted in concurrence with the factory functional testing, and a final inspection of the entire aeroplane before first flight. An action item process was used to ensure that all test findings were brought to a satisfactory closure. The safety reviews are another step in the development process to ensure that the safety requirements have been properly defined in the requirements, properly implemented in the designs and properly produced in the aeroplane hardware and software.

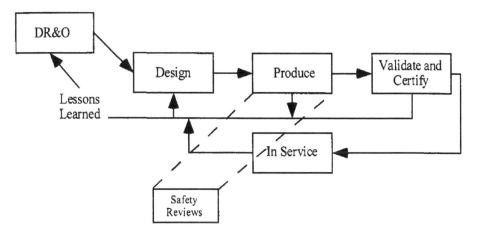

Figure 8   Safety reviews during production

Validation and certification

Validation and certification of the designs is the final phase in the development of a Boeing aeroplane. This phase, which is depicted in figure 9, includes all laboratory, ground and fight certification testing. Testing, together with analysis, are the two primary methods of showing compliance with the regulations.

Flight testing is done to validate laboratory testing and analysis, and to show compliance with regulatory requirements which cannot be shown by analysis. Many flight tests are aeroplane level in nature, such as the tests to demonstrate stall and maximum speeds. The flight test programme is also used to show compliance with many DRandO requirements defined early in the development programme.

The B777 flight test programme included a dedicated aeroplane for obtaining evidence of Part 121 readiness. These flight operations were conducted using final maintenance procedures, trouble-shooting equipment and spares. In later phases, testing included maintenance crews from airline customers for a more realistic test of the overall infrastructure needed for in-service support of the aeroplane.

Throughout the test phase, a problem reporting and tracking system was maintained by Systems Engineering and monitored by the safety organisation for any test results which had safety implications. Closure criteria were defined and then applied to each of the aeroplane level problems prior to closing the problem report.

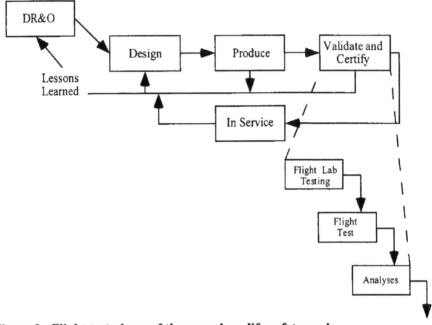

Figure 9   Flight test phase of the aeroplane life safety cycle

Continuing airworthiness

The Boeing safety process does not end with certification of the new aeroplane model. Data is collected from Customer Services for systems and component problems found in service, as shown in figure 10. These data, together with other data from accident investigations and from inspections of high-time aeroplanes, are utilised in several internal safety processes.

The initial use of this field operational data is in fulfilling the continuing airworthiness reporting requirements of FAR Part 21.3. There are also two parallel activities for incidents using the Accident/Incident Review Board and the Aeroplane Safety Awareness Process, which also reviews system and component data. The results of high-time inspections are reviewed by the Structural Analysis group. Together these activities are reviewed in the Service-Related Problems processes.

Changes in the design of aeroplanes are one result of the ongoing safety assessment process for operational problems. Service bulletins and changes in the maintenance or flight crew procedures may also result. The major lessons learned from this activity are incorporated into the requirements documents. This ensures that lessons learned from field problems will be reflected in the requirements for new aeroplane programmes.

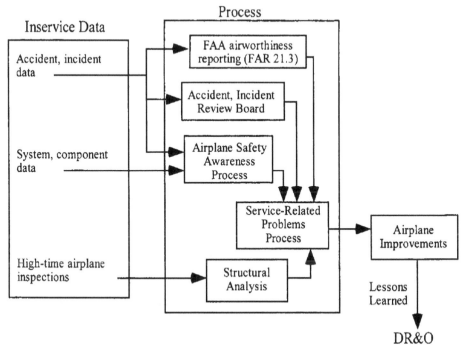

Figure 10 Continuing airworthiness

This completes the safety life cycle description for commercial aeroplanes at Boeing. This process yields improvements in the overall systems safety, starting with the requirements, continuing through the design, into the building of the test aeroplanes, through certification testing and finally into finding solutions for field problems. This end-to-end process was implemented successfully on the B777 programme. It has also been used on several derivative aeroplane programmes, such as the B737-600/700/800/900, B757-300 and B767-400.

Safety for future aeroplane development

The improvements in the overall lifetime safety cycle process applied to the B777 and later derivative programmes will not assure that safety goals for a two-fold decrease in the accident rate will be achieved in the future. Rather, these processes enabled the complex and highly integrated B777 architecture to be certified to the safety requirements proscribed by FAR/JAR 25.1309. Continued improvements in overall safety will require changes in the safety processes used to define, design, produce and certify systems, as well as changes in the ways aeroplanes are operated.

Requirements improvements

Requirements were implemented in a structured way on the B777 utilising a top-level document, the DRandO, followed by second-tier requirements in the SRandOs and finally, component specifications in the SCDs. Major improvements in the processes that create these documents are needed to implement the process recommendations of ARP4754 and to improve overall safety. It calls for assurance that errors or omissions in requirements or in the design have been identified and corrected in order to satisfy the certification requirements for complex or highly integrated systems. The development of top-level requirements is the first step in the ARP4754 process.

Functionality is another term to describe the behaviour of the aeroplane, in terms of the overall interaction of the systems in providing the aeroplane-level functions. Requirements definition efforts for the B777 captured the performance and regulatory requirements but the requirements for distributed functionality were less well documented. Additional work is needed in developing functional requirements to define how systems should behave, both in normal operations and following failures, and how the function relates to expected operational environments.

The top level functions, once defined, allow different proposed architectures to be compared with each other on the basis of weight, cost, complexity, risk and other factors. At the same time, the functions are used as the input to the functional hazard assessments. Each function can fail to be provided (i.e. loss of function), be provided in a degraded manner, or a malfunction can result, with or without crew alerts. The FHAs, performed in this manner, then determine the potential hazards associated with each failure type, thus driving the reliability requirements for the functions. These two activities will provide better top-level functional requirements and will drive the architecture selection based on the safety and functionality requirements of the aeroplane.

Crew performance predictability is still a major challenge in fully determining the total functional requirements. The diversity of human behaviour makes it highly unlikely that reliable quantitative estimates can ever be developed for crew performance under different failure conditions or flight situations. However, this is not to say that continued behavioural research and a greater emphasis on crew performance feedback in actual flight operations will not contribute to more reliable system functional requirements definition in the future. Success will depend on developing valid requirements that will support safe and efficient flight crew performance. Increased emphasis must be placed on obtaining crew performance data in a threat-free environment and on learning how to utilise such data better within the design process. This will be particularly important and extremely challenging when predictions must be made for novel systems or technologies that will not have the benefit of extensive in-flight experience. Of course, extensive simulation studies can help considerably, but only a limited number of simulations can be conducted and cannot possibly encompass the wide range in pilot capability and performance shaping factors. Hence, all manufacturers need better information on the types of simulations that will provide the greatest safety benefit for the particular design under consideration.

The concept of development assurance level, outlined in ARP4754, assigns a different level to each function, based on the criticality of that function. The development assurance levels are used later to determine the degree of requirements validation and design verification which are required for the systems which implement the functions. The development assurance levels define the degree of proof of process rigor that is required.

After the system architecture has been optimised, the sub-functions which result can be defined, along with their derived functional requirements. This allows functional requirements to be explicitly stated in the SRandO documents, together with the traditional requirements. Likewise, when the architectures of each system are defined using a second tier trade study of proposed sub-architectures, an additional tier of functional requirements can be assigned to the components. This process will result in improved architectures at all levels, and allow various candidates to be compared, using allocated safety and functional requirements as a major design driver.

Boeing is also implementing improvements in the requirements documentation process, using new software tools. These tools allow traceability to be captured from one level of requirement to another by establishing the parent-child relationship between the 'shall' statements. The new tools also allow attributes to be attached to the requirements to assist in the validation of each requirement statement at all levels. These attributes will include the rationale for the requirement and the method proposed to show compliance to the requirement later on in the development process. Figure 11 shows the relationship between the levels of functional requirements, the trade studies which were used and the attributes captured in the tool.

The assumptions made for the functional requirements can also be entered into the tool as attributes for each requirement. The overall validation of the assumptions is thus possible, as called out in ARP4754. The validation plan for the set of requirements documents, another ARP4754 recommended activity, is based on traceability and the rationale entered as attributes for each requirement, together with other validation methods such as experience with previous designs, testing and analysis.

Also, since the requirements documents can contain additional attributes to show the proposed methods to verify that the designs meet the requirements (compliance), the ARP4754 verification matrix can also be generated from the tool, ensuring that correlation exists between validation of the requirements and verification of the designs.

The two key improvements in new model requirements at Boeing include better functionality requirements driven from the safety assessments and better control of the validation and verification processes using the requirements management tool. This approach will also result in improved architecture for the aeroplane as a result of expanded functionality trade studies. Finally, this approach will allow us to implement key elements of both the ARP4754 and ARP4761 processes.

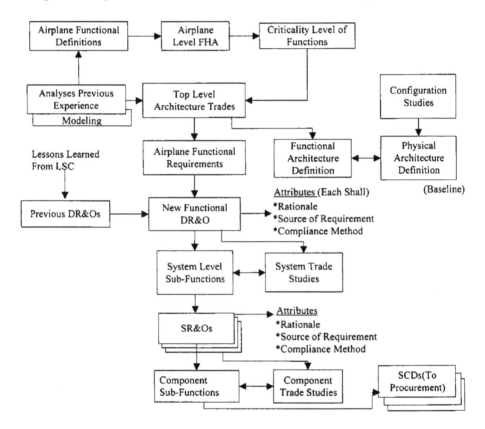

Figure 11 Structured functional requirements

Expanded use of modelling

There has been a long-term need for functionality modelling which is analogous to the digital pre-assembly of physical/spatial designs using CAD/CAM tools such as CATIA. A model of the aeroplane functional behaviour, if sufficiently detailed, would allow early analyses of proposed architectures for not only normal modes of operation but would also allow the investigation of failure modes and the behaviour which results from such failures at the aeroplane level. Further, the models would be used to drive out functional requirements of the systems and components by building a tiered set of models representing the three levels of the aeroplane architecture.

Boeing has been exploring the development of functional models to determine the practical aspects of their use. One example is shown in figure 12. This is a state model of the electrical functions for a large aeroplane. Each of the supporting systems has a behaviour model allowing the results of loss of the function performed by the sub-system to be captured. The model also generates the EICAS synoptic chart similar to one which would be provided to the flight crew along with proposed EICAS messages.

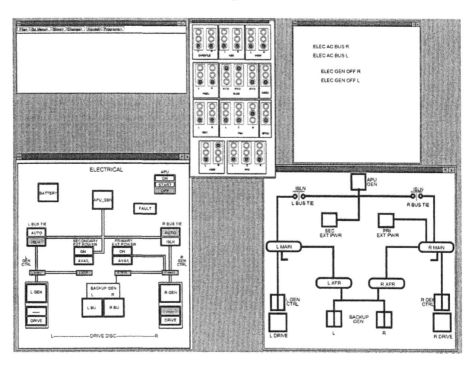

Figure 12 State model output

This model allows the design of the electrical system architecture to be thoroughly evaluated prior to the finalising the requirements documents. It would allow the functional requirements to be based on a complete assessment, not just the traditional scenarios of an engine out, or loss of one or more generators.

Functional modelling will be used in the future as one of the tools for requirements validation.

There is also a need to understand the functionality with respect to the human interface for different system modes and states. Crew responses to state changes may be different from the intended response according to the systems design. By combining such modelling with behavioural data on human-system interaction we will be able to make both system functionality and human error potential more visible to the design team. The result should be a reduction in crew errors when interacting with such systems and a corresponding increase in operational safety. In the future, more extensive and robust assessments of human-system interaction are likely to result if current efforts to model operator behaviour are successful.

Boeing intends to expand the use of functional models for future aeroplane programmes as one of the primary methods to improve the quality of the functional requirements and the resulting architecture of the overall aeroplane. Models will also be useful in later phases of the programme to assess the impact of changes. They can also be used to provide better requirements for the design of simulators and for the validation of flight crew procedures.

Expanded use of teaming

Recent Boeing programmes make wide use of teaming to allow concurrent engineering to occur. The Design Build Teams from the B777 programme have been expanded to become Integrated Product Teams and are now comprised of cross-functional members from many disciplines within Boeing. Of particular interest to this paper is the use of functional integration teams. The latter have a charter to ensure that the aeroplane's systems are integrated satisfactorily and that the resulting designs meet all of the requirements with no anomalous behaviour.

Safety and Systems Engineering are important members of the functional integration teams, together with the system design groups and other engineering disciplines, including Human Factors and Crew Operations. The sub-team concerned with requirements development has the responsibility to ensure that functional requirements are prepared together with the traditional requirements in a structured set of documents starting at the aeroplane level. This team is also responsible for processes used to validate requirements, to develop integrated verification plans and processes, and to prepare the ARP4754 plans and matrices. Functional analysis, including modelling, is also led by Systems Engineering under a different sub-team.

The safety organisation is responsible for leading the aeroplane-level safety assessment process as a sub-team under the primary Functional Integration team. This team ensures that the safety requirements are used to drive the functional requirements for the aeroplane, the systems and the components. It also ensures that a consistent safety design process is implemented across the overall programme, using ARP 4761 as a guide.

Summary

Improved safety of new large commercial aeroplanes will require changes in the processes employed during the development phases of a programme. The lifetime safety cycle process has enabled the more interdependent and highly integrated systems designs, such as the B777, to become certified and to enter airline service successfully. Further improvements are now underway in the area of better functional requirements definition driven by aeroplane-level safety assessments, wider use of modelling techniques to ensure that the functional requirements are correct and complete, and application of the guidance of ARP4754 and ARP4761. These efforts, coupled with widespread use of multi-discipline teaming will result in improved safety in future aeroplane designs and will facilitate the successful introduction of safer, more efficient new flight deck technologies.

References

ARP 4754. *Certification Considerations for Highly Integrated or Complex Airplane Systems.* Warrendale, Pennsylvania: SAE International.

ARP 4761. *Guidelines and Methods for Conducting the Safety Assessment Process on Civil Airborne Systems.* Warrendale, Pennsylvania: SAE International.

DO-178B. *Software Considerations in Airborne Systems and Equipment Certification.* Washington, DC.: RTCA Inc.

2 Head-up displays and visual attention: integrating data and theory

Geoffrey W. Stuart, Ken I. McAnally and
James W. Meehan

Abstract

Head-up displays (HUDs) are commonly used in military aviation, increasingly in commercial aviation, and are being considered for use in general aviation. In the last decade, a considerable amount of applied research has explored the phenomenon of 'attention capture' - the tendency for the pilot to pay attention to the display at the expense of events in the outside world. Awareness of these events, such as the presence of other aircraft during flight, or runway obstacles during landing, are critical to the safe operation of the aircraft. In order to understand the effects of HUDs on visual attention, we reviewed and critically analysed the applied literature in the context of current theories of visual attention. By integrating data from applied studies with theories derived from basic laboratory research, it should be possible to improve both the design of HUDs and methods for training in their use to minimise their adverse effects on visual attention.

Introduction

Advances in computer technology have affected the way information is displayed. Nowhere has the issue of human-system interaction been studied more intensively than in military aviation where the introduction into the cockpit first of the head-

This paper was first published in Human Factors and Aerospace Safety 1(2), 2001, pp. 103-124

up display (HUD) and now the helmet mounted display (HMD) have become the focus of a great deal of human factors research. The HUD is a device that interposes images on a transparent optical combiner in the pilot's line of sight. Normally it is mounted immediately above the instrument panel glare shield. The HMD is a display device that can be incorporated in a flight helmet and used to project images directly into the visual field of the pilot (usually on the helmet visor), allowing a view of the outside environment simultaneously with important flight information and other data. HMDs usually incorporate a head tracker that informs the on-board computer in real time where the pilot's head is directed. Information displayed in the HMD can therefore be made to change as the pilot's head moves, allowing symbology to remain linked spatially and temporally with the outside world. Unlike the HUD, the projection of information on the helmet visor means that it is always presented in, or close to, the pilot's line of sight.

Box 1

'The head-up display (HUD) projects instrument symbology onto a transparent screen in the pilot's forward field of view so that the pilot can concurrently monitor the display and maintain a view of the far domain environment...reducing the need to visually scan a number of instruments located on a conventional head-down instrument panel' (Martin-Emerson and Wickens, 1997).

Although for the most part HUDs and HMDs have led to improvements in efficiency, the undoubted benefits can also come with unwanted performance trade-offs. Perhaps the most important of these is the possible disruption to visual attention caused by the interposition of display information between the pilot and the outside world. For example, several simulation studies have demonstrated that when using a HUD to guide landing, pilots may fail to notice unexpected runway obstacles (Fischer, Haines and Price, 1980; Weintraub, Haines and Randle, 1985; Larish and Wickens, 1991; Wickens, Martin-Emerson and Larish, 1993; Wickens and Long, 1995). These findings highlight the need to give serious consideration to safety aspects of HUD use. The purpose of this paper is to review the literature on the effect of HUDs on visual attention (much of which to date has been available only in the form of technical reports), and to integrate that body of work with basic theories of attention derived from laboratory studies.

The principal argument in favour of the HUD and HMD for the display of information in the aircraft cockpit is that it obviates the need for the pilot to switch gaze between the instrument display and the operating environment. The main justification for the use of HUDs relates to two assumptions. The first is that when using such displays the pilot can monitor display and environment in parallel, that is, divide attention between them. The second is that there is less of a requirement for visual scanning. However, neither of these assumptions has been convincingly demonstrated to be universally true.

The potential disadvantage of such displays stems, paradoxically, from the same design feature that is claimed to confer the benefits: the two sources of information (display and real-world) spatially overlap. This overlap may lead to potential interference between the two sources of information, which may be characterised as *perceptual*, where one source of information masks the other, or *attentional*, where the information in one source captures the operator's attention so that important information in the other source does not reach conscious awareness.

Perceptual factors

Two properties of the HUD that are relevant when considering perceptual factors are collimation of the image and angular size of the symbols presented. The HUD presents collimated symbology superimposed on the pilot's view of the outside world. It is generally agreed that collimation, which removes the need to refocus the eyes when looking from the display and the outside environment, is a major advantage (Tufano, 1997). It has also been argued that the presentation of symbology in a head-up location reduces the need to make eye movements. However, the use of small symbology (approximately 28 min of arc in height, according to the recommendations of Weintraub and Ensing, 1992) in the typical HUD makes eye movements necessary, albeit smaller ones than would be required to look at the instrument panel, as shown by Dudfield and Hughes (1993). The major cost of an eye movement is in preparation for the movement, with large movements taking only slightly longer than small movements (Boghen, Troost, Daroff, Dell'Osso and Birkett, 1974; Zambarbieri, Schmid, Magenes and Prablanc, 1982). Thus, the advantage of head-up presentation is not as clear as originally argued (Martin-Emerson and Wickens, 1993).

The overlay of symbology onto the view of the outside world is likely to obscure or laterally mask objects in the environment (Wickens and Long, 1995; Martin-Emerson and Wickens, 1997) and may also disrupt effective scanning (Fischer, Haines and Price, 1980). Unpublished research from our laboratory (P. Hughes, unpublished observations) shows that both the average size of saccadic eye movements and the range of head movements are restricted when using a HUD. Qualitative analysis showed that a good deal of time was spent inspecting HUD symbology at the expense of the outside environment.

It is therefore generally agreed that symbology presented head-up should be sparse (Weintraub and Ensing, 1992; Wickens and Long, 1995, Ververs and Wickens, 1998). This recommendation is particularly relevant for central vision in a HMD where the display is tied to the head. For example, many designs include a velocity vector symbol that displays the predicted future position of the aircraft.

Considering this, it is interesting to note that a pilot training video (Flyright productions, 1993) shows HUD video from an F16 where a single engine Cessna was obscured by the velocity vector symbol, resulting in a near miss. An almost identical near-miss between an F16 and a single engine Cessna was also reported to the National Transport Safety Board of the USA (NTSB, 1999).

In summary, as the time taken to refocus the eyes is longer than that required to make eye movements (Weintraub, Haines and Randle, 1984; Weintraub, Haines and Randle, 1985), the major benefit of HUDs may be due to collimation and superior symbology rather than the head-up presentation. Although these perceptual factors associated with HUDs and HMDs are interesting and important, the emphasis of the present discussion is on attentional factors.

Attentional factors

One potential advantage of the HUD is that it increases the possibility that changes in the environment will be noticed. During the time spent looking down at a conventional instrument panel, as well as making eye movements between such a display and the outside world, changes in the outside world may be missed. A number of studies have demonstrated that changes are difficult to detect during saccadic eye movements (Carlson-Radvansky and Irwin, 1995), or following short intervals when the visual scene is not present (Simons, 1996). This phenomenon has been labelled 'change blindness'. Without obvious perceptual cues, e.g., flicker or motion, the observer needs to rely on visual memory of the prior scene to detect changes in it. This may be the basis of the consistent finding that HUDs lead to an improvement in the detection of expected events (Fadden, Ververs and Wickens, 1998). If the observer has an expectation that important events are likely to occur in the outside world, the HUD may allow effective monitoring to take place. However, this may not be the case if events in the outside world are unexpected, and attention is focused on the display (Fadden et al., 1998). The objective in the design of HUDs and HMDs is to enable the operator to use two sources of visual information concurrently when the task at hand demands it. There are two means by which this might be achieved which are not necessarily mutually exclusive. The operator may be able to process both sources of information in parallel, or he/she may be able to process information serially and efficiently, i.e., it may be possible to switch attention rapidly between the two sources of information by means of overt eye movements or by shifting attention covertly without accompanying eye movements (Pashler, 1997).

The demands of the task at hand usually determine what is the optimal mode of attention. A mismatch between the mode of the attention and task demands can arise. For example, if the observer tries to attend to two sources of information concurrently (through either parallel or efficient serial attention) and fails to do so, attention will be selective to one source at the expense of the other (attentional capture). On the other hand, if the task requires selective attention and there is failure to select, performance may be degraded due to interference from the task-irrelevant source (Brickner, 1989; McCann, Lynch, Foyle and Johnston, 1993b). Parallel or efficient serial attention can be difficult to discriminate between behaviourally, because if effective monitoring of the two domains does not require constant attention, the observer may be able to schedule attention effectively in a serial manner with no detectable adverse effect on performance. The distinction between efficient and inefficient serial attention reflects the ease and speed with which observers can switch attention. If such shifts in attention are slow or difficult, there is a greater chance that attention will be captured by either the display or the outside environment.

It is interesting to note that although some HUD proponents argue that the HUD allows simultaneous monitoring of the display and the outside environment (Naish, 1964; Martin-Emerson and Wickens, 1997), early studies of visual attention paid to two overlapping scenes suggest the opposite may be the case. In their pioneering study, Neisser and Becklen (1975) projected two films onto the same screen. One film was of people playing a ball game and the other was of people playing a hand-slapping game. Observers were asked to monitor these films for specific events. They were able to attend to one or other film successfully, but had great difficulty monitoring both films simultaneously. It was also apparent that no simple strategy was used to accomplish this task. The observers moved their eyes to monitor critical events, but it was also clear that attention was used to select and group the content of the relevant display so that the observer knew where to look. However, this example represents a very difficult task because there was complete overlap between comparatively similar scenes. As the HUD represents a much simpler array of visual elements, a greater degree of parallel processing may be possible.

Failure of parallel attention or efficient switching – attentional capture

As already described, a potential drawback of HUDs is that the continuous presence of the display may capture attention, at the expense of processing the external environment (Fischer, 1979; Fischer et al,. 1980; Hart and Brickner, 1987; Brickner, 1989; Foyle, McCann, Sanford and Schwirzke, 1993; McCann et al., 1993b; Wickens and Long, 1995, Martin-Emerson and Wickens, 1997). This problem is of particular relevance in the case of HMDs, where looking at the symbology is unavoidable. Attentional capture has been most clearly demonstrated in the context of unexpected events, for example runway incursions during simulated instrument landing using virtual symbology that directly overlapped the real runway so that it was possible to land without attending to the outside environment (see the meta-analysis by Fadden et al., 1998).

Box 2

'several pilots admitted that from time to time they caught themselves totally fixating on the symbology, oblivious of anything else, and had to consciously force their attention to the outside scene' (Fischer, Haines and Price, 1980).

In designing HUDs to minimise the possibility of attentional capture, it is important to understand how visual attention operates. The literature on this topic is extensive (see e.g., Pashler, 1997) so our discussion is confined to some key concepts. Although there is no generally agreed definition of attention, common to many viewpoints is the idea that the observer is bombarded with sensory information that exceeds processing capacity. This requires that information for further processing must be selected.

Orienting of attention

The process of selective attention begins with the orientation of attention to a particular source of information. The orientation of attention may be voluntary or it may be reflexive (e.g., in response to a sudden movement or a loud noise). These modes of orienting attention have been characterised as 'endogenous' and 'exogenous' respectively (Henderson and MacQuistan, 1993). It is well established that attention may be shifted voluntarily in a goal-directed manner to enable the processing of information relevant to the task at hand. On the other hand, rapid changes in the visual stimulus array, such as motion or flicker, automatically engage attention in a reflexive manner. Thus, this can be an effective way of breaking attentional capture. When considering the HUD it is important to note that capture by the HUD may be weaker in the case of external events that engage exogenous attention. For example, if an aircraft obstructing a runway during a HUD-guided landing had a flashing beacon, it is more likely that attention would be attracted to it, breaking any potential capture by HUD landing symbology.

However, in some circumstances important external events may not engage exogenous attention. For example, when on a collision course, the opposing aircraft appears motionless in space and the only cue to approach is looming. The problem is that size growth is only barely perceptible under these circumstances (e.g. NTSB, 1996). Thus, any capture of attention by the HUD is likely to be detrimental in cases where cues to exogenous attention are weak and the pilot is required to scan the outside environment voluntarily for potential hazards.

The basis for selection in visual attention

In order to attend to one source of information and ignore another (e.g., attend to the outside environment and ignore the HUD), there must be some basis for selective attention. In the visual domain, the most obvious means of selection is spatial location. As easy way to selectively attend is simply to look. Given that in human vision acuity is greatest in the fovea (the central or focal part of the visual field) and falls off into the visual periphery, this is an effective way of enhancing one part of the visual field at the expense of another. Using eye and head movements to orient towards a particular object or location is characterised as *overt* spatial attention. However, it has long been argued that spatial attention can be shifted *covert*ly, independently of eye movements, and experimental paradigms have now demonstrated this to be the case (Posner, 1980). While maintaining one's gaze, it is possible to covertly direct attention to different locations of the visual field. However, covert shifts of attention are usually part of a preparatory process for overt eye movements (Hoffman, 1998).

In addition to selection in two-dimensional space, other means of selection are possible. The third visual dimension (depth) can also be attended to selectively. Theeuwes, Atchley and Kramer (1998) found that observers could selectively attend to one of two depth planes when performing a visual search task. Andersen and Kramer (1993) showed that attention can be selective in depth using a variation of the flanker task (Eriksen and Eriksen, 1974). In the flanker task the observer is required to respond to a target in a known location in the close presence of task-relevant, but incongruent distractors. For example, people are slower to decide that a target letter in a known location is a 'T' rather than an 'S' when there are distracting letter 'S's nearby. This slowing of reaction time falls off with increasing separation of the distractors from the target. Andersen and Kramer (1993) found a similar effect when distractors were separated from the target in depth. However, when simply detecting the appearance of a target, it has been difficult to demonstrate selective attention in the third dimension (Ghirardelli and Folk, 1996).

An alternative view of selective attention is that rather than being directed to locations in space, attention is paid to objects, even when they occupy the same spatial location. A classic demonstration of object-based visual attention was carried out by Duncan (1984) who asked observers to report the features of a line intersecting a box. When inspection time was limited, observers found it easier to report two features of the same object than to report one feature each of two objects. This was attributed to the time needed to switch attention from one object to another, even though they occupied the same location. This finding has subsequently been confirmed by Lavie and Driver (1996). Observers also find it more difficult to ignore flankers that are grouped with the target to form a common 'object' than those that are not grouped with the target when the distance from the target is constant (Driver and Baylis, 1989, but see also Berry and Klein,

1993). Thus, when making visual discriminations it may be possible to switch attention from one depth plane to another, or from one perceptual group to another. However, for the detection of new objects in the visual field, two-dimensional spatial selection appears to occupy a privileged status, compared to object-based selection (Stuart, Maruff and Currie, 1997).

Selection may also be based on a common feature of elements of the visual array, such as common colour or motion. It has been proposed that common features may be selected directly (Wolfe, Cave and Franzel, 1989; Driver, McLeod and Dienes, 1992) or indirectly when they lead to elements being grouped together to form a single object to which attention is then directed (Duncan, 1995). This grouping is compelling in the case of common motion. Although such grouping has been characterised as forming objects, Palmer and Rock (1994) have pointed out that real objects are usually not dispersed across locations: they have the property of *uniform connectedness*.

What is selected in attentional capture?

There are several possible bases upon which attention may be selectively directed to the HUD or the environment. Wickens and Long (1995) have proposed two non-exclusive frameworks within which the operation of HUDs should be considered: two-dimensional space-based attention, and object-based attention. These frameworks may be extended to include selection based on three-dimensional space and selection based on common features, such as colour or motion. Common motion is a characteristic of HMDs when symbology is not stabilised for head movement, and is also characteristic of HUDs when manoeuvring the aircraft. Attention may be directed to the entire field of the display or to single elements within the HUD display area. The latter would represent two stages of selection, first to the HUD, and then to space within the HUD display area.

Four non-exclusive hypotheses arise from consideration of which part of the combined HUD/real-world display is selected in attentional capture. These are that attention is directed to (i) one of two planes in three-dimensional space, (ii) one of two overlapping fields in the same depth plane, (iii) one of two or more objects, which may combine elements from both of the overlapping fields, or (iv) a particular location in two-dimensional space.

Attention to one of two depth planes

It is often assumed that because the HUD/HMD is collimated, it is perceived to be located at a far depth plane. However, this assumption overlooks the fact that the display is transparent, and hence will always appear to overlay the external environment. Overlay is a powerful depth cue which is known to over-ride other depth cues such as stereoscopic disparity when these cues are placed into conflict. On a HMD the effects will be even more potent, because as the pilot moves his or her head, the visor-projected symbology will appear to pass in front of parts of the airframe and instrument panels within the cabin. The fact that the display may be out of focus when the pilot focuses on nearby features (such as the instrument panel) is not likely to over-ride this overlay cue. As a consequence, the pilot may be required to switch attention between the two depth planes, and this may incur performance costs (McCann et al., 1993). These costs may be asymmetrical - for example, it may be more difficult to attend to the far plane while ignoring the near plane.

Attention to one of two fields - display and environment

Visual attention may be directed selectively to the HUD because it forms a distinct field or group (by virtue of perceptual grouping factors such as common colour or motion), and only one such field or group may be attended to at a time (Foyle et al., 1993). A perceptual group or array might be regarded as higher-level organisation whose elements themselves are simple objects. Hence we can adopt the term *field* for such a grouping, following Fischer (1979). This is an important distinction, because if an entire field is selected, there is an implication that several elements can be attended to simultaneously, provided they are all visible and resolvable. Irrespective of a preference for one field over the other, there may be costs in disengaging attention from one field and switching it to the other (McCann et al, 1993; Martin-Emerson and Wickens, 1997).

Attention to one bounded or uniformly connected object including parts of display and environment

In the case of *conformal* symbology (that which bears a direct relationship with features of the outside world), an element of the display may be grouped with part of the environment such as a runway to form a single object (Wickens and Long, 1995). Attention to this object may be at the expense of other objects, either in the display or in the real world, including those at the same location as the attended object, such as a runway obstruction. Attention to the object may not represent parallel processing of the outside scene and the entire display as suggested by Martin-Emerson and Wickens (1997), because only one object (such as the combined virtual-plus-actual runway) might be attended to at a time. This would represent an instance of serial, undivided attention being directed to a single object.

Attention to a particular location or feature in either the display or the environment

Attention may be directed not to the entire display, but to a particular element that may be useful for the task at hand. Foyle et al. (1993) and Wickens and Long

(1995) argue that attention can be directed to only one location at a time. There may be costs associated with disengaging attention from one location (either in the display, environment or both) and shifting it to another. It should be noted that many studies of attention in HUDs have appealed to space-based selection of attention. For example, Foyle et al. (1993) found flying performance was better when two symbology sets were spatially well separated. This finding appeared not to support the space-based theory of selection. However, the alphanumeric symbols were small and probably required direct inspection. If eye movements were made to inspect the symbology, the results cannot be interpreted in terms of space-based selection of (covert) attention, which assumes an invariate locus of fixation. Rather, it reflects the distribution of overt attention. A more direct prediction from space-based selection is the degree to which there is interference from closely positioned symbology.

Reasons for attentional capture

The previous section addressed the question of *how* attention might be directed to the HUD at the expense of the outside world. In order to understand the phenomenon of attentional capture, we need also to consider *why* there is a bias in attention towards the HUD. Several possible explanations have been offered which likewise are not mutually-exclusive.

Salience/compellingness

It has been proposed that the HUD symbology attracts attention because of its perceptual characteristics such as sharpness, contrast, and colour, compared to the outside world (Fischer et al., 1980; May and Wickens, 1995; Ververs and Wickens, 1998). Laboratory research has confirmed the role of stimulus salience in attracting and retaining attention. However, it is not the case that attention is inexorably drawn to salient stimuli not relevant to the task (Yantis, 1998). Ververs and Wickens (1998) examined the effects of reducing the contrast of display elements (or in the case of a highly cluttered display, the task-irrelevant elements) to see if this improved the detection of other aircraft during cruise-flight simulation. Contrary to prediction, there was no effect of contrast reduction on the detection of other aircraft. Ververs and Wickens noted that in their study outside events were expected. It remains to be seen whether reducing the salience of some or all HUD elements improves the detection of unexpected events.

Clutter

There are two experimental paradigms that are relevant to the effect of clutter on visual attention; visual search (e.g. Treisman and Gormican, 1988) and the flanker interference effect (e.g., Eriksen and Eriksen, 1974). It is well established that clutter can affect the speed and accuracy of visual search for targets that are difficult to discriminate from other objects in the visual field. In the case of flanker interference, the time taken to report the features of a target item in a known location shows interference from items in nearby locations that are relevant to the task and not congruent with the target item (Maruff, Dankert, Camplin and Currie, 1999). This interference is modulated by the difficulty of the discrimination task (Lavie, 1995). Both visual search and flanker interference are modulated by perceptual grouping where distractors have less effect if they belong to a different perceptual group than the target item (Driver and Baylis, 1989).

The effect of clutter on visual attention in HUDs probably also depends on perceptual grouping, the relevance of the distractors and task difficulty. For example, if the observer can selectively attend to the HUD display or the outside world as a grouped array, this selection could ameliorate effects of clutter from the non-attended field. Moreover, given the different characteristics of HUD display elements and objects in the real world, it is possible that clutter may not present a major attentional problem in these particular circumstances. However, the perceptual effects of clutter (masking and disruption of scanning) remain.

Expectancy

A key feature of the studies that have demonstrated attentional capture was the unexpected nature of the critical events that were missed by the pilot (Fischer et al., 1980; Larish and Wickens, 1991; Wickens and Long, 1995). Detection of expected events in the far domain has been studied in marine navigation (Boston and Braun, 1996), taxiway navigation (Lasswell and Wickens, 1995) or 'highway in the sky' route guidance (Fadden and Wickens, 1997) and in these cases there was less evidence of attentional capture than when events were unexpected.

Some recent basic research into a phenomenon known as *inattentional blindness* (Mack and Rock, 1998) provides a useful theoretical framework for understanding attentional capture. In their task, observers were asked to judge which of the two arms of a cross was longer. Unexpectedly and without warning, another object (such as a small square) appeared in one of the quadrants defined by the cross. The experiment was then interrupted and the observers were asked if they had noticed anything apart from the cross during the critical trial. About 25% of observers failed to notice the extra stimulus, even though it was within the line of sight. This example of inattentional blindness increased in prevalence to between 60% and 80% of people when the cross was shifted away from the location of fixation so that the unexpected object appeared directly in the line of sight. Mack and Rock (1998) explained this counter-intuitive finding in terms of an inhibition of attention at the locus of fixation. Inattentional blindness was strongly modulated by expectation to the extent that only one inattention trial was possible for each subject. Once the observer was aware that something other than the cross might appear during a trial, a state of *implicit divided attention* was entered for subsequent trials in which the novel feature was much less likely to be missed. It should be noted that implicit divided attention may involve rapid switching of attention.

This evidence may explain why a proportion of pilots, when attending to the HUD landing symbology, failed to notice a runway obstruction during the simulated landing. Although the landing symbology and the runway occupied the same location, this did not guarantee that attention would be directed to the runway. Thus, the basis of selection is likely to have been object-based rather than space-based. Consistent with the laboratory studies of inattentional blindness, once pilots were alerted to a runway obstacle in a simulation study, they easily noticed it on subsequent trials (Fischer et al., 1980). This has clear implications for training of pilots in appropriate use of HUDs.

Redundancy

One reason that pilots may selectively attend to HUD symbology is that they do so voluntarily when the display itself contains all the necessary information required to perform the task. Hence, without instruction to the contrary, the system may induce pilots to fly by the instruments without reference to the outside world when information from the outside world is redundant (Fischer et al., 1980; May and Wickens, 1995). For example, when conformal runway symbology is used to assist landing, it is difficult to determine whether any attention at all is paid to the real runway, since the virtual runway on the HUD alone provides adequate cues for landing (Weintraub and Ensing, 1992). A related issue is that of automation-induced complacency (Lauber, Bray, Harrison, Hemingway and Scott, 1982), which occurs when the display operator relies excessively on automated processes to warn of critical events, such as when a HUD is used to cue target location in military applications (Yeh, Wickens and Seagull, 1999).

Box 3

'pilots prefer to use the HUD for the primary control of the flightpath, and to use the outside scene for monitoring purposes only, for the HUD provides more accurate guidance' (Fischer, Haines and Price, 1980).

Perceptual load

It has been argued that attentional capture is exacerbated when the task for which the HUD is being used is relatively demanding (Fischer et al., 1980; Larish and Wickens, 1991; Wickens, Martin-Emerson and Larish, 1993; May and Wickens, 1995). A corresponding effect has been shown in laboratory studies where attention becomes more focused on a primary task as it is increased in difficulty, thereby reducing the ability to process other stimuli (Lavie, 1995). This is evidently due to the increased resources demanded by the primary task as its difficulty is increased. This effect is likely to have adverse consequences for the ability to monitor the outside world while performing a demanding task - for example, a HUD-assisted landing during turbulence.

Avoiding attentional capture – facilitating concurrent processing

Martin-Emerson and Wickens (1997) have argued that only conformal symbology facilitates parallel or divided attention because elements of the display are fused with elements of the environment. However, perceptual fusion of real and virtual runways is a phenomenon that has not been clearly demonstrated. Also, it is not clear how much attention is paid to the real runway (Weintraub and Ensing, 1992). Therefore, this may not represent a case of true divided attention.

Scene-linking

It has been suggested that attentional capture may be avoided by removing any basis upon which the HUD can be segregated from the environment, such as relative motion. For example, Levy, Foyle and McCann (1998) found an advantage for displaying non-conformal symbology in a scene-linked manner where dials were 'painted' onto fixed locations in the environment with which they had no functional connection. Levy et al. (1998) argued this caused the display elements to combine with the outside scene to produce a single field within which spatial selection was possible. As with conformal symbology, perceptual fusion of non-conformal display elements with the environment into a single field has not been clearly demonstrated. However, in contrast to the situation for conformal symbology, the lack of redundancy of the non-conformal symbology could help to avoid insufficient attention being paid to the environment.

Peripheral symbology

Another manner in which parallel attention may be facilitated is the presentation of information to segregated perceptual modes, for example, to the visual and auditory modes - or within vision, to foveal and peripheral vision. Some display elements that can be seen without being deliberately looked at may be useable as cues in peripheral vision, and be processed without the pilot having to look away from an important environmental feature that is engaging focal vision. This strategy is of direct relevance to HMDs, as they offer the possibility of presenting visual information across a wide field-of-view. Thus, the potential of the HMD for concurrent processing of display and environment elements might be realised, in contrast to current designs that employ symbology that requires focal vision to view individual elements of the display.

Such a strategy is likely to be especially successful if consideration is given to the use of peripheral vision in the real world. The theoretical justification for peripheral-vision displays rests on the concept that there are two visual systems, the so-called *focal* and *ambient* visual systems (Trevarthen, 1968). It is argued the focal system is biased towards central vision, is used for fine-detail vision, is under conscious control, and is used for object recognition. Ambient vision, in contrast, uses the entire field of vision, works at a more reflexive level, and is used for spatial awareness, self-orientation, and guidance of motion. In a recent review, Previc (1998) has incorporated the distinction into a more general theory of space perception. The focal-ambient distinction is also consistent with the ecological theory of perception originally articulated by Gibson (1966), which addresses issues such as the visual guidance of locomotion through the analysis of optic flow. Proponents of the focal-ambient distinction have argued that ambient vision is direct in the Gibsonian sense, in that it may directly affect motor responses without the need for conscious analysis and decision. More controversially, it has also been argued that the ambient system does not impose an attentional or cognitive load (Hennessy and Sharkey, 1997).

There have been attempts to use peripheral or ambient vision to present flight information. The *Para-visual director* (Majendie, 1960) was a set of 'barber poles' which could be viewed peripherally to indicate bank and pitch in flight, but this work apparently did not progress beyond the experimental stage. The *Malcolm horizon* (Malcolm, 1984) was a virtual horizon line that was conformal with the real horizon and projected within the cockpit over a wide visual angle. Although it reached the flight-test stage, it was never adopted for either civilian or military use, due in part to technical reasons. Interest in peripheral-vision displays has nevertheless continued. Lentz, Turnipseed and Hixson (1987; 1991) have shown that a peripheral-vision virtual horizon, presented at eccentricities between 5 and 20 deg, offers significant advantages over conventional horizon indicators that require viewing with focal vision.

With a HUD it is relatively easy to look directly at elements within the display, although small saccadic eye movements may be necessary. In HMDs it may be more difficult to look directly at symbology that occupies peripheral locations of the display. In this case, peripheral symbology would only be useful if it did not require high visual acuity. Symbols suitable for peripheral stimulation are the horizon indicators (already described), and other symbols that have been enlarged to compensate for the loss of resolution with eccentricity (Anstis, 1974). Such enlarged symbology may permit the pilot to resolve alphanumeric or other symbols presented in para-foveal vision while keeping central vision free to view discrete features in the outside environment.

Multiple resources and workload

Modern theories of visual attention no longer consider attention as a single resource that must be divided among tasks. It is now recognised that the extent to which tasks can be carried out simultaneously depends on whether they tap the same resource (Navon and Gopher, 1979; Wickens, 1992). For example, North (1977) showed that it was more difficult to perform two tracking tasks or two digit-identification tasks at the same time than it was to simultaneously perform one of either task. Which factors govern the ability of humans to carry out tasks simultaneously is still a subject of active research (Pashler and Johnston, 1998). There is disagreement about where processing 'bottlenecks' occur, and how these may be avoided by using different input modalities, cognitive processes, or motor responses. There is a large body of research on the factors that determine cognitive workload, much of which is relevant to the question of how much information can be presented on a HUD or HMD, how this information should be presented, and how cognitive resources can be efficiently shared between concurrent tasks. Morey and Simon (1993) provide a detailed review of these issues in relation to HUDs and HMDs.

The use of peripheral displays represents a method by which multiple resources might be exploited. However, peripheral displays are not immune to conditions of high primary task workload. Malcolm (1984) has described inattention to a simple peripheral display when pilots were under high workload. Similarly, an analysis of HUD video from an accident involving an F/A-18 aircraft has concluded that under high stress, peripheral cues to spatial orientation, range, and motion were unattended (Sanders, 1989).

Training and practice

An important factor that may affect the ability to carry out tasks efficiently in parallel is the effect of training or practice. Fischer et al. (1980) suggested that one reason the HUD may capture pilots' attention is that the limits of training with the devices had not yet been reached. This is to suggest that with more training, it is possible that the HUD could be used while monitoring the external environment in parallel. Support for this possibility comes from a follow-up study of the overlaid movies of Neisser and Becklen (1975), carried out by Stoffregen and Becklen (1989). They found that with two days of practice, observers were able to monitor two superimposed video sequences simultaneously, achieving an accuracy of 75% if the events were in the same modality, rising to 89% when they were in different modalities (i.e., in visual mode for one video sequence, in auditory mode for the other). This demonstrates the beneficial effects of practice and of exploiting multiple attentional resources. It also demonstrates the usefulness of validating results obtained in controlled experiments under more realistic conditions that emulate aspects of pilot training and concurrent workload more closely.

In the inattentional blindness paradigm, detection of events not directly relevant to the primary task was increased by promoting a state of implicit divided attention through warning of their possible appearance. Attentional capture by HUDs is also likely to be minimised by promoting implicit divided attention through training in awareness of the non-redundancy of the environment, including the possibility of unexpected events.

Conclusions

HUDs are already in widespread use in military and commercial aircraft, and are being considered for general aviation. HMDs are also being adopted for military use. The collimation of these displays and their superior symbology represent advantages over traditional displays. The challenge for HUD designers is to retain these advantages while minimising the costs due to some of the attentional factors examined here. In particular, there is a need to consider the rapidly developing body of basic knowledge in human visual attention in order to understand and reduce adverse effects of HUDs on pilot performance. Such effects may be due to visual clutter, attentional capture associated with conformal symbology, or unnecessary eye movements necessitated by the use of small display elements.

We have described how symbology might be written to make better use of spatial separation for segmentation of symbols that represent distinct states of information. The dynamic functioning of symbols (i.e., the way they behave) also has potential for exploitation. Further experimental work is required for a more complete understanding of which functions might profitably address peripheral or foveal vision. The design of symbology is important in determining how it is processed by the visual system and in determining its perceptual task relevance and redundancy. Finally, the importance of training in the use of the HUD and the effects of expectancy should not be underestimated.

It should be emphasised that although there may be some room for improvement in HUD design and usage, the overall picture of HUD use has been positive, particularly in commercial aviation settings. Alaska airlines has reported that the introduction of HUDs to its Boeing-727 fleet supported extended operations under adverse weather conditions with no reported incidents (Kaiser, 1993). Indeed, the only serious incident listed in the databases of the Federal Aviation Administration and the National Transport Safety Board which was definitely attributed to the HUD was where the HUD combiner fell on the head of the pilot, necessitating the co-pilot to take over control of the aircraft (FAA, 1997)! There have been some incidents where the design of HUD symbology, rather than attentional capture, led to spatial disorientation (Kuipers, Kappers, van Holten, van Bergen and Oosterveld, 1989). However, this may have occurred irrespective of the head-up presentation of that symbology. While HUDs have undoubtedly been successful in extending the operational capability of commercial aviation, attentional capture is more likely to be a problem in military and general aviation where there is often an increased necessity to maintain a visual awareness of the environment. More ominously, pilots in general aviation are unlikely to receive specific training in the use of HUDs, and therefore may be more susceptible to attentional capture.

References

Andersen, G.J. and Kramer, G.J. (1993). Limits of focal attention in three-dimensional space. *Perception and Psychophysics, 53*, 658-667.

Anstis, S.M. (1974). A chart demonstrating variations in acuity with retinal position. *Vision Research, 14*, 589-592.

Berry, G. and Klein, R. (1993). Does motion-induced grouping modulate the flanker compatibility effect?: A failure to replicate. *Canadian Journal of Experimental Psychology, 47*, 714-729

Boghen, D., Troost, B.T., Daroff, R.B., Dell'Osso, L.F. and Birkett, J.E. (1974). Velocity characteristics of normal human saccades. *Investigative Opthalmology, 13*, 619-623.

Boston, B.N. and Braun, C.C. (1996). Clutter and display conformality: Changes in cognitive capture. In, *Proceedings of the Human Factors and Ergonomics Society 40th Annual Meeting* (pp. 57-61). Santa Monica: Human Factors and Ergonomics Society.

Brickner, M.S. (1989). Apparent limitations of head-up displays and thermal imaging systems. In, *Proceedings of the Fifth International Symposium on Aviation Psychology* (pp. 703-707) Columbus, OH: Ohio State University.

Carlson-Radvansky, L.A. and Irwin, D.E. (1995). Memory for structural information across saccadic eye movements. *Journal of Experimental Psychology: Learning, Memory and Cognition, 21*, 1441-1458.

Driver, J. and Baylis, G.C. (1989). Movement and visual attention: the spotlight metaphor breaks down. *Journal of Experimental Psychology: Human Perception and Performance, 15*, 448-456.

Driver, J., McLeod, P. and Dienes, Z. (1992). Motion coherence and conjunction search: implications for guided search theory. *Perception and Psychophysics, 51*, 79-85.

Dudfield, H.J. and Hughes, P.K. (1993). The use of redundant colour coding as an alerting mechanism in a fast jet head-up display. DRA Report AS/FS/TR93018/1. Farnborough: Defence Research Agency.

Duncan, J. (1984). Selective attention and the organisation of visual information. *Journal of Experimental Psychology: General, 113*, 501-517.

Duncan, J. (1995). Target and nontarget grouping in visual search. *Perception and Psychophysics, 57*, 117-120.

Eriksen, B.A. and Eriksen, C.W. (1974). Effects of noise letters upon the identification of a target letter in a non-search task. *Perception and Psychophysics, 16,* 143-149.

FAA (1997). FAA incident data system report 19971119041819C.

Fadden, S. and Wickens, C.D. (1997). *Maximizing traffic awareness with a head-up flightpath highway display.* Technical Report ARL-97-1/FAA-97-1, Aviation Research laboratory, Institute of Aviation, University of Illinois, Urbana-Champaign.

Fadden, S., Ververs, P.M. and Wickens, C.D. (1998). Costs and benefits of head-up display use: A meta-analytic approach. *In, Proceedings of the Human Factors and Ergonomics Society 42nd Annual Meeting* (pp. 16-20). Santa Monica: Human Factors and Ergonomocs Society.

Fischer, E. (1979). *The role of cognitive switching in head-up displays.* NASA CR-3137. Washington, DC: National Aeronautics and Space Administration.

Fischer, E., Haines, R.F. and Price, T.A. (1980). *Cognitive issues in head-up displays.* NASA Technical Paper 1711. Washington, DC: National Aeronautics and Space Administration.

Flyright Productions. (1993). *The 17 most popular ways to fall out of the sky ... and how to avoid them. Volume 2: Cruise and En-Route.* Van Nuys, CA: Flyright Productions.

Foyle, D.C., McCann, R.S., Sanford, B.D. and Schwirzke, M.F.J. (1993). Attentional effects with superimposed symbology: Implications for head-up displays (HUD). In, *Proceedings of the Human Factors and Ergonomics Society 37th Annual Meeting* (pp. 1340-1344). Santa Monica, CA: Human Factors and Ergonomics Society.

Ghirardelli, T.G. and Folk, C.L. (1996). Spatial cuing in a stereoscopic display: Evidence for a 'depth-blind' attentional spotlight. *Psychonomic Bulletin and Review, 3,* 81-86.

Gibson, J.J. (1966). *The senses considered as perceptual systems.* Prospect Heights, Illinois: Waveland Press, Inc.

Hart, S.G. and Brickner, M.S. (1987). Helmet-mounted pilot night-vision systems: Human factors issues. In, *Proceedings of the Spatial Displays and Spatial Instruments Conference* (pp. 13-1 to 13-21). Moffet Field, CA: NASA.

Henderson, J.M. and MacQuistan, A.D. (1993). The spatial distribution of attention following an exogenous cue. *Perception and Psychophysics, 53,* 221-230.

Hennessy, R.T. and Sharkey, TJ. (1997). *Display of aircraft state information for ambient vision processing using helmet mounted displays.* U.S. Army Aviation and Troop Command TR 97-D-5. Fort Eustis, VA: Aviation Applied Technology Directorate, Aviation Research, Development and Engineering Center (ATCOM).

Hoffman, J.E. (1998). Visual attention and eye movements. In, H. Pasher, (Ed.) *Attention* (pp. 119-153). Hove UK: Psychology Press.

Kaiser, K.J. (1993). The HUD experience at Alaska Airlines. In *Looking ahead: Proceedings of the international symposium on head-up display, enhanced vision and virtual reality*, Amsterdam Netherlands, (A95-24608 05-06). Amsterdam: Netherlands Association of Aeronautical Engineers.

Kuipers, A., Kappers, A., van Holten, C.R., van Bergen, J.H.W and Oosterveld, W.J. (1989). Spatial disorientation incidents in the R.N.L.A.F. F16 and F5 aircraft and suggestions for prevention (pp. OV-E-1-16). In, *AGARD conference on Situational Awareness in Aerospace Operations*, Copenhagen AGARD-CP-478.

Larish, I. and Wickens, C.D. (1991). *Divided attention with superimposed and separated imagery: Implications for head-up displays.* University of Illinois Institute of Aviation Technical Report (ARL-91-4/NASA HUD-91-1). Savoy, IL: Aviation Research Laboratory.

Laswell, J.W. and Wickens, C.D. (1995). *The effects of display location and dimensionality on taxi-way navigation.* University of Illinois Institute of Aviation Technical Report (ARL-95-5/NASA-95-2). Savoy, IL: Aviation Research Laboratory.

Lauber, J. K., Bray, R.S., Harrison, R.L., Hemingway, J.C. and Scott, B.C. (1982). *An operational evaluation of head-up displays for civil transport aircraft.* NASA/FAA Phase III final report. NASA (Ames) Technical Paper 1815.

Lavie, N. (1995). Perceptual load as a necessary condition for selective attention. *Journal of Experimental Psychology: Human Perception and Performance, 21,* 451-468.

Lavie, N. and Driver, J. (1996). On the spatial extent of attention in object-based visual selection. *Perception and Psychophysics, 58,* 1238-1251.

Lentz, J.M., Turnipseed, G.T. and Hixson, W.C. (1987). *Tracking a laser projected horizon indicator* (Report 1330) Pensacola, FL: Naval Aerospace Medical Research Laboratory.

Lentz, J.M., Turnipseed, G.T. and Hixson, W.C. (1991). *Tracking a laser projected horizon indicator: Some further developments* (Report 1351) Pensacola, FL: Naval Aerospace Medical Research Laboratory.

Levy, J.L., Foyle, D.C. and McCann, R.S. (1998). Performance benefits with scene-linked HUD symbology: An attentional phenomenon? In *Proceedings of the Human Factors and Ergonomics Society 42nd annual meeting.* pp. 11-15.

Mack, A. and Rock, I. (1998). *Inattentional blindness.* London, UK: Bradford.

Majendie, A.M.A. (1960). The para-visual director. *Journal of the Institute of Navigation, 13,* 447-454.

Malcolm, R. (1984). Pilot disorientation and the use of a peripheral vision display. *Aviation, Space and Environmental Medicine, 55,* 231-238.

Martin-Emerson, R. and Wickens, C.D. (1993). *Conformal symbology and the head-up display.* University of Illinois Institute of Aviation Technical Report (ARL 93-6/ NASA-HUD-93-1). Savoy, Illinois: Aviation Research Laboratory.

Martin-Emerson, R. and Wickens, C.D. (1997). Superimposition, symbology, visual attention and the head-up display. *Human Factors, 39,* 581-601.

Maruff, P., Dankert, J., Camplin, G. and Currie, J. (1999). Behavioural goals constrain the selection of visual information. *Psychological Science 10,* 52-525.

May, P. and Wickens, C.D. (1995). The role of visual attention in head-up displays: Design implications for varying symbology intensity. University of Illinois Institute of Aviation Technical Report (ARL 95-3/ NASA-HUD-95-1). Savoy, Illinois: Aviation Research Laboratory.

McCann, R.S., Foyle, D.C. and Johnston, J.C. (1993a). Attentional limitations with head-up displays. In, *Proceedings of the 7th International Symposium on Aviation Psychology.* Columbus, Ohio (pp. 70-75): Department of Aviation, Ohio State University.

McCann, R.S., Lynch, J., Foyle, D.C. and Johnston, J.C. (1993b). Modelling attentional effects with head-up displays. In, *Proceedings of the Human Factors and Ergonomics Society 37th Annual Meeting* (pp. 1345-1349). Santa Monica, CA: Human Factors and Ergonomics Society.

Morey, J.C. and Simon, R. (1993). *Attention factors associated with head-up display and helmet-mounted display systems.* ARI Research Note 93-12. Alexandria, VA: U.S. Army Research Institute for the Behavioral and Social Sciences.

Naish, J.M. (1964). Combination of information in superimposed visual fields. *Nature, 202,* 641-646.

Navon, D. and Gopher, D. (1979). On the economy of the human processing systems. *Psychological Review, 86,* 254-255.

Neisser, U. and Becklen, R. (1975). Selective looking: Attending to visually specified events. *Cognitive Psychology, 7,* 480-494.

North, R.A. (1977). Task functional demands as factors in dual task performance. In, *Proceedings of the 25th annual meeting of the Human Factors Society.* Santa Monica CA: Human Factors Society.

NTSB (1996). Aviation Safety Reporting System Report 332658. National Transport Safety Board, USA.

NTSB (1999). Near midair collisions systems report NGLFLAN990001. National Transport Safety Board, USA.

Palmer, S. and Rock, I. (1994). Rethinking perceptual organisation-the principal of uniform connectedness. *Psychonomic Bulletin and Review, 1,* 29-55.

Pashler, H.E. (1997). *The psychology of attention.* Cambridge, Massachusetts: MIT Press.

Pashler, H.E. and Johnston, J.C. (1998). Attentional limitations in dual-task performance. In, H. Pashler, (Ed.) *Attention* (pp. 155-189). Hove, UK: Psychology Press.

Posner, M.I. (1980). Orienting of attention. *Quarterly Journal of Experimental Psychology, 32,* 3-25.

Previc, F.H. (1998). The neuropsychology of 3-D space. *Psychological Bulletin, 124*, 123-164.

Sanders, F.C. (1989). The cobra in the basket – What you don't see can kill you. Cockpit 1989, pp. 4-10.

Simons, D.J. (1996). In sight, out of mind – when object representations fail. *Psychological Science, 7*, 301-305.

Stoffregren, T.A. and Becklen, R.C. (1989) Dual attention to dynamically structured naturalistic events. *Perceptual and Motor Skills*, 69, 1187-1201.

Stuart, G.W., Maruff, P. and Currie, J. (1997). Object-based visual attention in luminance increment detection? *Neuropsychologia, 35*, 843-853.

Theeuwes, J., Atchley, P. and Kramer, A.F. (1998). Attentional control within 3-D space. *Journal of Experimental Psychology: Human Perception and Performance, 24*, 1476-1485.

Treisman, A. and Gormican, S. (1988). Feature analysis in early vision: evidence from search asymmetries. *Psychological Review, 95*, 15-48.

Trevarthen, C. (1968). Two mechanisms of vision in primates. *Psychologische Forschung, 31*, 299-337.

Tufano, D.R. (1997). Automotive HUDs: The overlooked safety issues. *Human Factors, 39*, 303-311.

Ververs, P.M. and Wickens, C.D. (1998). Head-up displays: Effects of clutter, display intensity and display location on pilot performance. *International Journal of Aviation Psychology, 8*, 377-403.

Weintraub, D.J. and Ensing, M. (1992). *Human Factors Issues in Head-Up Display Design: The Book of HUD* (CSERIAC State of the Art Report). Wright-Patterson Air Force Base, Ohio: Crew System Ergonomics Information Analysis Center.

Weintraub, D.J., Haines, R.F. and Randle, R.J. (1984). The utility of head-up displays: Eye-focus vs. decision times. In, *Proceedings of the Human Factors Society, 28th Annual Meeting* (pp. 529-533). Santa Monica, CA: Human Factors Society.

Weintraub, D.J., Haines, R.F. and Randle, R.J. (1985). Head-up display (HUD) utility, II: Runway to HUD transitions monitoring eye-focus and decision times. In, *Proceedings of the Human Factors Society, 29th Annual Meeting* (pp. 615-619). Santa Monica, CA: Human Factors Society.

Wickens, C.D. (1992). *Engineering Psychology and Human Performance (2nd Edn.)*. New York: Harper Collins.

Wickens, C.D. and Long, J. (1995). Object vs space-based models of visual attention: Implications for the design of head-up displays. *Journal of Experimental Psychology: Applied, 1*, 179-193.

Wickens, C.D., Martin-Emerson, R. and Larish, I. (1993). Attentional tunneling and the head-up display. In, *Proceedings of the 7th International Symposium on Aviation Psychology* (pp. 865-870). Columbus, Ohio: Department of Aviation, Ohio State University.

Wolfe, J.M., Cave, K.R. and Franzel, S.L. (1989). Guided search: an alternative to the feature integration model of visual search. *Journal of Experimental Psychology: Human Perception and Performance, 15*, 419-433.

Yantis, S. (1998). Control of visual attention. In, H. Pashler (Ed.) *Attention* (pp. 223-256). Hove, UK: Psychology Press.

Yeh, M., Wickens, C.D. and Seagull, F.J. (1999). Target cuing in visual search: The effects of conformality and display location on the allocation of visual attention. *Human Factors, 41*, 524-542.

Zambarbieri, D., Schmid, R., Magenes, G. and Prablanc, C. (1982). Saccadic responses evoked by presentation of visual and auditory targets. *Experimental Brain Research, 47*, 417-427.

Acknowledgement

This work was supported by the Commonwealth of Australia Department of Defence under contract No. 647730.

3 Reviewing the role of cockpit alerting systems

Amy R. Pritchett

Abstract

Alerting systems are a prevalent part of modern cockpits, involved in a wide range of piloting tasks. This increasing prevalence corresponds with the increasing capability of modern alerting systems, which have sophisticated, complex algorithms referencing many input sources. The role(s) of the cockpit alerting system have expanded beyond the attention-director role normally covered in the research literature, including nuisances, desired cues, overloads, task management aids, initiators of procedures, and command devices. Some of these roles may be unintended by the designer, be problematic in terms of operational safety, or obstruct the pilot from having cognitive involvement in resolving hazards. These roles imply several problems which highlight operational issues and reveal open research topics. Some of these problems can be solved through widely-recognised measures, such as the reduction of false alarms. Other problems may be more difficult to solve; framed in automation terms, alerting systems are inherently clumsy with an opaque interface into their functioning. The most authoritative alerting systems are also prone to under- and over-reliance, and to conflicts between the authority and responsibility of the pilot. The safety benefits of alerting systems have been widely noted; however, without consideration of these human factors issues there may be a limit to further improvements in safety achievable by the addition of more alerting systems.

Introduction

Alerting systems are prevalent in modern cockpits. A Boeing 777, for example, may have an Engine Indication and Crew Alerting System (EICAS) dedicated to generating alerts and status messages about on-board systems, embedded alerting within other on-board systems, stall warnings, and advanced safety systems such

This paper was first published in Human Factors and Aerospace Safety 1(1), 2001, pp. 5-38

as windshear warnings, the Traffic alert and Collision Avoidance System (TCAS) and the Ground Proximity Warning System (GPWS) (United Airlines, 1998). The prevalence of cockpit alerting systems is also shown by their involvement in an increasingly comprehensive range of the pilot's tasks.

This increasing prevalence corresponds with the increasing capability of modern alerting systems. While simple alerting systems – detectors of a signal from a sensor – still abound, the most modern alerting systems may have input from multiple sensors and communications from other aircraft or the ground, and these inputs may be analysed by the alerting system using computationally intensive algorithms and large knowledge databases.

The role(s) of the cockpit alerting system have multiplied. This may be partly in response to their increased capabilities. Also, pilot familiarity with alerting systems changes the authority they allow the alerting system to have over them, ranging from a cessation of monitoring ('the alerting system will catch problems') to ignoring alerts ('the darn thing is wrong most of the time'). Finally, alerting systems maybe used in hitherto unintended situations, such as the stall warning becoming a cue to follow in high-performance manoeuvres.

In short, cockpit alerting systems have taken on a wide-range of roles beyond the attention-director role normally covered in the research literature. Describing these roles can be difficult to frame in 'automation' terms. Alerting systems are simultaneously highly and loosely automated: highly automated in that they are always monitoring and appear, from the pilot's point of view, to self-activate; loosely automated in that all but the most sophisticated can't actually control any aspect of the environment other than providing output to the pilot. Also, many alerting systems are considered safety-systems, whose actual role vis-à-vis the pilot, unlike an autopilot or flight management system, does not evolve through extended interaction in day-to-day operations but rather is selected by the pilot in the face of looming hazards.

This paper reviews the roles that cockpit alerting systems may assume, how these roles have changed with technological capability, and how effectively these roles allow alerting systems to function as pilot aids and safety systems. First, a denotation for alerting systems is proposed and contrasted with current connotations. A brief review of the technical considerations underlying alerting system design is provided. Then, the variety of roles of alerting systems noted both in the research literature and in studies of current operations are detailed. Finally, potential problems – and solutions – implied by these roles are discussed.

Denotation and connation of alerting systems

No industry standard definition of alerting systems exists which covers the full extent of current implementations. Formal definitions of automation typically imply the need for a level of control over the environment that the alerting system does not have (e.g. Sheridan, 1992, p. 3), or for novelty in having a machine involved in the task (e.g. Parasuraman and Riley, 1997, p. 231). This paper proposes the following formal denotation:

'An alerting system is an electro-mechanical system capable of monitoring for, detecting and announcing conditions anticipated (by the operator or the system designer) to impact the operator's near-term activities.'

While separate and different meanings are sometimes created for terms like *warning*, *alert*, and *alarm*, this definition does not create any distinction between them, while leaving room for implementation-specific meanings based on priority, likelihood or time-horizon (e.g. Sorkin, Kantowitz and Kantowitz, 1988; Veitengruber, 1977).

In contrasting this definition with the implicit use of the term 'alerting-system' in the literature, it is possible to illustrate alerting system qualities that have been well – and not-so-well – studied. For example, alerting systems are often thought of as safety systems, assisting the pilot in hazardous conditions (e.g. Riley et al, 1996), but they also may be used by the pilot as a desired cue, such as the stall warning during slow-flight training.

Likewise, alerting systems are often associated with aural alerts. However, the presence of an aural tone does not necessarily represent an alerting system (a crew-call sound, for example, may represent a signal rather than an alert), and an alerting system may not necessarily require an aural sound, but instead provide pop-up displays, warning lights, or tactile sensations.

Some traditional alerting systems have evolved to capabilities that include more than just alerting, yet remain in common parlance 'alerting systems'. For example, both TCAS and GPWS have executive capabilities, in that they can command the pilot to execute avoidance manoeuvres, and, in systems under test, automatically initiate manoeuvres. Although they may have outgrown the limited function of an alerting system, common connotations still refer to them as such.

Technical considerations in designing alerting systems

In designing an alerting system, fundamental decisions determine its capabilities, and by extension, the roles it can assume. This section briefly describes these design decisions, starting with the simplest alerting systems, signal detectors, and moving on to the more sophisticated systems, hazard detectors and hazard resolvers.

Signal detectors

The simplest alerting systems act as *signal detectors*, shown schematically in figure 1. The alerting system monitors a sensor input; when the input passes a threshold, an announcement is given to the pilot. Typically, the sensor input is also available to the pilot; as such, the alerting system has a direct correlate with a persistent display before the pilot, and may be thought of as an automated equivalent of a 'red-line'.

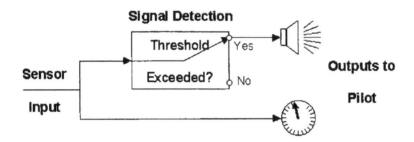

Figure 1   Schematic of signal detector

The threshold may be set in one of two ways. First, the alert threshold may be set by the alerting system operator with each use. This is common in domains where context sensitivities are important in determining the threshold, such as medicine. Such operator-determined alert thresholds can be found in aviation in less standardised operations such as general aviation. Not only may resourceful pilots implement their own simple alerting systems, but watch alarms and count-down-timers are common equipment for single-pilot Instrument Flight Rules (IFR) operations.

Conversely, the threshold may be set by the system designer when creating the alerting system, as is the case for the majority of aviation systems. The designer can build the alerting system around knowledge of sensor dynamics. For example, in developing an engine-fire alerting system from an engine temperature sensor, engineering analysis can identify the temperature readings expected during normal operations and the start of a fire. Also, pre-specified thresholds provide standardisation across a fleet of aircraft and multiple-person flight crews.

Selecting an alerting threshold is commonly described as a signal detection problem. The sensor's signal is presumed to be centred on one value if a condition exists, and another value if the condition does not exist; the signal varies around these values due to uncertainties, represented as noise. Hence, the threshold for detecting the existence of a condition mirrors statistical tests with their commensurate power to make correct detections and correct rejections, as well as their susceptibility to type I errors (missed detections) and type II errors (false alarms). At its heart, alerting remains a probabilistic venture, with the rates of missed detections and false alarms providing the core measure of alerting system efficacy.

An alerting system is limited by the ability of its sensor to observe the dynamics of interest. It is rare that a sensor provides a perfect assessment. Adding identical redundant sensors generally helps reduce the uncertainty bound, but also imposes more cost, weight, and potential for individual sensor failures. Sensors also indicate current values, whereas many thresholds must be set low enough to catch catastrophic conditions before they occur; such predictions therefore add extra uncertainty due to environmental unpredictability.

The trade-offs involved in the selection of an alerting threshold can be represented by a System Operating Characteristics curve (SOC), illustrated in figure 2. For a given sensor, a curve can be drawn that represents the loci of performance over all possible threshold settings. The SOC curves shown in figure 2 are smooth; in reality, they may have sudden jumps, such as with the TCAS SOC curves assembled by Kuchar (1996).

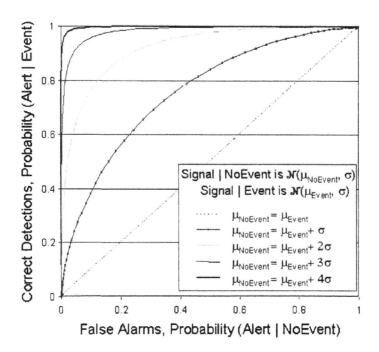

Figure 2 Representative system operating characteristics (SOC) curve

For systems evaluating, yes-or-no, whether a condition exists, the SOC directly portrays the factors to be considered in selecting a threshold. However, for continuously-evolving hazards, the factor of alert lead time is also an important consideration. For example, perfect yes-or-no detection of engine problems can be given by waiting until the engine fails; however, such an alerting system would be of limited use to the pilot. It is also useful to consider *when* an alert will go off; this may be measured by factors such as alert lead time (Bilimoria, 1998) or by the percentage of *late alarms* (alerts too late for an effective resolution) and the percentage of false alarms that will result in *caused accidents*.

Various mechanisms have been suggested for choosing the 'best' alerting threshold (e.g. Kuchar, 1996; Faitakis, Thapliyal and Kantor, 1998). A utility model is commonly used which considers the relative costs of false alarms (and caused accidents) versus missed detections (and late alarms), and finds the threshold value that minimises the expected cost. Quantifying these costs, however, can be difficult. Not only may it be controversial to assign a less-than-infinite cost to missed detections, but determining the cost of a false alarm can be problematic, due to its impact on day-to-day operations as well as its cumulative effects on pilot trust and non-conformance. Instead, in aviation it is common for an allowable missed detection rate to be set (often on the order of 10^{-3} to 10^{-9}) as an indicator of safety and as a certification standard, and subsequently verifying that the false alarm rate is not 'excessive.'

A common variant on a basic signal detector is the implementation of multi-phased alerts. The different phases may be intended as a more direct means of presenting likelihood (e.g. Sorkin, Kantowitz and Kantowitz, 1988), or they may serve as precautionary alerts, intended to prime the pilot as to the nature of a developing problem for a quicker and more accurate response to the ultimate alert.

Substantial research has also examined how the announcement function is best carried out; i.e. the mechanism by which the alerting system can inform the pilot of the event. For saliency, auditory and tactile mechanisms are typically used. These channels typically generate faster responses from operators, can convey urgency well, and require little directional search. The design requirement of making individual aural alerts salient and discriminate has a well-established set of knowledge and guidelines. General standards have been written for volume, length, on/off patterns, frequency, and spoken messages. A supplemental visual indication – warning flag on a dial, flashing light, etc. – may also be included (Stanton and Edworthy, 1999; Cooper, 1978; Veitengruber, 1977).

Tactile announcements are also being studied and implemented. The most common include stick-shaker/stick-pusher implementations for stall protection. Simple buzzers attached to the body are also being tried as a general indication to the pilot of events such as autopilot mode switches (Sklar and Sarter, 2000). The full extent to which tactile presentations can be used in operational environments remains an interesting topic of study.

In addition to their individual presentations, alerts need also be salient and discriminatable when multiple alerts are triggered at the same time. A range of conditions may trigger simultaneous alerts that will overlap to the extent that none can be distinguished. For example, in medicine, situations have been reported where 20 alarms may trigger simultaneously (Meredith and Edworthy, 1994).

Similar cases have been found in the nuclear power industry, process control, and, historically, in aviation (Woods, 1995; Cooper, 1978). As such, the technical capability represented by fully integrated cockpit systems is now being exercised to prioritise alerts and present them singly and sequentially (Proctor, 1998). This is less true in operations such as general aviation, where increasingly powerful alerting systems are now available but remain federated, preventing a central alert prioritisation scheme.

Hazard detectors

More complex alerting systems act as *hazard detectors*. Like signal detectors, they detect when a signal crosses a threshold; the difference is in what that signal represents. As shown in figure 3, multiple sensor signals feed into a pre-process that explicitly or implicitly derives a measure of 'hazard', which is then tested against a pre-specified hazard threshold. All, some or none of these sensor signals may also be available to the pilot.

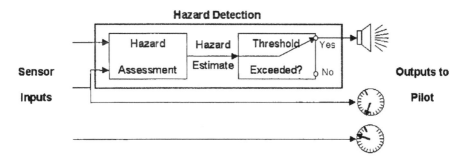

Figure 3   Schematic of a hazard detector

Such a design adds new challenges – namely, selection of a hazard metric and the means by which to calculate it. A common metric is projected time-to-accident. For example, both TCAS and GPWS calculate a projected time-to-impact; if it is less than an allowable threshold, then an alert is given. Another metric for assessing hazard is a direct prediction of hazard probability (e.g. Yang and Kuchar, 1997; Kuchar, 1996), representing one of several different things: the probability that an event is taking place; the probability that an event will occur if nothing is done; and the probability than an accident will occur if a standard resolution is effected. (Note that the probability threshold in this third case is normally quite small!)

The calculations assessing the hazard can be quite intricate. For example, TCAS's only sensor input about the vertical position of traffic is digitally-transmitted altitude rounded to the nearest 100 feet, updated approximately once per second. Through filtering algorithms and storing the measurements from the last several updates, estimates of both altitude and vertical speed are generated. Similar inaccuracies are found in the measurements in the horizontal plane, which software processing must address (RTCA, 1983). These algorithms can dramatically change the SOC curves, as was found with the dramatic reductions in false alarms enabled by software changes to TCAS (Klass, 1998). The on-board calculations may be made faster by pre-computing important values into a database, which the alerting system can then to refer to as a built-in knowledge base (Carpenter and Kuchar, 1997, Yang and Kuchar, 1997). Several different thresholds or alerting triggers may be considered (e.g. RTCA, 1983; Liu, Golborne, Bun and Bartel, 1998).

Some hazard detectors can act as diagnostic systems, in that they can also help identify the underlying cause of the hazard. In process control domains, for example, diagnosis can involve substantial reasoning about the causes of undesired conditions (Borndorff-Eccarius and Johannsen, 1993); this reasoning process can be sufficiently difficult that expert systems have been proposed (e.g., Stanton and Baber, 1995). Similar systems have been tried in aviation, although, from the pilot's point of view, the root-cause of the problem is not always as important as knowledge of a safe course of action (e.g. Davis and Pritchett, 1999).

Hazard resolvers

The most sophisticated safety systems have more than just alerting capabilities: they can also act as *hazard resolvers*. In this case, the purpose of the alert is to direct the attention of the pilot to a commanded resolution calculated and displayed by the system, as shown in figure 4. Aural alerts themselves may contain information, such as the climb or descend commands given by TCAS. Likewise, systems may identify specific configuration actions to take: for example, in the case of a fuel imbalance, a system could provide the pilot with a specific set of fuel feed settings to implement.

Such hazard resolvers are currently established for hazards which develop more fluidly and for which an exact, detailed procedure can not be pre-specified. For example, aircraft collision avoidance requires manoeuvres to be developed on the fly; TCAS additionally communicates with the other aircraft to agree on which direction each aircraft will go. In calculating these avoidance manoeuvres, assumptions must be made about pilot behaviour. For example, TCAS assumes that the pilot will follow a command within five seconds and will execute a 0.25 g pull-up or push-over, as commanded (RTCA, 1983).

Because the alerting and resolution tasks are intrinsically linked, there are benefits to combining them inside the same box. By knowing what the resolution will be, the system can delay the alert until that resolution is appropriate, potentially reducing false alarms, while also ensuring that the alert is early enough for an effective resolution. Likewise, at the point of an alert, much of the information needed for a resolution calculation is already available.

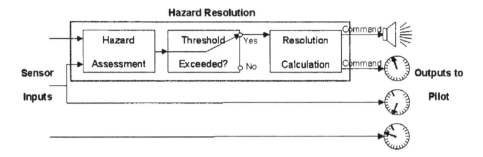

Figure 4   Schematic of Hazard Resolver

Once the system is capable of calculating a resolution, it is not a significant technical leap to give the alerting system control over the aircraft to enact the resolution (although it may be a practical problem in terms of cost, weight, and certification). Such systems are already being tested in the military for auto-ground collision avoidance (Scott, 1999), as well as being inherent parts of some flight control systems, such as the Airbus envelope protection systems.

Alerting system roles

Many different cockpit systems of varying sophistication may be denoted (or connoted) as alerting systems, and collectively they can perform a variety of roles. These roles may be categorised by their responses to the following questions:

- What will the pilot do in response to the alert? (From the point of view of the system designer, the certificator, the designer of the crew procedures, or the pilot.)
- What does the alerting system provide to the pilot – a simple signal verifiable by the pilot, or a determination of hazard or required action?
- Will the pilot try to avoid the alert, or try to get the alert to occur?

The pilot can allow an alerting system to have a number of different roles. Some of these roles were motivation to create the alerting system in the first place; others are more likely post-hoc capitalisation on the alerting system's capabilities; and others may be unwanted outcomes of negative experiences. With the increase in technical capability also comes the potential for new, more authoritative roles for alerting systems. The following sections outline the range of alerting system roles, starting with those associated with the simplest systems and ending with those achievable only with the most technologically advanced.

Alerting system role: attention-director

'DFW to LAW experienced a master warning light enroute to LAW. The right engine oil pressure annunciator light was confirmed by oil pressure gauge dropping.' (ACN 97054, 1988)[1]

The most common (and most studied) role of an alerting system is that of an *attention-director*; i.e. where the alerting system is intended to direct the pilot's attention to a signal deviation for the pilot to recognise, analyse, and resolve. As such, the alerting system is seen as providing a trigger to the pilot to start the diagnosis and, if necessary, resolution processes. The pilot is assumed to be in charge as a thoughtful, analytical being who may choose to ignore or disregard the alert based on experience or knowledge of other aspects of current context.

This attention-directing role brings to the cockpit a continual monitoring capability that the pilot can not provide. Beyond concerns with the boredom and fatigue of asking a human operator to continually monitor a signal, humans have been found to sample signals at a rate scaled to the frequency with which they change; so-called 'complacency' may actually be seen as a reasonable and approximating-rational coping mechanism in the face of competing workload demands (Kerstholt, Passenier, Houttuin and Schuffel, 1996; Molloy and Parasuraman, 1996; Parasuraman et al, 1996). As such, alerting systems can particularly aid the pilot in detecting a number of conditions: rare changes in the signal; sudden, quickly evolving signal changes that might develop between pilot samples; and signals revealing particularly catastrophic or irreversible conditions whose high cost merit a dedicated monitor.

Just as engineers use signal detection theory to analyse alerting systems, so has it been applied to modelling human behaviour. Such a model has had a strong empirical fit in laboratory studies. From these studies it was noted that subjects may tend to adjust their sensitivity to 'cancel' the alerting system: for example, subjects were found to respond later to earlier alerts, rather than following alerts with a fixed reaction time (Elvers and Elrif, 1997; Sorkin and Woods, 1985; Getty, Swets and Pickett, 1994; See et al, 1997).

Beyond signal detection theory, several other models of human event detection have been proposed (e.g., Rouse, 1983). Some of these – error and error rate thresholds, and Kalman filters with residual error tests – mirror engineering models sometimes used to design alerting system algorithms. Other models, such as pattern recognition and judgement analysis, are intended for analysing expert behaviour in naturalistic environments.

---

[1] Pilot report to the Aviation Safety Reporting System (ASRS), identified by report accession number and year.

While models of human event detection have been found fit well in laboratory tests, their predictive power for safety analysis of an aviation alerting system is limited for two significant reasons. First, the choice of 'mode' of behaviour is a pilot's opportunistic response to the full demands of the environment at the time of the alert, and is therefore hard to predict. Second, it is near-impossible to replicate in the laboratory the actual costs of the alert / no-alert decision. Laboratory studies need to create the ecology of the situation and tell their subjects the relative costs of a missed detection and false alarm; as such they can not reveal situations where an alerting system design varies in implicit-cost modelling from what the pilot would accept (Getty, Swets and Pickett, 1994).

This alerting system role is also characterised by what it does not do for the pilot. Dealing with an emergency might be characterised as a three-stage process: detection, diagnosis, and resolution (Rouse, 1983; Marshall and Baker, 1994). Obviously, an attention-director helps only with the first stage; subsequent steps are left to the pilot.

Alerting system role: nuisance

'I'm afraid the numerous false alarms, worse yet, the verbal distraction during critical phases, will cause the pilots to disarm [TCAS].' (ACN 171821, 1991)[1]

'The fire warning was false but occurred at a point in the flight where it was most likely, a hot day under load during engine start. Given the extreme seriousness of fire and no time for a lengthy verification of the warning, the evac was necessary.' (ACN 114636, 1989).

Alerting systems are typically viewed as safety systems installed to detect events that the pilot might otherwise not catch. With this emphasis on preventing high cost missed detections, the alerting threshold is typically set to a value which has extremely few missed detections, at the expense of potentially having a high false alarm rate. As a result, many alerting systems have become notorious for their false alarms and are sometimes viewed as a *nuisance*.

Engine indications, for example, have historically been viewed by pilots with a fair amount of scepticism. Also, TCAS and GPWS have also been reported by pilots as having a detrimental false alarm rate (Mellone, 1993; Hasse, 1992, Vallauri, 1995; Wiener and Curry, 1980). Problems with high false alarm rates are not unique to aviation, but can also be found in medicine, in process control, and in other forms of transportation, including trains and automobiles (Parasuraman and Riley, 1997; Dingus et al, 1997).

This high false alarm rate may be attributable to several factors. First and foremost, it is often a necessary consequence of setting the alerting system threshold to meet 'hard' missed detection standards. Additionally, designers may not have anticipated the range of extraneous conditions which lead to false alarms. For example, with engine fire alerting systems, several conditions may cause false alarms, such as extended ground idling, hot weather, and broken sensors or connectors (which may be more faulty than the engine itself).

Another factor contributing to a high false alarm rate is a poor understanding, on the part of the designer, of the true cost of a false alarm. As an isolated case a false alarm does not appear to have a high cost; other than requiring a diversion from the original flight plan, it seems like a safe move to avoid a potential catastrophe. Not until viewed in a longer-term sense does the true cost of false alarms come clear. While it is intended that the pilot should be able to disregard or over-ride the alerting system, he or she can not do so until they have regarded it sufficiently to decide that it is erroneous (Woods, 1995). If a pilot to chooses the follow a false alarm, then it has obstructed the outcome of the flight. If false alarms are frequent, then they can also start to obstruct the normal course of operations. For example, due to false GPWS alarms on approach to Cincinnati's runway 18L, special additions have been added to some airlines' briefings about conditions under which a GPWS alert may be disregarded for that approach.

For these reasons, false alarms can become such a nuisance that pilots may cease to respond, delay their response, turn off the alerting system, or discredit them to the extent that they ignore a correct detection. This so-called 'cry-wolf' phenomenon has been widely noted (e.g. Block, Nuutinen and Ballasts, 1999; Seminara, Gonzalez and Parsons 1997; Weiner and Curry, 1980; Paté-Cornell, 1986).

Alerting system role: final authority on problem

'It was possibly a false TCAS II alert, but like the GPWS, it's better to be safe than sorry.' (ACN 163373, 1990).

'... in IMC conditions the mode 2 GPWS warning occurred for 2 cycles. We immediately initiated climb to 8000 feet... After landing we phoned air traffic control and they became very defensive, assuring us that their minimum vector altitudes had not be violated...It was not a case of obvious false warning so we could not just disregard it, yet ATC was offended! We're alive!' (ACN 159794, 1990).

Just as a pilot may over-rely on the alerting system by not monitoring, so too may he or she 'catch' an oncoming problem before the alert, but rely on the alert as a *final authority on the problem*. For example, a pilot may notice that engine temperature is increasing. Uncertain whether the gauge is wrong and whether the problem warrants immediate action, the pilot may not take any drastic action until the problem is clearly defined. An alert provides that definition.

Likewise, the pilot may be reluctant to act based on uncertain information on matters over which he or she does not have complete authority. For example, Midkiff and Hansman (1993) found that pilots were reluctant to act based on overheard voice communications about possible traffic conflicts. In such

58

situations, the air traffic controller normally has authority over the pilot's actions. However, a TCAS advisory provides the pilot with the authority to act.

Alerting system role: trusted monitor

Just as pilots may under-rely on an alert when it is triggered, so may they over-rely on the alerting system as a *trusted monitor* when all appears to be going well, an effect Wiener and Curry (1980) termed 'primary-backup inversion.' The designer of an alerting system generally has an image of the role the pilot should play in monitoring independent of the alerting system. This intended role may vary: some alerting systems intend that the pilot should continue to monitor as before; others, such as with the dark cockpit philosophy, intend to take over much of the monitoring role, but still intend that the pilot should keep a general awareness of the flight and be observant for anomalies.

This over-reliance when all is going well may be correlated with under-reliance when an alert is given. Through nuisance alerts and system descriptions, the pilot may be well-convinced that the system's monitoring is continuous, albeit with conservative alerting criteria. While alerting systems are often thought of as interacting with the pilot when they activate, this role highlights how the presence of an alerting system can change patterns of behaviour in normal conditions in which the alerting system is silent.

Alerting system role: resolution assessor

'On climbout at approximately flight level 220, intermittent #1 engine overheat light on, followed by intermittent red fire handle light and bell. When throttle closed, all warning indications ceased. Initiated return to LAX. Later in descent all afore-mentioned indications returned. Shut down engine #1 and fired left extinguisher bottle... All warning indications ceased. Still further in descent same warning indications returned. Fired right extinguisher bottle. Indications again ceased. Landing at LAX uneventful.' (ACN 118275, 1989).

Most alerting systems, namely signal and hazard detectors, are thought of as providing an alert that an undesired event is occurring. Additionally, however, the disappearance of the alert can serve as a tool for assessing when this condition has been resolved; i.e. act as a *resolution-assessor* (e.g. Stanton and Baber, 1995). For example, consider the generation of an engine temperature warning. Not only does it indicate a potential problem with the engine, but it may also be a useful tool in resolving the problem – namely, the alert can let the pilot know whether throttling back the engine is sufficient, or whether more extreme action is needed.

Signal and hazard detectors do not provide open-loop guidance to the pilot about a resolution (i.e. they do not say 'do this and everything will be ok'). Instead, their alerts may be viewed as a feedback mechanism that lets pilots know the results of their efforts. This closed-loop process may be undertaken by the pilot in a deliberate, purposeful manner. Conversely, this process can also conceivably be undertaken in frustration (i.e. 'hit every button until the darn alert goes away').

In many situations this role of an alerting system can be positive in helping the pilot resolve a hazard quickly. Correspondingly, it suggests the danger of extending this alerting system role too far. Rather than viewing his or her task as keeping away from alerts, in most situations it is preferable for the pilot to view his or her role as keeping the aircraft near the desired condition, and to recognise that the absence of an alert does not imply the situation is completely satisfactory.

Alerting system role: desired cue

Normally, an alerting is something to be avoided when possible, and resolved when necessary. However, in some cases a system's alert may become a *desired cue*. For example, consider the stall warning. Implemented on the vast majority of aircraft flying today, it was initially motivated by a desire to alert the pilot when near an inadvertent stall and spin. However, most pilots trained on light general aviation aircraft are quickly introduced to another use for the stall warning – namely as a cue during slow flight training that the aircraft is truly just above stall speed, which the pilot should seek to keep on. This stall warning is also typically a desired cue when landing a light aircraft; if triggered with the wheels just off the ground, then it is a sign to all on board that the touchdown occurred properly just above stall.

This role of desired cue can even be capitalised upon explicitly in operating procedures. For example, current airline windshear avoidance procedures typically call for full-power and for the pilot to pull back on the flight controls until the onset of the stick-shaker (a tactile stall warning). Not only does it reduce the visual workload of the pilot, but it also provides a consistent cue during even the most extreme windshear events, in which aircraft airspeed indications may fluctuate rapidly in response to rapidly changing wind speeds. The role of desired cue has become sufficiently common in industry that other envelope-protection alerting systems have been proposed specifically for this role (e.g., Horn, 1999).

The use of cockpit alerts as a desired cue is made possible by a built-in safety margin. For example, stall warnings commonly trigger before stall; flap overspeed warnings initiate at 10 knots below the actual limit; and red-line alerts on airspeeds and engine speeds have a built in safety-margin of about 10%. As such, pilots often construe alerts as marking achievable – but not exceedable – flight conditions.

This role of alerting systems has evolved through pilot experience and, perhaps, with a perceived need for the cues they can provide. This evolution may be judged as having reached the point where this role is reinforced by training and procedures, and where the alerting system is used in response to situations beyond those it was originally intended to protect against.

Alerting system role: task management aid

The most wide-spread connotation of alerting systems is that they guard against unanticipated, hazardous conditions. However, in some situations alerts are anticipated and serve to direct the pilot's attention from one planned task to another (e.g. Hickling, 1994). In such cases, alerting systems can fill the role of *task management* aids. This role is illustrated by the use of watch alarms and timers in single-pilot Instrument Flight Rules (IFR) operations. The pilot may specifically choose to set the timer throughout the flight. It can be used to alert the pilot that something new needs to be started (e.g. radio call of waypoint passage), that something needs to be ended (e.g. the conclusion of a timed approach), that something needs to be checked (e.g. periodic reminders to check the aircraft systems' status), or that something ought to be happening (e.g. reaching an 'expect further clearance' time).

Such alerts can also be found in more sophisticated cockpits: for example, the 1000 feet-to-go horn alerts the pilot that he or she (or the autopilot) is transitioning into a level altitude. This role varies from the common conception of an alert – it is more mundane and less focused on emergencies. However, it does highlight the extent to which alerts may be not only expected, but can be cues within a pilot's plan.

Alerting system role: overload

'I find it very disturbing that a warning system like the GPWS can be allowed to disrupt air traffic control and cockpit communications because of its loud volume and its inability to be shut off.' (ACN 254544, 1993).

While an alerting system is normally intended to direct a pilot's attention to a problem, there are cases where an alert instead serves to *overload* the pilot and obstruct piloting tasks. Sometimes this overload may be purely physical in nature – due to the volume of the alert or the extreme brightness of a warning light, the pilot may not be able to recognise anything beyond the existence of the alert. For example, pilot reports filed with the Aviation Safety Reporting System (ASRS) have cited TCAS as the distraction precipitating unauthorised landings at Atlanta, Newark, and Salt Lake City (ACN 168712, 1991; ACN 178850, 1991; ACN 179521, 1991). This overload may also be more cognitive in nature. Because of the alert's saliency, the pilot may find it hard to ignore the alert (Mosier, 1996) and may prioritise the alert's subject before more important tasks, negating any task management and planning the pilot may have performed.

This overload may also occur in the presence of multiple alerts and many steps have been taken in aviation to resolve it, including allowing the pilot to silence some types of alerts, and prioritising and sequentially presenting alerts through a central alert-integration scheme (Proctor, 1998). While reducing overload, this solution has not proven able to totally prevent it. For example, in describing a recent crash of an MD-81, the co-pilot gave the following description:

'All the lamps are blinking and there are a lot of warning sounds in the cockpit. It is really a terrible environment. It is not possible to manage all this information. With so many malfunctions you stop analyzing them and concentrate on the flying. That's the only thing to do.' (Mårtensson, 1995, p. 315).

Integration is not an available solution for all aircraft. For example, sophisticated cockpit systems are now sufficiently affordable for general aviation. However, such systems are typically federated, i.e. they are independent units that do not co-ordinate their functions with other cockpit systems. With such installations the potential is growing for multiple alerts to create pilot overload.

Alerting system role: initiator of procedures

'Southbound approximately 80 nm north of ATL at flight level 290, the #2 fire warning activated. Engine was shutdown in accordance with emergency procedures and the flight diverted into ATL Hartsfield airport without further incident. To the best of my knowledge the warning was a false indication, but procedures required an immediate landing, which I did.' (ACN 89906, 1988).

The attention-director role assumes that the pilot will follow a fluid, cognitive diagnostic process in assessing the cause of an alert and the solution to the problem it identifies. In many operations, however, the alerting system instead acts as an *initiator of procedures*. These procedures can lead pilots through the diagnostic and resolution processes in a manner that can benefit from *a priori* study of the most likely and most hazardous situations. Procedures can also help pilots incorporate the temporal dynamics of the situation, such as engine-failure procedures in light aircraft that start with the potential resolutions requiring the most time to take effect (e.g. carb.-heat, fuel) and end with those with immediate effect (e.g. magnetos). If well-trained, pilots can use procedures to enact faster and more consistent reactions.

When alerting systems are intended to be initiators of procedures, there may be less of a desire for the alerting system to be given diagnostic and resolution capabilities, as these processes are built into the procedure. For example, in a flight simulator study of pilots' responses to onboard system failures, the pilots indicated few perceived benefits to enhanced alerting systems that presented diagnostic information in situations where a known procedure already existed (Davis and Pritchett, 1999).

The procedure can be a good way to actively draw the pilot into the diagnostic process. As an extreme example, the procedure following a fire-warning on the UH-60 'Blackhawk' helicopter has the pilot investigate the warning's veracity, including asking the crew-chief if there is smoke and monitoring the other gauges. In other words, the procedure can be a structure through which the pilot can verify the alert and evaluate the aircraft condition.

Conversely, in other situations the procedure may exist to essentially remove the pilot cognitively from the diagnosis and resolution task, and instead effect an autonomic response. In this situation, the alerting system has an executive role which is intended to require actions from pilots. For example, CFIT training material urges pilots to 'follow the GPWS alert'; likewise, with more reliable engine fire indications, pilots may be trained to activate the extinguishers without questioning.

Alerting system role: command device

'*Aircraft was not acquired visually until after evasive action was taken... TCAS and ATC saved the day. A collision would have occurred without the heads-up alert we got from TCAS.*' (ACN 179784, 1991)

'*The sequence of events transpired very fast – faster than you really can analyze the situation. The warnings and commands are very authoritative and you react almost out of fright.*' (ACN 165484, 1990)

A hazard-resolver-type alerting system may be implemented as a *command device*. In this role, the alerting system has an executive role in which pilots can be commanded, in real-time, to follow specific actions. For example, 'TCAS is a 'first' in a class of avionics that actually advises a manoeuvre, rather than the more conventional role of showing the situation to the pilot for his evaluation' (Williamson and Spencer, 1989, p. 1741). This implementation may be chosen when exact, specific procedures do not exist for every situation, and a resolution must instead be calculated on the fly; or this implementation and role may be chosen when there is a desire, by the alerting system designer, to reinforce a pre-specified procedure.

Within this alerting system role, it can be difficult – and sometimes undesired – for the pilot to become cognitively involved in the situation other than as an executor of the displayed commands. Not only may there be little time to delay, but also hazard-resolver alerting systems can be quite complex, making analysis of the reasoning behind the alert and commands difficult.

The pilot has two inter-related concepts to verify: the timing of the alert itself, and the substance of the subsequent resolution. The alerting system may have several different 'modes' of operation (such as the different thresholds and constraints on avoidance manoeuvres within TCAS as a function of altitude), and they may have several different alert triggers (such as GPWS, which has several different criteria that can trigger an alert). Most alerting systems do not present their underlying reasoning, so the pilot may not be aware of the assumptions and objectives underlying the system.

Also, from the pilot's point of view, the alerting system may now be presenting them with more than just information. Instead, the alerting system is now providing such a neat-and-tight package of information that it may be difficult to change their actions away from those commanded in any small way without the whole set unravelling. For example, TCAS not only calculates the projected efficacy of an avoidance manoeuvre on its own – it also communicates and co-ordinates with the other aircraft as to 'who goes where'. For a pilot to not-conform to a TCAS manoeuvre represents not just an over-ride of the command, but also the breaking of a hidden electronic contract made with the other aircraft.

In some sense, a safety system intended for this role may have advanced beyond the capabilities normally attributed to an alerting system. While it does generate alerts in response to hazardous situations, it also provides the analysis and command capability normally associated with other types of automation, such as expert systems, decision aids, and flight control systems.

Unlike many forms of advanced automation, however, the pilot is still physically involved in the control loop. Practical reasons for leaving the pilot in the control loop include concerns about the complexity and cost of creating, certifying and implementing a fully-automatic system, especially as an add-on into established cockpits. Also, the alerting system, as with automation in general, is often recognised as needing the pilot to assess its appropriateness within the current context (e.g. Rogers, Schutte and Latorella, 1996).

However, the decision to leave the pilot in the control loop may have an evolutionary explanation as well: current command device roles have evolved from roles associated with simpler alerting systems, in which the pilot has always been a fundamental part of the decision process. By leaving the pilot in the loop, there is often the appearance of the pilot remaining as the final authority in what action will be taken; however, with some systems this authority may not be balanced by the pilot having the ability to verify or question the alerting system due to time, workload, system complexity and lack of information.

With this alerting system role, pilots are typically measured as an actuator: i.e. by their reaction-time and command-following accuracy. For example, in recent tests of an automatic ground collision avoidance system (Auto-GCAS) for fighters, the following was noted:

'Because pilots are adamant about having final authority over their aircraft, the [flight test] team initially gave the pilot an ability to always override the Auto-GCAS. Extensive testing, plus discussion with F-22 test pilots, changed that attitude. During all-terrain testing, we found that even the slightest override of the GCAS autopilot in the wrong direction would blast you through the [minimum safe altitude] floor.' (Scott, 1999)

Potential problems with alerting systems roles

The just-completed review of alerting system roles revealed the good, the bad, and the unexpected. While alerting systems often meet their intended roles, they are also commonly ignored, used in unintended ways, and misunderstood. This section will discuss the problematic implications of the alerting system roles just discussed.

Problem: alerting systems function differently from other forms of cockpit automation

Alerting systems have a unique position in the cockpit, as they are often viewed as 'safety systems' intended to help the pilot predict, avoid and resolve hazardous situations. As such, several facets of discussions on automation design do not carry over well to alerting systems. For example, Woods (1986) suggested that 'good' automation would create a diverse, joint human-machine cognitive system; however, as a back-up monitor, alerting systems are inherently a redundant system performing many of the same monitoring, detection and diagnosis actions as the pilot. Likewise, 'normal' cockpit automation is activated and de-activated by the pilot. With this control, the pilot is comparatively free to determine his or her own fluid approach to the tasks at hand. Alerting systems are intended to disrupt this fluid process; they can not even be purposefully ignored without first requiring attention (Woods, 1995).

High pilot workload is generally considered undesirable. As such, reducing workload is generally a motivation for automation, and guidelines for designing automation for this purpose have been developed (e.g. Kantowitz and Caspar, 1988). In fact, the pejorative term *clumsy automation* has been applied to systems that require attention or increase workload at times when the pilot is already under high-workload and time-criticality (Weiner, 1989). Unfortunately, given that they are intended to activate in hazardous situations and demand attention, many alerting systems are fundamentally and irrevocably clumsy automation. At best, steps can be taken to reduce the potential for pilot overload through alert prioritisation (Proctor, 1998).

As such, much of the research and operational literature on the design and use of automation can not be directly applied. Likewise, measures of 'good' interaction with automation may not match measures commonly used for an alerting system. These differences are rooted in differences between 'efficiency' measures such as average performance and workload, and 'safety' measures that examine the frequencies and costs of hazardous occurrences.

In the same way, common fixes to problems with automation are not as easily applied to problems with alerting systems. For example, pilots typically receive formal flight training in the use of both alerting systems and 'normal' cockpit automation. However, many pilots report that a higher level of confidence in, and understanding of, automation (most notably the Flight Management System [FMS]) develops with on-the-job experience. This may be viewed as both a process for accumulating understanding of the system itself, as well as adapting his or her skills to the new environment including the automation (Kirlik, 1993). However, a pilot does not receive the same on-the-job training with many alerting

65

systems; they trigger so rarely that a pilot may see none, one or only a few in his or her career.

Problem: nuisance

'I don't know if you are tracking false GPWS warnings, but if you have any statistics I would like to see them. This system has given me enough false indications over the last five years, that I am suspect of its value to me or the flight deck.' (ACN 202795, 1992)

As noted earlier, alerting systems may take on the role of a nuisance, generally because of their high false alarm rate. This is obviously a problem, and one that can not be easily solved. An alerting system's fundamental limits (as illustrated by the false alarm – missed detection trade-off described by its SOC curve) are largely determined by its sensors and algorithms, and by environmental unpredictability. Ultimately, the best results will be attained through the use of the most accurate sensors and alerting algorithms. For example, significant reductions in false ground proximity warnings have been enabled through the Enhanced Ground Proximity Warning System's (EGPWS) inclusion of terrain databases as a reference for alerts, as compared to the older GPWS's ability to only consider radar altitude.

Within an alerting system's limits, it has been suggested that the base rate of the event should be considered, such that the alert threshold can be set to maximise the probability that any alert is correct (e.g. Parasuraman, Hancock and Olofinboba, 1997; Bliss, Gilson and Deaton, 1995). While it is correct to re-evaluate how the alert thresholds are set (and to re-adjust the cost of a false alarm), their common role in aviation as safety systems requires more emphasis on a low rate of missed detections for certification and for acceptance by the pilot community.

Other potential solutions include making the alert less strident so that the pilot is not as violently disrupted from his or her task. As a related solution, some systems have established phased alerts where the precautionary-phase alerts are less strident and serve to 'gently' prepare the pilot for a subsequent diversion of their full attention.

A third potential solution is to examine the intended role of the alerting system. Alerts intended to take over the pilot's actions, such as those demanding the execution of commands or procedures, may be perceived as more of a nuisance than those that function as attention-directors. In other words, the costs of false alarms from more authoritative systems may be higher and should be considered during design.

Likewise, alerts whose underlying basis are harder to perceive may appear erratic to the pilot. In such cases, the alerting system may be tasked with explaining itself, so that it is perceived as a consistent – albeit conservative – entity, rather than as a spurious nuisance.

Problem: trust in the alerting system

'When you've read the horror stories of others for not following GPWS warnings, and you believe your position to be safe in relation to the ground, it creates a tough conflict when the GPWS issues such a warning (most likely a false one).' (ACN 202384, 1992)

'There is a great lack of confidence in the TCAS system with the pilot group. I was one of them but I believe this saved a mid-air collision.' (ACN 185690, 1991)

The trust a pilot places in a system has been demonstrated to have a strong effect on his or her interaction with it. Trust in automation is typically associated with the dependability and predictability the operator has experienced in using it (Lee and Moray, 1992). However, most alerting systems interact with the pilot so little that a different basis for trust is relied upon, termed 'faith' by Lee and Moray (1992) and 'fiduciary responsibility' by Muir (1987).

Fiduciary responsibility is a measure of system capability inferred from certification by some outside, respected authority. It has the potential to provide a fair assessment of trust during the pilot's first interaction with an alerting system. However, it is extremely brittle to any perception of ill performance; trust in an alerting system be seriously damaged by a missed detection or false alarm. Once trust has been reduced to a level lower than justified by the performance of the system, it can be very hard to restore (Muir, 1994). This type of trust is not based solely on personal interaction. For example, in the case of TCAS, not only have pilots passed on their experiences – good and bad – by word-of-mouth, but the popular press has broadcast both situations where TCAS 'saved-the-day' and reports insinuating TCAS is unsafe. Such reports can impact perceptions of fiduciary responsibility.

Trust alone does not solely determine how the system will be used. Among several factors is the operator's own self-confidence in their ability to assess the relevant hazard independently (Lee and Moray, 1994; Riley, 1996). The impact of trust and self-confidence on pilot interaction with an alerting system is shown conceptually in figure 5. Each is broken down into two levels, high and low, representing four possible quadrants. When pilot self-confidence is high and his or her trust in the alerting system is low, it is reasonable to expect that the pilot will act primarily on their own assessment; when the pilot's self-confidence at the task is low and trust in the alerting system is high, then his or her action may be based primarily on the alerting system. Of note is the upper-left quadrant. Presumably we want the pilot to have both high self-confidence and high trust in the alerting system. However, in this condition, should a situation arise where the pilot not agree with the output of the alerting system, then he or she can be left in a conundrum about what actions to take, and it is impossible to predict with certainty what reasoning – the pilot's or the alerting system's – will determine the ultimate course of action.

Pilot Self-Confidence at Task

	High	*Low*
Trust in Alerting System *High*	Indeterminate	Pilot will probably follow alerting system
Low	Pilot will probably verify or ignore alerting system	Indeterminate

Figure 5   Trust in the alerting system and self-confidence as determinants of pilot action

Problem: alerting system complexity

As with other types of cockpit automation, pilot understanding of alerting systems may be difficult due to their complexity. The complexity of cockpit automation, especially Flight Management Systems (FMS), has been noted in many studies as an obstruction to good pilot understanding of the system. This complexity is often quantified in terms of the number of 'modes' within the system. While alerting systems may have modes in the form of context-sensitive alerting thresholds or multiple triggering criteria, a better measure of complexity – from the pilot's point of view – may be a rough categorisation of the amount of processing and fore-knowledge required to go from the information available to the pilot to the assessment made by the alerting system.

For simple signal detectors, this complexity measure would be very low – with a simple check of a gauge the pilot can verify the alerting system's output. At the other extreme are those hazard detectors and hazard resolvers that are intentionally designed for better overall performance than that expected from the pilot alone. Take TCAS, for example. Its alerts and commands are based on several processes not easily re-created by the pilot: memory of previous positions and convergence rates to estimate current conditions; filtering the assessment of convergence rate, tuned to the statistical properties of the sensor inputs; and communication with the intruding aeroplane to co-ordinate avoidance manoeuvres (RTCA, 1983). The logic to perform these calculations is intricate enough that specialised techniques had to be developed to certify its logic (e.g. Heimdahl, Leveson and Reese, 1998). Other alerting systems may also have built-in knowledge in the form of databases (Kuchar and Carpenter, 1997) or prioritisation schemes (Wiener and Curry, 1980; Proctor, 1998), adding to their apparent complexity.

Problem: presentation of feedforward and feedback information about the alerting system

Since the typical alerting system only provides visual and aural alerts – and possibly commands – its apparent functioning can be very 'opaque'; i.e. similar to effects found in studies of complex automated systems, the alerting system may not present the rationale, criteria, and determining factors for its actions to the operator to promote understanding (Sarter and Woods, 1992; Sarter and Woods, 1994; Hickling, 1994; Noyes and Starr, 2000).

An opaque interface with an alerting system may be solved by presenting more information about the alerting system's reasoning – such as a representation of the alerting system's threshold on a relevant situation display. Such *consonance* between an alerting system and a situation display can help pilots react in accordance with alerts that they might not otherwise agree with (Pritchett and Vandor, 1999). In creating such a consonant presentation, it is often important to have it available not just after the alert (when time can be critical), but also before the alert. Such a continuously-available display provides a predictive power found beneficial (Trujillo, 1994; Noyes, CresswellXStarr and Rankin, 1999; Noyes and Starr, 2000). Such a predictive power may also serve as feedforward information about the alerting system, allowing it to interact in a less disruptive manner with the pilot's planning and task management.

Treating the pilot's reaction to alerts as a logical process, the pilot's ability to understand the alerting system determines his or her ability to assess the validity of its alert and commands. Likewise, improving the pilot's ability to understand the system also serves implicitly to train the pilot on the dynamics of the hazard, potentially increasing the performance of his or her own independent judgements. As such, providing a better interface into the alerting system's functioning can serve as a parallel, co-ordinated effort to make the pilot *understand* the alerting system and to *agree* with it, and by extension to allow the pilot to develop a better basis for trust.

This solution may also extend to problems noted earlier. Having the alerting system provide both feedback (once the alert has occurred) and feedforward (before the alert) may, by extension, help reduce the negative impacts of alerting system complexity and of nuisance alerts, while helping the pilots form an appropriate trust in the alerting system (Bliss, Jeans and Prioux, 1996).

However, the correct presentation of this information may require a fundamental change in the way situation displays – and situation awareness – are viewed relative to the alerting task. Pilots' need for situation awareness is widely recognised (Endsley, 1995). To meet this need, situation displays are being widely implemented to provide the pilot with a clear picture of many aspects of the environment, such as aircraft system status, terrain, weather and traffic. However, these displays typically support a situation assessment that is independent of the alerting system. For example, the terrain shown on situation displays associated with EGPWS are typically colour-coded based on altitude, which is not the same schemata used for generating alerts. Based on aircraft configuration and vertical speed, it may be possible for 'yellow' terrain to not generate an alert, or for an alert to be triggered by potential impact with terrain shown in green.

As such, complete situation awareness may need to include 'alerting system awareness'. This poses not only a requirement on the situation display to provide alerting system awareness, but also a limitation on the alerting system: in order to *communicate* the its functioning, the alerting system's logic must be *communicable*, limiting its allowable complexity (Bainbridge, 1983).

Problem: unintended roles

The capabilities of an alerting system may be capitalised upon in ways not intended by its designer or not substantially discussed in the research literature. Pilots may opportunistically use the alerting system as a desired cue, as a resolution-assessor, or as a task management aid. These unintended roles may even be institutionalised through operating procedures and flight training.

These additional roles may sometimes be viewed as a side-benefit of alerting systems. However, the alerting system designer has neither the same level of control over their emergence, nor the ability to tailor the system to meet their needs. They can be difficult to predict; only the most general principles can help estimate what unintended roles may occur, such as estimating potential pilot actions when given the information the alerting system brings to the cockpit (e.g. Vallauri, 1997), or as a result of risk homeostasis.

Given that these unintended roles may occur, they may place additional requirements on alerting system design. For example, because some alerting systems may be used as resolution assessors or desired cues, they may require a built-in margin of play so that aircraft operation near their thresholds represents an acceptable level of safety.

Problem: procedural conflicts

'We were getting a TCAS [command] and the approach controller told us to ignore the TCAS... It put us in quite a dilemma with TCAS telling us to do one thing and the controller telling us to do another.' (ACN 177004, 1991)

Associated with many alerting systems are operating procedures dictating how they shall be used. For example, executive alerting systems such as GPWS and TCAS typically mandate a prompt reaction to their alerts, followed by conformance to their commands to resolve the hazard. However, other procedures may interact with the alerting system's procedure.

These interactions may be direct conflicts: for example, while the procedure for GPWS calls for an immediate pull-up, approach procedures for specific runways (such as Cincinnati's approach to runway 18L) give a detailed description of situations in which the pilot may elect to ignore a GPWS alert. Likewise, these interactions may represent the operator's reluctance to override standard operating procedures: for example, pilots have reported receiving conflicting commands from air traffic controllers and TCAS about how to resolve a potential collision hazard (Mellone, 1993; Vallauri, 1995). Finally, these conflicts may also result from conflicting procedures associated with simultaneous alerts from different alerting systems.

Obviously, the potential for procedural conflicts requires careful consideration during the design and testing of the alerting system. Likewise, procedural conflicts may also require consideration during implementation of new standard operating procedures. For example, changes in air traffic control procedures, such as closely-spaced parallel approaches, now require study for their impact on TCAS alerts; in some cases it may be necessary for the pilot to set TCAS to a less-authoritative alerting-only mode to prevent conflicts.

Problem: over- and under-reliance on the alerting system

'I believe the TCAS saved our lives and in retrospect I wish I had followed its advisories more aggressively.' (ACN 176015, 1991)

'We all should look into developing procedures involving TCAS II and when and at what times it should be used.' (ACN 176392, 1991)

The creation of a more capable alerting system implies that the pilot can – or should – rely upon it to some degree. Actually creating this level of reliance, however, may be difficult. Examining automation in general, problems with under- and over-reliance have been cited in many different domains, including aircraft, railroad, ship, process control, and medicine (Riley, 1996; Parasurman and Riley, 1997; Mosier and Skitka, 1996; Guerlain, 1999).

Under-reliance on automation is comparatively rare – for systems used on a day-to-day basis, the system must usually demonstrate during testing that it will be useful to the pilot before it is implemented. Predicting the reliance on an alerting system, on the other hand, is difficult based only upon the artificial conditions under which it must be tested (Pritchett, Vándor and Edwards, 1999). Hence the significant rate of non-conformance to alerting systems is commonly cited as the most visible example of under-reliance to automation (Parasuraman and Riley, 1997; Wiener and Curry, 1980). For example, one study of ASRS reports involving TCAS found a self-reported rate of non-conformance of 16%, one half of which were listed as conscious decisions by pilots at the time that another action would be better or the alert should be ignored (Mellone, 1993). Studies of GPWS reported a very high rate (73%) of 'delayed pilot reactions' to terrain alerts, with 64% of responding pilots citing their opinions that corrective action should not be initiated without first attempting to verify the warning (Hasse, 1992).

Over-reliance on alerting systems has also been identified. With the simplest alerting systems, this may be manifested as primary-backup-inversion, in which pilot behaviour during normal monitoring is not as involved as the designer had intended. As systems become more capable – and more authoritative – this over-reliance may transition from occurring just during normal monitoring to also allowing the alerting system to effectively make decisions in the face of hazards, opening the door to errors of commission in which a pilot acts upon faulty guidance.

As with automation, no tried-and-true set of solutions to over- and under-reliance has yet been identified. Many solutions stem from solving the more basic problems already described. Having the alerting system provide more information about its functioning – and hence its limitations – may enable the pilot to assess the alert's correctness within the immediate context. Likewise, reductions in false alarms through better sensors and alerting algorithms may help reduce under-reliance through improving trust.

More importantly, a potential solution may be found in clearly-defining the level of reliance expected from the pilot. Without this knowledge the pilot may not be aware that his or her behaviour does not match that assumed by the system designer. Likewise, without this knowledge, other processes such as training and drafting of procedures may not support appropriate reliance. This potential solution parallels calls for a clear and consistent philosophy of use for cockpit automation.

Problem: authority/responsibility double bind

'None of us even had time to look at the TCAS scope to see the aircraft providing the conflict. All we did was follow the command on the vertical velocity indicator and audio warning to descend.' (ACN 174742, 1991)

Typical measures of automation authority rate the amount of actuation performed by the automation, and the extent to which this actuation is initiated by the pilot (e.g. Billings, 1997; Sheridan, 1992). With alerting systems, however, actuation is performed by the pilot as initiated by the alerting system. Therefore, common classifications of automation authority do not capture the authority of an alerting system. Instead, the authority of the alerting system may be categorised by the level of control it has over the pilot. The simplest signal-detector alerting system may control the pilot only by inducing him or her to consider a gauge reading. With hazard-detector and hazard-resolver systems, a high degree of authority stems from their ability to 'cognitively railroad' the pilot into decisions that he or she can't verify due to lack of time, excessive workload, not having the same information as the alerting system, or an inaccurate conception of how the alerting system arrives at its decisions.

Beyond the practical under- and over-reliance issues, situations in which the pilot is cognitively railroaded raise more philosophical concerns about a condition termed by Woods (1986) as the 'authority/responsibility double bind'. Ultimate responsibility for flight safety rests with the captain. Historically, a commensurate complete level of authority stemmed from his or her almost complete level of control over how the flight was executed, within the constraints imposed by aircraft performance, air traffic control, and regulations (and the latter two can be negotiated or broken when needed). While the pilot is still nominally in charge, increasingly powerful alerting systems are assuming authority over specific hazards. At an extreme, the pilot may be responsible for – and required to execute – actions over which they can no longer hold authority.

Conclusions

'What with GPWS, windshear alerters, TCAS alerts, gear horns, bell, buzzers, clackers and split seconds to absorb, process and react, maybe we should re-evaluate the addition of more technology into our cockpits and whether it really improves safety?' (ACN 181018, 1991)

Because there is no perfect alerting system, the decision to implement an alerting system can be controversial. Normal guidelines for automated systems need often be broken when designing an alerting system for the rare, the hazardous, and the unexpected. In implementing alerting systems, the aviation industry must consider the '60 Minutes Test'[2], in which we ponder which question, given the capabilities of the alerting system, we feel we could better substantiate in a TV news interview:

'Why didn't you implement this alerting system earlier if it could have prevented an accident?'

or

'Why did you implement this alerting system when you knew there was a chance, albeit it small, that it might cause an accident?'

In other words, we sometimes need to violate our 'desired' human factors principles of happy co-existence between pilot and machine in order to implement alerting systems. While contentious, many cockpit systems are generally considered huge benefits to aviation safety. However, the capacity for pilots to deal with human-factors shortcomings may be limited while the number of alerting systems in growing, suggesting that their use may need to be carefully metered within the cockpit, and carefully delimited from mundane presentations of status. We may be reaching limits on the safety improvements achievable by adding more alerting systems to the cockpit.

However, there is much more insight that the human factors community can bring to the design and implementation of alerting systems. In 1980, Wiener and Curry suggested important questions about alerting systems. The answers to some of these are starting to be known: Why can alarms go unheeded? Why can a false

---

[2] American news programme which has debated the implementation of safety systems such as automotive airbags.

alarm rate be so high? Is there a need for a preview alert? Others are now become more pressing: Will/should the operators check the alarm? Will the alerting logic be too complex, especially in the case of prioritised alerts, for operators to perform validity checks and thus lead to over-reliance on the system? Will the system always be correct, and if not, will the operators recognise this?

Many aspects of these unanswered questions revolve around the role of the alerting system vis-à-vis the pilot. The bulk of human factors knowledge about pilot interaction with alerting systems covers primarily the attention-director role. Modern alerting systems are capable of many other roles, some of which are not always recognised during design and testing. As such, study is also required into the human factors issues with these roles, singly and collectively, and their impact on pilots in both normal operations and once an alert has been triggered.

As alerting systems become more capable, some of these human factors issues can become quite fundamental. Who's in charge? Is the entity with the responsibility also given the capacity to make a substantiated decision? These are not new questions; concerns raised at a 1963 autoland conference mirror current issues with alerting systems:

'A conclusion seems to follow from the above comments. If a suitable means is not provided to the pilot to enable him to land the airplane, then a suitable means should be provided to prevent the pilot from interfering with the automation during the last critical phase... It follows therefore that, if the full authority is left to the pilot, the actual reliability level is just that of the pilot himself with the information he has got, irrespective of the possible much higher reliability level of the black boxes – and the aircraft.' (Bartoli, 1963)

'[We] have been striving ... [to] retain the preponderance of the control in the hands of the captain and his crew not only in favor of their dignity but also in favor of overall safety... We would like to see the Autoland used as the autopilot is used during cruise, that is to say as an aid and a contribution to rest rather than a new pain in the neck.' (Turcat, 1963)

For systems where the desired role is to have the pilot actively involved in the control loop, the aviation community still has several large issues to solve. Mosier (1996) pointed out common myths in the use of automation, including that the operator can't disregard an authoritative and knowledgeable system, and that he or she can't always recognise when such a system is making a mistake. Eliminating these myths as design assumptions, and creating automation designs that prevent their associated problems, in practice, is at this time a fledgling endeavour compared to the volume of new technologies under development. Most alerting systems additionally must face these issues in the face of rare, hazardous, time-critical events, and often rely primarily on pilot trust in the alerting system.

For systems where it is not desired to have the pilot cognitively involved in diagnosis and resolution, the issue to be addressed is whether the pilot should be in the control loop at all. Bainbridge (1983) noted the tendency to automate the operator out of the system – in this case the issue is automating the operator into

74

the system. Without cognitive involvement, he or she is reduced to the level of an actuator with notoriously poor reaction time and accuracy. Rather than presenting the illusion that the pilot is in charge of a situation, it may be best to remove him or her from the control loop altogether, and place the burden of proof on the automated system's designer that it has the same performance, in the full range of operational contexts, as is normally expected from the pilot. Until such a design is demonstrated, every effort is required to keep the pilot cognitively involved in resolving critical hazards.

References

Bainbridge, L. (1983). Ironies of automation. *Automatica, 19*, 775-779.

Bartoli, G. (1963). Pilot and reliability. *5th technical conference on all-weather landing and take-off.* Lucerne.

Bilimoria, K.D. (1998). A methodology for the performance evaluation of a conflict probe. *Proceedings of the AIAA guidance, navigation and control conference.* Reston, VA: American Institute of Aeronautics and Astronautics.

Billings, C.E. (1997). *Aviation automation: the search for a human-centered approach.* Mahwah, NJ: Lawrence Erlbaum.

Bliss, J.P., Gilson, R.D., and Deaton, J.E. (1995). Human probability matching behaviour in response to alarms of varying reliability. *Ergonomics, 38*, 2300-2312.

Bliss, J.P., Jeans, S.M. and Prioux, H.J. (1996). 'Dual-task performance as a function of individual alarm validity and alarm system reliability information'. *Proceedings of the human factors and ergonomics society, 40th annual meeting.* Santa Monica, CA: Human Factors and Ergonomics Society.

Block, F.E., Nuutinen, L., and Ballast, B., (1999). Optimization of alarms: a study on alarm limits, alarm sounds and false alarms, intended to reduce annoyance. *Journal of clinical monitoring and computing, 15*, 75-83.

Borndorff-Eccarius, S. and Johannsen, G. (1993). Supporting diagnostic functions in human supervisory control. *Proceedings of the IEEE international conference on systems, man and cybernetics* (pp. 351-356). Piscataway, NJ: IEEE.

Cooper, G.E. (1977). *A survey of the status and philosophies relating to cockpit warning systems* (NASA Contractor Report CR-152071). Moffett Field, CA: NASA Ames Research Center.

Davis, S.D. and Pritchett, A.R. (1999). Alerting system assertiveness, knowledge, and over-reliance. *Journal of information technology impact, 3*, 119-143.

Dingus, T.A., McGehee, D.V., Manakkal, N., Jahns, S.K., Carney, C. and Hankey, J.M. (1997). Human factors field evaluation of automotive headway maintenance/ collision warning devices. *Human factors, 39*, 216-229.

Elvers, G.C., and Elrif, P. (1997). The effects of correlation and response bias in alerted monitor displays. *Human factors, 39*, 570-580.

Endsley, M. (1995). Toward a theory of situation awareness in dynamic systems. *Human factors special issue: Situation awareness 37*, 32-64.

Faitakis, Y.E., Thapliyal, S., and Kantor, J.C. (1998). An LMI approach to the evaluation of alarm thresholds. *International journal of robust and nonlinear control, 8*, 659-667.

Flight Safety Foundation (1997). *Controlled flight into terrain: education and training aid.* Arlington, VA: Flight Safety Foundation.

Getty, D.J., Swets, J.A., and Pickett, R.M. (1994). *The pilot's response to warnings: a laboratory investigation of the effects on human response time of the costs and benefits of responding* (Report No. 7947). Cambridge MA: BBN Systems and Technologies.

Guerlain, S.A., Smith, P.J., Obradovich, J.H., Rudmann, S., Strohm, P., Smith, J.W., Svirbely, J., and Sachs, L. (1999). Interactive critiquing as a form of decision support: An empirical evaluation. *Human factors 41*, 72-89.

Hasse, D. (1992). ALPA ground proximity warning system survey. *Proceedings of the flight safety foundation 45th annual international air safety seminar* (p. 38-44). Arlington, VA: Flight Safety Foundation.

Heimdahl, M., Leveson, N.G., and Reese, J.D. (1998). Experiences from specifying the TCAS II requirements using RSML. *Proceedings of the 1998 17th AIAA/IEEE/SAE digital avionics systems conference*, vol. 1, pp. C43-1 to C43-8. Piscataway, NJ: IEEE.

Hickling, E.M. (1994). Modern nuclear power plants: alarm system design. In, N. Stanton (Ed.) *Human factors in alarm design* (pp. 165-178). London: Taylor and Francis.

Horn, J. (1999). *Flight envelope limit detection and avoidance.* Unpublished doctoral dissertation, Georgia Institute of Technology, Atlanta.

Kantowitz, B.H. and Casper, P.A. (1988). Human workload in aviation. In, E.L. Wiener and D.C. Nagel (Eds.) *Human factors in aviation* (pp. 157-188). San Diego, CA: Academic Press.

Kerstholt, J.H., Passenier, P.O., Houttuin, K. and Schuffel, H. (1996). The effect of a priori probability and complexity on decision making in a supervisory control task. *Human factors, 38*, 65-78.

Kirlik, A (1993). Modeling strategic behavior in human-automation interaction: why an 'aid' can (and should) go unused. *Human factors, 35*, 221-242.

Klass, P.J. (1998, April 27). Eurocontrol mandates TCAS / 7.0 software installation. *Aviation week and space technology*, pp. 51-52.

Kuchar, J.K (1996). Methodology for alerting-system performance evaluation. *Journal of guidance, control and dynamics, 19*, 438-444.

Kuchar, J.K. and Carpenter, B.D. (1997). Airborne collision alerting logic for closely-spaced parallel approach. *Air traffic control quarterly, 5*, 1997.

Lee, J. and Moray, N. (1992). Trust, control strategies and allocation of function in human-machine systems. *Ergonomics, 35*, 1243-1270.

Lee, J. and Moray, N. (1994). Trust, self-confidence, and operator's adaptation to automation. *International journal of human-computer studies, 40*, 153-184.

Liu, H.T., Golborne, C., Bun, Y., and Martel, M. (1998). Surface windshear alert system, part 1: prototype development. *Journal of aircraft, 35*, 422-428.

Marshall, E. and Baker, S. (1994). Alarms in nuclear power plant control rooms. In, N. Stanton (Ed.) *Human factors in alarm design* (pp. 183-191). London: Taylor and Francis.

Mårtensson, L. (1995). The aircraft crash at Gottröra: experiences of the cockpit crew. *International journal of aviation psychology, 5*, 305-326.

Mellone, V.J. (1993, June). Genie out of the bottle? *ASRS directline*, Issue No. 4.

Meredith, C. and Edworthy, J. (1994). Sources of confusion in intensive therapy unit alarms. In, N. Stanton (Ed.) *Human factors in alarm design* (pp. 207-219). London: Taylor and Francis.

Midkiff and Hansman (1993). Identification of important 'party line' information elements and implications for situational awareness in the datalink environment. *Air traffic control quarterly, 1*, 5-30.

Molloy, R., and Parasuraman, R. (1996). Monitoring an automated system for a single failure: vigilance and task complexity effects. *Human factors, 38*, 311-322.

Mosier, K.L. (1996). Myths of expert decision making and automated decision aids. In, C.E. Zsambok and G. Klein (Eds.) *Naturalistic decision making* (pp. 319 – 330). Mahwah, NJ: Lawrence Erlbaum.

Mosier, K.L and Skitka, L.J. (1996). Human decision makers and automated decision aids: made for each other? In, R. Parasuraman and M. Mouloua (Eds.) *Automation and human performance: theory and applications* (pp. 201-220). Mahwah NJ: Lawrence Erlbaum.

Muir, B.M. (1987). Trust between humans and machines, and the design of decision aids. *International journal of man-machine studies, 27*, 527-539.

Muir, B.M. (1994). Trust in automation: I. Theoretical issues in the study of trust and human intervention in automated systems. *Ergonomics special issue: Cognitive ergonomics, 37*, 1905-1922.

Noyes, J.M, Cresswell-Starr, A.F., and Rankin, J.A. (1999). Designing aircraft warning systems: a case study. In, N.A. Stanton and J. Edworthy (Eds.), *Human factors in auditory warnings* (pp. 265-281). Aldershot, England: Ashgate.

Noyes, J.M. and Starr, A.F. (2000). Civil aircraft warning systems: future directions in information management and presentation. *International journal of aviation psychology, 10*, 169-188.

Parasuraman, R., Hancock, P.A., and Olofinboba, O. (1997). Alarm effectiveness in driver-centered collision-warning systems. *Ergonomics, 40*, 390-399.

Parasuraman, R., Molloy, R., Mouloua, M., and Hilburn, B. (1996). Monitoring of automated systems. In, R. Parasuraman and M. Mouloua (Eds.) *Automation and human performance: theory and applications* (pp. 91-115). Mahwah NJ: Lawrence Erlbaum.

Parasurman, R. and Riley, V. (1997). Humans and automation: use, misuse, disuse, abuse. *Human factors, 39*, 230-253.

Paté-Cornell, M.E. (1986). Warning systems in risk management. *Risk analysis, 6*, 223-234.

Pritchett, A.R., Vándor, B., and Edwards, K.E. (1999, June). Testing and implementing cockpit alerting systems. Presented at *Human error, safety, and system development*, Liége, Belgium.

Proctor, P. (1998, April 6). Integrated cockpit safety system certified. *Aviation week and space technology*, p. 61.

Radio Technical Commission for Aeronautics (RTCA) (1983). *Minimum operational performance standards for traffic alert and collision avoidance system (TCAS) airborne equipment*, (RTCA / DO – 185). Washington, DC: RTCA.

Riley, V. (1996). Operator reliance on automation: theory and data. In, R. Parasuraman and M. Mouloua (Eds.) *Automation and human performance: theory and applications* (pp. 19-35). Mahwah NJ: Lawrence Erlbaum.

Riley, V., DeMers, R., Good, M., Krishnan, K., Miller, C., and Misiak, C. (1996). *Crew-centered flight deck alerting*. Minneapolis, MN: Honeywell Technical Center.

Rogers, W.H., Schutte, P.C. and Latorella, K.A. (1996). Fault management in aviation systems. In, R. Parasuraman and M. Mouloua (Eds.) *Automation and human performance: theory and applications* (pp. 281-317). Mahwah NJ: Lawrence Erlbaum.

Rouse, W.B. (1983). Models of human problem solving: detection, diagnosis and compensation for system failures. *Automatica, 19*, 613-625.

Sarter, N.B. and Woods, D.D. (1992). Pilot interaction with cockpit automation: operational experiences with the flight management system. *International journal of aviation psychology, 2*, 303-321.

Sarter, N.B. and Woods, D.D. (1994). Pilot interaction with cockpit automation II: an experimental study of pilots' model and awareness of the flight management system. *International journal of aviation psychology, 4*, 1-28.

Scott, W.B. (1999, February 1). Automatic GCAS: 'you can't fly any lower'. *Aviation week and space technology*, pp. 76-80.

See, J.E., Warm, J.S., Dember, W.N., and Howe, S.R. (1997). Vigilance and signal detection theory: an empirical evaluation of five measures of response bias. *Human factors, 39*, 14-29.

Sheridan, T.B. (1992). *Telerobotics, automation and human supervisory control*. Cambridge, MA: MIT Press.

Sklar, A.E. and Sarter, N.B (2000). Good vibrations: tactile feedback in support of attention allocation and human-automation coordination in event-driven domains. *Human factors, 41*, 543-552.

Sorkin, R.D., Kantowitz, B.H. and Kantowitz, S.C. (1988). Likelihood alarm displays. *Human factors, 30*, 445-459.

Sorkin, R.D., and Woods, D.D. (1985). Systems with human monitors: a signal detection analysis. *Human-computer interaction, 1*, 49-75.

Stanton, N.A. and Baber, C. (1995). Alarm-initiated activities: An analysis of alarm handling by operators using text-based alarm systems in supervisory control systems. *Ergonomics special issue: Warnings in research and practice, 38*, 2414-2431.

Stanton, N.A. and Edworthy, J. (Eds.). (1999). *Human factors in auditory warnings.* Aldershot, England: Ashgate.

Trujillo, A.C. (1996, February) *Airline transport pilot preferences for predictive information.* NASA Technical Memorandum (NASA TM 4702). Hampton, VA: NASA Langley Research Center.

Turcat, A. (1963). The pilot and the all-weather landing. *5th technical conference on all-weather landing and take-off.* Lucerne.

United Airlines (1998). *B-777 Flight Manual.*

Vallauri, E. (1995). *Operational evaluation of TCAS II in France* (CENA/ R95-04). Toulouse: Centre D'Études de la Navigation Aérienne.

Vallauri, E. (1997). *Suivi de la mise en oeuvre du TCAS II en France en 1996* [1996 Survey of TCAS II implementation in France] (CENA/ R97-16). Toulouse: Centre D'Études de la Navigation Aérienne.

Vándor, B. and Pritchett, A.R. (1999, January). *Effects of displays and alerts on subject reactions to potential collisions during closely spaced parallel approaches* (ISyE Report R-99-02). Atlanta GA: Georgia Institute of Technology.

Veitengruber, J.E. (1977). Design criteria for aircraft warning, caution, and advisory alerting systems. *Journal of aircraft, 15*, 574-581.

Wiener, E.L. (1989). *Human factors of advanced technology ('glass cockpit') transport aircraft* (NASA Technical Report 117528). Moffett Field, CA: NASA Ames research center.

Wiener, E.L. and Curry, R.E. (1980). Flight-deck automation: Promises and problems. *Ergonomics, 23*, 995-1011.

Williamson, T. and Spencer, N.A. (1989). Development and operation of the traffic alert and collision avoidance system (TCAS). *Proceedings of the IEEE, 77*, 1735-1744.

Woods, D.D. (1986). Paradigms for decision support. In E. Hollnagel (Ed.), *Intelligent decision support in process environments* (NATA ASI Series, Vol. F21, 153-173). Heidelberg: Springer-Verlag.

Woods, D.D. (1995). The alarm problem and directed attention in dynamic fault management. *Ergonomics, 38*, 2371-2393.

Yang, L.C. and Kuchar, J.K. (1997). Prototype conflict alerting logic for free flight. *Journal of guidance, control and dynamics, 20*, 768-773.

4 Minimising pilot error by design: are test pilots doing a good enough job?

Gideon Singer

Background

It has been well documented that about 70% of commercial aircraft accidents in the last 15 years were human error related (FAA, 1996). The cockpit of an airliner is designed for a specific task of providing a safe and efficient interface with the operators, nowadays, mainly two pilots. Despite the similar tasks performed by all crews, designs vary greatly between manufacturers and hardly any standards exist for the interface methods. Design decisions in commercial projects have always been made based on subjective statements of test pilots. The test pilots rely on the certification regulations, company design philosophy and own previous experience (Singer, 1999). The design is scrutinised in reviews, flight tests and certification tests and is formally approved before it is allowed to enter service. And yet, most accidents lately have occurred despite this process. Can we, the test pilots, claim that we have been doing a good enough job?

The purpose of this paper

The purpose of this paper is twofold: The first part will try and convince you by accident data and specific design examples that we have not always done a good enough job. The second part will show the work being done by the Human Factors Harmonisation Working Group (HF-HWG, 2001) in order to improve the tools available to the design evaluator.

This paper was first published in Human Factors and Aerospace Safety 1(4), 2001, pp. 301-321

This paper will describe the present method of approval used by many manufacturers (especially the smaller ones), find the deficiencies in this method and especially the issues regarding the task of the test pilot. In order to be more convincing, several design examples from modern cockpits will be shown. Based on this review, recommendations for improvement will be made. These suggestions will include the need for providing the test pilots (and test engineers) with more efficient tools that will allow a more reliable cockpit design and validation process in the future. The emphasis will be made on the design evaluation methods although improvements can be made in other areas such as training and documentation.

The conclusion made will be that, *no*, we as test pilots have not done a good enough job in providing a safe and efficient cockpit interface. However, it was mainly due to the lack of usable tools, or maybe the lack of communication between the research institutes and the industry (Harris, 1997). Some criticism is raised towards the Test Pilot schools, still concentrating on the traditional subjective evaluation methods.

The international aviation community has been aware of the human factors issue in cockpit design. Triggered by the 'FAA Human Factors Study Team Report on the interface between flight crews and modern flight deck systems' (FAA, 1996), a FAA (Federal Aviation Administration) and JAA (Joint Airworthiness Authorities) harmonisation group has been tasked to follow the terms of reference agreed upon by the European and American industry and aviation authorities (Federal Register, 1997). The Human Factors Harmonisation Working Group (HF-HWG), was tasked to address the human factors certification deficiencies in the design related rules and advisory material for Large commercial aircraft the FAR 25 and JAR 25 (Federal Aviation Administration, 1998). The working group has been tasked to recommend changes based on existing requirement deficiencies and accident data. This group consists of experts in certification, human factors, flight-testing and operations from the USA, Europe and other countries that manufacture commercial aircraft. The group is half way through the task and has published an interim report that shows a structured review process of the regulatory material and a vast number of accident and incident reports with human factors issues. The group is in the process of making specific recommendations with the aim of formulating new regulatory and advisory material into the existing FAR/JAR design rules. Other recommendations might be implemented in the operational rules or training requirements.

The present evaluation method

The present method of evaluating a commercial cockpit design is based on contractual requirements, time and scope constraints and the trend to minimize certification risks. Unlike the two large manufacturers (Boeing and Airbus), the majority of the airframe manufacturers have very limited research resources and very compressed and infrequent new projects. In contrast to most military projects, commercial ones usually allow only two years for design and one year for development and certification flights (Singer, 2000). Due to these time constraints very little experimentation is done for validation of new design features and approvals are made based on 'good engineering practices'. In many cases the evaluations are done using paper mock-ups or early prototypes only and the final result is forced through the certification process as 'good enough'. Despite test pilot protests many design features are approved due to the lack of a 'certification paragraph' that could be used to force a change. Test pilots are often faced with a more or less finished design and have very little ability to require changes. Most of these change requests might be denied due to cost, scope or time frame with the typical promise of a next better version that never materialises. The test pilot is asked to make comments on error risks and the effect of such an error on flight safety without having the full background and tools to evaluate human error. When the design finally enters service, it usually lacks the proper means of training and documentation causing a gap between the designer's intentions and the way the line pilot uses the system.

All of the above factors have contributed to cockpit design solutions that lack a formal validation and therefore probably incorporate deficiencies that might cause or facilitate crew errors (Courteney, 1999). Some would claim that risks associated with such errors will usually be captured by other safety nets such as procedures and training but how reliable are these nets?

Design solutions using the present method

In order to substantiate the above accusations, several examples will be described in more detail. Some of these features have been identified as contributing factors to accidents in the past 15 years as stated in several reports such as the FAA Human Factors Study Team report (FAA, 1996), Flight Safety Foundation (FSF) yearly accident summary 1999 and the HF-HWG accident data review (HF-HWG, 2001).

The examples used in this paper are just some of the issues that the author has been personally engaged in. As identified in the HF-HWG report there are many more. The examples range from basic flight instrument conventions, to warning information display, the form given to text messages and the lack of specific requirements for flight management systems (FMS) interface design. These examples have all been taken from FAR/JAR 25 projects in the past 10 years (Singer, 2000).

Attitude indicator conventions

In the report mentioned above loss of control has been determined to be one of the main causes of several incidents and accidents involving large transport category. The loss of the SAAB 340 after taking off from Zurich in early 2000 (FOCA,

2000) is suspected to have been caused by loss of control. According to the interim report of the Swiss Federal Office of Civil Aviation (FOCA) the aircraft banked slowly to one direction and then after a hesitation, bank angle increased to an attitude that made recovery impossible. As test pilots performing manoeuvres requiring accurate bank angle capture, we have certainly all seen a tendency to initially recover from a steady bank angle in the wrong direction. This is evident only when using the attitude display indicator (ADI) as reference. This tendency has not been as evident in military aircraft that have a different position to their roll (bank) angle index.

The form and function of the artificial horizon has hardly changed in the past 50 years. The western concept in commercial and military aviation has always been the one mimicking the outside world horizon as the moving part and the aircraft reference as an index fixed to the aircraft structure as seen from inside the cockpit (the inside-out concept). The moving part consists of a two colour moving background (earth and sky) with pitch scales depicted. The fixed index includes the pitch reference (aircraft symbol) and roll scale (bank angle). The pitch index is usually positioned on the horizon in the middle of the display when in level flight. The roll index though can be placed either at the top or bottom of the display and points straight up (sky pointer) or straight down (earth pointer).

The general inside-out convention has been adapted and seldom questioned despite substantial experimental data from the 1960s (Roscoe, 1968) showing results that favour the opposite convention (outside-in) used in the east. According to modern aviation research the convention of the moving horizon gives a consistent frame of reference for a pilot sitting in the cockpit but violates the principle of the moving part (the aircraft banks in reality). Since the introduction of head up displays (HUD), the principal of conformity has made the western ADI convention more intuitive when overlaying the outside world.

Addressing the inside–out convention as a given standard in most commercial aircraft, several other questions arise when investigating the differences between military and commercial attitude displays. The position of the roll index in military aircraft is predominantly the one pointing down (earth pointer) while the commercial one is almost always pointing up (sky pointer). This feature has also been transferred to the HUD symbology philosophy of commercial versus military aircraft. Could this be the reason for temporary loss of bank angle perception when using commercial ADIs? One needs to address several parameters first in order to reach a higher confidence level that the probable critical parameter is the position of the roll index:

- Military aircraft are more agile and wrong roll angle can be quickly corrected without noticeable effects. Can we conclude that military pilots actually do not roll in the wrong direction due to display misinterpretation?
- Military pilots manoeuvre the aircraft to a higher degree and are better trained to perceive attitude correctly and react quickly. Could this training be the determining factor that improves military pilots performance in roll?

- Military pilots usually look outside during manoeuvring or use the head-up display that is projected directly onto the outside world. Could these features explain the different tendency to roll in the wrong direction?
- Modern military ADIs are actually three-dimensional and show also the tendency to change heading (a grid of heading arcs is depicted on the background to form a globe feature). Could this be the extra cue that helps the military pilots to determine roll direction?
- In many commercial aircraft today the mechanical ADI has been replaced with an electronic ADI (EADI). This is a replica of the conventional instrument without any moving parts but using a cathode ray tube (CRT) or liquid crystal display (LCD) instead. Could the loss of the three-dimensional depth of the mechanical parts (shadow, structure and layers of details in the display) in the flat electronic display have caused the deficient ability to determine bank angle?

It would be impossible to discredit the above concerns as probable features affecting the response of commercial pilots by means of analysis or interviews. The issue is that the changes in display technology, the position of the roll index (sky-pointer or ground pointer) or the use of the pointer as a 'fly-to' index compared with a 'status' index are never evaluated objectively.

Simple experiments can point towards the more reliable display method and show what effect previous training has on the intuitive response in cases of stress.

What information does the pilot need?

The information overload in the cockpit of a commercial aircraft during malfunctions or emergencies is one issue, a concern which originates from several aircraft accidents (FAA, 1996; Billings, 1997).

In one accident case (Gottröra, Sweden 1991) with both engines failing after takeoff, the MD80 crew was presented with an unusual amount of critical information. Visual and aural warnings were given as well as alert messages on the overhead annunciator panel, all at the same time (Mårtensson, 1995). The pilots were overloaded with information, and in interviews (Mårtensson and Singer, 1998) the pilots suggested that information in the warning system should be prioritised in a way that the pilots could perceive it properly and act accordingly (Woods, 1995).

The crew alerting systems of the modern transport aircraft can handle almost any malfunction that the pilot is expected to deal with. These features are tested, certified and trained by crews in simulator training. There are variations in the philosophy of display in the alerting information between the manufacturers but many methods implemented in today's aircraft show satisfactory results and good human integration for the task defined (Pritchett, 2001).

However, in case of multiple faults in a high workload situation, the warning system of the modern cockpit is not always easy to use and understand. The tendency is to overload the display with warnings, cautions and inoperative system information accompanied by various aural warnings and cues. The pilot becomes overloaded with information and cannot handle all at one time. The result is that the pilot may disregard the information, return to 'basic flying', and rely on his own perception of the situation, a strategy which turned out to be the correct one in the accident mentioned above, but might have catastrophic effects in other emergencies.

The present regulations define only few individual warnings in detail (red and amber colour use, landing gear warning, etc). Several standards have been developed, some giving the pilot all the information available, some implementing a certain level of prioritisation and other providing high levels of automation followed by system guidance. All of these methods have been approved but none was scrutinised by objective criteria of fail or pass based on operator response.

As test pilots faced with these systems we often revert to a subjective evaluation that tries to look at the consistency, readability and lack of ambiguity of the displays. Despite many simulator sessions for evaluating failures, these are done by a prepared crew and in a sterile environment. How many of us can recall inviting the minimum qualifications pilot to participate in the certification system failure evaluations of a new design?

Easy to read TEXT messages

When reviewing several modern commercial cockpits it becomes clear that different means of presenting text messages are used for information and warning. Each method usually has a philosophy behind it, some based on pilot action required and some based on an index system.

Examples of three methods to display text of a hydraulic failure are given below. They are based on aircraft types commonly in use:

- Side – system – function – status   (R HYD PRESS LO)
- System – side – function – status   (HYD R PRESS LO)
- System – function – status – side   (HYD PRESS LO L)

It is surprising to discover that very few experiments have been done in the design phase to evaluate the ease of readability and perception of each display method. Cultural and language differences are seldom considered when determining text interface and the assumption is that all users are fluent in the English language. In many cases the design is driven by the actions the crew has to take (like selecting a certain system page) but in other cases it is more of an administrative decision such as the ease of applying an alphabetical index system for documentation.

The assumption regarding crew error

When evaluating pure system failures, the certification process is based on a probability analysis that looks into the relation between the effect of a failure and the probability of its occurrence. This process is driven for single and multiple failures and is strictly regulated by the requirements (FAR/JAR 25.1309) (FAA, 1998). The most probable failures must not have more that a minor effect on safety margins; workload and passenger comfort while the improbable ones may have hazardous effects. Failure combinations that have a catastrophic effect may not be more than extremely improbable (the magic number 10^{-9}).

When addressing crew error we are very inconsistent in the way we value crew monitoring and action. This can be the use of crew procedure as an assumption for safe operations (the reliance on checklist, airmanship, crew coordination) or the reliability of the crew to follow checklists without error. At present there is a reluctance to give probability numbers to crew errors since the numbers will be very dependant on external factors such as stress, workload and flight phase. Crew correct action or error is usually used as a 'yes' or 'no' (probability 1 or 0) for different design requirements.

For clarity here are some examples of conditions where crew error is assumed to be a significant safety risk. These are specifically mandated by a prescriptive regulation such as FAR 25.703 (FAA, 1998):

Crew is *assumed to make an error:*

- Gear extension prior to landing – mandated specific warnings.
- Takeoff with the a non- takeoff configuration – mandated warning.
- Crew shutting down the wrong engine when on fire – lit handles mandatory.
- Crew exceeding the approved operating speed – mandatory warning.

Crew is *assumed to act correctly:* these conditions are not specifically addressed by the rules but have been found to be safety critical in flight test:

- FMS aircraft weight entry (define the Vspeeds) – no warning.
- Takeoff with a wrong takeoff (approved) configuration – no warning.
- Crew shutting down the wrong engine following a failure– no warning.
- Crew not setting rudder pedals or seat to enable full yaw control – no warning.
- Crew neglecting to disconnect AP prior to landing (non-autoland) – no warning.

These examples highlight the need to apply a more systematic approach to crew error, whether for errors in normal conditions or error following a system failure. The only valid approach seems to be the future integration of the crew error probabilities into the basic system safety assessment. This evaluation will determine whether the effect of each combination requires a 'fool proof' design or whether a warning will be sufficient.

Design solutions can be an indication to the correct lever (fire handle), a warning when a wrong setting is attempted (flap selection at an excessive speed) or an inhibition (gear retraction on the ground). Each solution has its technical drawbacks in the form of reliability, nuisance warnings and cost. A probabilistic approach to crew error will allow a systematic approach that will be followed by all and apply the correct levels of defence for each condition depending on the predicted effects.

Integration of FMS

In commercial flight, on most modern aircraft today, navigation and flight path are being controlled by a system generally called the flight management system (FMS). The interface with the crew in the cockpit is achieved by an active display that is usually called the control display unit (CDU) and is the input/output channel. In addition, the system displays its planned/executed route on a navigation display (ND) and flight path guidance by means of a flight director on the primary flight displays (PFD).

The technical requirements and methods for testing system performance, accuracy and fault analysis are well established and are defined in the certification requirements for such systems and aircraft. The methods for technical validation of such systems have been used successfully in many types of aircraft avionics and have shown very high level of reliability. However, validation of the way the system interfaces with the crew, displays information or reacts to crew inputs is not well defined and each manufacturer or vendor is free to adapt its own philosophy and methods of showing compliance (Singer, 1999).

In the late nineties, new ATC regulations that mandate the installation of FMS into *all* aircraft that use medium and upper airspace in Europe were published. This produced growing demand for cheap 'add-on', 'off-the-shelf' systems for integration in older aircraft of all sizes.

Many of the transport category aircraft flying today have not been designed with a FMS as part of the cockpit. Many aircraft are still featuring the so-called 'classic cockpit' and are lacking the modern avionics bus communication technique used on the integrated cockpits. When such designs are evaluated, it is for the correct function of the system during normal operation but not for possible error modes and crew mismanagement.

When the test team is faced with the task of approving a system such as an FMS only the following design requirements are mandatory for compliance regarding human factors when applying for a certification (FAA, 1998):
- FAR/JAR 25.671(a):
  *Each control and control system must operate with the ease **smoothness** and **positiveness** appropriate to its functions.*
- FAR/JAR 25.771(a):
  *Each pilot compartment and its equipment must allow the minimum flight crew to perform their duties without **unreasonable concentration** or fatigue.*

- FAR/JAR 25.777(a):
  *Each cockpit control must be located to provide **convenient operation** and to **prevent confusion and inadvertent operation**.*
- FAR/JAR 25.1301(b):
  *Each item of installed equipment must be labelled as to its identification, function or **operating** limitations, or any applicable combination of these factors.*
    *(d) ...**function properly** when installed.*
- FAR/JAR 25.1329(f):
  *The system must be designed and adjusted so that, within the range of adjustment available to the human pilot it cannot produce hazardous loads on the airplane, or create hazardous deviations in the flight path, under any condition of flight appropriate to its use, either during normal operation or in the event of a malfunction, assuming that corrective action begins **within a reasonable period of time**.*
- FAR/JAR 25.1523(a):
  The minimum flight crew must be established so that it is sufficient for safe operation considering the workload on individual crew members (see Appendix D).
- FAR 25 Appendix D:
  *Criteria for determining minimum flight crew (a)(3) Basic workload functions ... Navigation. (b) Workload factors. The following workload factors are considered significant when analysing and demonstrating workload for minimum crew determination: (1) **The accessibility ease and simplicity** of operation of all necessary flight, power, and equipment controls... (8)The communications and navigation workload.*

The FAA has also published advisory circulars (AC) that add methods for the acceptable means of compliance with the rules above. In the case of the FMS, AC 25-15 addresses the means for approval of FMS features, mainly those regarding the vertical navigation functions (FAA, 1989). Taking a closer look at the AC, one notices that the human performance and human error issues have been neglected and are not included in the method of compliance.

It becomes clear that the existing requirements are general, vague and do not aid the manufacturer or authority evaluation groups in their decisions. Even if a reviewer sets a requirement for a workload experiment with the system, he would have difficulties in substantiating the request against cost and schedule constraints. None of the above paragraphs (or their related advisory material) (FAA, 1989) include any method or criteria for compliance.

The nature of the requirements often results in reviewer statements of a successful result that are just as vague and generic since they mimic the requirement text to the letter. The statement is very subjective and usually based on a very limited exposure to the system in very few operational conditions. 'Workload', 'fatigue', 'ease' and 'simplicity' are meaningless terms without a

89

frame of reference to them. An example of such a review could be one of a new FMS in an existing aircraft. The reviewing pilot's previous skills, background and exposure are not questioned. As a reviewing pilot he/she is always very experienced and involved in previous development and testing of the system. The reviewers are always biased by other factors that affect their judgment and they do not represent the average user's background in service.

In order to explain the problem in more detail, examples from present modern designs will be described and deficiencies highlighted. The risk involved in these features will be shown and possible effects of making an error will be discussed.

CDU design

The CDU is the main interactive interface between the crew and the FMS. The standard interface includes a screen, line select keys, alphanumeric keys, specific function keys and warning lights. This design is typical to all manufacturers, but unlike the typewriter (or PC), there is no standard position for the letter keys. In addition, each specific function key has a different use in each design. The NAV key for example; on one design is used for *navigating* while on another design it is used for *planning* only. The FPLN (flight plan) key; on one design used for *planning* while on the other used for *navigating*. These features increase the risk of negative transfer when transitioning between systems.

CDU menu layers

The CDU has a limited display area (usually capable of 8-12 rows of text) and in order to integrate all the functions required for navigation and performance, several menu layers are needed. The limited display area, when interfacing with large size navigation and performance data required for today's airspace, emphasise the 'keyhole effect' (Sarter and Woods, 1997). This effect is the property of having a small view port relative to the large size data it is used to interface with. Since layers are unavoidable, the design aim should be to minimise the number of layers and more importantly, to keep the operator oriented at all times as to his position and his possible hidden options. The fact that the positioning of these functions is not logical to the operator means that the pilot needs to search by means of 'trial and error' through up to 10-15 menus until finding the right function. Since no cues are available for this search the pilot has to rely on memory or perform the time consuming search. This is a characteristic that increases workload and frustration and should not be a feature in a modern interactive display.

Feedback of changes

For flight critical actions, like changing flight plan or selecting a direct route to a new waypoint, some designs allow the pilot to review the navigational change and then accept or cancel it before the change is implemented. Other designs are much less tolerant and once a change is initially prompted it is immediately implemented. *Direct to* and *delete* functions are the normal methods for the pilot to modify a flight plan in flight. These modifications affect the aircraft flight path when implemented and therefore must include cues for crew verification. Since slips and errors are quite common in the cockpit environment due to turbulence, parallax errors or procedural errors, it is essential to have a review function for critical changes. The system in this case must be fault tolerant and include clear review functions.

Display on ND

The CDU, being an alphanumeric display, is not the most optimal display for building pilot situation awareness of aircraft position, trend and navigational forecast. When making a change such as *direct-to* or *delete,* some designs depict both the active track and suggested change for the pilot to review prior to activation. This display on the ND gives the pilot a graphical depiction of the CDU change in form of a temporary route change overlaying the active route. This feature allows all crewmembers to review the change before activation and has been found to increase system fault tolerance. Other designs display the change in aircraft track only after it has been activated and executed. Such changes to active flight path without crew confirmation have been known to cause confusion and reduce safety margins if error made in congested airspace.

Database ambiguity

Today's databases of waypoints, navigation aids and procedures are enormous. The same identification in the database may define several waypoints around the world. Usually the risk for selecting the wrong waypoint is mitigated by suggesting the nearest one at the top of the list. *Non-directional beacons* (NDB) and marker beacons have a two-letter code and can therefore describe several beacons. On some designs the NDB code is not accepted without a dedicated suffix to minimize error, while on other designs an input without the suffix will be accepted without feedback to the pilot that another (non-NDB) waypoint has been selected. With increased database complexity and error potential it is essential to insert reasonability check functions to minimize the risk for selecting the wrong waypoints.

UNDO functions

Any user of PC software expects an *UNDO* function in order to recall incorrect inputs, whether they are due to errors or slips. This function is not a standard feature in CDU software and each design has its own criteria for providing an

UNDO feature. This feature may be lacking even in the flight critical parameters such as *direct-to* and *delete*. In some cases the selection of *delete* to the wrong line select key cancels the whole flight plan without any *review* or *UNDO* options.

Colour logic CDU/ND

In today's cockpits, interfaces between EFIS and FMS of different makes are becoming more common. This may highlight differences in communication standards with the effect that the different displays show different colours for the same waypoint. Combine this with aircraft manufacturers who have different colour standards, and the resulting display might be confusing and misleading. The lack of industry standards for coding-coding makes the task of integrating avionics difficult and usually with unexpected results.

As test pilots encountering such deficiencies we are often confronted with the statement 'has been certified previously'. The large manufacturers usually have more leverage for making improvements while the smaller ones are forced to accept the system as it is. The lack of more specific requirements, objective criteria and reliable methods result in the inability of the test teams to enforce improvements to known risk areas.

Improvements required

The examples above highlight the need for a more systematic approach to crew performance and error in the design process of a new cockpit. It seems that the complexity of modern avionics systems and cockpit controls and displays have become too large for individual experts such as test pilots to validate. Better tools are needed (Wise, 1993; Wise, 1994). Tools for defining crew tasks, acceptable performance and error modes for each cockpit are required. The definition of the tasks and acceptable performance must be made using objective terms to enable a more uniform and unbiased approach by the evaluators. The methods must be acceptable by all manufacturers in order to achieve a standard minimum safety level. The correlation between design, procedures and training of each system must be established. Clear means of compliance must be made available to improve design teamwork and minimize final certification risks.

The conclusion is that the long-term solutions must be the improvement of design criteria and the introduction of more guidance material for the design and test teams to follow. A more detailed requirement basis will also reduce the development risk for each manufacturer allowing an early evaluation to known specifications. This method has been the acceptable mean of compliance for hardware and software and to a certain extent it must be applied to crew errors. Another area of improvement is the use of limited scale experiments exposing it to the end user (the line pilot) to help and validate design assumptions made by the experts. In such a way the test teams will be able to substantiate their conclusions early in the design phase (avionics logic, display, FMS etc) and compare several options when changes are still feasible.

At present such experiments are performed but at a very small scale and only if management allows this optional activity. These experiments require simple tools but usually highly trained and dedicated personnel, that are rare during the development phase.

Test case of a new methodology – the DIVA project

The author of this paper participated as a test pilot in a new role in a recent project that addressed several of the deficiencies described above. This project can be used as a good example of a new structure Human Centred and Performance Based approach to cockpit design. The DIVA (design of human/machine and their validation in aeronautics) project (Nibbelke et al., 2001) used the experience of the aviation industry and research institutes and addressed the issues of controlled flight into terrain (CFIT) displays and system failure presentation. The project utilized a step-by-step approach making use of accepted methods of management and cognitive tools. The method consisted of three phases.

The first phase was gathering the user requirements with the help of a management tool QFD (quality function deployment). This tool was developed to fit the cockpit environment, and included a large matrix that converted customer requirements into lower level engineering requirements. The tool also allowed for subjective ratings of importance and relative importance of the parameters.

The second phase included the review of relevant accident data in order to construct realistic scenarios in which the new design feature could be validated. The scenarios were determined based on expert inputs including test pilots. The scenarios were built around simulation tools that allowed exposure of a non-expert crew to time and flight phase limited scenarios. Objective measuring equipment such as eye tracking devices and data recording equipment were combined with subjective evaluations. Uninvolved experts such as test pilots and test engineers performed a structured design review. This was to get a second opinion of the experiment layout and correlation with the initial customer requirements. The review also considered whether known human factor guidelines were implemented in the design.

The last phase was the actual evaluation performed by airline pilots of varying experience and recording objective and subjective data. The simulations were performed with and without the new design features or with different levels of automation of the features. This data was then compared with the initial management tool and correlation was evaluated.

The DIVA project implemented the new approach of systematically using customer requirement criteria, accident data, to base modern technical solutions. The design was determined by experts such as test pilots and validated in simulators using line pilots.

Several of the DIVA design features are considered for implementations in future designs. Despite the improved approach used by this project, the time scale and simulation complexity encountered requires a simplification of the process in order to become usable for the process of design and validation of a 'live' aircraft project.

Regulatory work in progress

One effective method of improving future designs is undoubtedly the improvement of the design certification requirements and advisories. For the transport category aircraft this is mainly the FAR/JAR 25. The Human Factors Harmonization Working Group (HF-HWG) has been tasked to recommend such changes based on existing requirement deficiencies and accident data.

The HF HWG was created in August 1999 per the tasking published in Federal Register, July 22, 1999 (FAA, 1999). The tasking can be summarised as follows:

- Review the relevant existing FAA/JAA 25 rules and regulatory material applicable to flight deck design, to determine their adequacy to consistently address design-related flight crew performance vulnerabilities and the prevention and management of flight crew errors.
- Based on this review, recommend the updating of existing rules and advisory material or development of new rules, new advisory materials and the associated implementation plan.
- As work progresses, identify implications for qualifications and operations to be communicated to and addressed by other appropriate groups.

The group first met in October 1999. It was constituted in such a way as to intentionally balance the various types of expertise needed by the group (human factors, piloting, aircraft design, certification, rulemaking...) as well as the national and organizational (North America vs. JAA nations, authorities vs. industry) ties of the members. Today the group consists of 42 members who meet on a quarterly basis, usually alternating between North American and European locations. To date, six meetings have been held.

After defining the work plan and having it approved by Transport Airplane and Engine Issues Group (TAIEG), the HF-HWG defined its working method:

1. First, the HWG needed to define the material to be reviewed as instructed by the Aviation Rulemaking Advisory Committee (ARAC) tasking. A subgroup was tasked to provide the list of regulatory material to be reviewed.
2. Second, the HF-HWG decided to employ two different but complementary approaches to identify deficiencies in the rules.

- The first approach consisted of a direct review of the regulatory material by using a carefully constructed list of human factors topics to examine each component of the rules and associated advisory documents to determine if the topics were consistently addressed or not, and why (or why not).
- The second approach was experience based. It started from a collection of data describing either human performance problems (e.g., accidents or incident reports, experience of airline pilots or test pilots) or actual instances in which certification experts could not find regulatory material with which to address an obvious human factors design issue. This approach enabled the group to find data driven evidence of 'holes in the regulations'.

3. Third, starting from an integrated list of the deficiencies identified by both approaches, the Group will use predefined criteria to derive recommendations for developing or updating relevant Part 25 rules and advisory material. These criteria will evaluate the safety benefit as well as the expected acceptance and efficiency of these recommendations and will indicate priority of implementation.

If needed, the Group will also issue recommendations for additional work that should be carried out on non-part 25 rules.

To work effectively, the HF-HWG was split into 4 subgroups (A, B, C and D) to address the various aspects of task 1 (see figure1):

- Subgroup A: Materials to be reviewed.
- Subgroup B: Top-down/concept-based process for reviewing the regulatory material.
- Subgroup C: Bottom-up/case-based process for reviewing the regulatory material.
- Subgroup D: Criteria for assessing the expected success of the product(s) of the working group.

Because the two approaches taken by subgroup B and subgroup C had to stay independent to remain effectively as exhaustive and complementary as possible, a need to create a process to integrate their outcomes arose. An Integration team was created for this purpose.

The following types of documents were identified as relevant to the working group's task and were made available on the HWG website:

- Part 25 FARs (133 regulations and 3 appendices) at amendment 87.
- FAA Advisory Circulars (AC) - 20 series (19 ACs).
- FAA Advisory Circulars (AC) - 25 series (22 ACs).
- FAA Advisory Circulars (AC) - 120/121 series (10 ACs).
- JAR-25 (136 regulations) at change 15.
- JAA Advisory Circulars (ACJ) 25 series (108 ACJs).
- Temporary Guidance Leaflets (TGL) 25 series (10 TGLs).

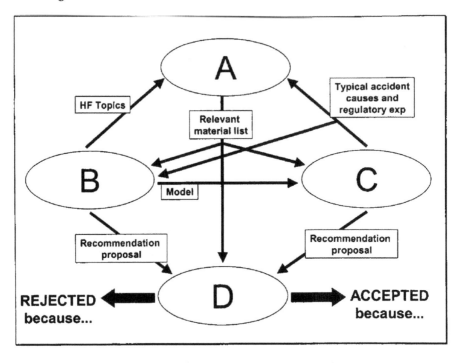

Figure 1 **The subgroup A, B, C and D processes and the interface between the groups that will result in recommendations of rule changes (HF-HWG, 2001)**

These regulations were reviewed for a list of human factors topics. A conceptual model of human/system interaction to ensure that the group of topics was inclusive of all known human factors considerations related to flight deck design guided the development. The topics each describe some type of information that may be useful to include in regulations and advisory material documents.

The topics are organized into seven categories:

- Information.
- Controls.
- Means to communicate.
- Human/machine integration.
- Pilot characteristics.
- Flight deck environment.
- External environment.

The objective of subgroup C was to take a data driven, experienced based approach at identifying human performance design related deficiencies within and across the part 25 regulatory material. The subgroup was tasked with reviewing a set of published reports that document analyses of accidents, incidents, and safety related events and research studies. To supplement this literature, the subgroup was also tasked with reviewing experience-based items from the manufacturers' databases; in-flight operational experience collected from airline pilots and test pilots; and regulatory experience compiled from various certification projects. The list of issues compiled from these published and unpublished sources was used to identify deficiencies of the regulatory material. This approach ensures that the resulting list of deficiencies addresses issues that have been documented in the literature, experienced in the field and derived from research. Furthermore, it ensures the final recommendations are data driven.

The process included the following steps:

- *Identify the list of sources* Identify a list of sources for obtaining relevant Part 25 human performance experience-based issues. Forty-five sources were reviewed including documents which summarized accident and incident data, research literature, experience-based items from the manufacturers' databases, in-flight operational experience collected from airline pilots, test pilots and regulatory experience compiled from various certification projects.
- *The matrix* Relevant issues were entered into a spreadsheet, referred to as 'the matrix'. Data collected included, but were not limited to, a description of each human performance issue or scenario, potential consequences, related regulatory material, and the regulatory issue were raised.
- *The filter* Issues that did not have a FAR/JAR 25 component were not entered into the matrix. The group was conservative and inclusive in its approach by keeping issues, which could have a design solution to guard against the risk of not considering potentially useful data just because one solution could be training. All issues not related to human performance were screened out.
- *Linking to the specific regulatory paragraphs* Since the working group task was to identify deficiencies within and across the FAR/JAR 25 regulatory material, issues were linked to the associated individual regulatory paragraphs.
- *Linking to equipment types* A second methodology had to be used to link other types of experienced-based issues that were not easily linked to the equipment type-FARs; for example, issues associated with new technologies not specifically called out in the FARs, such as global positioning systems (GPS).
- *Identify issue categories* The matrix items were also classified by category. These categories are more general in nature, such as issues with a flight crew lack of situation awareness. These general issues were linked, where possible, to specific regulations. Alternatively, some categories of issues

could not be mapped back to specific regulatory material, and were flagged as a general deficiency across the regulatory material.

- *Consolidation* Once the matrix data was complete, the next step in the subgroup C process was organizing and consolidating the issues. This was critical since subgroup C identified over *400* individual issues.

The method used to define the best criteria was based on the review of the literature and expertise of the subgroup D members. The evaluation criteria are based on the expected safety improvement which will result from the modifications introduced by the HF-HWG, as well as the feasibility of the recommendations, based on technical issues, cost-effectiveness, and the expected level of acceptance by both the regulatory authorities and industry. The prioritisation of the recommendations will be based on the methodology used on previous programs addressing safety initiatives by regulation. This process, which will be modified as needed to fit the HF-HWG task, uses expert judgment to evaluate recommendations against a set of rating scales, which are then combined partly through the use of a mathematical algorithm.

The review process showed clearly the weakness of the structure and philosophy of the present regulation framework. The regulations are based on old design solutions, are either very generic and difficult to show objective compliance with or specify outdated solutions. The index system is system based and does not fit the modern integrated cockpit where many systems are cross woven in function, logic and failure modes. The role of crew resource management has not been addressed in the design and the usability issues are mentioned only in general. The main dilemma of the working group is how to turn the rules and regulations into a flexible but consistent tool that will also address future designs and fit with the operational rules that address the cockpit and crew.

The HF-HWG Interim report bases its conclusions and recommendations on the extensive work that the subgroups have performed and the data they have collected.

Summary

The modern test pilot can no longer rely only on his 'Cooper-Harper' scale for evaluation of new complex cockpits. Objective criteria and clear methods to obtain the data from the end user population are to be used based on detailed requirements and guidance material. The test pilot with his/her experience should help develop these tests and recommend improvements. Design related certification material to support this process is being recommended by the HF-HWG and will hopefully be implemented in the design regulations in several years.

The future role of the test pilot will be as an expert in the planning of the tests, evaluating the test conditions and analysing the test results of development and certification flights or simulations. Based on performance based regulations and guidance material rather than the existing prescriptive ones, the applicant will have more flexibility to determine the design features. The test pilot will be involved in the philosophy of the design, checking consistency and determining relevant flying tasks in all flight conditions and unusual situations. The evaluation criteria for certification will be performance and error rate and type using a wide population of the end user, the line pilot, to be exposed to the new design in the most realistic scenarios. If the results require, the test pilot will be involved in modifying the design or the procedures and recommending training requirements in order to meet the performance criteria during reruns

Since rules alone cannot improve the design, evaluators such as test pilots must be trained in using and accepting these new means of compliance. New design features must not only be seen as barriers in the certification process but also as means of getting credit for good features and being able to reduce training and procedures.

References

Billings, C.E. (1997). *Aviation Aautomation – the search for a human-centered approach*. Mahwah, New Jersey: Lawrence Erlbaum Associates.

Courteney, H. (1999). Human factors of automation: The regulator's challenge. In, S.W.A. Dekker and E. Hollnagel (Eds), *Coping with computers in the cockpit* (pp. 109-130). Aldershot, UK: Ashgate.

Federal Aviation Administration (1989). FAA Advisory Circular 25-15, *Approval of Flight Management Systems in Transport Category Airplanes*. Washington, DC: Federal Aviation Administration.

Federal Aviation Administration (1996). *FAA Human Factors Study Team Report on the interface between flightcrews and modern flight deck systems*, Washington, DC: Federal Aviation Administration.

Federal Aviation Administration (1998). *Code of Federal Regulations*, Aeronautics and Space, Parts 1-59. Washington, DC: Federal Aviation Administration.

Federal Register (1999). Human Factors Harmonisation Working Group. http://www.researchintegrations.com/hf-hwg/fed-reg-tasking-index.htm

FOCA Saab 340 accident report (Crossair Flug CRX 498 vom 10. Januar 2000 bei Nassenwil), 2001, http://www.bazl.ch/

Harris, D. (1997). Human Factors for Flight Deck Certification. *Proceedings of the European Workshop to Develop Human Factors Guidelines for Flight Deck Certification*. London, UK: Cranfield University Press.

Hopkin, V.D. (1993). *Verification and validation: Concepts, issues and applications. In, J.A. Wise, V.D. Hopkin, and P. Stager (Eds) Verification and validation of complex systems: Human factors issues. NATO ASI series F, Vol. 110, pp. 9-34. Berlin: Springer-Verlag.*

Human Factors Harmonisation Working Group (2001). Interim report: *http://www.researchintegrations.com/hf-hwg/index.htm*

Mårtensson, L. and Singer, G. (1998) *Warning Systems in Commercial Aircraft - an Analysis of Existing Systems.* Royal Inst of Technology, Dept of Industrial Economics and Management, report TRITA-IEO-1998:01, ISSN 1100-7982. Stockholm: Royal Institute of Technology.

Mårtensson, L. (1995). The aircraft crash at Gottröra: Experiences of the cockpit crew. *International Journal of Aviation Psychology, 5*, 305-326.

Nibbelke, R., Pritchard, C., Emmerson, P., Leggatt, A. and Davies, K. (2001). Where do we go from here? Navigation decision aiding in the case of sub-system failure. In, D. Harris (Ed.) *Engineering Psychology and Cognitive Ergonomics – Volume 5* (pp. 135-142). Aldershot: Ashgate.

Pritchett, A. (2001). Reviewing the role of cockpit systems, *Human Factors and Aerospace Safety, 1*, 5-38.

Roscoe, S, N. (1968). Airborne displays for flight and navigation. *Human Factors, 10*, 321-332.

Sarter N.B., Woods D.D., Billings C.E. (1997). Automation Surprises. In, G. Salvendy (Ed), *Handbook of Human Factors and Ergonomics* (pp. 1926-1943). Mahwah, NJ: Erlbaum.

Singer, G. (1999). Filling the gaps in the human factors certification net. In, S.W.A. Dekker and E. Hollnagel (Eds), *Coping with computers in the cockpit*, (pp. 87-108). Aldershot, UK: Ashgate.

Singer, G. (2000). Towards a safer cockpit – Improving cockpit interface through flight test. *Licentiate thesis, Report 2000-8*, Royal Institute of Technology, Stockholm, Sweden. ISSN 0280-4646.

Wise, J.A., and Wise, M.A. (1993). *Basic considerations in verification and validation. In, J.A. Wise, V.D. Hopkin, and P. Stager (Eds)* Verification and validation of complex systems: Human factors issues. NATO ASI series F, *Vol. 110, pp. 87-96. Berlin: Springer-Verlag.*

Wise, J.A., Hopkin, V.D., and Stager, P. (Eds.) (1993). Verification and validation of complex systems: Human factors issues. NATO ASI series F, *Vol. 110. Berlin: Springer-Verlag.*

Woods, D.D. (1995). The alarm problem and directed attention in dynamic fault management. *Ergonomics, 38*, 2371-2393.

Editor's note

A response to this paper by Richard L. Newman and Kevin W. Greeley appears in *Human Factors and Aerospace Safety 2(3), 277-285* which is immediately followed by a rejoinder by Gideon Singer.

5   Passenger safety in future very large transport aircraft

Helen C. Muir, Lauren Thomas
and Rebecca Wilson

Abstract

The development of Very Large Transport Aircraft (VLTAs) presents some exciting opportunities and challenges. Of major importance will be taking steps to ensure that the current high standards of passenger safety which have been achieved in the current aircraft fleets is maintained. Many of the issues which will require consideration in order to achieve this goal are discussed in the paper.

Background

Since the introduction of commercial jet transportation, aviation has achieved a remarkable safety record. In addition to a 95% reduction in the accident rate, steps have been taken by all of the regulatory authorities to reduce the number of fatalities. Improvements have included the introduction of floor proximity lighting, fire-blocking materials in seats, smoke detectors in the cargo bay and toilets, and additional space adjacent to exits. The behaviour of passengers and their impact on emergency evacuations has also come under scrutiny since it is believed that with a comprehensive understanding of behaviour in highly stressful and disorientating conditions, steps could be taken to improve the probability of a successful evacuation of all of the passengers from the aircraft.

For the future Very Large Transport Aircraft (VLTA), the challenge for both the manufacturers and the regulators will be to ensure that with passenger loads of between 400 and 800, together with cabin interiors which may differ significantly

This paper was first published in Human Factors and Aerospace Safety 4(3), 2004, pp. 259-271

from the current fleet, e.g. two decks or multi aisles, the high standards of safety and survival which have been achieved in the past, can be maintained.

Factors influencing passenger survival

Much of the information which has been gained about passenger survival has been gained from accident investigation. Whilst no two accidents can ever be the same, it is possible to learn from the similarities and differences between the causes of the accidents, their location and the environmental conditions present, the types of passengers onboard and their responses to the emergency. For instance, there were many similarities between the accident at Manchester in 1985 (Air Accidents Investigation Branch, 1985) and the one which occurred at Calgary in 1984 (ICAO, 1984), in that they were both caused by an engine fire at take off. However, they differed in one important respect, namely that at Manchester there were 55 fatalities whereas in Calgary everyone survived. We know that in some aircraft accidents everyone files out of the plane in a rapid although orderly manner, for example, in the evacuation of a British Airways 747 at Los Angeles in 1987 (Civil Aviation Authority, 1991) as a result of a bomb scare. In other accidents however, the orderly process breaks down and confusion in the cabin can lead to blockages in the aisles and at exits, with a consequent loss of life (Air Accidents Investigation Branch, 1985).

In 1989 it was suggested that one of the primary reasons for the differences in behaviour between the orderly and disorderly situations arose from the motivation of individual passengers (Muir, Marrison, and Evans, 1989). It was pointed out that in some accidents, as in the aircraft certification evacuations, all of the passengers assume that the objective is to get everyone out of the aircraft as quickly as possible, and they therefore all work collaboratively. In other emergencies, however, the motivation of individual passengers could be very different, especially in the presence of smoke and fire. In a situation where an immediate threat to life is perceived, rather than all passengers being motivated to help each other, the main objective which governs their behaviour becomes survival for themselves, and in some instances, members of their family. In this situation, when the primary survival instinct takes over, people do not work collaboratively. This can lead to the evacuation becoming very disorganised, with some individuals competing to get through the exits. The behaviour observed in the accident which occurred at Manchester (Air Accidents Investigation Branch, 1985), and other accidents, including the fire at Bradford City Football Stadium, UK (Taylor, 1990) supports this interpretation.

The findings from the accident data suggest that for future VLTAs it will be important to ensure that the professional cabin crew are able to control and direct passengers in an emergency. It will also be important to ensure that the configuration of the cabin is such that blockages will not occur in the event of passengers starting to panic in the event of a fire.

Airframe configuration

The findings from the accident data suggest that evaluation of the ergonomic issues associated with use of a VLTA airframe in an emergency will require consideration by the manufacturers and regulatory authorities. For either airframes with twin decks or multi aisles, these configurational issues will include the following factors.

Size, location and access to exits

The size, location at access to exits can all influence the opportunity for passengers to survive an accident. For all aircraft the current regulation stipulates that the maximum number of passengers that can be carried is dependent on the number and types of exits available on each side of the fuselage. These conditions will apply to VLTAs (US Department of Transportation, 1974 and UK Civil Aviation Authority, 1978). There are five types of emergency exits (see table 1).

Table 1   Exit Types (From, Edwards, M. and Edwards, E. (1990). *The Aircraft Cabin*. Aldershot: Gower Technical).

Type	Minimum height		Minimum width		Maximum step up	
	Inches	mm	Inches	mm	Inches	mm
A	72	1830	42	1067	0	0
I	48	1220	24	610	0	0
II	44	1118	20	508	10	254
III	36	914	20	508	20	508
IV	26	660	19	483	29	737

For passenger seating configurations of more than 110 seats, the emergency exits in each side of the fuselage must include at least two Type I or larger exits. Each emergency exit must be easily accessible, and must also meet the requirements in terms of exit arrangement, assist means, escape routes, exit marking and emergency lighting. All passenger emergency exits should be distributed throughout the cabin as uniformly as practical, taking into account passenger seat distribution, and exits should be located where they afford the most effective means of passenger evacuation. The current regulations also state that no passenger emergency exit shall be located more than 60 feet from any adjacent passenger exit on the same side of the same deck of the fuselage. Type A floor level exits are required to have an escape passageway at least 36 inches wide. In addition, the assist means for each Type A exit must be self-supporting, and must be capable of simultaneously carrying two parallel lines of evacuees.

In a study conducted by the NTSB of passengers and crew involved in 46 evacuations, all of the 67 floor level exits used, were opened without difficulty during these evacuations. (National Transportation Safety Board, 2000). This suggests that providing there is no deformation to the structure of the exit or doorframe there are unlikely to be exit operational problems in the event of an emergency. In general passengers were able to access exits without difficulty except for one accident in which the interior cabin furnishings became dislodged and were obstacles to some passengers' access to exits. There are no known reports of accidents in which the size of a floor level exit caused problems for passenger egress, in contrast to Type III exits where this has been a problem and on which extensive research has been conducted (Air Accidents Investigation Branch, 1986, Muir, Marrison, and Evans, 1989).

Accident severity has also been found to influence the ease with which passengers will be able to reach an exit. Severe damage to the fuselage, for example, can cause interior furnishings to be dislodged and become obstacles for passengers attempting to exit an aeroplane. In the MD-82 accident in Little Rock, Arkansas (National Transportation Safety Board, 2000) the crash forces caused seats to break free from their seat tracks and block aisles. In the forward portion of the cabin, passengers had to navigate around fallen overhead bins and across a severely deformed floor. Fortunately, the crash caused several gaps in the fuselage that passengers were able to use for egress.

Other factors which have been reported as restricting the ability of passengers to access operational exits have included broken interiors, overhead bins, the seatback in front of them and aisle width. In addition flight attendants have reported that their seat obstructed the evacuation and that galley items obstructed the evacuation. Although it must be recognised that in the majority of accidents, passengers have been able to access operational exits without difficulty, the size and location of exits in the future VLTAs will require serious consideration.

Location and size of aisles and cross aisles.

Other factors which will require consideration will be the location and size of aisles and cross aisles. The regulations state that there must be a passageway leading from the nearest main aisle to each floor level emergency exit (US Department of Transportation, 1974, UK Civil Aviation Authority, 1978). Each passageway leading to a floor level exit must be unobstructed and at least 36 inches wide. If two or more main aisles are provided, there must be unobstructed cross-aisles at least 20 inches wide between main aisles. Passenger aisles within the cabin should be a minimum width of 15 inches less than 25 inches from the floor and a minimum width of 20 inches at 25 inches and more above the floor.

In the accident which happened in the UK at Manchester airport in 1985 (Air Accidents Investigation Branch, 1985) the accident investigators concluded that the bulkheads at the front of the cabin had severely restricted the ability of some passengers to access the exits at the front of the airframe.

The research, which was conducted in the UK following the Manchester Accident (Muir, Marrison, and Evans, 1989) clearly indicated that when the aperture between the bulkheads at the front of the cabin was increased from 20 inches to 30 inches, the speed of passengers able to pass through the aperture was significantly increased. Making the gap even wider did not significantly increase the flow rate and on occasions led to problems. These included the occurrence of the flight attendant being pushed out through the exit by the rush of passengers at the start of the evacuation (an occurrence which has also occurred in some accidents) because she had no bulkhead to protect her. This is a factor which will require consideration in the design of the cabin adjacent to the exits, in future VLTAs. The other problem was that in dense smoke, the passengers tended to hesitate when they got to the end of the aisle and found that there was no easy hand hold between the end of the aisle and the exit aperture. By contrast when there was only a small bulkhead they were able to feel this with their hands and use this to enable them to guide themselves to the exit. These findings may have implications for the design and location of the monuments in future VLTAs.

There do not appear to be reports of the cross aisles in the currently configured wide-bodied airframes causing problems during either evacuation certification tests or in evacuations in an actual emergency. If it was possible to establish dual flows down the cabin aisles this could significantly improve the evacuation rate. It may also be the case that if exits are located exactly at the end of each aisle, rather than being hidden behind a bulkhead, passengers can then leave their seats, move into the aisle and will be immediately able to see an operational exit. This may well increase the speed of their progress down the aisle in an emergency.

Individual cabin capacity limitations

The seating and space for passengers may also be a factor potentially capable of influencing survival in VLTAs. The regulated minimum space requirements for seated passengers are contained within the UK CAA regulations (Civil Aviation Authority, 1989). These regulations were developed based on anthropometric data for 5th percentile females and 95th percentile British males, and also took into account the minimum distance and the vertically projected distance between any seat, and the seat (or other fixed structure) immediately in front of it.

Currently, the minimum distance required between the back of a seat and the back of the seat in front (the seat pitch) is 26 inches, and the minimum vertically projected distance between seat rows is 3 inches. These minima were originally set in order to provide adequate space for passengers to both occupy a seat, and to stand and vacate the seat in order to move to the main aisle. While these standards have recently been reviewed in a study conducted for the Joint Aviation Authorities (Quigley et al, 2001), there have as yet been no regulatory changes based on this research.

In principle, there would appear to be no reason why the regulations regarding seat pitch and seating density for wide-bodied aircraft should be any different on a VLTA airframe. The key consideration should be the evacuation performance, and ensuring that this can be achieved to a satisfactory standard.

Sill heights for VLTAs

The future VLTAs involving two decks might have Type A exits and a sill height of 5 metres at the lower deck and 8 metres at the upper deck. In order to achieve a rapid evacuation of all of the passengers in an emergency it is essential that the time passengers take to jump onto the slide is kept to an absolute minimum. Reports from airline operators in company training schools, indicate that as the height of the sill increases, hesitation time before jumping onto the slide also tends to increase. Over the course of an evacuation of an airframe a significant number of passengers hesitating will inevitably increase the overall evacuation time.

Research has shown that the most effective method to overcome the tendency by passengers to hesitate, or in some instances to sit rather than to jump onto the slide, is to ensure that all of the flight attendants are trained to act assertively (Muir and Cobbett, 1995). In addition, anything which can be achieved by improvements to the slide design to encourage passengers to feel more confident and to overcome their natural tendency to hesitate will be of advantage. It will be important that when future VLTAs are certificated that sufficient tests are conducted to ensure that a representative group of passengers will jump rapidly onto the slides.

Slides and post egress factors

In an aircraft accident, when a rapid evacuation of the passengers is required, slides are used to enable passengers to escape from the aircraft. The Emergency Evacuation Slides Technical Standard Order (Federal Aviation Administration 1999) states that all slides must be capable of demonstrating rates of at least 70 passengers per minute, per lane. Therefore, for dual lane slides, the chutes must be capable of supporting a flow rate of 140 passengers per minute. In full-scale evacuation demonstrations, as with experimental evacuations and evacuation models, the actual flow rate obtained will depend on many factors.

Research has indicated that injuries during egress are frequently associated with the use of the slide. The reasons for these include the airframe coming to rest at an unlevel attitude making some of the slides too short, severe weather conditions e.g. strong winds making the slide use hazardous, passengers endeavouring to use the slide before it is fully deployed, passengers falling off the side of the slide, or sustaining injuries either during their descent or at the bottom of the slide. The design of the escape slides will therefore require serious consideration in order to minimise the potential for injuries to passengers. Research is being undertaken at the University of Newcastle in UK into alternate slide design (Gosling, 1998).

The reported injuries which have been associated with the use of slides, have frequently occurred as a consequence of congestion at the bottom of the slides. The development of some new technology and procedures for marshalling passengers away from the airframe following an evacuation will be required for future VLTAs.

There have also tragically been instances of numbers of passengers and occasionally crew who have successfully evacuated the aircraft but have subsequently sustained serious injury or loss of life. There have been instances of passengers being run over by rescue personnel arriving at the scene of the accident, an instance of the passengers re-boarding the aircraft to search for missing hand luggage only to be overcome by a fire which broke out in the cabin while they were on board. It is frequently not possible to trace all of the passengers who have been on board the aircraft following an accident. All of these factors indicate importance of designing procedures for handling such a large number of passengers, post evacuation, in order to ensure their safety.

Emergency exit lighting

An emergency lighting system, independent of the main lighting system, is installed on all aeroplanes. The regulations require that the emergency lighting system must include the following: illuminated emergency exit marking and locating signs, sources of general cabin illumination, interior lighting in emergency exit areas, floor proximity escape path marking, and exterior emergency lighting (US Department of Transportation, 1974, US Civil Aviation Authority, 1978).

The effectiveness of the emergency lighting systems was reviewed by the NTSB (National Transportation Safety Board, 1992). Of the 36 flight attendants who responded, there were only two reports of failed lights, both from flight attendants in the Little Rock accident (National Transportation Safety Board, 2000). Further, five flight crew members and 10 flight attendants reported that emergency lighting systems assisted evacuations in which visibility was restricted. All of these crew members were involved in five night evacuations. The Safety Board concluded therefore, that emergency lighting systems functioned as intended in the 30 evacuation cases investigated in detail. This supports the case for the continued use of emergency lighting to assist passengers evacuate in smoke in VLTAs.

Access to upper deck

For VLTAs involving two decks, the extent to which the stairs used for passengers to board the upper deck may be available for use in various aircraft emergencies will require careful consideration. It is anticipated that the certification process will be based on the passengers evacuating from each floor using the slides from the exits on their floor. In this situation the stairs will not be used. In an actual emergency this may not always be easy to achieve, especially if the slides are not available, for a variety of reasons. Some passengers on the upper deck may have to be physically restrained from using the stairs which could present a serious challenge for cabin crew.

Novel interiors

The suggestion has been made that in future VLTAs, some operators may request novel configurations including recreational and exercise areas. If these are to be introduced, the safety implications for their use in flight will require special consideration, especially with respect to turbulence. However it will be assumed that all passengers will be required to be seated in a normal 16g seat for takeoff and landing or in the event of a pre-warned emergency such as aircraft coming into land with a damaged undercarriage.

Cabin crew

The successful management of between 400 and 800 passengers will be the responsibility of the cabin crew. Cabin crew issues for future VLTAs will include the following.

Numbers of flight attendants

There is extensive evidence from both research (Muir and Cobbett, 1995) and from accidents (National Transportation Safety Board, 1992) that the flight attendants can be the most important determinant of the successful evacuation of all of the passengers in an emergency.

The usual maximum number of passengers per flight attendant is 50:1. However Scandinavian Airlines fly with one flight attendant per 30 passengers and indeed many other operators fly with more than the minimum number. It should be recognised, however that those operators who fly with additional crew usually do so for reasons of service as well as safety. Future aircraft designs, with multi-aisles and large number of passengers, raise the question of whether a ratio of one flight attendant per 50 passengers will be sufficient. The manufacturers and regulatory authorities could determine by testing, how many flight attendants will be required, and in which locations in the event of an emergency on VLTA.

Flight attendant assist space

From the videotapes for certification evacuations, it becomes apparent that the size of adequate assist space can lead to the flight attendants being unable to stay in the assist space when they are assisting the passengers to evacuate in quick succession down the slides. Thus the size of the assist space can mean that the flight attendant reduces the probability of continuous dual lane slide usage. It could be that increasing the size of the assist space will enable the flight assistants to provide sufficient assistance to the passengers to ensure that there is continuous dual lane slide use.

Direct view

The regulations require all of the flight attendants to have an unrestricted view of the passengers in the cabin when seated for takeoff or landing. The rationale for this is that despite the presence of warning signs in the cabin to make passengers remain seated in a safe position during critical phases of flight, passengers do not always respect these cabin signs. There have been numerous instances of passengers attempting to pick up their belongings from overhead bins on final approach, standing up during taxiing and putting their carry on baggage into the aisle. In the event of an emergency landing, passengers often tend to leave their brace for impact position as soon as the aircraft is on the ground. Flight attendants need to visually monitor these situations to prevent this from happening. On rare occasions it has been necessary for cabin crew to relay instructions over a public address system, by megaphone, or simply by shouting. Not only the increased passenger load, but the two deck or multi aisle configuration will make this issue even more important in the future.

Injuries to flight attendants and passengers

In a study to investigate the sources of injury to flight attendants and passengers in flight, (National Transportation Safety Board, 1992), it was found that the main causes were injuries as a consequence of lack of stability of the aircraft in turbulence, trolleys going out of control, passenger luggage or safety equipment falling from overhead bins, and in-flight fires. The large numbers of crew and passengers on future VLTAs, mean that unless consideration is given to ways of minimising the injuries which can arise from these sources, there could be an unacceptable number of injuries on any one flight.

Passengers

In order to enable passengers to perform optimally in an emergency, the following areas will require consideration.

Provision of safety information for passengers

The regulations (US Department of Transportation, 1974) require that passenger carrying aeroplane operators shall ensure that all passengers are orally briefed by the appropriate crew member before take-off. This briefing should include restrictions on smoking, the location of the emergency exits, the use of safety belts and when to use them, and the location and use of any required flotation means. In addition, each passenger-carrying operator must provide a safety card in a convenient location for use by each passenger. This card should supplement the oral briefing and should contain diagrams of, and methods of operating, the emergency exits, and other instructions necessary for the use of emergency equipment. However, providing this information will not necessarily ensure that all of the passengers have retained the relevant information and are able to apply it appropriately in an emergency.

Passenger performance in an evacuation is dependent on how well they have prepared for such an eventuality. A large part of this preparedness is their knowledge of exit location and operation, which is normally information by provided either by the oral briefing or by the safety card. There is a considerable body of evidence which suggests that passengers do not pay attention to this safety information. For example, the recent NTSB Safety Study (National Transportation Safety Board, 2000) examined 46 evacuations, sending questionnaires to all passengers involved. Of 457 passengers who returned questionnaires, 54% (457 people) reported that they had not watched the entire briefing because they had seen it before. Of 431 passengers who answered the question relating to the safety card, 68% (293 people) said that they had not read it. Furthermore, even those passengers who do read the safety card may not necessarily understand it. In a recent study, 36 pictorial diagrams randomly chosen from 50 safety cards were presented to 113 people. Twenty of these 36 diagrams were understood by less than 50% of those tested (Caird, et al, 1997). As a result, the NTSB has recommended that the FAA require minimum comprehension testing standards for safety briefing. With the large numbers of passengers on VLTAs it will be important to ensure that they all understand what they should do in the event of an emergency.

Future issues

Precautionary evacuations

The proposed VLTAs will require passengers to evacuate from a sill height of 8 metres. The majority of aircraft evacuations are in fact precautionary evacuations. The public may be prepared to tolerate a small number of serious injuries from slides in the event of an aircraft fire. Were a significant number of serious injuries to occur in the precautionary evacuations this could make the public lose confidence in the safety of VLTAs.

Enhanced directional information

One of the challenges for the future is that as airframes become bigger there will be an increasing demand for innovation which will assist passengers to locate available exits and to access them quickly even in the presence of smoke in the cabin. Recent innovations in the UK which are currently being used to assist members of the public to evacuate from buildings in the event of a fire have included electroluminescent way guidance systems incorporating tactile cues (Thomas, Muir, Niazi, 2001), photoluminescent or 'glow in the dark' way guidance, and directional noise (Rutherford and Withington, 1998). These systems could merit further exploration.

Another possibility might be to explore whether the currently used lighting, signs and floor proximity systems are currently being employed to maximum advantage. It could be that changes to their location or in the case of luminescent material, the size of the area which they cover could assist the speed of the evacuation, especially when there is smoke in the cabin.

Emergency command and control procedures

The procedures currently used by flight attendants for an emergency evacuation have been carefully developed and standardised. Following the call to evacuate each attendant is required to independently assess the situation outside their exit and if the conditions are acceptable open the exit and once the slide has deployed, assist the passengers to evacuate onto the slide as rapidly as possible. If, upon inspection, the flight attendant finds the external conditions are such that it will be unsafe to evacuate through their exit, they must then redirect their passengers to the nearest operational exit. These procedures originally developed when aeroplanes were relatively small and attendants could hear and see each other relatively easily.

As airframes become larger consideration should be given to whether or not these procedures continue to be adequate. The practice in other scenarios where large numbers of people are required to evacuate quickly in the event of a fire (e.g. football stadiums, oil rigs) is that a commander works at a control station and manages the evacuation in order to ensure that all of the escape opportunities are used to maximum advantage. With the advent of new technologies (e.g. small video recorders, mobile phones) it should be possible for the commander to have a small control station from which he/she can monitor the conditions inside and outside the cabin. He/she can then provide additional information to the attendants at the exits as required. The control station could be located immediately outside the flight deck so that the evacuation commander can have easy access to the captain of the aircraft. Such a system could also be of benefit in the event of medical emergencies, in-flight fires, hijack, etc.

Threat from fire

The fact that the smoke from a fire frequently enters the cabin and can have such catastrophic consequences is a major concern with so many passengers in the cabin. The first approach must be to explore whether with these larger airframes, additional safeguards can be designed into the fuselage to reduce the probability of the smoke entering the cabin. Another consideration could be consideration of the introduction of some form of cabin water mist system to reduce the rate at which the smoke can spread through the cabin.

Conclusions

Information from accidents, cabin safety research, and safety monitoring all provide knowledge that can be used to support the design of future VLTA cabins. For future VLTAs of twin-deck or multiple aisle design, the challenge for both the manufacturers and the regulators will be to ensure that, on aircraft carrying between 400 and 800 passengers, the impressive safety record of the aviation industry is maintained.

References

Air Accidents Investigation Branch, Department of Transport (1985). *Report on the accident to Boeing 737-236 Series 1 G-BGJL at Manchester International Airport on 22 August 1985. Aircraft Accident Report 8/88.* London: HMSO.

Caird, J.K., Wheat, B., McIntosh, K.R. and Dewar, R.E. (1997*).* The comprehensibility of airline safety card pictorials. *In, Proceedings of Human Factors and Ergonomics Society 41st Annual Meeting, Alberquerque, NM.* Santa Barbara: Human Factors and Ergonomics Society.

Civil Aviation Authority (1978). Joint Airworthiness Requirements, (JAR 25 – Large Aeroplanes). London: Author.

Civil Aviation Authority (1989) *Minimum Space for Seated Passengers Airworthiness Notice 64, Issue 1.* London: Author.

Civil Aviation Authority (1991). *Report on the accident to Boeing 737 N388US at Los Angeles. Airport World Airline Accident Summary CAP 479.* London: Author.

Edwards, M. and Edwards, E. (1990). *The Aircraft Cabin.* Aldershot: Gower Technical.

Federal Aviation Administration (1999). *Emergency evacuation slides, ramps, ramp/slides and slide/rafts Technical Standard Order C69c.* Washington DC: Author.

Gosling, P.D. (1998). A new philosophy applied to the design of pneumatic aircraft evacuation slides and slide-rafts The VLTA Conference, Noordwijkerhout, The Netherlands.

International Civil Aviation Organisation (1984). *Report on the accident to Boeing 737 C-GQPW at Calgary Airport ICAO Summary 1984-2*. Montreal: Author.

Muir, H., Marrison, C. and Evans A, (1989). *Aircraft evacuations: The effect of passengers motivation and cabin configuration adjacent to the exit. CAA Paper 89019*. London: Author.

Muir, H.C. and Cobbett, A.M. (1995). *Cabin crew behaviour in emergency evacuations. Civil Aviation Authority/Federal Aviation Administration Paper DOT/FAA/CT-95/16*. London: Author.

National Transportation Safety Board (2000). *Emergency evacuation of commercial airplanes Ref. NTSB/SS-00/01, PB2000-917002 Notation 7266*. Washington DC: Author.

National Transportation Safety Board (1992). *Flight attendant training and performance during emergency situations. Special Investigation Report NTSB/SIR-92-02*. Washington DC: Author.

Quigley, C., Southall, D., Freer, M., Moody, A. and Porter, M. (2001) *Anthropometric Study to Update Minimum Aircraft Seating Standards. Report prepared for the Joint Aviation Authorities*.

Rutherford P and Withington D J. (1998). Sound Location for Aiding Emergency Egress. *Fire Safety Engineering, 5*, 14-17.

Taylor, P. (1990). *Hillsborough Stadium Disaster – Final report on enquiry by Rt.Hon.Justice Taylor*. London: HMSO.

Thomas, L.J, Muir H.C. and Niazi, F. (2001). *Preliminary evaluation of an electroluminescent Floor Proximity Emergency Escape Path Marking System (FPEEPMS) incorporating tactile cues*. Cranfield: Cranfield University.

US Department of Transportation (1974). *Federal Aviation Regulations Part 25 – Airworthiness Standards*. Washington, DC: Author.

US Department of Transportation (1974). *Federal Aviation Regulations Part 121 – Operating Requirements*. Washington, DC: Author.

Section Two
Operations and Training

6 A review of the benefits of aviation human factors training

Graham D. Edkins

Abstract

This paper reviews the available evidence for the benefits of aviation human factors training. Despite the proliferation of human factors training programmes across the aviation industry since the 1980s there are few published studies that demonstrate positive shifts in attitude or behaviour following the introduction of such training. Those studies reporting benefits suffer from a number of methodological weaknesses including the failure to use control groups, lack of longitudinal evaluation and small sample sizes. Of significant concern is a lack of cost effectiveness data demonstrating a return on investment from human factors training. Recommendations for future research are made in the light of consolidating existing evidence on the commercial benefits of human factors training.

Introduction

Over the past twenty years, there has been an increasing recognition that human factors training can have a significant impact on safety, particularly within high-risk domains such as transport, mining and energy. The aviation industry has been at the forefront of this trend. Human error has been consistently identified as contributing to the majority of air crashes since the late 1970s (FAA, 1995; Johnson, 2000a; Salas, Prince, Bowers, Stout, Oser and Cannon-Bowers, 1999b). In most cases, these human errors occurred despite the operators' technical competence. Highly trained people committed what seemed to be trivial errors. Usually these errors involved factors such as breakdown in communications, poor

This paper was first published in Human Factors and Aerospace Safety 2(3), 2002, pp. 201-216

decision-making and failures in leadership (Helmreich, 1996) and in some cases resulted in tragic loss of human life, as well as huge financial and public relations costs for those organisations involved.

To minimise human error, the aviation industry introduced a series of cockpit resource management training programmes in the early 1980s. These resource management programmes have typically raised awareness about human factors concepts, such as communication, decision-making and teamwork, within the flight crew working environment. Airlines throughout the world have progressed from cockpit orientated training programmes to Crew Resource Management (CRM) and Advanced Crew Resource Management (ACRM). Subsequently, these programmes have expanded into a plethora of different forms across a wide variety of industries. For example, the air traffic control domain has adapted airline CRM training into a set of Team Resource Management programmes (Andersen and Bove, 2000). Outside aviation, CRM-style training has been applied within the nuclear industry (Harrington and Kelso, 1991), the medical fraternity (Davies and Helmreich, 1996; Fisher, Phillips, and Mather, 2000; Howard, Gaba, Fish, Yang and Sarnquist, 1992), for maritime crews (Andersen, Soerensen, Weber and Soerensen, 1996; Bydorf, 1998), and in the offshore oil industry (Flin, 1995; Flin and O'Connor, 2001). Variants of CRM have also been used to enhance decision-making and team skills training for emergency services personnel. Similarly, team based safety behaviour training, which is analogous to human factors training, has been incorporated into industries such as construction (e.g. Raya, Bishop, and Qi, 1997). Regardless of industry application, these human factors training programmes have similar foci on safety and human behaviour.

Despite the widespread use of human factors training programmes, there is a lack of longitudinal studies examining their effectiveness. For example, do human factors training programmes have a significant impact on error management? Is there a relationship between human factors training and improved safety performance? The answers to these questions are particularly important for organisations questioning whether such programmes are a sound investment in times when training budgets may be scarce.

The purpose of this paper is to critically review the current state of human factors training within the aviation industry with specific regard to: studies that claim a successful link between human factors training and improved safety performance; and programmes that appear to demonstrate a return on investment. In particular, attention is paid to those studies reporting benefits from human factors training application in non-flight crew areas. It is hoped that this review may provide a précis of the status of human factors work on this subject as well as offer a useful resource for organisations to build a stronger human factors business case.

An empirical analysis of human factors training

While human factors training is becoming established across many industries, it remains most widespread in aviation. Successive generations of training programmes have refined the concepts and added to their scope. However, from the outset, doubts have been expressed about the validity of programmes. Initial doubters described the courses as 'charm school' and irrelevant to aviation (Helmreich, 1996). Since then, programme content has matured and the training methods have become increasingly sophisticated, but the doubters persist. Steps to overcome these doubters' resistance have usually been fruitless. But do the doubters have the evidence on their side?

At first glance, the best method to evaluate human factors training programmes would appear to be simple: rates of accidents. This approach seems logical given that the first programmes were introduced to reduce the incidence of human error in accident rates. Yet despite twenty years of human factors training, human error continues to be involved in the majority of aviation accidents. Johnson (2000a) recently found that while CRM style courses have been used in many airlines, there has not been any noteworthy reduction in rates of incidents and accidents resulting from crew teamwork and communication failures.

However, using accident rates to evaluate human factors training is futile, due to significant changes over this period in the way aviation accidents are analysed. Aircraft safety occurrences are now investigated in much greater detail, with 'multiple causality' now typically identifying a chain of events that leads to an accident (ICAO, 1992; Reason, 1992). Detailed systemic investigations almost inevitably lead to the identification of human error at one or more points along the chain. Such detailed analysis allows greater understanding of the causes of accidents, but it also means that the rate of accidents classified as 'human error' has increased.

With the increasing sophistication of investigation techniques, accident rates cannot be used as a broad method of evaluating training success. In addition, because accident rates in commercial aviation are already low, the infrequency of events makes any detection in improvement difficult even with identical accident investigation techniques (Helmreich, Chidester, Foushee, Gregorich and Wilhelm, 1990; Salas et al., 1999a). Accident rates could only provide valid comparisons if pre-training and post-training accident rates are available, *and* if the methods of analysing cause and the error classification system are identical. Without such data, human factors training has to be evaluated in other ways.

However, there are examples of when human factors training *has* been cited as preventing accidents. For example, potential disasters with two United Airlines flights[3] were averted and attributed to successful training in communication and

---

[3] In United Airlines Flight 811, a cargo door blew out on a Boeing 747 causing significant damage and the loss of two engines. United Airlines Flight 232, a DC10, suffered a catastrophic failure of the centre engine, resulting in the loss of all hydraulics and flight control systems.

teamwork (Salas, Rhodenizer, and Bowers, 2000). While such incidents are suggestive of benefits, anecdotal evidence is difficult to evaluate scientifically. Without rigorous controls, it cannot be determined if human factors training prevented the occurrence of accidents in these or other cases.

A review of the literature reveals that there are two approaches to evaluating the effectiveness of human factors training programmes; attitudinal and behavioural.

Attitudinal based methods of evaluating human factors training effectiveness

In the early development of human factors training, emphasis was often placed on attitudes. This was typically true in both training and in evaluation. In the aviation industry, formative courses sought to modify trainee's attitudes toward teamwork and other human performance issues. The effectiveness of these programmes was usually evaluated by measuring employee attitudes after training (Helmreich, 1999). This approach has been typical of human factors programmes in other industries as well. For example, air medical programmes have been evaluated by questionnaires, which aimed to measure individuals' attitudes towards team awareness and effective communication (Fisher et al., 2000). Similarly, crisis resource management training in medical operating rooms has been assessed by questionnaires, where participants where asked to rate themselves on their performance (Holzman, Cooper, Gaba, Philip, Small and Feinstein, 1995).

This reliance on attitude measurement does not provide sufficient evidence for the effectiveness of human factors training. Surveying attitudes is relevant to some parts of programme evaluation, such as judging employee reactions and detecting potential morale problems. However, when evaluating the benefits of a training programme, attitudes are an unsuitable measure, for two reasons. Firstly, it is a debatable assumption that attitudes have a direct effect on behaviour. It is possible that trainees have simply learned the right thing to say and are responding appropriately. Even if trainees have absorbed the concepts being taught, attitudes give no indication of whether they know how to apply what they have learned. Secondly, and more importantly, attitudinal assessment is not appropriate for an objective evaluation of what an individual has learned. When psychologists wish to test a person's intelligence, they do not give them a questionnaire asking them how intelligent they are. Instead, they use a set of performance items, which are compared to objective and standardised normative data points. Such behavioural methods of evaluation are applicable for human factors training programmes.

Despite such flaws, many human factors training programmes continue to rely on attitudes as a prime measure of programme effectiveness. However, some sections of the aviation industry are shifting to behavioural methods of training and evaluation (see Flin and Martin, 2001 for a review). This illustrates another significant problem; namely that human factors training programmes have not developed as a unified field with standardised methods. Rather, the area can be characterised as a diverse range of programmes and concepts developed by separate airlines and government agencies (Salas et al., 1999b).

As a result, any evaluation of the effectiveness of human factors training needs to consider the diversity in the field, including the impact of different organisational cultures, the operating environments and the types of programme conducted. Studies that claim to demonstrate the apparent failure or success of human factors training often need to distinguish which form or type of programme is being used. All forms of human factors training are not created equal and without further probing of the type of courses participants underwent, a well-intentioned evaluation may not provide substantive evidence against the field as a whole.

The use of behaviour based evaluation criteria

In recent years, some human factors training programmes have started to develop more rigorous criteria for training and evaluation. Behavioural competencies have begun to replace training for attitudes and awareness (e.g. van Amermaete and Krujisen, 1998). The development of behavioural competencies allows trainees to learn specific skills, which can be employed in work settings. Furthermore, the evaluation of specific competencies allows greater accuracy in assessing those areas in which individual trainees perform well, and those areas they need to improve. While behavioural human factors training is not universally applied, its acceptance appears to be spreading.

In contrast to the initial development of CRM style programmes, characterised by their wide variety, different assumptions, different training methods, and a lack of common content, the recent growth of behavioural human factors training has been accompanied by a shift toward standardised programmes. The involvement of regulatory bodies such as the Joint Aviation Authority (JAA) has led to increased standardisation of training methods and course content.

In the United States, the Federal Aviation Administration (FAA) has sponsored the development of Advanced Crew Resource Management (ACRM). This system is not a single package for all airlines, but a basis for individual airlines do develop their own programmes. Significantly, the ACRM programme includes skill-based, behavioural measures of crew performance, as well as standardisation of trainers.

In Europe, the Joint Aviation Authority has produced the NOTECHS system, an amalgamation of existing methods to measure non-technical skills. In this system, non-technical skills are defined as 'attitudes and behaviours in the cockpit not directly related to aircraft control, system management, or standard operating procedures' (van Avermaete and Krujisen, 1998). Non-technical skills are divided into four categories: cooperation, leadership and/or management skills, situation awareness, and decision-making. The NOTECHS system also includes five principles, which are intended to provide objective assessment. The first requirement is that only observable behaviour is assessed. Secondly, for behaviour to be rated unacceptable, it is a requirement that there be a threat to flight safety. The third requirement is that unacceptable behaviour must be repeated during a check to determine if there is a substantive problem. Fourthly, each behaviour must be rated as either acceptable or unacceptable. Finally, an explanation is required for each unacceptable rating.

While the shift from attitude based evaluation to a focus on behavioural training and assessment of flight crew skills is promising (Flin and Martin, 2001), human factors training is now being increasingly applied to other areas of aviation such as maintenance (e.g. Johnson, 2000b; Stelly and Poehlmann, 2000). With the broader application of human factors programmes, it has become even more imperative to evaluate the evidence for their effectiveness.

Evidence for the effectiveness of human factors training

When considering the effectiveness of human factors training, it should be noted that some researchers believed that training effectiveness had already been validated *before* the development of behavioural programmes like NOTECHS (Helmreich, 1996). However, most of the evidence cited above measured attitudes rather than behaviour, so that even when studies found that flight crew attitudes were improved (e.g. Helmreich and Wilhelm, 1991), this did not constitute reliable evidence. Indeed, some researchers concluded that evidence for human factors training success was sorely lacking (eg. Novick, 1997;Wise, 1996).

With the spread of behavioural programmes, there is now new scope for evaluating human factors training effectiveness. However, as behavioural programmes have only been applied since the mid-1990s, empirical evaluations have been understandably limited in both military and commercial aviation contexts.

Human factors training effectiveness within military aviation

To date, the most convincing evidence of human factors training effectiveness within the military aviation environment has been published by Salas, et al., (1999a). In a recent paper, these authors reported two evaluation studies of CRM style training applied in naval aviation. The first study included 35 pilots and 34 enlisted aircrew from U.S. Naval transport helicopters, taking part in the research programme through their annual CRM training. The participants were trained in four skill areas (communication, assertiveness, mission analysis, and situational awareness) as part of a behavioural-focused programme. The study used a combination of attitudinal and behavioural indices, which were measured pre and post training. However, no control group was used. The results of the attitudinal evaluation were generally positive, which was consistent with previous research. More importantly, the study included a behavioural evaluation where participants received specific opportunities to demonstrate team behaviour. Trained teams performed significantly better than baseline teams on the teamwork behaviours. These results suggest that the CRM training produced at least short-term improvements in teamwork behaviour.

However, Salas et al., (1999a) noted one substantial problem with their first study. That is, organisational constraints had prevented them from establishing whether trainees were equally capable in team behaviour before the training commenced. Therefore, they conducted a second study with a similar structure to the first, but which incorporated a control group that received no training. This second study used 27 naval aviators, also taking part in the research as part of their annual CRM training. The training course addressed a greater variety of skill areas (decision making, assertiveness, mission analysis, communication, coordination, leadership, adaptability/flexibility, and situational awareness). The evaluation used similar attitudinal and behavioural indices to the first study, but the behavioural evaluation included a larger number of test items. This study found that teamwork behaviours improved when compared to the control group. Therefore, both studies reported by Salas et al., (1999a) demonstrated that the CRM training produced behavioural improvements in human performance.

The studies cited above are consistent with previous research by Salas and associates, which, demonstrate modest but consistent improvement in teamwork behaviour after CRM training, even with already experienced aviators. Further supporting evidence has come from other areas of military aviation. In a comprehensive paper, Diehl (1991) reviewed the evidence for CRM within the military field with particular application to rotary wing aircraft, which tend to have higher accident rates compared to their fixed wing counterparts. Data from a variety of sources indicated that training programmes reduced error rates. In one example, Bell Helicopters Textron Inc incorporated CRM training principles into crew operating their Jetranger helicopter. The global human error accident rate for this aircraft type fell 36% for the four-year period after the introduction of training, when compared to the preceding four-year period. In another instance, Petroleum Helicopter Inc, then the largest U.S. operator of commercial helicopters, introduced CRM training. The accident rate dropped 54% in the following two years, whereas it had remained relatively stable in the six preceding years. However, the substantive evidence came from the USAF Military Airlift Command (MAC). In 1985, MAC introduced a CRM-style programme. According to Diehl (1991), in the following five-year period, accident rates fell 52% and serious flight-related mishaps fell 51% when compared to the preceding five-year period. Accident and serious mishap rates in other parts of the USAF fell 18% and 21% respectively in the corresponding periods. The main difference between MAC and other air commands was CRM training.

Graham D. Edkins

While the above research does seem to support the effectiveness of human factors training, it has one substantial drawback: the evidence comes from military applications. The military is different from commercial aviation in both its operating environment and its training programmes. For example, military aviation accepts relatively risky procedures, which would not be tolerated in the conservative commercial arena. This means that the impact on teamwork in training will also be different, both in the outlook of pilots and in the specific behaviours used as skill markers. Nevertheless, the methodology developed for evaluation within the military appears to be suitable for adaptation in a commercial environment.

Human factors training effectiveness within commercial aviation

Behavioural evidence for the effectiveness of human factors training within commercial aviation has been scarce to date. Historically research based on positive attitude change has provided evidence supporting the impact of training programmes. For example, Byrnes and Black (1993) utilised the Cockpit Management Attitudes Questionnaire (CMAQ; Gregorich and Wilhelm, 1993) to assess attitude change in a group of U.S airline pilots, and found that human factors training produced a positive attitude shift, which remained stable for up to five years. Other studies using the CMAQ have supported these results reporting a positive shift in pilot attitudes towards human factors concepts following a training course (Gregorich, 1993; Gregorich, Helmreich and Wilhelm, 1990; Incalcaterra and Holt, 1999).

In perhaps the best empirical evaluation before the advent of behavioural human factors training, Helmreich and Foushee (1993) reported on a programme, which included the use of line-oriented flight training (LOFT) and periodic training. They found that ratings of human performance in line operations improved substantially after training. While this study did not use specific behavioural markers it does provide additional supporting evidence for the use of human factors training within commercial operations.

More recent attempts to evaluate human factors training effectiveness within aviation have focused on behavioural change. Boehm-Davis, Holt and Seamster (2001) report on a training programme, which used Line Orientated Evaluation's (LOE's) and line checks as performance indicators. Data from the first year, before the introduction of the programme, functioned as a baseline, and was compared with data from the next two years. The participants were evaluated using standardised behavioural assessments. From this, the authors deduced that the training improved observable performance in CRM skills. The authors argued that this study provided supporting evidence to a previous application of the LOE in which one fleet (human factors training) outperformed another (non-human factors training) on half of the check items (Holt, Boehm-Davis and Hpansberger, 1999).

Other studies reporting behavioural change following human factors training include Clothier (1991) who used the LINE LOS Checklist (LLC). Comparison between trained and untrained crews in LOFT and line observations indicated that there was a significant difference after training on 12 of the 14 LLC categories. This was supported by Helmreich and Foushee (1993) who found significant positive differences on all 14 categories of the LLC, over a three-year period, following human factors training.

Gunther (2000) reported that over a two year period at Continental Airlines, the introduction of the Line Operations Safety Audit (LOSA), a non-jeopardy, normal operations audit programme, and subsequent introduction of human factors training in threat and error management, resulted in some remarkable improvements on behavioural safety indices. In 1996, studies indicated that on average flight crew detected 15% of internal errors. After the introduction of a threat and error management course, 55% of internal errors were detected. In the same period, flight crews achieved a 78% reduction in unstable approaches at 1000ft above ground level, and a 40% reduction in unstable approaches at 500ft.

While the papers by Boehm-Davis et al., (2001), Clothier (1991), Gunther (2000) and Helmreich and Foushee (1993) are some of the few published studies that can be found in commercial aviation, there appears to be a lack of scientifically rigorous research, which in part has ensured that there remains little confidence in the effectiveness of human factor training programmes. The few studies that are published tend to rely on a combination of rational and anecdotal information, do not use control participants, and do not clearly specify the intervention that was applied. Furthermore, there does not appear to be any studies that have attempted to measure where human factors training programmes demonstrate a return on investment. In contrast, it is the aviation maintenance area, which is leading the way in cost effectiveness research.

Evidence for the cost effectiveness of human factors training

Several studies have examined the financial efficacy of human factors training on aviation maintenance. These have generally found investment returns on training programmes, in the form of reductions in equipment damage incidents, employee down time, or lost time injuries. These reductions have provided significant cost savings for operators.

Johnson (2000b) reported on the outcome of a two day human factors training course for maintenance staff, which led to a reduction of ground towing damage events by 75%, with a resultant cost saving of US$195,000 per year. Similarly, Eiff (2000) described the implementation of a human factors education programme on shift turnover. This demonstrated a reduction in average man-hours (by 2,474 hours) to complete a 'D' check, with a reported cost saving of US$94,000 per year. In addition, Stelly and Poehlmann (2000) reported on the outcome of a two-day human factors training course for Continental Airlines. The course produced several behavioural outcomes; a 68% reduction in ground damage incidents, a 12% decrease in job injuries, and 10% reduction in staff overtime. The total cost saving was US$60,000 per year for five years. However, the most impressive cost benefit research to date is that of Taylor (2000). The introduction of a maintenance resource management programme at a U.S. airline reduced lost-time injuries (LTIs) by 80% over two years, with a total claimed cost saving of US$1,300,000 over that period.

While, the above maintenance studies provide useful cost efficacy data there are no published studies in other areas of aviation, such as ramp, freight or catering. Furthermore, several methodological weaknesses limit their application.

Flaws with current human factors training evidence

The most common problem of many evaluations of aviation human factors training is the lack of a control group to determine if any observed effects are a result of the training, and not some other cause. This is a shortcoming across other industries as well (e.g. Fisher et al, 2000; Holzman et al, 1995). Of the studies reviewed in this paper, the vast majority did not include a control group to verify the effects of training.

A second methodological weakness is the relative lack of longitudinal evaluation. Short-term behavioural evaluation methods give a useful indication that human factors training may be effective, but without a longitudinal evaluation, it is impossible to determine if the effects of training diminish over time, and if so, does recurrent training have any effect? While the review by Diehl (1991) included some examples of longitudinal evaluation, these lacked formal control groups. Furthermore, it is unfortunate that an otherwise very impressive study by Salas et al., (1999a), lacked longitudinal evaluation. Some researchers have included longitudinal evaluation, and others have included control groups, but none have reported the application of both.

The third methodological weakness is specific to the Salas et al., (1999a) paper. While this paper provided useful behavioural data, the relatively low numbers of participants weakens what conclusions can be drawn. Given cost and logistical constraints, it is understandable why this and similar studies use a small number of participants, but the lack of large sample sizes nonetheless remains a problem when deciding what weight should be given to research findings.

A fourth methodological shortcoming is a lack of information about training programme cost-effectiveness, with the exception of the maintenance studies cited above. While studies into aviation maintenance provide measurements of cost, savings and return on investment, similar information is unavailable for other areas such as flight operations or the airport/ramp environment. This is most probably due to the costs of incidents being harder to document outside of maintenance. What is lacking is a definable set of cost indices, which can be used to measure the effectiveness of a human factors training programme. Moreover, the maintenance studies that have been cited in this paper do not appear to have been published in peer-reviewed literature. Therefore, it is difficult to determine if the claims made in return of investment are valid.

From a comprehensive review of 48 studies that claimed to evaluate the effectiveness of CRM training in the aviation industry, O'Connor, Flin and Fletcher (2001) suggest, that while there appears to be some evidence demonstrating a positive change in attitude, knowledge and behaviour following CRM training, training evaluation is not the norm. This is despite the prolific use of human factors training programmes throughout the aviation industry.

Conclusions and recommendations

For those aviation organisations contemplating human factors training, or who have an existing programme but wish to expand it into other areas such as maintenance or airport/ramp operations, do the studies reviewed above provide conclusive evidence for justifying capital expenditure?

The return on investment studies (Stelly and Poehlmann, 2000; Taylor, 2000) conducted within aviation maintenance provide some solid evidence upon which to base a business case. However, the cost effectiveness evidence from operational areas outside of aviation maintenance, are lacking despite some recent studies in the flight operations environment supporting behavioural safety improvements following the introduction of human factors training (Boehm-Davis et al, 2000; Gunther, 2000).

Clearly, more cost effectiveness data is needed to add weight to the argument. Measuring costs is relatively easy in some areas of aviation, as the evidence has shown in maintenance. Other areas, such as airport/ramp operations, also have relatively quantifiable measures of cost efficacy, although the evidence for the effectiveness of human factors training to date is less clear-cut in this area (e.g. McDonald, Cromie and Ward, 1997).

One of the most promising indicators appears to be lost time injuries (LTIs). LTIs represent direct, measurable costs to airlines. They also provide an objective measurement, which can be used as a criterion for evaluating human factors training. It has been estimated that 96% of LTIs are behavioural in nature (Dupont, 2000). Given that the focus of contemporary human factors training programmes is to modify and reinforce effective safety behaviour, it is reasonable to assume that LTIs will be reduced. A reduction in LTIs from human factors training has already been demonstrated in some aviation maintenance human factors programmes (e.g. Taylor, 2000). One current study being conducted at Qantas Airways (Edkins, 2000; Edkins and Pietrovitch, in preparation) may provide further supporting evidence. This longitudinal Australian study is being conducted within airport/ramp operations to determine the impact of a behaviour based human factors training programme on a number of safety indices including workers compensation claims (LTIs).

Those researchers intending to evaluate the effectiveness of human factors training programmes need to ensure that an appropriate methodology is employed, that includes sound evaluation criteria. The training should be evaluated by behavioural-based methods, using specific competencies to assess non-technical skills. Such evaluations should be longitudinal, otherwise any observed effects may merely be manifested in short-term benefits. Control groups are also needed to determine if training has produced any observed effects. O'Connor et al (2001) suggest a multifaceted evaluation approach that employs a combination of attitude, knowledge, behavioural and organizational measures.

Furthermore, human factors programmes implemented across the aviation industry need to more consistently report on cost indices, as a measure of programme success. These indices may include objective criteria such as reduction in LTIs, equipment damage, employee work time, employee over time etc. Tracking and reporting on costs will help to ensure that operators, who are struggling to rationalise expenditure, have a stronger business case upon which to justify an expected return on investment.

References

Amermaete, J.A.G. van and Krujisen, E.A.C. (Eds) (1998). *NOTECHS: The evaluation of non-technical skills of multi-pilot aircrew in relation to JAR-FCL requirements.* Amsterdam: National Aerospace Laboratory NLR.

Andersen, H.B., Soerensen, P.K., Weber, S., and Soerensen, C. (1996). *A study of the performance of captains and crews in a full mission simulator.* Roskilde, Denmark: Risoe National Laboratory.

Andersen, V. and Bove, T. (2000). A feasibility study in the use of incidents and accidents reports to evaluate effects of Team Resource Management in Air Traffic Control. *Safety Science, 35*, 87-94.

Boehm-Davis, D.A., Holt, R.W., and Seamster, T.L. (2001). Airline resource management programs. In, E. Salas, C. Bowers and E. Edens (Eds.), *Improving teamwork in organizations: Applications of resource management training.* Mahwah, NJ: Lawrence Erlbaum Associates.

Bydorf, P. (1998). *Human factors and crew resource management: An example of successfully applying the experience from CRM programmes in the aviation world to the maritime world.* Paper presented at the 23rd conference of the European Association for Aviation Psychology, Vienna.

Byrnes, R.E., and Black, R. (1993). Developing and implementing CRM programmes: The Delta experience. In, E. Weiner, B. Kanki and R. Helmreich (Eds.), *Cockpit resource management.* San Diego: Academic Press.

Clothier, C. (1991). Behavioural interactions across various aircraft types: Results of systematic observations of line operations and simulations. In R.S. Jensen (Ed.), *Proceedings of the 6th International Symposium on Aviation Psychology,* Columbus, Ohio: Ohio State University Press. pp. 332-337.

Davies, J.M. and Helmreich, R.L. (1996). Simulation: It's a start. [Editorial]. *Canadian Journal of Anaesthesia, 43,* 425-429.

Diehl, A.E. (1991). Does Cockpit Management Training Reduce Aircrew Error? *Paper presented at 22nd International Seminar, International Society of Air Safety Investigators.* Canada.

Du Pont (2000). *Briefing to Qantas safety management by David Hainsworth, Senior Account Manager.* 26 October, Melbourne.

Duncan, J.C. and Feterle, L.C. (2000). The use of personal computer-based aviation training devices to teach aircrew decision making, teamwork and resource management. *Journal of Aviation/Aerospace education and research (Winter 2000),* 421-426.

Edkins, G. (2000). *Business Case: Development, implementation and evaluation of a human factors training and assessment program for operational staff.* Qantas Airways, Sydney.

Edkins, G. and Pietrovitch, M. (in preparation). *Human factors training on the ramp: The cost, impact and effect on employee safety behaviour.* Qantas Airways: Sydney.

Eiff, G. (2000). Human factors and a strategic approach to return on investment. *SAE Advances in Aviation Safety Conference,* Daytona Beach, April 11-13.

FAA (1995). *Crew Resource Management Training* (Advisory Circular No. AC120-51B). Washington, DC: Department of Transportation, Federal Aviation Administration.

Fisher, J., Phillips, E. and Mather, J. (2000). Does crew resource management training work? *Air Medical Journal, 19,* 137-139.

Flin, R.H. (1995). Crew Resource Management for Teams in the Offshore Oil Industry. *Journal of European Industrial Training, 19,* 23-27.

Flin, R. and Martin, L. (2001). Behavioural markers for Crew Resource Management: A survey of current practice. *International Journal of Aviation Psychology, 11,* 95-118.

Flin, R. and O'Connor, P. (2001). Applying crew resource management on offshore oil platforms. In, E. Salas, C. Bowers E. and Edens, E. (Eds.), *Improving teamwork in organizations: Applications of resource management training.* Mahwah, NJ: Erlbaum.

Gregorich, S.E. (1993). The dynamics of CRM attitude change: Attitude stability. In, R.S. Jensen (Ed.), *Proceedings of the 7th International Symposium of Aviation Psychology.* Columbus, Ohio: Ohio State University Press. pp. 509-512.

Gregorich, S.E., Helmreich, R.L., and Wilhelm, J.A. (1990). The structure of cockpit resource management attitudes. *Journal of Applied Psychology, 75,* 682-690.

Gregorich, S.E., and Wilhelm, J.A. (1993). Crew resource management training assessment. In, E.L. Wiener, B.G. Kanki and R.L. Helmreich (Eds.), *Cockpit resource management*. San Diego: Academic Press.

Gunther, D. (2000). Corporate culture and error. *IATA/ICAO Aviation Safety and Human Factors Seminar*, Rio de Janeiro, 17-18 August.

Hansberger, J.T., Holt, R.W. and Boehm-Davis, D. (1999). Instructor/evaluator evaluations of ACRM effectiveness. In, R.S. Jensen (Ed), *Proceedings of the 10th International Symposium on Aviation Psychology*. Columbus, Ohio: Ohio State University Press.

Harrington, D. and Kello, J. (1991). Systematic evaluation of nuclear operator team skills training. *Paper presented at the American Nuclear Society*, San Francisco, CA, November.

Helmreich, R.L. (1996). The Evolution of Crew Resource Management. *Presented at the IATA Human Factors Seminar*, Warsaw, Poland, October 31.

Helmreich, R.L., Chidester, T.R., Foushee, H.C., Gregorich, S.E., and Wilhelm, J.A. (1990). How effective is cockpit resource management training? Issues in evaluating the impact of programs to enhance crew coordination. *Flight Safety Digest, 9*, 1-17.

Helmreich, R.L. and Foushee, H.C. (1993). Why crew resource management? Empirical and theoretical bases of human factors training in aviation. In, E.L. Wiener, B.G., Kanki, and R.L. Helmreich, (Eds). *Cockpit resource management*. San Diego, CA: Academic Press.

Helmreich, R.L., Merritt, A.C. and Wilhelm, J.A. (1999). The evolution of crew resource management training in commercial aviation. *International Journal of Aviation Psychology, 9*, 19-32.

Helmreich, R.L. and Wilhelm, J.A. (1991). Outcomes of crew resource management training. *International Journal of Aviation Psychology, 1*, 287-300.

Holt, R.W., Boehm-Davis, D., and Hansberger, J.T. (1999). Evaluating effectiveness of ACRM using LOE and line-check data. In, R.S. Jensen (Ed), *Proceedings of the 10th International Symposium on Aviation Psychology*. Columbus, Ohio: Ohio State University Press. pp. 273-288.

Holzman, R.S., Cooper, J.B., Gaba, D.M., Philip, J.H., Small, S.D. and Feinstein, D. (1995). Anesthesia Crisis Resource Management: Real-Life Simulation Training in Operating Room Crises. *Journal of Clinical Anesthesia, 7*, 675-687.

Howard, S., Gaba, D., Fish, K., Yang, G., and Sarnquist, F. (1992). Anaesthesia crisis resource management training: Teaching anaesthesiologists to handle critical incidents. *Aviation, Space and Environmental Medicine, 63*, 765-770.

Incalcaterra, K.A., and Holt, R.W. (1999). Pilot evaluation of ACRM programs. In, R.S. Jensen (Ed), *Proceedings of the 10th International Symposium on Aviation Psychology*. Columbus, Ohio: Ohio State University Press. pp 285-291.

International Civil Aviation Organisation (1992). *Human factors digest No. 10: Human factors, management and organization.* Montreal, Canada.

Johnson, C. (2000a). Reasons for the failure of CRM training in aviation. In, K. Abbott, J.J. Speyer and G. Boy, (Eds) *HCI Aero 2000: International Conference on Human-Computer Interfaces in Aeronautics.* Cepadues-Editions: Toulouse, France.

Johnson, W.B. (2000b). Return on investment in maintenance human factors. *Presented at the 14th Annual Human Factors in Aviation Maintenance Symposium.* Vancouver B.C. 17-18 April.

Lingard, H. and Rowlinson, S. (1997). Behavior-based safety management in Hong Kong's construction industry. *Journal of Safety Research, 28,* 243-256.

McDonald, N., Cromie, S. and Ward, M. (1997). The impact of safety training on safety climate and attitudes. In, H. Soekkha (Ed.) *Aviation Safety.* Utrecht: VSP.

Novick, D.G. (1997). What is Effectiveness? *Position paper for the CHI '97 Workshop on HCI Research and Practice Agenda.*

O'Connor, P., Flin, R. and Fletcher, G. (2001). *Methods used to evaluate the effectiveness of CRM training in the aviation industry.* UK Civil Aviation Authority Project 121/SRG/RandAD/1.

Raya, P.S., Bishop, P.A. and Qi, W.M. (1997). Efficacy of the components of a behavioral safety program. *International Journal of Industrial Ergonomics, 19,* 19-29.

Reason, J. (1992). *Human error.* Cambridge: Cambridge University Press.

Salas, E., Fowlkes, J.E., Stout, R.J., Milanovich, D.M. and Prince, C. (1999a). Does CRM training improve teamwork skills in the cockpit? Two evaluation studies. *Human Factors, 41,* 326-343.

Salas, E. Prince, C., Bowers, C.A., Stout, R.J., Oser, R.L. and Cannon-Bowers, J.A. (1999b). A methodology for enhancing crew resource management training. *Human Factors, 41,* 161-172.

Salas, E., Rhodenizer, L. and Bowers, C.A. (2000). The Design and Delivery of Crew Resource Management Training: Exploiting Available Resources. *Human Factors, 42,* 490-511.

Stelly, J. and Poehlmann, K.L. (2000). Investing in human factors training: Assessing the bottom line. *Presented at the 14th Annual Human Factors in Aviation Maintenance Symposium,* Vancouver B.C. 17-18 April.

Taylor, J.C. (2000). A new model of return on investment for MRM programs. *Presented at the 14th Annual Human Factors in Aviation Maintenance Symposium.* Vancouver, B.C. 17-18 April.

Wise, J.A. (1996). CRM and 'The Emperor's New Clothes'. *Presented at and in the Proceedings of the Third Global Flight Safety and Human Factors Symposium.* Auckland, New Zealand, 9-12 April.

7 Development of the NOTECHS (non-technical skills) system for assessing pilots' CRM skills

Rhona Flin, Lynne Martin, Klaus-Martin Goeters,
Hans-Jürgen Hörmann, René Amalberti,
Claude Valot and Herman Nijhuis

Abstract

Crew Resource Management (CRM) courses are designed to teach pilots about non-technical (cognitive and social) skills that are essential for effective and safe flight operations. This article presents a summary of the empirical development of the European taxonomy of pilots' non-technical skills (NOTECHS) and associated rating method. It describes the system components and the experimental validation. The system has four Categories: *Co-operation, Leadership and Managerial Skills, Situation Awareness, Decision Making*, each subdivided into Elements and behavioural markers. The latter are examples of effective and ineffective behaviours supporting the evaluation and debriefing, as well as giving indications for retraining, if this is required. Operational principles for fair and objective use of the NOTECHS system and training guidelines for raters are outlined.

This paper was first published in Human Factors and Aerospace Safety 3(2), 2003, pp. 97-119

Introduction

The aviation community has put considerable emphasis in the last decade on flight crew members' non-technical skills as a crucial factor for enhanced safety. Crew Resource Management (CRM) courses are designed to teach pilots about these 'cognitive and interpersonal skills needed to manage the flight within an organized aviation system' (CAA, 2003, p1). The CRM training appears to result in effective transfer of the desired behaviours to the flight deck (Gregorich and Wilhelm, 1993; O'Connor, Flin and Fletcher, 2002a; Salas, et al, 2001). Additional mandatory regulations have recently appeared in Europe, that require a more formal incorporation of non-technical (CRM) skills evaluation into all levels of training and checking flight crew members' performance.

The European Joint Aviation Authorities (JAA) require the training and assessment of Crew Resource Management (CRM) skills as set out in the CRM regulations included in JAR OPS (2001) 1.940, 1.945, 1.955, and 1.965, asking for an evaluation of flight crews' CRM skills. For example, '*the flight crew must be assessed on their CRM skills in accordance with a methodology acceptable to the Authority and published in the Operations Manual. The purpose of such an assessment is to: provide feedback to the crew collectively and individually and serve to identify retraining; and be used to improve the CRM training system.*' (1.965).

This legislation resulted from a desire by the JAA from the mid 1990s, to achieve a generic method of evaluation of non-technical skills throughout the JAA countries and JAA operators. Such a generic method would minimize cultural and corporate differences, and maximize practicability and effectiveness for airline instructors and examiners. As a consequence, in 1996, the JAA Project Advisory Group on Human Factors initiated a project group that was sponsored by four European Civil Aviation Authorities (Germany, France, Netherlands, UK). A research consortium consisting of members from DLR (Germany), IMASSA (France), NLR (Netherlands) and University of Aberdeen (UK) was established to work on what was called the NOTECHS (Non-Technical Skills) project. The group was required to identify or to develop a feasible and efficient methodology for assessing pilots' non-technical (CRM) skills. (For the purpose of the project, these were defined as the cognitive and social skills of flight crew members in the cockpit, not directly related to aircraft control, system management, and standard operating procedures – SOPs). The design requirements were (i) that the system was to be used to assess the skills of an individual pilot, rather than a crew, and (ii) it was to be suitable for use across Europe, by both large and small operators, i.e. it was to be culturally-robust. This article presents a summary of the development of the European taxonomy of pilots' non-technical skills (NOTECHS) and describes the system components. For a more comprehensive account, see the final project report (van Avermaete and Kruijsen, 1998).

Method

After reviewing alternative methods, it became obvious for various reasons that none of the existing systems could be adopted in their original form. Nor did any single system provide a suitable basis for simple amendment that could be taken as an Acceptable Means of Compliance under the scope of JAR. The reasons for this were that the existing systems were either too complex to be used on a pan-European basis, or too specific to a particular airline, or were designed to assess crews rather than individual pilots (e.g. University of Texas LLC (Line/Line Oriented Simulation Checklist system, Helmreich et al, 1995). Therefore, the NOTECHS group decided that it would have to design a new taxonomy of non-technical skills, (see Seamster and Kaempf, 2001 for a good description of techniques that can be used for this).

The identification of the basic set of non-technical skills for the NOTECHS system consisted of three interleaved phases of work.

(i) Review of existing systems to evaluate proficiency in pilots' non-technical skills to identify common categories and elements of behaviour (NOTECHS Report, work package 2; see also Flin and Martin, 1998; 2001).

(ii) Literature search for relevant research findings relating to key categories of non- technical skills identified in existing systems (NOTECHS Report, work package 3).

(iii) Extended discussions with subject matter experts, in this case - KLM pilots experienced in evaluating non-technical skills, at NOTECHS working group meetings. Particular attention was paid to two of the principal CRM skills frameworks, namely the KLM WILSC/ SHAPE systems (Antersijn and Verhoef, 1995; KLM, 1996) and the University of Texas LLC system (Helmreich, et al, 1995). The systems in use by Air France, RLD (Dutch CAA) and Lufthansa (Quick Reference System) to evaluate pilots' non-technical skills during checks were also reviewed.

It is important to note that the required system was to be usable on a pan-European basis. This means that the majority of instructors/ examiners would not have English as their native language and would be based in very small companies, as well as in the large airlines. Consequently, the following design principles were used to guide the final choice of components and descriptor terms.

(i) The basic categories and elements should be formulated with the maximum mutual exclusivity. This is only achievable to a certain degree, given the interdependence of the various non-technical skills in flight deck operations.

(ii) A rule of parsimony was applied, in that the system should contain the minimum number of categories and elements in order to encompass the critical behaviours.

(iii) The terminology used should reflect everyday language for behaviour, rather than psychological jargon.

135

(iv) The skills listed at the behaviour level should be directly observable in the case of social skills or could be inferred from communication, in the case of the cognitive skills.

On the basis of these design principles, a prototype system was developed from non-technical skill set identified from the three work packages described above. Following extended discussions at two project meetings, and a subsequent two-day workshop involving four psychologists from the team, a draft taxonomy was prepared. This was circulated to group members for comments. Then the revised components and structure were extensively reviewed at a group meeting with the whole team, including the KLM pilots.

Structure of the NOTECHS system

The NOTECHS framework consists of four main categories: *Co-operation, Leadership and Managerial Skills, Situation Awareness, Decision Making*, each of them being subdivided into elements and behavioural markers (see figure 1). The latter are examples of effective and ineffective behaviours supporting the evaluation and debriefing, as well as giving indications for retraining, if this is required.

The four primary categories subdivide into two social skills (*Co-operation; Leadership and Management*) and two cognitive skills (*Situation Awareness; Decision Making*); it was judged to be unnecessary to add another level to the system by introducing this distinction explicitly. It should be noted that for the social skills, behaviours are generally in the form of communication (verbal and non-verbal) which can be directly observed. The cognitive skills are not directly observable since they do not directly materialise in overt behaviour but occur 'in the head of the pilot'. Hence for evaluation purposes, these cognitive processes must be inferred from observable behaviours, (e.g. specific actions or verbalisations – thus when a pilot states a decision, the observer can infer that some option selection has taken place; discussion of alternative divert airports reveals that option generation and comparison processes are being employed). Not all non-technical rating systems include cognitive skills explicitly, due to the indirect methods which must be used for their evaluation. Nevertheless, a basic tenet of CRM is that pilots should communicate in a manner that reveals their mental models and thinking processes to the other crew members. Thus it was deemed appropriate to evaluate these critical cognitive skills which have been shown to contribute to flight safety, and which are taught to pilots as fundamental components of CRM.

Two further points should be noted with regard to the system components. The category 'Communication' is featured in a number of systems but is not shown in NOTECHS as a separate category. This is because communication skills are inherent in all four categories and the listed behaviours all involve communication. A category of 'Personal Awareness' skills (e.g. coping with stress or fatigue) was considered but rejected due to difficulties in observing, or inferring except in the most extreme cases.

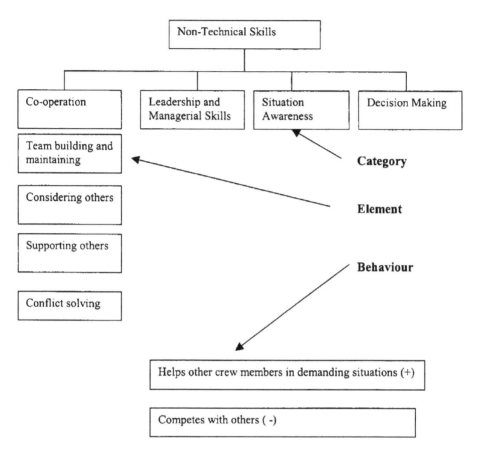

Figure 1   Basic structure of the NOTECHS system

In relation to the four categories, a number of derived elements were examined and for each element a series of indicative behaviours were identified. At the elemental level, this set was compared against the KLM SHAPE system and the LLC system to confirm that essential elements had been encompassed. In the final version, three to four elements for each of the four categories were selected, giving a total of 15 elements (see table 1). For each element a number of exemplar behaviours were included. The exemplar behaviours were phrased as generic (e.g., closes loop for communications), rather than specific (e.g., reads back to ATC), to give an indication of type, and to avoid specifying particular behaviours which should be observed. This should also ensure that the system is as widely applicable as possible. Accompanying guidance notes to the system provide further details.

Table 1   Categories and elements of NOTECHS

Category	Elements
1. Co-operation	- Team-building and maintaining
	- Considering others
	- Supporting others
	- Conflict solving
2. Leadership and Managerial Skills	- Use of authority and assertiveness
	- Providing and maintaining standards
	- Planning and co-ordination
	- Workload management
3. Situation Awareness	- Awareness of aircraft systems
	- Awareness of external environment
	- Awareness of time
4. Decision Making	- Problem definition and diagnosis
	- Option generation
	- Risk assessment and option selection
	- Outcome review

Description of the four categories

Co-operation

Defined as 'the ability to work effectively in a team/ crew'. *Co-operation* requires team building and maintaining, so that co-operative actions are based on mutual agreement by crew members in a positive group climate. Such a climate is also created by factors like consideration/support of other crew members and conflict solving skills. *Co-operation* deals with the question of how people function as a working group. It does not refer to the work itself, such as the quality/quantity of output.

Good co-operation is largely dependent on active and open communication between crew members. However, communication is not a basic element of co-operation alone, as mentioned above, it is a general mediator of all four non-technical skills Categories. Some aspects of communication may fall more into one than another category, thus these particular aspects become secondary descriptors. The aspects of communication which belong to *Co-operation* deal with building a climate for open communication, sensitivity for different aspects of messages (e.g. also the emotional component) and awareness of the difference of verbal vs. non-verbal communication.

The category *Co-operation* comprises four elements (see table 2).

- *Team building and maintaining:* Establishing positive interpersonal relations and active participation of crew members in fulfilling the tasks.
- *Considering others:* Acceptance of others and understanding their personal condition.
- *Supporting others:* Giving help to other crew members in cases where they need assistance.
- *Conflict solving:* Articulation of different interpersonal positions with suggestions for solutions.

The two interpersonal categories of the NOTECHS system, namely *Co-operation* and *Leadership and Managerial Skills* are overlapping to a certain degree, since both refer to group processes. The solution for reaching a clearer distinction is that in the NOTECHS system, co-operation involves team building and maintaining (in some other systems this is subsumed in leadership and managerial skills). On the other hand, the aspects of coordination and responsibility, although often discussed as parts of co-operation, became elements of leadership and managerial skills in the NOTECHS terminology. The conceptual difference is that *Co-operation* is concerned with mutual assistance and team atmosphere during work, while *Leadership and Managerial Skills* covers all aspects of initiative, coordination and goal setting. Considering and supporting others could be grouped together as one element, since in practice both aspects are very closely interrelated, but for the sake of clarity these concepts were separated.

Leadership and managerial Skills

Defined as: 'effective leadership and managerial skills achieve joint task completion within a motivated, fully functioning team through coordination and persuasion'. The core of effective leadership is to set the highest priority on the joint completion of a given task. Leadership responsibilities include the active and goal-directed coordination of the working activities within the crew. This is always a reciprocal process. Without complementary behaviour of the crew, leadership behaviour is less effective. All crew members are expected to dedicate their efforts and initiative to the safe and efficient achievement of the flight goals. However, the final and legal responsibility for the operation on the whole is undivided, resting with the pilot in command (PIC). Crew responsibilities include monitoring and challenging each other whenever differences in concepts or actions are perceived. Within the scope of delegated tasks crew members have the same responsibilities as the PIC.

139

Table 2   Co-operation category: elements and behavioural markers (examples)

Element	Good practice	Poor practice
Team building and maintaining	Establishes atmosphere for open communication	Blocks open communication
	Encourages inputs and feedback from others	Keeps barriers between crewmembers (CM)
	Does not compete with others	Competes with others
Considering others	Takes notice of the suggestions of other CM even if s/he does not agree	Ignores suggestions of other CM
	Takes condition of other CM into account	Does not take account of the condition of other CM
	Gives personal feedback	Shows no reaction to other CM
Supporting others	Helps other CM in demanding situations	Hesitates to help other CM in demanding situations
	Offers assistance	Does not offer assistance
Conflict solving	Keeps calm in interpersonal conflicts	Overreacts in interpersonal conflicts
	Suggests conflict solutions	Sticks to own position without considering a compromise
	Concentrates on what is right rather than who is wrong	Accuses other CM of making errors

The International Civil Aviation Organisation (ICAO) has defined a leader as 'a person whose ideas and actions influence the thought and the behaviour of others. Through the use of example and persuasion, and an understanding of the goals and desires of the group, the leader becomes a means of change and influence' (ICAO, 1989a). It is important to distinguish between leadership, which is acquired and authority, which is assigned. Leadership is one aspect of teamwork, and the success of a leader depends on the quality of his/her relationship in the team. The crew members should feel that they are an integral part of a well-run, well-organised operation in which their inputs are essential to reach commonly valued goals and overall success of the operation.

In comparison to the category *Co-operation, Leadership and Managerial skills* focuses more on the goal-directed initiative the respective crewmember is investing into management and coordination functions. This includes also positive influences on the motivation and morale of the crew. Whereas *Co-operation* is more focused on interactive processes without explicit appointed roles and independently of authority differences of the individuals.

The leader has a clear concept for the operation and provides general standards and directions for the completion of the different tasks. The tasks are allocated according to defined roles, specific experience, as well as to the present level of workload of the crewmembers. This concept for the operation is interactively briefed and always open for contributions from other crew members. In order to ensure proper support and the participation from all parts of the crew, active care is taken to establish and maintain closed loop communication. A leader motivates, activates, and monitors others and encourages the crew to monitor and challenge her/himself and each other in a non-degrading way.

It was decided to extract four major elements for *Leadership and Managerial skills* from the existing systems (see table 3). The skills themselves should be the same for leaders and followers. The way they are implemented in behaviour may differ according to position.

- *Use of authority and assertiveness:* Creating a proper challenge and response atmosphere. The given command authority of the PIC should be adequately balanced with assertiveness and crew member participation. If the situation requires, decisive actions are expected.
- *Providing and maintaining standards:* The compliance with essential standards (SOPs and others) for the task completion should be ensured. Therefore the crew should mutually supervise and intervene in case of deviations from standards. If the situation requires, it may be necessary to apply non-standard procedures. Such deviations should be announced and consultation should take place.
- *Planning and coordination:* In order to achieve high performance and to prevent workload peaks or dips, an appropriate concept for organised task sharing and delegation has to be established. Plans and intentions have to be communicated so that the whole crew understands the goals and that the activities conducted by the crew do reflect proper coordination.
- *Workload management:* Clear prioritisation of primary and secondary operational tasks. Based on sound planning, tasks are distributed appropriately among the crew. Signs of stress and fatigue are

141

communicated and taken into account as performance affecting factors. Available external and internal resources (including automation) are used to accomplish task completion in time.

Table 3   Leadership and Managerial skills category: elements and behavioural markers (examples)

Element	Good practice	Poor practice
Use of authority and assertiveness	Takes initiative to ensure crew involvement and task completion	Hinders or withholds crew involvement
	Takes command if situation requires, advocates own position	Passive, does not show initiative for decisions, own position not recognisable
	Reflects on suggestions of others	Ignores suggestions of others
	Motivates crew by appreciation and coaches when necessary	Does not show appreciation for the crew, coaches very little or too much
Providing and maintaining standards	Subscribes to SOPs, makes sure SOP compliance in crew	Does not comply to SOPs, does not monitor crew for SOP compliance
	Intervenes if task completion deviates from standards	Does not intervene in case of deviations
	With crew being consulted, deviates from standards if necessary	Deviations from standards are neither announced nor consulted
	Demonstrates will to achieve top performance	Does not care for performance effectiveness

Table 3   Leadership and Managerial skills category: elements and behavioural markers (continued)

Element	Good practice	Poor practice
Planning and co-ordination	Encourages crew participation in planning and task completion	Plans only for him/herself, crew not involved
	Plan is clearly stated and confirmed	Intentions not stated or confirmed
	With crew being consulted, changes plan if necessary	Changes plan without informing crew or follows plan blindly
	Clearly states goals and boundaries for task completion	Goals and boundaries remain unclear
Workload management	Distributes tasks among the crew, checks and corrects appropriately	Flying 'solo' without other crewmembers involved
	Secondary operational tasks are prioritised to retain sufficient resources for primary flight duties	Secondary operational tasks interfere with primary flight duties
	Allots adequate time to complete tasks	Workload is increased through inadequate planning
	Notifies signs of stress and fatigue	Ignores signs of stress and fatigue

Situation awareness

Situation awareness can be defined as 'one's ability to accurately perceive what is in the cockpit and outside the aircraft' (ICAO, 1989b, p13); or simply as 'knowing what is going on'; or more precisely as, 'the perception of the elements in the environment within a volume of time and space, the comprehension of their meaning, and the projection of their status in the near future' (Endsley, 1995, p36). Shrestha, et al (1995, p.52) suggest an alternative version as a result of their review of ten definitions of situation awareness: 'situation awareness is a dynamic, multifaceted construct that involves the maintenance and anticipation of critical task performance events. Crew members must also have temporal awareness, anticipating future events based on knowledge of both the past and the present. It is crucial that individuals monitor the environment so that potential problems can be corrected before they escalate.

Table 4   Situation   Awareness   category: elements   and   behavioural markers (examples)

Element	Good practice	Poor practice
Awareness of aircraft systems	Monitors and reports changes in systems' states	Does not ask for updates
	Acknowledges entries and changes to systems	Does not signal awareness of changing systems
Awareness of external environment	Collects information about environment (position, weather and traffic)	Does not enquire about environmental changes
	Shares key information about environment with crew	Does not comment on relevant environmental factors, or is surprised by them
	Contacts outside resources when needed (to maintain situation awareness)	Operates a 'closed shop'
Awareness of time	Discusses time constraints with crew	Does not set priorities regarding time limits
	Discusses contingency strategies	Does not discuss relationship between past events and present/future
	Identifies possible future problems	Is surprised by outcomes of past events

ICAO (1989b) lists situation awareness topics that should be taught in CRM training:

- Total awareness of surrounding environment
- Reality vs. perception of reality
- Fixation
- Monitoring
- Incapacitation (partial/ total, physical, psychological).

Pilots sometimes define situation awareness as 'being ahead of your aircraft'. This implies that the pilot is prepared and is in control, has command of the aircraft and the current tasks. For all of the elements of situation awareness, the pilot needs to not only know their present state but also to be able to predict their future states, so anticipation covers this predictive aspect. Communication is the medium through which situation awareness can be assessed. It is not only *knowing something* that is crucial to good situation awareness, it is being able to fit this information into the right place in a mental model of the situation so that if it is important it triggers problem recognition. This definition stresses the ever-changing nature of the cockpit environment and the need for the crew to continually monitor and update their model of the situation by collecting information from all the sources that are available to them. The three Elements and behaviours in the NOTECHS Category *Situation Awareness* were selected to reflect this concept (see table 4).

- *Awareness of aircraft systems:* active knowledge of mode and state of systems, aircraft energy states (e.g. fuel).
- *Awareness of environment:* active knowledge of current and future position, weather, air traffic, terrain.
- *Awareness of time:* sense of available time and thinking ahead to consider future conditions and contingencies.

Decision Making

Decision Making is defined as 'The process of reaching a judgement or choosing an option'. This definition of decision making is not generally disputed in the aviation literature although it may be labelled aeronautical decision making (Kaempf and Klein, 1995) or pilot judgement. Pilot decision making does not just involve one strategy - different types of decisions are made at different times. Decision events differ enormously in what they demand of the crew, what options and supports exist in standard procedures and policies for making decisions and in features that may make the situation complex. Orasanu (1993), a NASA research psychologist, has studied the styles of decision making used by pilots in different situations. '... *crew decision making is not one thing. Crews make many different kinds of decisions, but all involve situation assessment, choice among alternatives, and assessment of risk.*' (p.138). Hence, pilots' decisions differ in the degrees to which they call on various cognitive processes depending on the decision structure and task conditions. Whilst the captain has responsibility, he or she is supported by the other members of the team in cockpit decision making, therefore, crew decision making is managed decision making. Within the NOTECHS system, the Category *Decision Making* is narrower than pilot judgement as defined by Jensen (1996). His model encompasses decision making in its wider context, taking into account all the contributory factors of the individual as well as the situation. Rather, the focus for NOTECHS was on an information processing framework based on current research from applied cognitive psychology (e.g. Stokes, Kemper and Kite, 1997).

Table 5   Decision Making category: elements and behavioural markers (examples)

Element	Good practice	Poor practice
Problem definition and diagnosis	Gathers information to identify problem	Nature of problem not stated or failure to diagnose
	Reviews causal factors with other crew members	No discussion of probable causes
Option generation	States alternative options	Does not search for information
	Asks crew members for options	Does not ask crew for alternatives
Risk assessment and option selection	Considers and shares estimated risk of alternative options	Inadequate discussion of limiting factors with crew
	Talks about possible risks for action in terms of crew limits	No consideration of limiting factors
	Confirms and states selected option/ agreed action	Does not inform crew of decision path being taken
Outcome review	Checks outcome against plan	Fails to check selected outcome against goal

The elements which are integrated into *Decision Making* (see table 5) were derived principally from the FOR-DEC model (Hörmann, 1995) and the pilot decision making taxonomy developed by Orasanu (1993).

- *Problem definition and diagnosis:* gathering information and determining the nature of the situation. Considering alternative explanations for observed conditions.
- *Option generation:* formulating alternative approaches to dealing with the situation. The opportunity for this will depend on available time and information.
- *Risk assessment and option selection:* making a judgement or evaluation of the level of risk/ hazard in the alternative approaches and choosing a preferred approach.
- *Outcome review:* considering the effectiveness/suitability of the selected option against the current plan, once the course of action has been implemented.

The measurement of decision making follows the same lines as that for situation awareness. As decision making is a cognitive process, it is not possible to observe it directly and it has to be inferred from pilot behaviours. Again, this will be through communication - the crew telling each other what point their thinking has reached, stating diagnoses and courses of action, as well as discussing alternatives to undertake a risk assessment.

Rating system

The NOTECHS categories and elements are rated on a five-point scale – 'very good, good, acceptable, poor, very poor'. In addition an overall rating of 'acceptable/ not acceptable' is required. The five-point scale design was chosen after reviewing other systems and on the advice of subject matter experts (instructors/ examiners).

Operational principles for using the NOTECHS system

Five operational principles were established to ensure that each crewmember receives as fair and as objective an assessment as possible with the NOTECHS system.

1. *Only observable behaviour is to be assessed* – The evaluation must exclude reference to a crewmember's personality or emotional attitude and should be based only on observable behaviour. Behavioural markers were designed to support an objective judgement.
2. *Need for technical consequence* – For a pilot's non-technical skills to be rated as unacceptable, flight safety must be actually (or potentially) compromised. This requires a related objective technical consequence.

147

3. *Acceptable or unacceptable rating required* – The JAR-OPS requires the airlines to indicate whether the observed non-technical skills are acceptable or unacceptable.
4. *Repetition required* – Repetition of unacceptable behaviour during the check must be observed to conclude that there is a significant problem. If, according to the JAR-paragraph concerned, the nature of a technical failure allows for a second attempt, this should be granted, regardless of the non-technical rating.
5. *Explanation required* – For each Category rated as unacceptable the examiner must: a) Indicate the Element(s) in that Category where the unacceptable behaviour was observed. b) Explain where the observed NTS (potentially) led to safety consequences. c) Give a free-text explanation on each of the Categories rated unacceptable, using standard phraseology.

Judging behaviour is always more subjective than judging technical facts. NOTECHS has been designed to minimise ambiguities in the evaluation of non-technical skills. However there are several factors that can occur in the evaluation process. The first relates to the unit of observation, i.e. who is evaluated: the crew globally, the captain, or the co-pilot. The NOTECHS system is designed to be used to assess individual pilots. When an evaluation relates to individuals, a potential difficulty is to disentangle individual contributions to overall crew performance. But this difficulty already exists during checks when considering technical performance. NOTECHS does not magically solve this problem, but may serve to objectively point to behaviours that are related more to one crew member than the other, therefore allowing examiners to differentiate the judgement of the two crew members.

The second factor relates to any concern that raters are simply judging non-technical skills on the basis of intuition. Again, NOTECHS requires the instructor/ examiner to justify any criticisms at a professional level, and with a standardised vocabulary. Furthermore, a judgement should not be based on a vague global impression or on an isolated behaviour or action. Repetition of the behaviour during the flight is usually required to explicitly identify the nature of the problem.

The NOTECHS method is designed to be a guiding tool to look beyond failure during recurrent checks or training, and to help point out possible underlying deficiencies in CRM competence in relation to technical failures. NOTECHS is not intended to fail additional crew members during mandatory checks, or indeed on any other occasion, as compared to the present situation. The evaluation of non-technical skills in a check using NOTECHS should not provoke a failed (not acceptable) rating without a related objective technical consequence, leading to compromised flight safety in the short or long term. In the event of a crew member failing a check for any technical reason, NOTECHS can provide useful insights into the contributing individual human factors for the technical failure. Used in this way, the method can provide valuable assistance for debriefing and orienting tailored retraining.

Preliminary test of NOTECHS: the JARTEL project

The prototype NOTECHS system offered a systematic approach for assessing pilots' non-technical skills in simulator and flight missions. Testing of the basic usability and psychometric properties of the NOTECHS system was then required. The Directorate General Transportation (DGTREN) of the European Community, in co-ordination with the JAA research committee tasked a consortium of five aviation research centres (NLR (N), DLR (G), University of Aberdeen (UK), DERA (UK) and IMASSA (F)) and four aviation business centres (Sofreavia (F), British Airways (UK), Alitalia (I), and Airbus) to test the NOTECHS method. A European research project JARTEL (Joint Aviation Requirements - Translation and Elaboration of Legislation) began in January 1998 and was completed in 2001. The main goals of this project were to assess:

- Usability of the NOTECHS system as an assessment tool.
- Reliability and validity of the assessment tool.
- Influence of cultural differences on the use of the NOTECHS system within Europe.

Experimental study

The experimental study was carried out using eight video scenarios filmed in a Boeing 757 simulator, with current pilots as actors. The scenarios showed simulated flight situations with predefined behaviours (from the NOTECHS elements) exhibited by the pilots of varying quality ('very poor' to 'very good' standard). The pilots' behaviours were rated using the NOTECHS systems by 105 instructors, recruited from 14 airlines in 12 European countries. The airlines represented large and smaller carriers within five different European cultural groups.

Each of the experimental sessions was conducted within an airline training centre. It began in the morning with a standard briefing on the NOTECHS method (the participants had previously been supplied with background information on the NOTECHS system), and a practice session. Questionnaires were also completed by the instructors, providing data on their background and experience. During the subsequent afternoon session, the captain's and first officer's behaviour in each of the eight cockpit scenarios was rated by the instructors using the NOTECHS score forms. At the end of the experimental session, a second questionnaire was given to the instructors for evaluating the NOTECHS rating process and material.

In summary, the results indicated that 80% of the instructors were consistent in their ratings, 88% of them were satisfied with the consistency of the method. On average, the difference between a reference rating (established for benchmarking by consensus ratings in a set of trained expert instructors), and the instructors' ratings was less than one point on the five-point scale, confirming an acceptable level of accuracy. In the evaluation questionnaire, the instructors were very satisfied with the NOTECHS rating system, especially with the five-point scale (98%). Cultural differences (relating to five European regions) were found to be less significant than other background variables, such as English language proficiency, experience with non-technical skills evaluation, and different role perceptions of captain and first officer (see Hörmann, 2001) for details of the cultural analysis. Full details of the experimental method and the results can be found in the JARTEL project reports for work packages 2 and 3 (Sofreavia web site: sofreavia.com/jartel/) or see O'Connor, et al (2002).

A subsequent operational trial of NOTECHS was run with several airlines (see JARTEL work package 4 Report). It confirmed the applicability and feasibility of the system in real check events.

These first experimental and operational tests of the NOTECHS system showed that it was usable by instructors and appeared to have acceptable psychometric properties. These results were achieved with a minimal training period of half a day due to difficulties in recruiting experienced instructors to take part in the study, especially from the small companies. This level of training would be insufficient for using the NOTECHS system for regular training or assessment purposes. It is recommended that the basic training period is two full days or longer (depending on the level of previous experience of rating pilots' non-technical skills).

Training requirements for users of the NOTECHS system

Users of NOTECHS are certified flight instructors and authorized examiners. It is necessary to train all raters in the application of the method. NOTECHS presupposes sufficient knowledge of concepts included in the JAR-FCL theoretical program on human performance and limitations (JAR-FCL1.125/1.160/1.165-Theoretical knowledge instruction PPL/ATPL). No additional theoretical knowledge is required. Being current in CRM training and recurrent CRM is required, at least as a participant. Experience of CRM instruction is a facilitating factor for standardisation, but is not a prerequisite (see CAA 2003 for the current UK position on CRM Instructors and CRM Instructor Examiners). Most of the training effort should be devoted to the understanding of the NOTECHS methodology, the specific use of the evaluation grid, the calibration process of judgement and the debriefing phase. As the NOTECHS system is primarily used as a tool for debriefing and identification of training needs, then it is important to ensure that in debriefing an emphasis is placed on skill components, rather than more 'global' analyses of performance. (For general advice on training and other practical aspects of the use of behavioural marker systems, such as NOTECHS, for evaluating non-technical (CRM) skills, see Baker and Dismukes, 2002; Baker, Mulqueen and Dismukes, 2001; Klampfer, Flin, Helmreich, et al., 2001.)

In the UK the CAA (2003, Chapter 7, p2) has recently published the following guidance on CRM skills assessment:

For individual CRM skills assessment, the following methodology is considered appropriate:

- *An operator should establish the CRM training programme including an agreed terminology. This should be evaluated with regard to methods, length of training, depth of subjects and effectiveness.*
- *The CRM standards to be used (e.g. NOTECHS) have been agreed by crews, operators and regulators, and reflect best practice.*
- *The standards are clear, brief, and published (in the Operations Manual).*
- *The methodology for assessing, recording and feeding back has been agreed and validated.*
- *Training courses are provided to ensure that crews can achieve the agreed standards.*
- *Procedures are in place for individuals who do not achieve the agreed standards to have access to additional training, and independent third party appeal.*
- *Instructors and examiners are qualified to standards agreed by all parties, and are required to demonstrate their competency to the CAA or such persons as the CAA may nominate.*
- *A training and standardisation programme for training personnel should be established.*

Conclusions

In summary, NOTECHS was designed as: (i) A professional pragmatic tool for instructors and authorised examiners; (ii) A tool to be used by non-psychologists; (iii) A tool using common professional aviation language, with the primary intention of debriefing pilots and communicating concrete directions for improvements. NOTECHS was not designed as: (i) A research tool (although it can be used for this purpose, see Goeters, 2002); (ii) A tool for judging flight-crew personality on the basis of instructors' or authorised examiners' personal opinions; (iii) A tool for introducing psychological jargon into the evaluation.

The preliminary evaluation of the NOTECHS system from the experimental and operational trials indicated that the basic psychometric properties were acceptable and that the method was usable and accepted by practitioners. Clearly a more extensive test of the psychometric quality of NOTECHS would be desirable but this would require a large data set collected under standardised conditions.

In response to the JAA requirements on evaluation of CRM skills, many airlines have now developed their own systems, several of which are at an advanced stage such as the KLM SHAPE system, the Lufthansa System 'Basic

Competence for Optimum Performance' (Burger, Neb and Hörmann (2002), and the Alitalia PENTAPERF system (Polo, 2002). The Alitalia and Lufthansa systems have made use of the basic NOTECHS framework in the design of their own customised systems (Hörmann, Burger and Neb, 2002). Several other airlines are currently using NOTECHS or their own versions of it to complement their proficiency evaluation methods both in Europe (e.g. Finnair, Eastern Airways, Iberia) and beyond (e.g., Gulf Air). One important aspect of any skills training programme, such as CRM, is that the transfer of skills to the workplace should be established (Boehm-Davis, et al., 2001; O'Connor, et al., 2002b). The NOTECHS system offers one method of ascertaining whether the CRM training provided to pilots is actually enhancing effectiveness of overall crew performance on the flight deck (Goeters, 2002).

References

Antersijn, P. and Verhoef, M. (1995). Assessment of non-technical skills: is it possible? In, N. McDonald, N. Johnston and R. Fuller (Eds.) *Applications of Psychology to the Aviation System.* Aldershot: Avebury.

Avermaete, van J. and Kruijsen, E. (Eds.) (1998). *NOTECHS. The Evaluation of Non-Technical Skills of Multi-Pilot Aircrew in Relation to the JAR-FCL Requirements.* Final Report NLR-CR-98443. Amsterdam: National Aerospace Laboratory (NLR).

Baker, D. and Dismukes, K. (2002). Special issue on training instructors to evaluate aircrew performance. *International Journal of Aviation Psychology, 12,* 203-222.

Baker, D., Mulqueen, C. and Dismukes, K. (2001). Training raters to assess resource management skills. In, E. Salas, C. Bowers and E. Edens (2001) (Eds.) *Improving Teamwork in Organizations. Applications of Resource Management Training.* Mahwah, N.J.: LEA.

Boehm-Davis, D., Holt, R. and Seamster, T. (2001). Airline resource management programs. In, E. Salas, C. Bowers and E. Edens (2001) (Eds.). *Improving Teamwork in Organizations. Applications of Resource Management Training.* Mahwah, N.J.: LEA.

Burger, K.-H., Neb, H. and Hörmann, H.-J. (2002). Basic Performance of Flight Crew – A concept of competence based markers for defining pilots performance profile. *Proceedings of the 25th European Aviation Psychology Conference, Warsaw.* Warsaw: Polish Airforce.

CAA (2003). *Crew Resource Management (CRM) Training. Guidance for Flight Crew, CRM Instructors (CRMIs) and CRM Instructor-Examiners (CRMIEs).* Gatwick, Sussex: Safety Regulation Group, Civil Aviation Authority. Available on www.caa.co.uk

Endsley, M. (1995). Toward a theory of situation awareness in dynamic systems. *Human Factors, 37*, 32-64.

Flin, R. and Martin, L. (1998). *Behavioural Markers for CRM.* CAA Report 98005 London: Civil Aviation Authority.

Flin, R. and Martin, L. (2001). Behavioural markers for Crew Resource Management: A review of current practice. *International Journal of Aviation Psychology, 11*, 95-118.

Goeters, K.-M. (2002). Evaluation of the effects of CRM training by the assessment of non-technical skills under LOFT. *Human Factors and Aerospace Safety, 2*, 71- 86.

Gregorich, S. and Wilhelm, J. (1993). Crew resource management training assessed. In, E. Wiener, B. Kanki and R. Helmreich, (Eds.) *Cockpit Resource Management.* San Diego: Academic Press.

Helmreich, R. (2000). The Line Oriented Safety Audit (LOSA) system. Paper presented at the *Australian Aviation Psychology Conference*, Manly, November.

Helmreich, R., Butler, R., Taggart, W. and Wilhelm, J. (1995). The NASA/ University of Texas/ FAA Line/ LOS checklist: A behavioural marker-based checklist for CRM skills assessment. Version 4. Technical Paper 94-02 (Revised 12/8/95). Austin, Texas: University of Texas Aerospace Research Project.

Hörmann, H.-J. (1995). FOR-DEC: A prescriptive model for aeronautical decision making. In, R. Fuller, N. Johnston, and N. McDonald, (Eds.) *Human Factors in Aviation Operations.* Aldershot: Avebury.

Hörmann, H.-J. (2001). Cultural variations of perceptions of crew behaviour in multi-pilot aircraft. *Le Travail Humain, 64, 247-268.*

Hörmann, H.-J., Burger, K-H. and Neb, H. (2002). Integration of interpersonal skills into a pilot's proficiency reporting system. First results of a usability study at Lufthansa. In, O. Truszczynski (Ed.) *Proceedings of the 25th European Aviation Psychology Conference, Warsaw.* Warsaw: Polish Airforce.

ICAO (1989a). *Human factors digest no. 1. Fundamental human factors concepts.* Montreal, Canada: International Civil Aviation Organization.

ICAO (1989b). *Human factors digest no. 2. Flight crew training: Cockpit resource management (CRM) and line-oriented flight training (LOFT).* Montreal, Canada: International Civil Aviation Organization.

Jensen, R. (1996). *Pilot Judgment and Crew Resource Management.* Aldershot: Avebury.

Kaempf, G. and Klein, G. (1995). Aeronautical decision making: The next generation. In, N. Johnston, N. McDonald and R. Fuller (Eds.) *Aviation Psychology in Practice.* Aldershot: Avebury.

Klampfer, B., Flin. R., Helmreich R.,. et al (2001). *Enhancing performance in high risk environments: Recommendations for the use of Behavioural Markers.* Daimler Benz Foundation. Available as pdf file on www.psyc.abdn.ac.uk/serv02.htm.

KLM (1996). Feedback and Appraisal System. Amsterdam: KLM Internal Paper.

O'Connor, P., Flin, R. and Fletcher, G. (2002a). Techniques used to evaluate Crew Resource Management training: A literature review. *Human Factors and Aerospace Safety, 2, 217-233.*

O'Connor, P., Flin, R. and Fletcher, G. (2002b). Methods used to evaluate the effectiveness of flightcrew CRM training in the UK aviation industry. *Human Factors and Aerospace Safety, 2, 235-255.*

O'Connor, P., Hörmann, H.-J., Flin, R., Lodge, M., Goeters, K.-M. and the JARTEL group (2002). Developing a method for evaluating crew resource management skills: A European perspective. *International Journal of Aviation Psychology, 12,* 265-288.

Orasanu, J. (1993). Decision making in the cockpit. In, R. Helmreich, E. Weiner and B. Kanki (Eds.) *Cockpit Resource Management.* San Diego: Academic Press.

Polo, L. (2002). Evaluation of flight crew members' performance. Is evaluation a product or a tool? In, O. Truszczynski (Ed.) *Proceedings of the 25th European Aviation Psychology Conference, Warsaw.* Warsaw: Polish Airforce.

Salas, E., Burke, S., Bowers, C. and Wilson, K. (2001). Team training in the skies. Does Crew Resource Management (CRM) training work? *Human Factors, 43,* 641-674.

Seamster, T. and Keampf, G. (2001). Identifying resource management skills for pilots. In, E. Salas, C. Bowers and E. Edens (Eds.) *Improving Teamwork in Organizations. Applications of Resource Management Training.* Mahwah, N.J.: LEA.

Shrestha, L., Prince, C., Baker, D. and Salas, E. (1995). Understanding situation awareness: Concepts, methods and training. In, W. Rouse (Ed) *Human/ Technology Interaction in Complex Systems.* Vol 7. Greenwich, CT: JAI.

Stokes, A., Kemper, K. and Kite, K. (1997). Aeronautical decision making, cue recognition and expertise under pressure. In, C. Zsambok and G. Klein. (Eds.) *Naturalistic Decision Making.* New Jersey: LEA.

Acknowledgements

We would like to acknowledge the contribution of the other members of the NOTECHS project group: Eric Kruijsen, Hans Sypkens, Jurgen van Avermaete, Cees van Gelderen. Mike Lodge and Paul Field provided helpful comments on the draft manuscript. The development work for NOTECHS was funded by CAA (GB), DGAC (F), LBA (D), RLD (NL), and EC DG VII. The views presented are those of the authors and should not be taken to represent the position or policy of the funding bodies.

Lynne Martin is now at NASA Ames, California; Hans-Jürgen Hörmann is now at the Boeing Research and Teaching Center, Madrid.

8　Teamwork at 35,000 feet: enhancing safety through team training

C. Shawn Burke, Katherine A. Wilson
and Eduardo Salas

Abstract

The aviation industry has been commended for its ability to maintain a high
level of safety despite operating in a mission critical, high impact work
environment.　This commitment to mindfulness and safety has led to the
aviation community's transition to a high reliability organisation (HRO).　A
key factor in this transition was its commitment to team training and belief that
collaboration among crew-members can be used as a key strategy by which
errors can be managed.　This recognition led to the development of a highly
successful team training program (i.e., crew resource management, CRM).
CRM's touted success within aviation has led to its adoption by many
industries outside CRM.　Therefore, it becomes important to delineate how
aviation made this progression through the use of CRM as well as identify
areas that have posed key challenges in making this transition.　Therefore, the
purpose of this paper is twofold.　First, to review how aviation has used CRM
to become a mindful HRO.　In doing this, we briefly review the theoretical
drivers behind CRM.　Second, to provide principles concerning how
organisations outside of aviation can use lessons learned within aviation to
move towards becoming an HRO.　In highlighting principles we also identify
those areas that continue to pose challenges in aviation's quest to maintain
HRO status and continually improve.

This paper was first published in Human Factors and Aerospace Safety 3(4), 2003, pp. 287-312

155

Teamwork at 35,000 feet: enhancing safety through team training

The events of September 11, 2001, have left many doubting the safety of our airways and the classification of the aviation industry as a high reliability organisation. However, in terms of safety, the airline industry has been repeatedly commended as being one of the most reliable organisations, despite the fact that the skies are becoming increasingly crowded (Orlady and Orlady, 1999; Sarter and Alexander, 2000). For example, in 2000 approximately 25,000 flights departed daily from airports nationwide (US Department of Transportation, 2001), yet the number of fatal accidents of scheduled commercial airliners nationwide remains negligible with 3 fatal accidents during that year resulting in 92 deaths (Sietzan, 2001). Over the past two years, US commercial aviation has seen only 1 fatal accident resulting in 21 deaths (Borenstein, 2003; www.ntsb.gov).

Organisations, such as aviation, that function within complex, fast-paced and ambiguous operational environments, yet are able to consistently maintain a high safety record are known as high reliability organisations (HROs) (others include nuclear power plants and military organisations). One characteristic that distinguishes HROs from non-HROs is a focus on minimising the number of accidents and incidents due to the severe consequences of error (Westrum and Adamski, 1999). To combat error severity, HROs develop a culture which promotes safety, continuous learning, and a focus on the 'big picture' to make the unexpected the expected (Roberts and Bea, 2001a; Weick and Sutcliffe, 2001).

Within aviation, the primary mechanism by which safety and mindfulness are created is through a large investment in team training (see Wiener, Kanki and Helmreich, 1993). The aviation industry maintains its status as a high reliability organisation by: (a) recognising the complexity of the environment, (b) recognising that interdependencies exist between crew members, (c) training members to be mindful, and (d) taking advantage of all the resources at their disposal, both equipment and personnel. To accomplish this, they have invested heavily in team training, specifically, the development and application of Crew Resource Management (CRM) training. CRM represents a human factors intervention which attempts to mitigate the effects of stress on performance through the promotion of teamwork (Salas, Bowers, and Edens, 2001).

In light of the above, the purpose of this paper will be twofold. First, we illustrate how aviation has used CRM to create and maintain its status as a HRO. This is accomplished by briefly reviewing the theoretical foundation behind CRM and then illustrating how components of CRM fit within the HRO framework. Second, we provide principles concerning how organisations that work in mission critical, high impact work environments outside of aviation can use what has been learned within the aviation industry as a mechanism to become a HRO. In providing principles we also identify areas that have proved especially challenging to the aviation community – where mindfulness has not yet been met.

Background

In 1978, a United Airlines aircraft crashed near Portland, Oregon due to the failure of junior crewmembers to assert to the captain the low fuel state of the aircraft while the crew attempted to deal with a landing gear malfunction (www.airdisaster.com). The National Transportation Safety Board (NTSB, 1979) cited a breakdown in teamwork as the primary cause of the accident in that crewmembers failed to monitor one another and provide the requisite back-up needed (as cited in Driskell, Salas, and Johnston 1999).

The above incident is indicative of the environment within the aviation industry during the mid to late 1970s. During this time the NTSB began to see a trend among the causes of aviation accidents – human error related to failures in teamwork. More specifically, research has suggested that 60-80 % of aviation accidents can be attributed to human error (Freeman and Simmon, 1991; Taggart, 1994; Foushee, 1984). Similarly, the Government Accounting Office (GAO) found that teamwork deficiencies (e.g., lack of coordination among cockpit crews, captain's failure to assign tasks to other members, and a lack of effective crew supervision) were a contributing cause in approximately ½ of the accidents reported by major airlines that involved one or more fatalities during the time period covering 1983-1985 (U.S. GAO, 1997). The recognition of the fact that teams are not automatically effective (Hackman, 1990) led the aviation industry to become one of the largest investors in team training, resulting in the construction and application of CRM. Initially, CRM was introduced as a means to manage issues with teamwork among aircrews and the consequent safety issues (Wiener et al., 1993; Salas et al., 2001). The purpose of CRM was to train crewmembers to use all the resources available to them – equipment, people, and information – through team communication and coordination. Similarly, Salas and colleagues (1999) have defined CRM training as a set of instructional strategies with the purpose of improving teamwork within the cockpit through the application of tested training tools (e.g., lectures, simulations) that target specific content related to teamwork (i.e., knowledge, skills, and attitudes).

CRM was introduced over two decades ago and has evolved through several stages as changes have occurred within the aviation community (Helmreich, Merritt, and Wilhelm, 1999; Helmreich and Foushee, 1993; Maurino, 1999). Since its inception in 1981, the focus of CRM training has ranged from psychological testing of crewmembers to cockpit group dynamics to the integration of training for the cockpit and cabin crewmembers and maintenance personnel (Helmreich et al., 1999). Recently, the Advanced Qualification Program (AQP) was implemented allowing airlines to tailor training to fit their own needs, while still requiring that both CRM and line-orientated flight training (LOFT) (i.e. simulation-based training) be provided to all crews. The implementation of AQP also signalled a greater push to integrate the concepts included in CRM training with those in technical training. The foundation for the latest generation of CRM is the acceptance that human error is inevitable and an emphasis on the importance of error management (Helmreich, 1997; 2000). This generation attempts to manage errors through training that focuses on teamwork skills that will support: (a) error avoidance, (b) detection of errors before they occur, and (c) mitigation of consequences as a result of errors not being avoided or detected. Some programs have even broadened the scope of their programs to emphasise threat recognition and management. The success of CRM has been a key factor in the aviation industry's status as a high reliability organisation (Helmreich and Merritt, 1998a). However, prior to illustrating the use of CRM as a tool through which aviation maintains their HRO status, we will first review the theoretical drivers for its use.

Theoretical drivers for CRM training

Although the aviation industry has long used teams as a key organisational strategy, there have been several advances in the team literature within the past 20 years (Guzzo and Dickson, 1996). These advances have served to strengthen our understanding of the factors related to team effectiveness, as well as methods by which to train teams. In turn, the advances in theory have served as drivers for the design and delivery of CRM training. These advances in theory can be broken down into three areas, those dealing with: (a) teamwork, (b) team competencies (i.e. knowledge, skills, and attitudes), and (c) shared mental models.

Teamwork

The past 20 years has witnessed many advances in what is known about teamwork (Guzzo and Dickson, 1996; Ilgen, Major, Hollenbeck, and Sago, 1993). As a result, many conceptual and empirically-based models depicting the relationship between input variables (e.g., team characteristics, individual characteristics), process variables (e.g. communication, coordination, decision-making, back-up behaviour, compatible cognitive structures, compensatory behaviour, and leadership), and outcome variables (e.g., increased productivity, increased safety, increased job satisfaction) have been developed (see Swezey and Salas, 1992, for a representative sample). These models, as well as empirical research, have not only illustrated the dynamic and multi-dimensional nature of teamwork, but have also shown the importance of process variables in determining the relationship between team input and team output (Wiener et al., 1993; Swezey and Salas, 1992; Guzzo and Dickson, 1996). For example, it has been argued that skills such as adaptability, communication, coordination, decision-making, leadership, and back-up behaviour are important process (i.e. teamwork) variables (Cannon-Bowers, Tannenbaum, Salas, and Volpe, 1995, see table 1).

In addition, it has been argued that teams are dynamic and evolve over time (Gersick, 1988; Morgan, Glickman, Woodard, Blaiwes, and Salas, 1986; Kozlowski et al., 1996). Related to this is that many have argued that there are two tracks of skills that must be mastered within teams, task-work and teamwork. Task-work skills are those skills that members must understand and acquire for actual task performance, while teamwork skills are the behavioural and attitudinal responses that members need to function effectively as part of an interdependent team (Morgan et al., 1986). In terms of training, most would argue that task-work skills need to be trained prior to teamwork skills. Moreover, it has been argued that the relationship between task-work skills and team effectiveness is mediated by teamwork skills (Hackman and Morris, 1975; Bass, 1990; Brannick, Roach, and Salas, 1993).

Team competencies

As the theory behind teamwork advanced, researchers began to further delineate the concept of teamwork. More specifically, researchers began to argue that teamwork is comprised of a core set of competencies that involve knowledges (what team members 'think'), skills (what team members 'do'), and attitudes (what team members 'feel') (i.e. KSAs) (Cannon-Bowers et al., 1995; Salas, Burke, and Cannon-Bowers, 2000). For example, Cannon-Bowers et al. identified eight major teamwork skills that are transportable across situations (see table 1).

The recognition of teamwork competencies represented an important development in the theory behind teams and teamwork in that up to this point the focus during training was primarily on the behavioural side of teamwork, neglecting the cognitive and affective components of it. Recent work within the team literature has begun to focus on examining team cognition and exactly how cognitive processes relate to teamwork (e.g., shared mental models, Cannon-Bowers, Salas, and Converse, 1993), metacognition (Klein, 2000), and shared situation assessment (Burke, Fiore, and Salas, 2003).

Another important advance in terms of team competencies came with the recognition that there are many types of teams (Sundstrom, DeMeuse, and Futrell, 1990). More specifically, the recognition that due to the differences in function, composition, and interdependencies present within various teams, the importance of specific teamwork competencies will vary. While researchers have argued for a set of generic, transportable competencies (see table 1), the weight of each one may differ dependent on the situation. Furthermore, other teamwork competencies have been identified to be dependent on team characteristics such as whether: (a) team membership is stable or unstable and (b) the team focuses on the same tasks or completes several different types of tasks.

Table 1   Major team skill dimensions. Adapted from 'Defining team competencies and establishing team training requirements,' by J.A. Cannon-Bowers, S.I. Tannenbaum, E. Salas, and C.E. Volpe, 1995, in R. Guzzo, E. Salas et al. (Eds.), *Team effectiveness and decision making in organizations*, pp. 344-346, San Francisco, CA: Jossey-Bass

Skill dimension	Definition
Adaptability	Team's ability to gather information from the task environment and adjust their strategies by reallocating their resources and using compensatory behaviours (e.g., back-up behaviour).
Communication	Team's ability to exchange information accurately and clearly and to acknowledge receipt of information.
Coordination	Team's ability to organise their activities, responses, and resources in order to achieve synchronisation.
Decision making	Team's ability to gather information and integrate it with their knowledge to make sound judgments, identify alternative solutions, decide on the best solution, and evaluate the results of the chosen solution.
Interpersonal Relations	Team's ability to improve the interactions between team members using motivational techniques and cooperative behaviours.
Leadership/team management	Team's ability to guide and coordinate team members' activities, plan, be organised, evaluate team performance, motivate team members, and create a positive atmosphere.
Performance monitoring and feedback	Team's ability to monitor team members' performance to provide constructive feedback, seek feedback on own performance, and accept feedback from others.
Shared situation awareness	Team's ability to develop shared mental models of the environment (internal and external) to apply correct task strategies.

Shared mental models

The last theoretical driver for CRM training originates with what is known about the impact of shared mental models on teamwork and team performance. Shared mental models refer to team members possessing compatible or similar knowledge structures with regard to the equipment, task, and team (Rouse and Morris, 1986; Rouse, Cannon-Bowers, and Salas, 1992). The sharing of cognitive structures allows teams to better combat human error, as well as catch system errors in that these cognitive structures allow teams to generate descriptions of systems and make predictions about future system states (e.g., Rouse et al., 1992). Furthermore, when operating in dynamic, complex environments explicit coordination and/or communication may not be possible. Many have begun to argue, and research has begun to suggest, that shared mental models allow effective teams to remain consistent in terms of their performance within complex, stressful environments (Cannon-Bowers et al., 1993; Burke, 1999; Marks, Zacarro, and Mathieu, 2000; Orasanu, 1990) by allowing members to coordinate implicitly (i.e., without explicit communication).

A commitment towards becoming a HRO

We now turn the focus of this paper to the specific application of how aviation has used CRM training to realise a commitment towards becoming a HRO. Weick and Sutcliffe (2001) state that there are five characteristics exhibited by HROs – commitment to resilience, deference to expertise, sensitivity to operations, reluctance to simplify, and preoccupation with failure. These characteristics will be expanded upon to show how the aviation community uses CRM to accomplish each as well as areas that have remained challenging for aviation.

Commitment to resilience One of the key characteristics of a HRO is its ability to identify, control and recover from errors (Weick and Sutcliff, 2001). This ability is facilitated by an effort to keep errors small, practice worst case scenarios and develop general strategies to expect and react to the unexpected. The aviation community has witnessed their commitment to resilience primarily through four avenues: use of teams, focus on promoting compatible cognitive frameworks, use of simulation and provision of timely feedback.

Helmreich and Merritt (1998a) have argued that the greatest countermeasure to human error is collaboration among crewmembers (i.e. teamwork). Teamwork encourages resilience to errors in that members may serve as redundant systems by providing back-up and monitoring behaviours. Back up behaviours and monitoring provide crews with an effective means to managing errors that occur by avoiding, trapping, or mitigating the consequences of errors (Helmreich and Merritt, 1998b). In order to manage errors within teams, one of three things must happen: (a) team members must ask for help when overloaded, (b) team members monitor each others performance to notice any performance decreases, or (c) team members take an active role in assisting other team members who are in need of help. This recognition along with the realisation that teams are not automatically effective (Hackman, 1990) provides the foundation for aviation's use of CRM. CRM training focuses on informing crew members on the inevitability of human error and the importance of error management through teamwork by teaching such behaviours as: decision making, cross-checking, monitoring, leadership and review and modification of plans (Helmreich, 1997, 2000).

Principle 1: Organisations operating in mission critical, high impact work environments where interdependent action is required must use teams to facilitate the identification, control and recovery from errors where members are trained in requisite teamwork competencies.

A second way that the aviation community shows a commitment to resilience is through a commitment to training that develops compatible cognitive frameworks (i.e. shared mental models) among crewmembers. Based on the effectiveness of cognitive structures to combat human error, the aviation community uses several strategies to help foster compatible cognitive frameworks among crewmembers (e.g. cross-training, Stout, Cannon-Bowers and Salas, 1996; pre-mission briefings, Burke, 1999). The first strategy mentioned, cross-training, is a team-based instructional strategy that provides exposure to and/or practice with other team mates' tasks, roles and responsibilities (Stout et al.). The goal of this instructional strategy is for team members to develop a clear understanding of the entire team function and the importance of each member, including the interdependencies present.

Pre-mission briefings may also serve as an instructional strategy in that they provide a mechanism by which the leader can communicate a mental model of the problem situation and required team interaction to the rest of the team (Burke, 1999), thereby creating compatible cognitive frameworks. For example, Ginnett (1993) found evidence for the usefulness of pre-mission briefings within aircrews in that captains of highly effective crews were found to brief their crewmembers prior to mission engagement on four basic themes (i.e. the task, crew boundaries, standards and expected behaviours and authority dynamics).

Both of the above methods are commonly used within the aviation community as ways to form compatible knowledge structures, resulting in the ability to implicitly coordinate actions as well as knowing where expertise within the team lies according to the situation. In addition, by facilitating compatible knowledge structures they serve to provide a common mental picture that team members can compare current events against to identify errors and concurrently serve to guide the identification of whom has the expertise or role to combat the error.

Principle 2: To become a HRO, organisations must train team members to develop compatible cognitive frameworks concerning the equipment, task and team such that they are better able to identify errors early and facilitate the team's operation under stress by enabling implicit coordination.

A third way in which the aviation community shows a commitment to resilience is through the large investment in training crewmembers to not only recognise irregularities, but also to respond to them (Roberts and Bea, 2001b). The primary way that aviation has accomplished this is through the use of simulation that allows trainees to practice the worst-case scenario, as well as develop general strategies for reacting to both expected and unexpected events. By combining an event-based approach to training with the use of simulation, trainees are able to practice important, but infrequently occurring events. In addition, through the incorporation of a scenario-based approach, events within the simulation can be systematically varied based on training objectives (see Principle 6). The use of this type of simulation is witnessed through Line-Orientated Flight Training (LOFT) and Line-Operational Simulation (LOS).

Principle 3: Simulation must be used to assist crews in practicing irregular events or events too dangerous to practice during line operations.

A final component that allows the aviation community to keep errors small and enables a timely response to irregularities is the use of timely, diagnostic feedback. Timely feedback serves as input that allows members to correct and learn from their actions, as well as serving to integrate this information into their knowledge structures (i.e. mental models) that guide team action. Although timely feedback is important for the updating of member mental models, feedback must also be diagnostic. While many organisations provide feedback, most solely provide feedback related to individual or team outcomes. In terms of CRM training, this would be akin to informing the trainee that they passed or failed a training module, without any further elaboration. In order for learning to occur, outcome feedback, while important, is not enough – process feedback must also occur.

Process feedback revolves around '…gathering information on a collection of activities, strategies, responses and behaviors employed in task accomplishment' (Cannon-Bowers and Salas, 1997, p. 51). It relates to 'how' and 'why' the trainee performed as he/she did. The diagnostic capabilities of process measures also provide information as to the exact areas, if any, that are in need of remediation (Cannon-Bowers and Salas, 1997). Feedback must be explicit and constructive (i.e. positive and not critical of the individual), directing the trainee's attention and giving him/her an indication of how to improve, as knowledge of results, in and of itself, is not necessarily informative. Finally, the feedback must be meaningful and delivered at both the individual and team levels.

Principle 4: In order to maintain HRO status, organisations must incorporate process feedback that allows team members to keep errors small by quickly correcting deficient teamwork competencies and actions.

While the aviation community has shown a commitment to resilience through its commitment to develop general strategies that allow crews to expect and react to unexpected events, there still remains a need for improvement within this regard. Specifically, the aviation community must not only broaden its view of team training to move beyond CRM, but must also enact a mandate for existing

CRM training. The aviation community has taken what has proven to be a step in the right direction by focusing on improving teamwork as a way to combat errors and allow crews to develop strategies by which error can be combated. However, aviation has tended to restrict this focus to CRM training without taking advantage of what has been learned within team training since CRM's inception. Specifically, there are a number of relevant instructional strategies that when combined with CRM training may prove to aid in the on-going quest to create and maintain resilience. Examples of team training strategies that have proven successful in other domains include, but are not limited to, team leader training (Salas, Burke and Stagl, 2004), self-correction training (Blickensderfer, Cannon-Bowers and Salas, 1997) and metacognitive training (Zaccaro, Rittman and Marks, 2001).

Combined with a narrow view of team training is the fact that even when team training implemented (i.e. CRM), there exists no mandate or standardisation for the design, implementation, or evaluation of such training. Specifically, while Advisory Circular 120-51D presents guidelines for CRM training programmes in commercial aviation, the circular explicitly states that it 'presents one way, but not necessarily the only way, that CRM training may be addressed' (p. 1). Furthermore, the circular states that CRM training focuses on situation awareness, communication skills, teamwork, task allocation and decision-making, however a recent evaluation of CRM training reveals that there are a very disparate set of skills trained across airlines. For example, skills trained as a part of CRM range from (a) leadership/followership, communication, decision-making and stress management (Byrnes and Black, 1993) to (b) communication, situation assessment and decision-making (Ikomi, Boehm-Davis, Holt and Incalcaterra, 1999) to (c) inquiry, advocacy, conflict resolution, critique and decision-making (Jackson, 1983). This lack of agreement as to the competencies to be trained and methods utilised in CRM is also noted by Driskell and Adams (1992).

This state of affairs is not only evident within the commercial community, but also within the military community (see Salas, Burke, Bowers and Wilson, 2001). The lack of standardisation across similar platforms not only has implications for crews that change carriers during their career, but has implications for trying to ascertain the effectiveness of such programmes. There currently exists no 'gold' standard for CRM programmes. As many of these programmes train a disparate range of knowledges, attitudes and behaviours it makes it difficult to generalise findings from one evaluation study to the next to ascertain the effectiveness of CRM training within the aviation community as a whole.

Principle 5: Organisations seeking to create resilience by developing organisation wide strategies to combat human error must implement a mandate for training such that the competencies trained, methods of implementation and evaluation are standardised throughout the industry.

Deference to expertise Another characteristic that sets HROs apart from non-HROs is the creation of a culture where deference to expertise is encouraged. More specifically, while many organisations use status or member rank to determine how heavily to weigh the advice or input that members offer, HROs use member expertise – regardless of rank. Organisations that work in mission critical environments, yet are able to maintain their high reliability status, recognise the value in expertise and seek to train and use this expertise, regardless of the level at which it resides. Within such an environment diversity is cultivated and decisions are made on the front line.

With regard to aviation, CRM training seeks to not only build crewmember expertise, but to also train crewmembers to recognise and value expertise among others. The aviation community accomplishes this via two mechanisms (i.e. event-based simulation and assertiveness training). One way in which the aviation community has increased the efficiency of skill acquisition and requisite expertise is through the use of event-based simulation. Event-based simulation builds on the fact that simulation alone cannot ensure training success (Salas, Bowers and Rhodenizer, 1998). Rather, it is important that events related to the trained KSAs be embedded into the simulation (Salas and Cannon-Bowers, 2001). To better observe specific target behaviours, these events are embedded into the simulation at pre-specified times so that they may be recorded (Fowlkes, Dwyer, Oser and Salas, 1998). For example, an instructor playing the role of flight leader provides erroneous navigation information. Based on the given scenario, instructors observe the behaviours of the crewmembers (e.g. do they question the erroneous information?). By observers knowing when and what events will occur within the simulation, relevant data is more easily captured and feedback provided to trainees. This, in turn, increases the efficiency by which trainees learn by: (a) ensuring that targeted competencies are practiced and (b) providing trainees with near real-time feedback.

Principle 6: Organisations performing mission critical tasks must not only realise the value of expertise, but that it can be efficiently created through the use of event-based simulation.

The second way in which aviation encourages the use of expertise is through assertiveness training of junior crew members. As it may not always be senior crew members who have the most expertise in a given situation, it is important for junior crew members to feel free to speak up and offer their expertise. Assertiveness training involves teaching individuals to clearly and directly communicate their concerns, ideas, feelings and needs to others (Jentsch and Smith-Jentsch, 2001). Assertiveness is trained not only so that junior crew members feel comfortable offering their perceptions to higher status members, but also so that communication is delivered in a manner that does not demean

165

others or infringe upon their rights. In turn, this allows aviation crews to take full advantage of the potential synergy available within the team by deferring to expertise in any given situation, regardless of rank.

Principle 7: To become a high reliability organisation, deference to expertise must be the organisational norm such that low status members are encouraged to assert themselves.

Sensitivity to operations A third characteristic of HROs is their sensitivity to operations. This is evident by an organisation's ongoing concern with the unexpected, attentiveness to those on the front line and acknowledgement that the cause of an accident is often not the result of a single, active error. Rather, many errors remain latent, embedded in the operational system until just the right combination of adverse events occurs – having the potential to lead to a catastrophic accident (Roberts and Bea, 2001b; Maurino, Johnston, Reason and Lee, 1995). Given this realisation, HROs focus on everyone knowing the 'big picture'. Within this type of environment, clear, concise communication and well-developed situational awareness is key.

The aviation community shows its sensitivity to operations by stressing the importance of information gathering, closed-loop communication, shared situation awareness among crewmembers and de-briefing. More specifically, the importance of situation awareness and closed-loop communication are two of the specific behaviours taught within a predominant number of CRM training programmes. Additionally, the aviation community encourages two prerequisites for the possession of shared situation awareness in a team environment – open communication (seen in assertiveness training for junior crew members) and diagnostic feedback.

The process of situation assessment and the resulting situational awareness is foundational to the creation of mindfulness of crewmembers. Mindfulness has been defined as 'the combination of ongoing scrutiny of existing expectations, continuous refinement and differentiation of expectations based on newer experiences, willingness and capability to create new expectations that make sense of unprecedented events…' (Weick and Sutcliffe, 2001, p. 42). Situation assessment involves the scanning of the environment and the perceiving of cues and patterns in a dynamic context. Information gained during this assessment process is then integrated into existing knowledge structures serving to update members' shared mental models (Salas, Cannon-Bowers, Fiore and Stout, 2001). This process culminates in a shared awareness of the situation among crewmembers (see Cannon-Bowers et al., 1995; Endsley, 1999). The resultant awareness helps to alert members to latent errors, as well as impacting decisions in terms of strategy and team co-ordination efforts to contain and minimise errors that do occur.

Principle 8: In becoming a high reliability organisation, a mindful organisation must encourage team members to continuously assess their environment and share relevant information to create a shared understanding.

A final way in which the aviation community exhibits a sensitivity to operations is through the recognition that errors often remain latent and that learning opportunities come in many forms. As such, after training episodes (i.e. LOFT, LOS) and operational flights crews progress through a debriefing session in which the crew's performance is reviewed, lessons discussed and areas for improvement are noted and plans made. It is important to note that an effective debriefing session is not an endeavour that happens automatically. For example, crews conducting debriefs for line operations must be trained in techniques that facilitate self-debriefing (see Blickensderfer et al., 1997), while within a training environment instructors should be trained in the facilitation of the debriefing process (Dismukes and Smith, 2000). The debriefing process must be interactive and one in which crew input is valued. Despite the importance of such techniques, effective debriefings have proved to be a challenging area for the aviation community often due to the hierarchical nature of the team.

Dismukes, Jobe and McDonnell (2000) conducted a study to examine the effectiveness of LOFT debriefs. Results indicated that while the great majority of instructors were highly competent, conscientious and displayed strong interpersonal skills, they were not highly effective as facilitators. For example: (a) rarely did instructors engage crew members in setting an agenda for the discussion, (b) instructors talked much more than crew, (c) most instructors were found to ask a large number of questions to the exclusion of other techniques, (d) crew responses tended to be brief and back and forth discussion among crew members limited and (e) instructors devoted substantially more time to positive aspects rather than ways to improve negative aspects of performance. In addition, findings indicated that debriefings often did not occur immediately after LOFT and on several occasions crew members spontaneously mentioned having trouble remembering relevant aspects of the simulation. Finally, within each airline scores of individual instructors and crews varied over a wide range for most variables. This, in turn, has implications for standardisation of training as previously discussed.

Since delivering their initial report to the FAA, several airlines have responded by expanding their training for instructors. However, important to note is that effective debriefing techniques are not an automatic skill and have posed challenging to the aviation community.

Principle 9: Systematic training must be delivered in order for instructors or crews to be able to conduct debriefs in which latent errors are found and learning occurs.

Reluctance to simplify Another important characteristic of HROs is the unwillingness to simplify a situation. This characteristic is witnessed through an environment and culture which encourages spanning of boundaries, negotiating, scepticism and differences of opinion. While an environment simplified by expectations can help reduce the complexity and promote coordination among interdependent members, if simplified too much it can also be harmful to the organisation. For example, inflexible expectations can lead to disconfirming or novel evidence being ignored or misinterpreted. Within the aviation community environmental complexity and unpredictability is not only recognised (Weick and Sutcliff, 2001), but the aviation community stresses the importance of being prepared for both the expected (e.g. routine) and unexpected (e.g. novel) events.

One way in which the aviation community stresses the importance of complexity is by providing a combination of on-line and simulator-based training and recurrent evaluation. Simulators are a key part of the individual crewmembers' annual Proficiency Check to assess technical competence via the successful completion of specified manoeuvres (Helmreich, 1997). Simulators are also used as part of CRM training during LOFT. LOFT provides crews with an opportunity to practice management of error-inducing situations (e.g. stalls, engine failures), which would otherwise be dangerous to conduct in the actual aircraft (Helmreich, 1997, 2000). This not only allows crews to experience what works and does not work in particularly dangerous situations (Roberts and Bea, 2001b), but allows them to receive diagnostic feedback concerning their performance. During these training events, crews are also presented with situations where the procedural solutions are not clear, encouraging them to expand their thinking and response repertoire. This training may be beneficial and is reflective of a reluctance to simplify complex situations in that it trains pilots to make few assumptions within the cockpit (Weick and Sutcliff, 2000).

In order to best prepare crew members for complex environments there are several components built into CRM training systems. The following are a few more instances of the aviation community's reluctance to simplify operations. First, it is recognised that team training is complex. Recently, Salas and Cannon-Bowers (2000) have defined team training as, 'a set of tools and methods, that in combination with required competencies and training objectives, form an instructional strategy' (p. 313). This definition alludes to the complexity of team training, yet many organisations do not realise this complexity. The aviation community has arguably been the biggest advocate of team training (see Helmreich et al., 1993) and as such has learned that training is more than just simulation and it's more than just a place. Training is about changing behavioural, cognitive and attitudinal phenomena (Goldstein, 1993) – it's about learning, application and transfer. Moreover, there are many barriers that may block trainees from learning, applying and transferring targeted competencies back to the job.

In order to combat organisational and individual barriers to training, as well as create a systematic training programme, the aviation community has learned to take advantage of what is known about how people learn and retain knowledge. Only people who are knowledgeable about the science of training should be responsible for the creation, implementation and evaluation of training programmes. For example, we know that before a training programme is created a training needs assessment should be conducted to determine: (a) what needs to be trained, (b) who needs to be trained and (c) organisational constraints/barriers. This needs assessment serves to guide the development of training objectives, specification of training content, media and strategies by which training is delivered and evaluated (see Salas and Cannon-Bowers, 2000, 2001).

Principle 10: To become a HRO, organisations must exploit the findings, caveats and lessons learned from simulation and team training.

The addition of simulation to training programmes within the aviation community has been a huge success. Allowing team members the ability to practice learned KSAs in a training environment helps in the transfer of these KSAs to the actual job. However, for training to be successful, it takes more than just good simulation—as simulation is only a tool for training (Salas et al., 1998). More specifically, practice in simulations must be guided. Next, events should be embedded into the simulation to help determine training's success. Additionally, high physical fidelity simulations (e.g. motion-based, detailed scenes) do not ensure training success. In fact, it is argued that low physical fidelity simulations may be just as effective as long as trainees must perform the cognitive and behavioural requirements of the task (Bowers and Jentsch, 2001). In short, more may not be better. Finally, training success is determined by the amount of feedback provided to trainees. However, feedback should be provided to trainees not only at the individual level, but also at the team level.

Principle 11: While mission critical organisations are increasingly using simulation as a training tool, they must incorporate what is known about learning into its use.

Another way in which complexity is realised is that the aviation community recognises that the key to an effective CRM programme involves more than just getting the right 'text' in the programme. The environment outside the training setting must be prepared so that the trained competencies (i.e. KSAs) will transfer to the actual job. This is important for if trainees learn the requisite competencies, but meet resistance once they are back on the job the competencies are not likely to be practically useful and will not transfer. Some things that can be done to help trainees overcome this hurdle are the following: (a) ensure supervisory support, (b) explain the benefits of these new competencies to those outside the training environment, (c) implement relapse prevention procedures and (d) during training highlight possible roadblocks for trainees, as well as strategies to deal with these roadblocks (Salas and Cannon-Bowers, 2000). While early generations of CRM witnessed difficulties in gaining 'buy-in' from pilots, later generations have been much more successful.

Principle 12: HROs must not only witness a reluctance to simplify the operational environment, but must realise the impact that factors outside the training environment may have on the success of training.

While aviation is often mindful of the 'big picture', it tends to not oversimplify situations. One area in which this line of thought has not been followed is in the recognition that cultural differences (i.e. national, organisational, professional) may impact teamwork both within and outside the cockpit and crew. Specifically, with the exception of a handful of researchers who are beginning to examine this issue (e.g. Helmreich and Merritt, 1998b; Hutchins, Holder and Perez, 2002; Helmreich, Wilhelm, Klinect and Merritt, 2001) culture is typically treated as a mute point. However, experience has shown that when attempting to apply U.S. developed CRM training packages abroad the concepts within them don' t always translate well (Helmreich et al., 2001). Moreover, within other domains cultural factors have been shown to influence individuals attitudes, beliefs and behaviours (Thomas, 1999; Adler, 1997; Triandis, 2000; Helmeich, 1994) and interacting within a multicultural environment is often viewed as challenging and frustrating (Helmreich and Merritt, 1998b). As the aviation industry is repeatedly placed within situations where interaction across cultural boundaries is necessary, it seems that this is an issue that needs to be studied. For examples of how culture may impact the aviation industry the reader is referred to the crash of Avianca Flight 52 in 1990.

Principle 13: As organisations continue to become more global, the complexity added by cultural factors must not be underestimated.

Preoccupation with failure   The final characteristic of an HRO that the aviation community has exhibited through the use of CRM training is a preoccupation with failure. This refers to a culture where error reporting is encouraged, an acceptance that human error is inevitable and an obsession with success liabilities.   There are at least four mechanisms that show aviation's commitment to this value: non-punitive reporting, recurrent training, evaluation of CRM programmes and access to data.

Often the latent errors that are present within a system are trapped by crewmembers before they result in an accident or incident. Klair (2000) states that 'lessons can...be learned from flights that do not end in accidents' (p. 72). Klair's statement is characteristic of organisations (e.g. aviation) where the culture is one that not only permits, but also encourages preoccupation with failure. Preoccupation with failure within the aviation industry is evidenced by the creation of a learning climate which consists of: debriefing, evaluation of CRM programmes and encouragement of crewmembers to report near misses and lesser incidents, as well as accidents.

To encourage this type of reporting, the National Aeronautics and Space Administration (NASA) developed the Aviation Safety Reporting System (ASRS). ASRS is a voluntary, non-punitive reporting system allowing pilots or crewmembers to report errors or unsafe acts that occurred during the flight. The end result of ASRS is that it allows the aviation community to handle errors proactively (Sexton, Thomas and Helmreich, 2000). Each year the ASRS database receives approximately 32,000 reports (Orlady and Orlady, 1999). NASA employs expert analysts to review the reports contained in the database and report the trends being seen through various aviation-related publications (e.g. CALLBACK, Directline), as well as the Internet. These reports provide information that is invaluable to the aviation community in terms of the types of errors committed by crewmembers (Sarter and Alexander, 2000). This information is, in turn, used to train crewmembers during CRM and recurrent training to better prepare for those events that are becoming an increased concern, due to frequency or severity.

The success of this system is due to several characteristics: (a) it is overseen by an independent organisation (i.e. NASA), (b) reports are filed anonymously with no fear of punishment and (c) problems or trends identified from the filed reports can be addressed and included as part of crewmembers' training. As a result of ASRS's success, other highly reliable organisations have implemented their own voluntary reporting systems, for example the nuclear and petrochemical domains (Kohn, Corrigan and Donaldson, 1999).

Principle 14: Organisations wishing to become or maintain the status of high reliability must recognise that incidents and minor mishaps that occur represent key learning opportunities.

Another way in of which the aviation community shows its preoccupation with failure and obsession with success liabilities is the requirement that all crewmembers attend recurrent training (Helmreich, 2000). The Federal Aviation Regulations (FARs) require that captains be retrained every six months and first officers be retrained every 12 months (Orlady, 1993). This training has two purposes: (a) to ensure flight proficiency, skills and knowledge and (b) to reinforce pilot knowledge of current operational information. The type of knowledge and skills emphasised during training is platform specific (e.g. specific to the type of equipment that each pilot is involved with). Recurrent training contributes to aviation's resilience to errors in that without it trained attitudes concerning teamwork, error management and safety decay over time (Irwin, 1991; Gregorich, 1993; Helmreich, 1991; Helmreich et al., 1999).

Principle 15: HROs recognise *that skill decay is inevitable and must design training requirements accordingly.*

The final way in which the aviation community illustrates a preoccupation with failure is in its evaluation of CRM training programmes. Training evaluation has been defined as 'the systematic collection of descriptive and judgmental information necessary to make effective training decisions related to the selection, adoption, value and modification of various instructional activities' (Goldstein, 1993, p. 147). Although systematic evaluations of training programmes may be time and labour intensive, they are the only way to ensure that programmes are truly effective. In turn, this promotes resilience to errors by ensuring that training is having the intended impact.

There are several types of data that may be collected when evaluating training programmes. Perhaps the most common training evaluation typology is that proposed by Kirkpatrick (1976), consisting of: (1) reactions, (2) learning, (3) behaviour (i.e. extent of performance change) and (4) results (i.e. degree of impact on organisational effectiveness or mission success). Within recent years, this typology has been expanded by several researchers (see Kraiger, Ford and Salas, 1993; Salas and Cannon-Bowers, 2001). Salas, Burke et al. (2001) conducted a review of 58 published studies containing some level of evaluation (via Kirkpatrick's typology) pertaining to CRM training. CRM training was found to generally produce (a) positive reactions (affective, utility based), (b) enhanced learning (primarily measured through attitude change) and (c) desired behaviour change in the cockpit. However, due to a lack of studies which tested systematically (and directly) the effects of CRM training, its true impact on safety was unable to be determined. Recently, other researchers drawing from the same studies found similar results (see O'Connor, Flin, Fletcher and Hemsley, 2003).

The reviews conducted by Salas, Burke et al (2001) and O'Connor et al (2003) contain a double-edged sword. On the one hand, the aviation community has shown a relatively large commitment to evaluation in that many of the studies collected training evaluation data at multiple levels. Specifically, of the 58 studies reviewed 24 collected evaluation data using more than one type of evaluation data, as suggested by Kirkpatrick (1976). The important point here is that the different levels suggested by Kirkpatrick provide different types of information that can be used to not only improve the training programme, but also serve as the basis for feedback to participants concerning their strengths and weaknesses.

Principle 16: If organisations are to witness an obsession with success liabilities they must conduct continual, systematic evaluations of training programmes and recognise that all training is not equally effective.

The other side of these results is that after 20 years of implementation the picture is not as clear as it should be. One reason for the lack of clarity is that researchers need more access (Salas, Wilson-Donnelly, Burke and Wightman, under review). In addition, there needs to be a commitment to systematic long-term longitudinal studies that will serve to illustrate the impact that CRM training has on safety. It is particularly important that the aviation community heed this call as other industries are adopting CRM practices based on some empirical evidence, but more frequently on anecdotal evidence.

Principle 17: While challenging within complex operational environments, longitudinal evaluations of training's impact on the bottom line must be implemented as they are a necessary part of organisations seeking to maintain HRO status.

Concluding remarks

Despite the fact that the skies are becoming increasingly crowded and technology is putting increased cognitive demands on airline crews, the airline industry has been repeatedly commended for its safety record. Many have argued that a commitment to team training, as evidenced by the creation and implementation of crew resource management (CRM) training, is a key factor in aviation's ability to maintain a high safety record despite a complex environment. The theoretical knowledge that the team literature provides concerning the complexity of teamwork and factors that impact its effectiveness have served as drivers for the creation of CRM. Moreover, it is through the basic tenets and content contained within CRM that one can see the processes through which the aviation industry has created and maintained its status as a high reliability organisation. Specifically, CRM training promotes a: (a) commitment to resilience, (b) deference to expertise, (c) sensitivity to operations and (d) reluctance to simplify the environment. Moreover, the aviation industry exhibits a preoccupation with failure in its use of incident and mishap data, as well as accident data, as learning opportunities which are then fed into initial CRM training, as well as recurrent training.

The successfulness of CRM training has been strongly suggested as indicated by: (a) positive participant reactions and much anecdotal evidence, (b) learning and (c) the ability of trainees to apply learned competencies (see Salas et al., 2001). Due to the touted success of CRM, many organisations outside of the aviation community are beginning to adopt aviation training practices (e.g. firefighting, Lubnau and Okray, 2001; pharmacies, Jaklevic, 1997; merchant navy ships, Flin, 1995, nuclear plants, Helmreich, 1997; and medical service nursing, Brannon, 2001). As the use of this application of team training is beginning to generalise to other domains it becomes useful to extract some of the lessons that have been learned by the aviation community and propose how they may generalise to other organisations. Moreover, as we argue that CRM training has been a key driver of the aviation community's ability to become a high reliability organisation, we also hope that the evidence offered herein and the corresponding principles can further the progression toward an organisation's (including those in aviation) status as a HRO as well as highlighting some of the challenges that may be faced along the way.

References

Adler, N.J. (1997). *International dimensions of organizational behavior* (3rd edition). Cincinnati, OH: International Thomson Publishing.

Bass, B. (1990). *Bass and Stogdill's handbook of leadership (3rd ed.)*. New York: The Free Press.

Blickensderfer, E.L., Cannon-Bowers, J.A. and Salas, E. (1997). Training teams to self-correct: An empirical investigation. *Paper presented at the 12th annual meeting of the Society for Industrial and Organizational Psychology*, St. Louis, MO.

Bowers, C.A. and Jentsch, F. (2001). Use of commercial off-the-shelf, simulations for team research. In, *Advances in human performance and cognitive engineering research* (Vol. 1, pp. 293-317). Greenwich, CT: JAI Press.

Brannick, M., Roach, R. and Salas, E. (1993). Understanding team performance: A multimethod study. *Human Performance, 6*, 287-308.

Brannon, B.C. (2001, June 28). *Keeping government nurses on the job.* Department of the Air Force Presentation to the Committee on Appropriations Subcommittee on Defense United States Senate. Retrieved February 6, 2002, from the World Wide Web: http://ehostvgw8.epnet.com/ehost.asp?key=204.179.122.141_8000_2009 355424andsite=ehostandreturn=y.

Burke, C.S. (1999). *Examination of the cognitive mechanisms through which team leaders promote effective team processes and adaptive team performance.* Unpublished doctoral dissertation, George Mason University, Virginia.

Burke, C.S., Fiore, S. and Salas, E. (in press). The role of shared cognition in enabling shared leadership and team adaptability. To appear in J. Conger and C. Pearce (Eds.), *Shared leadership: Reframing the how's and why's of leadership.* London: Sage Publishers.

Byrnes, R.E. and Black, R. (1993). Developing and implementing CRM programs: The Delta experience. In, E.L. Wiener, B.G. Kanki and R.L. Helmreich (Eds.), *Cockpit resource management* (pp. 421-443). San Diego CA: Academic Press.

Cannon-Bowers J.A. and Salas E. (1997). A framework for developing team performance measures in training. In, M.T. Brannick, E. Salas and C. Prince (Eds.), *Team performance assessment and measurement: Theory, research and applications* (pp.45-62). Mahwah, NJ: Lawrence Erlbaum Associates.

Cannon-Bowers, J., Salas, E. and Converse, S. (1993). Shared mental models in expert team decision making. In, N.J. Castellan Jr. (Ed.). *Individual and group decision making: Current issues* (pp. 221-246). Hillsdale, NJ: Lawrence Erlbaum Associates.

Cannon-Bowers, J.A., Tannenbaum, S.I., Salas, E. and Volpe, C.E. (1995). Defining team competencies and establishing team training requirements. In, R. Guzzo, E. Salas and Associates (Eds.), *Team effectiveness and decision making in organizations* (pp. 333-380). San Francisco, CA: Jossey-Bass.

Dismukes, R.K., Jobe, K.K. and McDonnell, L.K. (2000). Facilitating LOFT debriefings: A critical analysis. In, R.K. Dismukes and G.M. Smith (Eds.), *Facilitation and debriefing in aviation training and operations* (pp. 13-25). Aldershot: Ashgate Publishing.

Dismukes, R.K and Smith, G.M. (Eds.) (2000). *Facilitation and debriefing in aviation training and operations.* Aldershot: Ashgate Publishing.

Driskell, J.E. and Adams, R.J. (1992). *Crew resource management: An introductory handbook.* Final Report. U.S. Department of Transportation: Federal Aviation Administration.

Driskell, J.E., Salas, E. and Johnston, J.H. (1999). Does stress lead to a loss of team performance? *Group Dynamics, 3,* 291-302.

Endsley, M.R. (1999). Situation awareness in aviation systems. In, D.J. Garland, J.A. Wise and V.D. Hopkin (Eds.), *Handbook of aviation human factors* (pp. 257-276). Mahwah, NJ: Lawrence Erlbaum Associates.

Flin, R.H. (1995). Crew resource management for teams in the offshore oil industry. *Journal of European Industrial Training, 19,* 23-27.

Fowlkes, J.E., Dwyer, D.J., Oser, R.L., Salas, E. (1998). Event-based approach to training (EBAT). *International Journal of Aviation Psychology, 8,* 209-221.

Foushee, H.C. (1984). Dyads and triads at 35,000 feet. *American Psychologist, 39,* 885-893.

Freeman, C. and Simmon, D.A. (1991). Taxonomy of crew resource management: information processing domain. In, R.S. Jensen (Ed.), *Proceedings of 6th Annual International Symposium on Aviation Psychology* (pp. 391-397). OH: The Ohio State University.

Gersick, C.J.G. (1988). Time and transition in work teams: Towards a new model of group development. *Academy of Management Review, 31,* 9-41.

Ginnett, R.C. (1993). Crews as groups: Their formation and their leadership. In, E.L. Wiener, B.G. Kanki and R.L. Helmreich (Eds.), *Cockpit resource management* (pp. 71-98). San Diego, CA: Academic Press.

Goldstein, I.L. (1993). *Training in organizations: Needs assessment, development and evaluation (3rd ed).* Monterey, CA: Brooks/Cole Publishing Company.

Gregorich, S.E. (1993). The dynamics of CRM attitude change: Attitude stability. In, *Proceedings of the 7th International Symposium on Aviation Psychology* (pp. 509-512). OH: The Ohio State University.

175

Guzzo, R.A. and Dickson, M.W. (1996). Teams and organizations: Recent research on performance and effectiveness. *Annual Review of Psychology, 47,* 307-338.

Hackman, J.R. and Morris, C.G. (1975). Group task, group interaction processes and group performance effectiveness: A review and proposed integration. *Advances in experimental social psychology, 8,* 45-99. New York: Academic Press.

Hackman, R.A. (Ed.). (1990). *Groups that work (and those that don't): Creating conditions for effective team work.* San Francisco: Jossey-Bass.

Helmreich, R.L. (1991). Strategies for the study of flightcrew behavior. In, R.S. Jensen (Ed.), *Proceedings of the 6th International Symposium on Aviation Psychology* (pp. 338-343). OH: The Ohio State University.

Helmreich, R.L. (1994). Anatomy of a system accident: The crash of Avianca Flight 052. *International Journal of Aviation Psychology, 4,* 265-284.

Helmreich, R.L. (1997). Training and evaluation through simulation in aviation and medicine. *Proceedings of the 1997 AERA Annual Meeting,* Chicago, IL.

Helmreich, R.L. (2000). On error management: lessons from aviation. *British Management Journal, 320,* 781-785.

Helmreich, R.L. and Foushee, H.C. (1993). Why crew resource management? Empirical and theoretical bases of human factors in aviation. In, E.L. Wiener, B.G. Kanki and R.L. Helmreich (Eds.), *Cockpit resource management* (pp. 3-45). San Diego, CA: Academic Press.

Helmreich, R.L. and Merritt, A.C. (1998a). *Error and error management.* Technical Report 98-03.

Helmreich, R. L. and Merritt, A. C. (1998b). *Culture at work in aviation and medicine: National, organizational and professional influences.* Aldershot: Ashgate Publishing.

Helmreich, R.L., Merritt, A.C. and Wilhelm, J.A. (1999). The evolution of crew resource management training in commercial aviation. *The International Journal of Aviation Psychology, 9,* 19-32.

Helmreich, R.L., Wiener, E.L. and Kanki, B.G. (1993). The future of crew resource management in the cockpit and elsewhere. In, E.L. Wiener, B.G. Kanki and R.L. Helmreich (Eds.), *Cockpit resource management* (pp. 479-501). San Diego, CA: Academic.

Helmreich, R.L., Wilhelm, J.A., Klinect, J.R. and Merritt, A.C. (2001). Culture, error and Crew Resource Management. In, E. Salas, C.A. Bowers and E. Edens (Eds.), *Improving Teamwork in Organizations: Applications of Resource Management Training* (pp. 305-331). Hillsdale, NJ: Erlbaum. (UTHFRP Pub254).

Hutchins, E., Holder, B.E. and Pérez, R.A. (2002). Culture and Flight Deck Operations. *Unpublished internal report prepared for the Boeing Company* [Sponsored Research Agreement 22-5003]. San Diego: University of California San Diego.

Ikomi, P.A., Boehm-Davis, D.A., Holt, R.W. and Incalcaterra, K.A. (1999). Jump seat observations of advanced crew resource management (ACRM) effectiveness. In, R.S. Jensen, B.Cox, J.D. Callister and R.Lavis (Eds.), *Proceedings of the 10th International Symposium on Aviation Psychology* (pp. 292-297). OH: The Ohio State University.

Ilgen, D.R., Major, D.A., Hollenbeck, J.R., Sego, D.J. (1993). Team research in the 1990s. In, M.M. Chemers and R. Ayman (Eds.), *Leadership theory and research* (pp. 245-271). San Diego, CA: Academic Press.

Irwin, C.M. (1991). The impact of initial and recurrent cockpit resource management training on attitudes. In, R.S. Jensen (Ed.), *Proceedings of the 6th International Symposium on Aviation Psychology* (pp. 344-349). OH: The Ohio State University.

Jackson, D.L. (1983). United Airlines' cockpit resource management training. In, R.S. Jensen (Ed.), *Proceedings of the 2nd Symposium on Aviation Psychology* (pp. 131-137). OH: The Ohio State University.

Jaklevic, M.C. (1997). *AMA group to look at quality issues. Modern Healthcare, 27*, 27.

Jentsch, F. and Smith-Jentsch, K.A. (2001). Assertiveness and team performance: More than 'just say no'. In, E. Salas, C.A. Bowers and E. Edens (Eds.), *Improving teamwork in organizations: Applications of resource management training* (pp. 73-94). Mahwah: New Jersey: Lawrence Erlbaum and Associates.

Kirkpatrick, D.L. (1976). Evaluation of training. In, R.L. Craig (Ed.), *Training and development handbook: A guide to human resources development* (pp. 18.1-18.27). New York, NY: McGraw-Hill.

Klair, M.B. (2000). The mediated debrief of problem flights. In, R.K. Dismukes and G.M. Smith (Eds.), *Facilitation and debriefing in aviation training and operations* (pp. 72-92). Aldershot: Ashgate Publishing.

Klein, G. (2000). Cognitive task analysis of teams. In, J.M. Schraagen and S.F. Chipman et al. (Eds), *Cognitive task analysis* (pp. 417-429). Mahwah, NJ: Lawrence Erlbaum Associates.

Kohn, L., Corrigan, J., Donaldson, M. (Eds.) (1999). *To Err is Human: Building a Safer Health System. Institute of Medicine.* Washington DC: National Academy Press.

Kozlowski, S.W.J., Gully, S.M., Nason, E.R., Ford, J.K., Smith, E.M., Smith, M.R. and Futch, C.J. (1994). A composition theory of team development: Levels, content, process and learning outcomes. In, J. Mathieu (Chair), *Developmental views of team processes and performance. Symposium conducted at the 9th annual conference of the Society for Industrial and Organizational Psychology,* Nashville, TN.

Kraiger K., Ford, J.K. and Salas, E. (1993). Application of cognitive, skill-based and affective theories of learning outcomes to new methods of training evaluation. *Journal of Applied Psychology, 78*, 311-328.

Lubnau, T.E. and Okray, R. (2001). Crew resource management for the fire service. *Fire Engineering, 154*, 99-107.

Marks, M.A., Zaccaro, S.J. and Mathieu, J.E. (2000). Performance implications of leader briefings and team interaction training for team adaptation to novel environments. *Journal of Applied Psychology, 85*, 971-986.

Maurino, D.E. (1999). Safety prejudices, training practices and CRM: A mid-point perspective. *The International Journal of Aviation Psychology, 9*, 413-427.

Maurino, D.E., Johnston, N., Reason, J. and Lee, R.B. (1995). *Beyond aviation human factors*. Aldershot, England: Avebury Aviation.

Morgan, B.B., Jr., Glickman, A.S., Woodard, E.A., Blaiwes, A.S. and Salas, E. (1986). *Measurement of team behaviors in a Navy environment* (Technical Report Number 86-014). Orlando, FL: Naval Training Systems Center.

National Transportation Safety Board (NTSB). (1979). *Aircraft accident report. United Airlines, Inc. McDonnell-Douglas DC-8-61, N8082U, Portland, Oregon, December 28, 1978 (Report No. NTSB-AAR-82-8)*. Washington, DC: Author.

O'Connor, P., Flin, R., Fletcher, G. and Hemsley, P. (2003). Methods used to evaluate the effectiveness of flightcrew CRM training in the UK aviation industry. *Human Factors and Aerospace Safety, 3, 1-17*.

Orasanu, J.M. (1990). *Shared mental models and crew performance*. Paper presented at the 34th annual meeting of the Human Factors Society, Orlando, FL.

Orlady, H.W. (1993). Airline pilot training today and tomorrow. In, E.L. Wiener, B.G. Kanki and R.L. Helmreich (Eds.), *Cockpit resource management* (pp. 447-477). San Diego, CA: Academic Press.

Orlady, H.W. and Orlady, L.M. (1999). *Human factors in multi-crew flight operations*. Aldershot: Ashgate Publishing.

Roberts, K.H. and Bea, R. (2001a). When systems fail. *Organizational Dynamics, 29*, 179-191.

Roberts, K.H. and Bea, R. (2001b). Must accidents happen? Lessons from high-reliability organizations. *Academy of Management Executive, 15*, 70-79.

Rouse, W.B., Cannon-Bowers, J.A. and Salas, E. (1992). The role of mental models in team performance in complex systems. *IEEE Transactions on Systems, Man and Cybernetics, 22*, 1296-1308.

Rouse, W.B. and Morris, N.M. (1986). On looking into the black box: Prospects and limits in the search for mental models. *Psychological Bulletin, 100*, 349-363.

Salas, E., Bowers, C.A. and Edens, E. (Eds.). (2001). *Improving teamwork in organizations: Applications of resource management training*. Mahwah, NJ: Lawrence Erlbaum Associates.

Salas, E., Bowers, C.A. and Rhodenizer, L. (1998). It is not how much you have but how you use it: Toward a rational use of simulation to support aviation training. *International Journal of Aviation Psychology, 8*, 197-208.

Salas, E., Burke, C.S. and Cannon-Bowers, J.A. (2000). Teamwork: Emerging principles. *International Journal of Management Reviews, 2*, 339-356.

Salas, E., Burke, C.S., Bowers, C.A. and Wilson, K.A. (in press). Team training in the skies: Does crew resource management (CRM) training work? To appear in Human Factors.

Salas, E., Burke, C.S. and Stagl, K. (2004). Developing teams and team leaders: Strategies and principles. In, D. Day, S.J. Zaccaro and S.M. Halpin (Eds.), *Leader development for transforming organizations* (pp. 325-355). Mahwah, NJ: Lawrence Erlbaum Associates, Inc.

Salas, E. and Cannon-Bowers, J.A. (2000). The anatomy of team training. In, S. Tobias and J.D. Fletcher (Eds.), *Training and retraining: A handbook for business, industry, government and the military* (pp. 312-335). New York: Macmillan Reference.

Salas, E. and Cannon-Bowers, J.A. (2001). The science of training: A decade of progress. *Annual Review of Psychology, 52*, 471-499.

Salas, E., Cannon-Bowers, J.A., Fiore, S.M. and Stout, R.J. (2001). Cue-recognition training to enhance team situation awareness. In, M. McNeese, E. Salas and M. Endsley (Eds.), *New trends in cooperative activities: Understanding system dynamics in complex environments* (pp. 169-190). Santa Monica, CA: Human Factors and Ergonomics Society.

Salas, E., Prince, C., Bowers, C., Stout, R., Oser, R.L. and Cannon-Bowers, J.A. (1999). A methodology for enhancing crew resource management training. *Human Factors, 41*, 161-172.

Salas, E., Wilson-Donnelly, K.A., Burke, C.S. and Wightman, D.C. (under review). Does CRM training work? An update, extension and some critical needs. Submitted to Human Factors Journal.

Sarter, N.B. and Alexander, H.M. (2000). Error types and related error detection mechanisms in the aviation domain: An analysis of Aviation Safety Reporting System incident reports. *The International Journal of Aviation Psychology, 10*, 189-206.

Sexton, J.B., Thomas, E.J. and Helmreich, R.L. (2000). Error, stress and teamwork in medicine and aviation: cross sectional surveys. *British Management Journal, 320*, 745-749.

Sietzen, F. (2001). Without WTC - air accidents down in 2001. *MedServ Medical News*. Retrieved March 12, 2002 from http://www.medserv.no/article.php? sid=1225.

Stout, R.J., Cannon-Bowers, J.A. and Salas, E. (1996). The role of shared mental models in developing team situational awareness: Implications for training. *Training Research Journal, 2*, 85-116.

Sundstrom, E., deMeuse, K. and Futrell, D. (1990). Work teams: Applications and effectiveness. *American Psychologist, 45*, 120-133.

Swezey, R.W. and Salas, E. (1992). (Eds.), *Teams: Their training and performance*. Norwood, NJ: Ablex.

Taggart, W.R. (1994). Crew resource management: Achieving enhanced flight. In, N. Johnston, N. McDonald and R. Fuller (Eds.), *Aviation psychology in practice*. England: Avebury.

Thomas, D.C. (1999). Cultural diversity and work group effectiveness. *Journal of Cross-cultural Psychology, 30*, 242-263.

Triandis, H.C. (2000). Culture and conflict. *International Journal of Psychology, 35*, 145-152.

US Department of Transportation Bureau of Statistics. (2001). *Airport Activity Statistics of Certificated Air Carriers Summary Tables: Twelve Months Ending December 31, 2000* (Report No. BTS01-05). Retrieved February 15, 2002, from http://www.bts.gov/publications/airactstats2000/.

US Department of Transportation (2001). *Crew resource management training. Advisory Circular #120-51D*. Federal Aviation Administration.

United States General Accounting Office (1997). *Human Factors: FAA's guidance and oversight of pilot crew resource management training can be improved.* (GAO/RCED-98-7). Washington, DC: GAO Report to Congressional Requesters.

Weick, K.E. and Sutcliffe, K.M. (2001). *Managing the unexpected: Assuring high performance in an age of complexity*. San Francisco: Jossey-Bass.

Westrum, R. and Adamski, A.J. (1999). Organizational factors associated with safety and mission success in aviation environments. In, D.J. Garland and J.A. Wise (Eds.), *Handbook of aviation human factors* (pp. 67-104). Mahwah, NJ: Lawrence Erlbaum Associates.

Wiener, E.L., Kanki, B.G. and Helmreich, R.L. (Eds.). (1993). *Cockpit resource management*. San Diego CA: Academic Press.

Zaccaro, S.J., Rittman, A. and Marks, M.A. (2001). Team leadership. *Leadership Quarterly, 12*, 451-483.

9 Why we need new accident models

Sidney W.A. Dekker

Abstract

The models we currently use to understand aerospace safety and accidents are based on a structuralist vocabulary, with mechanistic metaphors that describe the internal workings or failings of operators and their surrounding organisations. Such a view may be increasingly at odds with interpretative demands posed by recent accidents in otherwise very safe systems. Particularly the drift into failure, which represents a large category of residual risk in aerospace, is hard to model (and thereby understand and predict) with structuralist approaches. Drifting into failure is not so much about breakdowns or malfunctioning of components, but about an organisation not adapting effectively to the complexity of its structure and environment. This requires aerospace to adopt a true systems approach, which sees sociotechnical complexity not as constituted of parts and their interactions, but as a web of dynamic, evolving relationships and transactions. This can lead to models that can make processes of drift come alive, and help point to more productive countermeasures.

Introduction

The greatest residual risk in today's safe aerospace systems is drift into failure. Drift into failure is a slow, incremental movement of systems operations towards the edge of their safety envelope. This movement is driven by pressures of scarcity and competition that subtly influence the many decisions and trade-offs made daily by operators and management hierarchies. The intransparency of complex sociotechnical systems that surround the operation of uncertain technology makes that people do not stop the drift (e.g. Perrow, 1984; Vaughan, 1996). Often they do not even see it. Accidents that lie at the end of drift are 'the effect of a systematic migration of organisational behaviour toward accidents

This paper was first published in Human Factors and Aerospace Safety 4(1), 2004, pp. 1-18

under the influence of pressure towards cost-effectiveness in an aggressive, competitive environment' (Rasmussen and Svedung, 2000, p. 14). Drift into failure is hard to recognise because it is about normal people doing normal work in (seemingly) normal organisations, not about obvious breakdowns or failures or errors. Drift into failure is scary for all kinds of stakeholders because it reveals how harm can occur in organisations designed to prevent it. Drift into failure is also difficult to model and predict using current approaches in aerospace human factors. These are largely limited to a structuralist vocabulary. Our language of failures is a language of mechanics. We describe accident 'trajectories', we seek causes and effects, interactions. We look for 'initiating failures', or triggering events, and trace the successive domino-like collapse of the system that follows it. This worldview sees sociotechnical systems as machines with parts in a particular arrangement (blunt versus sharp ends, defenses layered throughout), with particular interactions (trajectories, domino effects, triggers, initiators), and a mix of independent or intervening variables (blame culture versus safety culture). This is the worldview inherited from Descartes and Newton, the worldview that has successfully driven technological development since the scientific revolution half a millennium ago. The worldview, and the language that accompanies it, is based on particular notions of natural science, and exercises a subtle but very powerful influence on our understanding of sociotechnical success and failure today. Yet this worldview may be lagging behind the sociotechnical developments that have taken place in aerospace, leaving us less than well equipped to understand failure, let alone anticipate or prevent it. This paper looks at a case of drift into failure, and proposes how we may need new kinds of models to capture the workings and predict

Drifting into failure

The 2000 Alaska Airlines 261 accident is an example of drift. The MD-80 crashed into the Ocean off California after the trim system in its tail snapped. *Prima facie*, the accident seems to fit a simple category that has come to dominate recent accident statistics: mechanical failures as a result of poor maintenance. A single component failed because people did not maintain it well. Indeed, there was a catastrophic failure of a single component (a jackscrew-nut assembly). A mechanical failure, in other words. The break instantly rendered the aircraft uncontrollable and sent it plummeting into the Pacific. But such accidents do not happen just because somebody suddenly errs or something suddenly breaks: there is supposed to be too much built-in protection against the effects of single failures. Consistent with the patterns of drift into failure, it were the protective structures, the surrounding organisations (including the regulator) that themselves contributed, in ways inadvertent, unforeseen and hard to detect. The organised social complexity surrounding the technological operation, the maintenance committees, working groups, regulatory interventions and approvals, manufacturer inputs, all intended to protect the system from breakdown, actually helped set its course to the edge of the envelope and across.

In Alaska 261, the drift towards the accident that happened in 2000 had begun decades before, during the first flights of the 1965 Douglas DC-9 that preceded the MD-80 type. In the MD-80 trim system, the front part of the horizontal stabiliser is connected to a nut which drives up and down a vertical jackscrew. An electrical trim motor rotates the jackscrew, which in turn drives the nut up or down. The nut then pushes the whole horizontal tail up or down. Adequate lubrication is critical for the functioning of a jackscrew and nut assembly. Without enough grease, the constant grinding will wear out the thread on either the nut or the screw (in this case the screw is deliberately made of harder material, wearing the nut out first). The thread actually carries the entire load that is imposed on the vertical tail during flight. This is a load of around 5,000 pounds, similar to the weight of a whole family sedan hanging by the thread of a jackscrew and nut assembly. Were the thread to wear out on an MD-80, the nut would fail to catch the threads of the jackscrew. Aerodynamic forces then push the horizontal tailplane (and the nut) to its stop way out of the normal range, rendering the aircraft uncontrollable in the pitch axis. Which is essentially what happened to Alaska 261. Even the stop failed because of the pressure. A so-called torque tube runs through the jackscrew in order to provide redundancy (instead of having two jackscrews, like in the preceding DC-8 model). But even the torque tube failed in Alaska 261.

None of this is supposed to happen of course. When it first launched the aircraft in the mid 1960s, Douglas recommended that operators lubricate the trim jackscrew assembly every 300 to 350 flight hours. For typical commercial usage that could mean grounding the aeroplane for such maintenance every few weeks. Immediately, the socio-technical, organisational systems surrounding the operation of the technology began to adapt. And set the system on its course to drift. Through a variety of changes and developments in maintenance guidance for the DC-9/MD-80 series aircraft, the lubrication interval was extended. A complex and constantly evolving web of committees with representatives from regulators, manufacturers, subcontractors and operators was at the heart of a development of maintenance standards, documents and specifications. Rationality for maintenance interval decisions was produced relatively locally, relying on incomplete, emerging information about what was, for all its deceiving basicness, still uncertain technology. While each decision was locally rational, making sense for decision makers in their time and place, the global picture became one of drift towards disaster.

Significant drift, in fact. Starting from a lubrication interval of 300 hours, the interval at the time of the Alaska 261 accident had moved up to 2,550 hours, almost an order of magnitude more. As is typical in the drift towards failure, this distance was not bridged in one leap. The slide was incremental: step by step; decision by decision. In 1985, jackscrew lubrication was to be accomplished every 700 hours, at every other so-called maintenance 'B check' (which occurs every 350 flight hours). In 1987, the B-check interval itself was increased to 500 flight hours, pushing lubrication intervals to 1000 hours. In 1988, B checks were eliminated altogether, and tasks to be accomplished were redistributed over A and C checks. The jackscrew assembly lubrication was to be done each eighth 125-hour A check: still every 1,000 flight hours. But in 1991, A check intervals were extended to 150 flight hours, leaving a lubrication every 1,200 hours. Three years later the A check interval was extended again, this time to 200 hours. Lubrication would now happen every 1,600 flight hours. In 1996, the jackscrew assembly lubrication task was removed from the A check and moved instead to a so-called task card that specified lubrication every eight months. There was no longer an accompanying flight hour limit. For Alaska Airlines eight months translated to about 2,550 flight hours. The jackscrew recovered from the ocean floor, however, revealed no evidence that there had been adequate lubrication at the previous interval at all. It might have been more than 5,000 hours since it last received a coat of fresh grease.

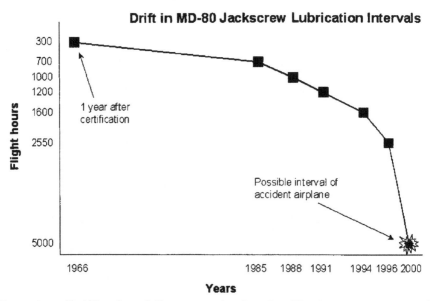

Figure 1   **Drifting into failure over the decades. The jackscrew lubrication interval gradually got extended (almost by a factor of 10) until the Alaska Airlines 261 accident**

After only a year of DC-9 flying, Douglas received reports of thread wear significantly in excess of what had been predicted. In response, the manufacturer recommended that operators perform a so-called end-play check on the jackscrew assembly at every maintenance C-check, or every 3,600 flight hours. The end-play check uses a restraining fixture that puts pressure on the jackscrew assembly, simulating the aerodynamic load during normal flight. The amount of play between nut and screw, gauged in thousandths of an inch, can then be read off an instrument. The play is a direct measure of the amount of thread wear.

From 1985 onwards, end-play checks at Alaska became subject to the same kind of drift as the lubrication intervals. In 1985, end-play checks were scheduled every other C check, since the required C checks consistently came in at 2,500 hours. 2,500 hours was rather ahead of the recommended 3,600 flight hours, unnecessarily grounding aircraft. By scheduling an end-play test every other C check, though, the interval was extended to 5000 hours. By 1988, C check intervals themselves were extended to 13 months, with no accompanying flight-hour limit. End-play checks were now performed every 26 months, or about every 6,400 flight hours. In 1996, C check intervals were extended once again, this time to 15 months. This stretched the flight hours between end-play tests to about 9,550. The last end-play check of the accident aeroplane was conducted at the airline maintenance facility in Oakland, California in 1997. At that time, play between nut and screw was found to be exactly at the allowable limit of .040 inch. This introduced considerable uncertainty. With play at the allowable limit, what to do? Release the aeroplane and replace parts the next time, or replace the parts now? The rules were not clear. The so-called AOL 9-48A said 'that jackscrew assemblies could remain in service as long as the end-play measurement remained within the tolerances (between 0.003 and 0.040 inch)' (NTSB, 2002; p. 29). It was still 0.040 inch, so the aircraft could technically remain in service. Or? How quickly would the thread wear from there on? Six days, several shift changes and another, more favourable end-play check later, the aeroplane was released. No parts were replaced: they were not even in stock in Oakland. The aeroplane 'departed 0300 local time. So far so good', the graveyard shift turnover plan noted (ibid. p. 53). Three years later the trim system snapped and the aircraft disappeared into the ocean not far away. Between 2,500 hours to 9,550 hours there is more drift toward failure. Again, each extension made local sense, and was only an increment away from the previously established norm. No rules were violated, no laws broken. Even the regulator concurred with the changes in end-play check intervals. Normal people doing normal work around seemingly normal, stable technology.

MD-80 maintenance technicians were never required to record or keep track of the end-play on the trim systems they measured. Even the manufacturer had expressed no interest in seeing these numbers or the slow, steady degeneration they may have revealed. If there was drift, in other words, no institutional or organisational memory would know it. The decisions, trade-offs, preferences and priorities which seem so out of the ordinary and immoral after an accident, were once normal and common sensical to those who contributed to its incubation.

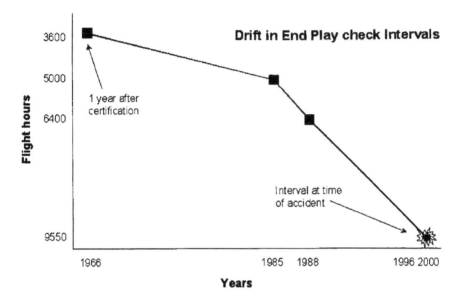

Figure 2   **More drift into failure. The end-play check interval (which gauges thread wear on the jackscrew-nut assembly) was stretched from 3,600 to 9,550 flight hours**

Banality, conflict and incrementalism

Sociological research (e.g. Perrow, 1984; Weick, 1995; Vaughan, 1996; Snook, 2000) as well as prescient human factors work (Rasmussen and Svedung, 2000) and research on system safety (Leveson, 2004) has begun to sketch some of the internal workings of drift. They converge on some important commonalities. First, accidents, and the drift that precedes them, are associated with normal people doing normal work in normal organisations -- not with miscreants engaging in immoral deviance. We can call this the 'banality of accidents' thesis. Second, at the heart of trouble lies a conflictual model: organisations that involve safety-critical work are essentially trying to reconcile irreconcilable goals (staying safe *and* staying in business). Third, drifting into failure is incremental. Accidents do not happen suddenly, nor are they preceded by monumentally bad decisions or bizarrely huge steps away from the ruling norm.

    The banality of accidents thesis says that the potential for having an accident grows as a normal by-product of doing normal business under normal pressures of resource scarcity and competition. No system is immune to the pressures of scarcity and competition (not even (or certainly not) regulators). The chief engine of drift hides somewhere in this conflict, in this tension between operating safely and operating at all.

In trade-offs between safety and efficiency there is a feedback imbalance. Information on whether a decision is cost-effective or efficient can be relatively easy to get. An early arrival time is measurable and has immediate, tangible benefits. How much is or was borrowed from safety in order to achieve that goal, however, is much more difficult to quantify and compare. If it was followed by a safe landing, apparently it must have been a safe decision. Extending a lubrication interval similarly saves immediately measurable time and money, while borrowing from the future of an apparently problem-free jackscrew assembly. Each consecutive empirical success (the early arrival time is still a 'safe' landing; the jackscrew assembly is still operational) seems to confirm that fine-tuning (Starbuck and Milliken, 1988) is working well: the system can operate equally safely, yet more efficiently. As Weick (1993) points out, however, safety in those cases may not at all be the result of the decisions that were or were not made, but rather an underlying stochastic variation that hinges on a host of other factors, many not easily within the control of those who engage in the fine-tuning process. Empirical success, in other words, is not proof of safety. Past success does not guarantee future safety. Borrowing more and more from safety may go well for a while, but you never know when you are going to hit. This moves Langewiesche (1998) to say that Murphy's law is wrong: everything that can go wrong usually goes right. And then we draw the wrong conclusion.

The nature of this dynamic, this fine-tuning, this adaptation, is incremental (Vaughan, 1996). The organisational decisions that are seen as 'bad decisions' after the accident (even though they seemed like perfectly acceptable ideas at the time) are seldom big, risky steps. Rather, there is a long and steady progression of small, incremental steps that unwittingly take an operation toward its boundaries. Each step away from the original norm that meets with empirical success (and no obvious sacrifice of safety) is used as the next basis from which to depart just that little bit more. It is this incrementalism that makes distinguishing the abnormal from the normal so difficult. If the difference between what 'should be done' (or what was done successfully yesterday) and what is done successfully today is minute, then this slight departure from an earlier established norm is not worth remarking or reporting on.

Drift into failure and incident reporting

This makes the definition of an incident deeply problematic. Before 1985, failing to perform an end-play check every 2,500 hours could be considered an 'incident', and given that the organisation had a means for reporting it, it may even have been considered as such. But by 1996, the same deviance was normal. Regulated even. By 1996, the same failure was no longer an incident.

And there was more. Why report that lubricating the jackscrew assembly often had to be done at night, in the dark, outside the hanger, standing in the little basket of a lift truck at a soaring height above the ground? Even when it was raining (which it does do in San Francisco)? Why report that you, as a mechanic have to fumble your way through two small access panels that hardly allow room for one human hand – let alone space for eyes to see what is going on inside and what needs to be lubricated – if that is what you have to do all the time? It was normal work; it was required to get the job done. The mechanic responsible for the last lubrication of the accident aeroplane told investigators that he had taken to wearing a battery-operated head lamp during night lubrication tasks, so that he had his hands free and could see at least something (NTSB, 2002). Though perhaps remarkable after the fact, these things were 'normal' then, they were not reportworthy. They were not 'incidents'. Why report that the end-play checks were performed with one restraining fixture (the only one in the entire airline, fabricated in-house, nowhere near the manufacturer's specifications), if that is what you used every time you did an end-play check? Why report that end-play checks, either on the aeroplane or on the bench, generated widely varying measures, if that is what they did all the time, and if that is what maintenance work is often about? It is normal; it is not an incident. Even if the airline had a reporting culture, even if it had a 'learning culture', even if it had a 'just' culture so that people would feel secure in sending in their reports without fear of retribution, these would not be 'incidents' that would turn up in the system. The failure to adequately see the part to be lubricated (that non-redundant, single-point, ultra safety-critical part), the failure to adequately and reliably perform an end-play check – none of this appears in incident reports. But it is deemed 'causal' or 'contributory' in the accident report. These were not incidents. In very safe systems, such as commercial aviation in the Western world, incidents do not precede accidents. Normal work does. In these systems, the common cause hypothesis (that incidents and accidents stem from the same root) is false, and the value of incident reporting for making even greater progress on safety is dubious:

> accidents are different in nature from those occurring in safe systems: in this case accidents usually occur in the absence of any serious breakdown or even of any serious error. They result from a combination of factors, none of which can alone cause an accident, or even a serious incident; therefore these combinations remain difficult to detect and to recover using traditional safety analysis logic. For the same reason, reporting becomes less relevant in predicting major disasters. (Amalberti, 2001, p. 112).

Despite this insight, independent errors and failures are still the major return of any accident investigation today. The 2002 NTSB report on flight 261, following Newtonian-Cartesian logic, speaks of deficiencies in Alaska Airlines' maintenance programme, of shortcomings in regulatory oversight, of responsibilities not fulfilled, of flaws and failures and breakdowns. Of course, in hindsight they may well be just that. And finding faults and failures is fine because it gives the system something to fix. But why did nobody at the time see these so very apparent faults and failures for what they (in hindsight) were? This is where the structuralist vocabulary of traditional human factors and systems safety is most limited, and limiting. The 'holes' found in the 'layers of defence' (respectively the regulator, the manufacturer, the operator, the maintenance facility and lastly the technician) are easy to discover once the rubble is strewn before one's feet. But these deficiencies and failures are not seen as such, nor easy to see as such, by those on the inside (or even those relatively on the outside, like the regulator!) before the accident happens. Indeed, structuralist models can capture the 'deficiencies' that result from drift very well: it accurately identifies latent failures, resident pathogens in organisations and locates the holes in the layers of defence. But the build-up of 'latent failures', if that is what you want to call them, is not modelled. The *process* of erosion, of attrition of safety norms, of drift towards margins, cannot be captured well by structuralist approaches, for those are inherently metaphors for resulting *forms*, not models oriented at processes of *formation*. Structuralist models are static.

Although the structuralist models of the 1990s are often called system models or systemic models, they are a far cry from what actually is considered systems thinking (e.g. Capra, 1982). The systems part of structuralist models has so far been limited to identifying, and providing a vocabulary for the upstream structures (blunt ends) behind the production of 'errors' at the sharp end. The systems part of these models is a reminder that there is context; that we cannot understand errors without going into the organisational background from which they hail. All of this is necessary, of course, as 'errors' are still all to often seen as the legitimate conclusion of an investigation (although under more fashionable labels such as 'breakdown in CRM'). But reminding people of context is no substitute for beginning to explain the dynamics; the subtle, incremental processes that lead to, and normalise, the behaviour eventually observed. This requires us to take a different perspective on the messy interior of organisations, and a different language to cast the observations in.

Systems as dynamic relationships

Capturing and describing the processes by which organisations drift into failure requires systems thinking. Systems thinking is about relationships and integration. It sees a sociotechnical system not as a structure consisting of constituent departments, blunt ends and sharp ends, deficiencies and flaws, but as a complex web of dynamic, evolving relationships and transactions. Instead of building blocks, the systems approach emphasises principles of organisation. Understanding the whole is quite different from understanding an assembly of separate components. Instead of mechanical linkages between components (with a cause and an effect), it sees transactions – simultaneous and mutually interdependent interactions. Such emergent properties are destroyed when the system is dissected and studied as a bunch of isolated components (a manager, department, regulator, manufacturer, operator). Emergent properties do not exist at lower levels; they cannot even be described meaningfully with languages appropriate for those lower levels.

Take the lengthy, multiple processes by which maintenance guidance was produced for the DC-9 and later the MD-80 series aircraft. Separate components (such as regulator, manufacturer, operator) are difficult to distinguish, and the interesting behaviour, the kind of behaviour that helps drive drift into failure, emerges only as a result of complex relationships and transactions. At first thought the creation of maintenance guidance would seem a solved problem. You build a product, you get the regulator to certify it as safe to use, and then you tell the user how to maintain it in order to keep it safe. Even the second step (getting it certified as safe) is nowhere near a solved problem, and deeply intertwined with the third. But more about that later. First the maintenance guidance. Alaska 261 reveals a large gap between the production of a system and its operation. Inklings of the gap appeared in observations of jackscrew wear that was higher than what the manufacturer expected. Not long after the certification of the DC-9, people began work to try to bridge the gap. An aviation industry team Maintenance Guidance Steering Group (MSG) was set up to develop guidance documentation for maintaining large transport aircraft (particularly the Boeing 747) (see NTSB, 2002). Using this experience, another MSG developed a new guidance document in 1970, called MSG-2, which was intended to present a means for developing a maintenance program acceptable to the regulator, the operator and the manufacturer. The many discussions, negotiations and inter-organisational collaborations underlying the development of an 'acceptable maintenance program' showed that how to maintain a once certified piece of complex technology was not at all a solved problem. In fact, it was very much an emergent thing: technology proved less certain than it had seemed on the drawing board (e.g. the DC-9 jackscrew wear rates were higher than predicted), and it was not before it hit the field of practice that 'deficiencies' became apparent. If you knew where to look, that is.

In 1980, through combined efforts of the regulator, trade and industry groups and manufacturers of both aircraft and engines in the US as well as Europe, a third guidance document was produced, called MSG-3. This document had to de-confound earlier confusions, for example between 'hard-time' maintenance, 'on-condition' maintenance, 'condition-monitoring' maintenance, and 'overhaul' maintenance. Revisions to MSG-3 were issued in 1988 and 1993. The MSG guidance documents and their revisions were accepted by the regulators, and used by so-called Maintenance Review Boards (MRB) that convene to develop guidance for specific aircraft models. The MRB does not write guidance itself, however, this is done by industry steering committees, often headed by a regulator. These committees in turn direct various working groups. Through all of this, so-called on-aircraft maintenance planning (OAMP) documents get produced, as well as generic task cards that outline specific maintenance jobs. Both the lubrication interval and the end-play check for MD-80 trim jackscrews were the constantly changing products of these evolving webs of relationships between manufacturers, regulators, trade groups, and operators, who were operating off of continuously renewed operational experience, and a perpetually incomplete knowledge base about the still uncertain technology (remember, end-play check results, for example, were not recorded or tracked). What are the rules? What should the standards be? The introduction of a new piece of technology is followed by negotiation, by discovery, by the creation of new relationships and rationalities. 'Technical systems turn into models for themselves', says Weingart (1991, p. 8): 'the observation of their functioning, and especially their malfunctioning, on a real scale is required as a basis for further technical development.' Rules and standards do not exist as unequivocal, aboriginal markers against a tide of incoming operational data (and if they do, they are quickly proven useless or out of date). Rather, rules and standards are the constantly updated products of the processes of conciliation, of give and take, of the detection and rationalisation of new data. Setting up the various teams, working groups and committees was a way of bridging the gap between building and maintaining a system, between producing it and operating it. Bridging the gap is about adaptation – adaptation to newly emerging data (e.g. surprising wear rates) about an uncertain technology. But adaptation can mean drift. And drift can mean breakdown.

Modelling live sociotechnical systems

What kind of safety model could capture such adaptation, and predict its eventual collapse? Structuralist models are limited. Of course, we could claim that the lengthy lubrication interval and the unreliable end-play check were structural deficiencies. That they were holes in layers of defence? Absolutely. But such metaphors do not help us look for where the hole occurred, or why. There is something complexly organic about MSG's, something ecological, that is lost when we model them as a layer of defence with a hole in it; when we see them as a mere 'deficiency' or a latent failure. When we see systems instead as internally plastic, as flexible, we can begin to see them as organic. Their functioning is controlled by dynamic relations and ecological adaptation, rather than by rigid mechanical structures. They also exhibit self-organisation (from year to year, the make-up of MSG's was different) in response to environmental changes, and self-transcendence: the ability to reach out beyond currently known boundaries and

191

learn, develop and perhaps improve. What is needed is not yet another structural account of the end result of organisational deficiency. What is needed instead is a more functional account of living processes that co-evolve with respect to a set of environmental conditions, and that maintain a dynamic and reciprocal relation with those conditions (see Heft, 2001). Such accounts need to capture what happens within an organisation, with the gathering of knowledge and creation of rationality within workgroups, once a technology gets fielded. A functional account could cover the organic organisation of maintenance steering groups and committees, whose make-up, focus, problem definition and understanding co-evolved with emerging anomalies and growing knowledge about an uncertain technology.

A model that is sensitive to the *creation* of deficiencies, not just to their eventual presence, makes a sociotechnical system come alive, rather than the static simile of a structuralist metaphor. It must be a model of processes, not just a model of structure. Extending a lineage of cybernetic and systems engineering research, Nancy Leveson (2002) proposes that control models can fulfil part of this task. Control models use the ideas of hierarchies and constraints to represent the emergent interactions of a complex system. In their conceptualisation, a sociotechnical system consists of different levels, where each super-ordinate level imposes constraints on (or controls what is going on in) subordinate levels. Control models are one way to begin to map the dynamic relationships between different levels within a system – a critical ingredient of moving toward true systems thinking (where dynamic relationships and transactions are dominant, not structure and components). Emergent behaviour is associated with the limits or constraints on the degrees of freedom of a particular level.

The division into hierarchical levels is an analytic artefact necessary to see how system behaviour can emerge from those interactions and relationships. The resulting levels in a control model are of course a product of the analyst who maps the model onto the sociotechnical system. Rather than reflections of some reality out there, the patterns are constructions of a human mind looking for answers to particular questions. For example, a particular MSG would probably not see how it is super-ordinate to some level and imposing constraints on it, or subordinate to some other and thus subject to its constraints. In fact, a one-dimensional hierarchical representation (with only up and down along one direction) probably oversimplifies the dynamic web of relationships surrounding (and determining the functioning of) any such multi-party, evolving group as an MSG. But all models are simplifications, and the levels analogy can be helpful for an analyst who has particular questions in mind (why did these people at this level or in this group make the decisions they did, and why did they see that as the only rational way to go?).

Control among levels in a sociotechnical system is hardly ever perfect. In order to control effectively, any controller needs a good model of what it is supposed to control, and it requires feedback about the effectiveness of its control. But such internal models of the controllers easily become inconsistent with, and do not match the system to be controlled (Leveson, 2002). Buggy control models are true especially with uncertain, emerging technology (including trim jackscrews) and the maintenance requirements surrounding them. Feedback about the effectiveness of control is incomplete and can be unreliable too. A lack of jackscrew-related incidents may provide the illusion that maintenance control is effective and that intervals can be extended, while the paucity of risk actually depends on factors quite outside the controller's scope. In this sense, the imposition of constraints on the degrees of freedom is mutual between levels and not just top-down: if subordinate levels generate imperfect feedback about their functioning, then higher-order levels do not have adequate resources (degrees of freedom) to act as would be necessary. Thus the subordinate level imposes constraints on the superordinate level by not telling (or not being able to tell) what is really going on. Such a dynamic has been noted in various cases of drift into failure, including the Challenger Space Shuttle disaster (see Feynman, 1988).

Drift into failure as erosion of constraints and eventual loss of control

Nested control loops can make a model of a sociotechnical system come alive more easily than a line of layers of defence. And in order to model drift, it *has* to come alive. Control theory sees drift into failure as a gradual erosion of the quality or the enforcement of safety constraints on the behaviour of subordinate levels. Drift results from either missing or inadequate constraints on what goes on at other levels. Modelling an accident as a sequence of events, in contrast, is really only modelling the end-product of such erosion and loss of control. If safety is seen as a control problem, then events (just like the 'holes' in layers of defence) are the *results* of control problems, not the causes that drive a system into disaster. A sequence of events, in other words, is at best the starting point of modelling an accident, not the analytic conclusion. The processes that generate these weaknesses are in need of a model.

One type of erosion of control occurs because original engineering constraints (e.g. 300-hour intervals) are loosened in response to the accumulation of operational experience. Such loosening occurs in response to local concerns with limited time-horizons and based on uncertain, incomplete knowledge. Often it is not even clear to insiders that constraints have become less tight as a result of their decisions in the first place, or that it at all matters if they have. And even when it is clear, the consequences may be hard to foresee, and judged to be a small potential loss in relation to the immediate gains. As Leveson (2002) puts it, experts do their best to meet local conditions, and in the busy daily flow and complexity of activities they may be unaware of any potentially dangerous side effects of those decisions. It is only with the benefit of hindsight or omniscient oversight (which is utopian) that these side-effects can be linked to actual risk.

Being a member of a system, then, can make systems thinking all but impossible. Perrow (1984) makes this argument very persuasively, and not just for the system's insiders. An increase in system complexity diminishes the system's transparency: diverse elements interact in a greater variety of ways that are difficult to foresee, detect, or even comprehend. Influences from outside the technical knowledge base exert a subtle but powerful pressure on the kinds of decisions and trade-offs that people will make, and constrain what will be seen as a rational decision or course of action at the time (Vaughan, 1996). It is in these normal, day-to-day processes that we can find the seeds of organisational failure and success. And it is these processes we must turn to in order to find leverage for making further progress on safety. As Rasmussen and Svedung (2000, p. 14) put it:

> To plan for a proactive risk management strategy, we have to understand the mechanisms generating the actual behavior of decision-makers at all levels ... an approach to proactive risk management involves the following analyses:
> - a study of normal activities of the actors who are preparing the landscape of accidents during their normal work, together with an analysis of the work features that shape their decision making behavior
> - A study of the present information environment of these actors and the information flow structure, analyzed from a control theoretic point of view.

Reconstructing or studying the 'information environment' in which actual decisions are shaped; in which local rationality is constructed, can help us penetrate processes of organisational sense-making. These processes lie at the root of organisational learning and adaptation, and thereby at the source of drift into failure. The narrowness and incompleteness of the niche in which decision makers find themselves can come across as disquieting to retrospective observers, including people inside and outside the organisation. It was after the Space Shuttle Columbia accident that the Mission Management Team 'admitted that the analysis used to continue flying was, in a word, 'lousy'. This admission – that the rationale to fly was rubber-stamped – is, to say the least, unsettling.' (CAIB, 2003; p. 190)

'Unsettling' it may be, and probably is – in hindsight. But from the inside, people in organisations do not spend a professional life making 'unsettling' decisions. Rather, they do mostly normal work. Again, how can a manager see a 'lousy' process to evaluate flight safety as normal, as not something that is worthy reporting or repairing? How could this process be normal? The CAIB itself provides clues to answers in their allusion to pressures of scarcity and competition:

> The Flight Readiness process is supposed to be shielded from outside influence, and is viewed as both rigorous and systematic. Yet the Shuttle

Program is inevitably influenced by external factors, including, in the case of STS-107, schedule demands. Collectively, such factors shape how the Program establishes mission schedules and sets budget priorities, which affects safety oversight, workforce levels, facility maintenance, and contractor workloads. Ultimately, external expectations and pressures impact even data collection, trend analysis, information development, and the reporting and disposition of anomalies. These realities contradict NASA's optimistic belief that pre-flight reviews provide true safeguards against unacceptable hazards. (2003, p. 191).

Perhaps there is no such thing as 'rigorous and systematic' decision-making based on technical expertise alone. This is probably an illusion. Expectations and pressures, budget priorities and mission schedules, contractor workloads and workforce levels all impact technical decision making. All these factors determine and constrain what people there and then see as rational or unremarkable. While the intention was that NASA's flight safety evaluations were 'shielded' from those external pressures, these pressures nonetheless seeped into even the collection of data, analysis of trends and reporting of anomalies. The information environments thus created for decision makers were continuously and insidiously tainted by pressures of production and scarcity (and in which organisation are they not?), pre-rationally influencing the way people saw the world. Yet even this 'lousy' process was considered 'normal' – normal or inevitable enough, in any case, to not warrant the expense of energy and political capital on trying to change it. Drift into failure can be the result.

Engineering resilience into organisations

All open systems are continually adrift inside their safety envelopes. Pressures of scarcity and competition, the intransparency and size of complex systems, the patterns of information that surround decision makers, and the incrementalist nature of their decisions over time, can make that systems drift into failure. Drift is generated by normal processes of reconciling differential pressures on an organisation (efficiency, capacity utilisation, safety) against a background of uncertain technology and imperfect knowledge. Drift is about incrementalism contributing to extraordinary events, about the transformation of pressures of scarcity and competition into organisational mandates, and about the normalisation of signals of danger so that organisational goals and 'normal' assessments and decisions become aligned. In safe systems, the very processes that normally guarantee safety and generate organisational success, can also be responsible for organisational demise. The same complex, intertwined sociotechnical life that surrounds the operation of successful technology, is to a large extent responsible for its potential failure. Because these processes are normal, because they are part and parcel of normal, functional organisational life, they are difficult to identify and disentangle. The role of these invisible and unacknowledged forces can be frightening. Harmful consequences can occur in organisations constructed to prevent them. Harmful consequences can occur even when everybody follows the rules (Vaughan, 1996).

The direction in which drift takes pushes the operation of the technology can be hard to detect, also or perhaps especially for those on the inside. It can be even harder to stop. Given the diversity of forces (political, financial, and economic pressures, technical uncertainty, incomplete knowledge, fragmented problem solving processes) both on the inside and outside, the large, complex sociotechnical systems that operate some of our most hazardous technologies today seem capable of generating an obscure energy and drift of their own, relatively impervious to outside inspection or inside control.

Recall that in normal flight, the jackscrew assembly of an MD-80 is supposed to carry a load of about 5,000 pounds. But in effect this load was borne by a leaky, porous, continuously changing system of ill-taught and impractical procedures delegated to operator level that anxiously, but always unsuccessfully, tried to close the gap between production and operation, between making and maintaining. Five thousand pounds of load on a loose and varying collection of procedures and practices, were slowly, incrementally grinding their way through the jackscrew threads. It was the sociotechnical system designed to support and protect the uncertain technology, not the mechanical part, that had to carry the load. It gave. The accident report acknowledged that eliminating the risk of single catastrophic failures may not always be possible through design (as design is reconciliation between irreconcilable constraints). It concluded that 'when practicable design alternatives do not exist, a comprehensive systemic maintenance and inspection process is necessary' (p. 180). The conclusion, in other words, became to have a non-redundant system (the single jackscrew and torque tube) be made redundant through an organisational system of maintenance and airworthiness checking. The report was forced to conclude that the last resort should be a countermeasure which it just spent 250 pages proving does not work.

Drifting into failure is not so much about breakdowns or malfunctioning of components, as it is about an organisation not adapting effectively to cope with the complexity of its own structure and environment (see Woods, 2003). Organisational resilience is not a property, it is a capability. A capability to recognise the boundaries of safe operations, a capability to steer back from them in a controlled manner, a capability to recover from a loss of control if it does occur. This means that human factors and system safety must find new ways of engineering resilience into organisations, of equipping organisations with a capability to recognise, and recover from, a loss of control. How can an organisation monitor its own adaptations (and how these bound the rationality of decision makers) to pressures of scarcity and competition, while dealing with imperfect knowledge and uncertain technology? How can an organisation become aware, and remain aware of its models of risk and danger? Answers to these questions hinge on our ability to develop more organic, co-evolutionary accident models. Organisational resilience is about finding means to invest in safety even under pressures of scarcity and competition, since that may be when such investments are needed most. Preventing drift into failure requires a different kind of organisational monitoring and learning. It means fixing on higher-order variables; adding a new level of intelligence and analysis to the incident reporting and error counting that is done today.

References

Amalberti, R. (2001). The paradoxes of almost totally safe transportation systems. *Safety Science, 37*, 109-126.

Capra, F. (1982). *The turning point*. New York: Simon and Schuster.

Columbia Accident Investigation Board (2003). *Report Volume 1*, August 2003. Washington, D.C.: Government Printing Office.

Feynman, R.P. (1988). *'What do you care what other people think?' Further adventures of a curious character*. New York: Norton.

Heft, H. (2001). *Ecological psychology in context: James Gibson, Roger Barker and the legacy of William James's radical empiricism*. Mahwah, NJ: Lawrence Erlbaum Associates.

Langewiesche, W. (1998). *Inside the sky: A meditation on flight*. New York: Pantheon Books.

Leveson, N. (2004). A new approach to system safety engineering. *Safety Science, 42*, 237-270.

National Transportation Safety Board (2002). Loss of control and impact with Pacific Ocean, Alaska Airlines Flight 261 McDonnell Douglas MD-83, N963AS, about 2.7 miles north of Anacapa Island, California, January 31, 2000 (AAR-02/01). Washington, D.C.: NTSB.

Perrow, C. (1984). *Normal accidents: Living with high-risk technologies*. New York, NY: Basic books.

Rasmussen, J. and Svedung, I. (2000). *Proactive risk management in a dynamic society*. Karlstad, Sweden: Swedish Rescue Services Agency.

Snook, S.A. (2000). *Friendly fire: The accidental shootdown of US Black Hawks over Northern Iraq*. Princeton, NJ: Princeton University Press.

Starbuck, W.H. and Milliken, F.J. (1988). Challenger: Fine-tuning the odds until something breaks. *Journal of Management Studies, 25*, 319-340.

Vaughan, D. (1996). *The Challenger launch decision: Risky technology, culture and deviance at NASA*. Chicago, IL: University of Chicago Press.

Weick, K.E. (1993). The collapse of sensemaking in organizations. *Administrative Science Quarterly, 38*, 628-652.

Weick, K.E. (1995). *Sensemaking in organizations*. London: Sage.

Weingart, P. (1991). Large technical systems, real life experiments, and the legitimation trap of technology assessment: The contribution of science and technology to constituting risk perception. In T.R. LaPorte (Ed.), *Social responses to large technial systems: Control or anticipation*, pp. 8-9. Amsterdam, NL: Kluwer.

Woods, D.D. (2003). Creating foresight: How resilience engineering can transform NASA's approach to risky decision-making. *US Senate Testimony for the Committee on Commerce, Science and Transportation*, John McCain, Chair. Washington, D.C., 29 October 2003.

10 Drinking and flying: causes, effects and the development of effective countermeasures

Don Harris

Abstract

Drinking and flying is a relatively rare event, yet one which has immense potential to compromise safety. When pilots are caught flying an aircraft under the influence of alcohol, because such instances are so rare it often becomes a newsworthy item. Commencing in the mid-1980s, regulations have been introduced both in the USA and Europe to specify a peak blood alcohol concentration (BAC), above which it is illegal to act as a crewmember of an aircraft. Research suggests that these regulations may not be as effective as intended, though, either because the BAC specified is too high to promote safety (USA) or that there is no effective way of enforcing the regulations (Europe). Furthermore, it is also argued that there is no one 'best' way of deterring drinking and flying. Effective countermeasures can only be specified with respect to the root cause of the problem. To be effective the enforcement of the regulations needs to be supplemented with educational propaganda and remedial actions and these actions need to be appropriately targeted with respect to the root cause of the drinking and flying behaviour.

Background

In the United Kingdom, a relatively recent, if slightly sensationalist, television documentary programme brought the issue of drinking and flying in commercial aircraft crews to the attention of the public (Dispatches, 12 October, 2000). While

This paper was first published in Human Factors and Aerospace Safety 2(4), 2002, pp. 297-317

the scientific and safety-related merit of such programmes may initially be thought to be questionable, some interesting attitudes toward the use of alcohol in the secret filming of the crews emerged. Of particular note was one opinion expressed that even in the event of a hangover when flying the following morning, everything would be 'OK' and safety would not be compromised as the automated systems would look after the aircraft during critical phases of flight. The programme also suggested that there was an 'endemic drinking culture' within some parts of the airline involved. The issues directly and indirectly surrounding these opinions are worth exploring in some greater detail.

Recent accident statistics suggest that alcohol has not been implicated in a commercial aircraft accident for several years, however, there have been several instances of commercial pilots being disciplined or dismissed for consuming excessive amounts of alcohol before flying. In 1997, a major British airline sacked a pilot for arriving at work at Los Angeles under the influence of alcohol. In January 2000 the Captain of a Moroccan aircraft was refused permission to take off at Schipol airport as he was suspected of being drunk. More recently, in 2002 one American pilot resigned prior to being investigated for drinking and flying and two other pilots were arrested for operating an aircraft under the influence of alcohol when taxiing their aircraft prior to take-off.

In 1985, the US Federal Aviation Administration (FAA) established an upper blood alcohol concentration (BAC) of 40mg per 100ml of blood (also expressed as 40mg/dl – milligrams per decilitre). Above this BAC, it was expressly prohibited to act as a crewmember of a civil aircraft (Code of Federal Regulations, Title 14; part 121.458 and 121.459). In 1995 this rule was amended to incorporate the provision for evidentiary breath testing. In the case of a pilot producing a positive breath test with an indicated BAC of between 20mg/dl and 39mg/dl, that person is prohibited from flying until a repeat test indicates that their BAC is below 20mg/dl or at least eight hours have elapsed from taking the initial test. The US regulations also include provision for the suspension or revocation of an offender's licence and for random testing for alcohol of designated employees in 'safety-sensitive' roles. Each year, the regulatory authority requires at least 10% of all airline employees, including pilots, to be randomly selected for drug and alcohol testing. The regulator may require up to 50% of employees in these safety-critical roles to be tested in any calendar year. This may be reduced to 25% when the level of positive tests for alcohol falls below 1% and be further reduced to 10% when the level of positive tests falls below 0.5%. This rule was introduced to supplement the eight-hour 'bottle-to-throttle' rule, which was widely regarded as being inadequate (see Modell and Mountz, 1990). Cook (1997b) calculated that the consumption of 20 units of alcohol (the equivalent less than 10 pints of normal strength beer or five cans of extra strong lager) would, eight hours later, result in a BAC of approximately 30mg/dl. To attain a BAC of less that 5mg/dl would take an average male about 20 hours. In such a case, even a 24-hour 'bottle to throttle' rule would leave an inadequate margin for error and would also not account for impairment in performance as a result of any post alcohol impairment – PAI (better known as 'hangover') effects. However, Modell and Mountz (1990) also suggested that the compliance with drinking and flying regulations was likely to decrease with an increase in the abstinence period required before taking command of an aircraft.

In the UK, until April 1998, article 57 of the UK Air Navigation (No. 2) Order (1985) merely stated that 'the limit of drinking or drug taking is any extent at which the capacity to act as a crewmember would be impaired'. This regulation was subsequently amended to incorporate a revision to the European Joint Aviation Authorities operations regulations (JAR OPS, Part 1), which now specifically prohibits a pilot to act as a crewmember with a BAC of greater than 20mg/dl. For an 80kg male, this equates to drinking just over one half pint (254ml) of normal strength beer. This regulation effectively requires a longer abstinence period from drinking before flying (which may decrease the likelihood of compliance) and/or an increase in 'technical' (as opposed to deliberate) breaches of the regulation as a result of not allowing the body long enough to metabolise the alcohol in it.

At present in the UK there is no regulatory provision for random drug and alcohol testing in the aviation industry, although it is being introduced in other safety-critical industries (e.g. the rail sector). After the documentary programme 'exposing' the drinking and flying 'problem' in British airlines, it was proposed by the airline in question to introduce random testing, however, this would have required a change in the terms and conditions of employment of their crews. It will be suggested later in this paper, though, that random alcohol tests may not be the best way to eradicate drinking and flying behaviour in all cases. It is argued that there is no one 'best' way to reduce the incidence of drinking and flying. The root of the problem needs to be understood before effective remedial actions may be taken. This will be discussed at greater length in a subsequent section.

Epidemiological studies

Early epidemiological studies of fatally injured pilots suggested that alcohol was implicated in a relatively high percentage of aviation accidents, although these estimates varied considerably. Harper and Albers (1964) found that 35.5% of fatally injured general aviation pilots had BACs greater than 15mg/dl. This observation was corroborated by Gibbons and Plechus (1965) and Ryan and Mohler (1972), who also found that approximately 30% of fatalities had BACs of this order. However, the statistics are complicated to some extent by the occurrence of naturally produced ethanol in decomposing tissue (Canfield, Kuipec and Huffine, 1993). As a result, the high incidence of fatal alcohol-related accidents in general aviation during the 1960s and early 1970s could well be a considerable over estimate. Nevertheless, over the last quarter of a century there has been a decline in the number of fatally injured pilots with significant levels of alcohol in their bloodstream. Lacefield, Roberts and Blossom (1975) reported that 19.5% of civil pilots killed between 1968-74 had BACs in excess of 15mg/dl. NTSB figures for the years 1975-81 implicated alcohol in 10.1% of general aviation accidents and 9.1% in 1983. Between 1989 and 1993, the figure again dropped slightly to between 7.3 and 8.0% of all fatally-injured pilots in the USA having a BAC in excess of 40mg/dl (Canfield, Hordinsky, Millett, Endecott and Smith, 2000). Between 1994 and 1998, an average of 7.0% of US-licensed pilots involved in a fatal accident had a BAC in excess of the prescribed American limit (Canfield, Hordinsky, Millett, Endecott and Smith, 2000), with a low of just 4.0% in 1995. During the period 1994-1998 no fatal accidents involving a US part 121 operation (large commercial aircraft) had a pilot with a BAC in excess of 40mg/dl, however, 5.0% of all accidents in the same period involving a pilot with a class 1 medical certificate did show the pilot to have a BAC in excess of the prescribed limit.

Alcohol and flying performance

The effects of alcohol upon many facets of human performance have been examined using a variety of paradigms and dosages. For example, alcohol has been found to impair: the acquisition of new information (Parker, Alkana, Birnbaum, Hartley and Noble, 1974); performance on divided-attention tasks (Moskowitz and DePry, 1968; and Moskowitz, Marcelline, Burns and Williams, 1985), the rate of information-processing (Moskowitz and Murray, 1976) and verbal skills (Tharp, Rundell, Lester and Williams, 1974; and Hashtroudi, Parker, DeLisi and Wyatt, 1983). It is often assumed that the higher processes are more impaired by alcohol than are the lower ones, but there is some confusion in the literature regarding the relative effects of alcohol on the cognitive and sensory-perceptual domains. Nevertheless, there appears to be a general consensus that the motor domain is the most resilient to alcohol (e.g. Moskowitz and Murray, 1976; Stein and Allen, 1986; Hindmarch, Kerr and Sherwood, 1991). Levine, Kramer and Levine (1975) performed a meta-analysis of the literature to assess the relationship between alcohol and performance in three ability domains; the cognitive domain; the perceptual-sensory domain and the psychomotor domain. It was found that as BAC increased, performance deteriorated in each of the domains, however psychomotor tasks seemed to be the least impaired.

A more recent extensive review of the literature specifically concentrating on the effects of low BACs by Moskowitz and Fiorentino (2000) examined the effects of alcohol in 13 main behavioural areas. In several studies impairment was demonstrated at a BAC of less than 10mg/dl. The results of the meta-analysis suggested that driving tasks, flying tasks and divided attention tasks were the categories most sensitive to low concentrations of blood alcohol. These categories were followed (respectively, and in decreasing order of sensitivity) by vigilance tasks; perception and visual functions; tracking tasks; general cognitive tasks; psychomotor skills and choice reaction time tasks. Simple reaction times and critical flicker fusion were found to be relatively insensitive to the effects of alcohol.

Flying an aircraft manually is a complex, divided-attention task, requiring the integration and co-ordination of a large number of sources of information, actions and procedures. In addition to the fine physical control of the aircraft in three axes to achieve the desired altitude, speed and heading, a pilot must simultaneously monitor the cockpit instruments, navigate, communicate with Air Traffic Control and take account of weather conditions and other aircraft. Each activity competes for limited processing capacity in the pilots' working memory. If the task demands exceed the pilots' available capacity, decrements in performance may occur in some tasks. While flying a highly automated airliner often does not require the fine psychomotor skill it does make heavy cognitive demands on its pilots. Communicating with Air Traffic Control is still essential as is communicating with the other crewmembers. As can be seen, from the results of the meta-analysis undertaken by Moskowitz and Fiorentino (2000), many of the categories of task most affected are more related to the supervisory control tasks of flying a high-technology modern airliner, than they are to the 'hands-on' control of a general aviation aeroplane.

The majority of studies of the effects of alcohol on flying have primarily investigated its effects on the psychomotor skills involved in controlling the aircraft although its effects on other aspects of the flying task have also been logged. Billings, Wick, Gerke and Chase (1973) conducted the only study (to date) of the effects of alcohol on pilots' performance in flight itself. They reported decrements in the performance of pilots flying a light aircraft during Instrument Landing System (ILS) approaches at blood alcohol concentrations of 40, 80 and 120mg/dl. In addition, the number and seriousness of the procedural errors committed by both experienced and less experienced pilots rose as their blood alcohol concentration increased. Performance on secondary tasks also deteriorated as information processing capacity was reduced under the influence of alcohol, and pilots preferentially focused their attention on the primary tasks. Many other studies have also noted a decrement in the psychomotor flying performance of pilots with alcohol. For example, Henry, Davis, Engelken, Triebwasser and Lancaster (1974) noted a deterioration in pilot performance during a long series of demanding manoeuvres conducted in a simulator, but only at BACs of greater than 60mg/dl. Although these findings are interesting, they are only of marginal interest herein.

Of more pertinence to the present discussion, in a study by Billings, Demosthenes, White and O'Hara (1991), pilots undertook simulated flights between Los Angeles and San Francisco in a Boeing 727 airliner. It was noted that serious errors increased at BACs of greater than 25mg/dl. Most errors were

203

associated with planning, procedural errors, and failures of vigilance rather than errors in the psychomotor domain. Morrow, Leirer and Yesavage (1990) investigated the effects of alcohol and age upon the more cognitive types of flying-related task, for example radio communication. Pilots in the alcohol condition made more communication-related errors than in the placebo condition, with impairment increasing from a BAC of 40mg/dl to 100mg/dl. Older pilots made both more course and radio errors than did the younger pilots at the higher BAC. Both age and alcohol significantly increased the frequency of severe course errors that would have endangered safety in actual flight.

Of greatest concern is the accumulating collection of studies which indicate that pilots' performance may be impaired at BACs well below the 40mg/dl limit specified in the FAA regulations, especially in the more cognitive tasks which are now of central importance in flying a modern, highly automated airliner. As previously noted, Billings et al. noted a significant increase in serious errors (defined as those which could have resulted in loss of terrain separation) at BACs of 25mg/dl. Under the 1998 revision to JAR OPS (part 1) it has been prohibited to act as a crewmember of a European aircraft with a BAC of greater than 20mg/dl. However, even at this level there is evidence that alcohol still can impair performance, especially in the more cognitively demanding tasks. Smith and Harris, (1994) observed that radio communication errors increased at BACs as low as 20mg/dl. Davenport and Harris (1992) found decrements in performance at BACs of 11mg/dl during a series of demanding simulated ILS (instrument landing system) approaches.

Unfortunately, even with a BAC of zero, performance decrements as a result of PAI (a hangover) may be detected. Several studies have shown that alcohol hangovers affect the complex cognitive and motor performance required to fly an aircraft (e.g. Collins and Chiles, 1979). Yesavage and Leirer (1986) found that pilots who had ingested enough alcohol to achieve a BAC in excess of 100mg/dl were still showing significant performance decrements 14 hours later and at a time when their BAC had retuned to below zero. Bates (2002) examined PAI effects after an intervening night of sleep. The results showed that alcohol impaired performance at 10 hours after reaching a BAC of 100mg/dl.

In short, there is considerable, incontrovertible evidence that even the smallest amounts of alcohol impair performance and that consuming any amount of alcohol before flying is unwise. For further information on the effects of alcohol on pilot performance see the excellent reviews by Modell and Mountz (1990), Ross and Mundt (1996) and Cook (1997a). However, to expect pilots to abstain totally from drinking is not really practical. No one enjoys flying that much! The problem therefore becomes how to mix safely the consumption of alcohol and the operation of an aircraft. This is of particular importance to professional pilots. As will be discussed in the following sections, there are several reasons why a professional pilot may drink, which also includes for social reasons or enjoyment. As the reasons for drinking and flying may therefore vary, the remedies to avoid drinking and flying will also vary with respect to the fundamental underlying cause for the consumption of alcohol. There is no simple 'one size fits all' remedy to prevent pilots flying when under the influence of alcohol. With the introduction of the 20mg/dl BAC limit in Europe, this further complicates the drinking and flying problem, especially when it comes to the matter of deterrence.

The reasons for drinking and flying

It is only for legal purposes that performing certain activities is prohibited above a specified BAC. Unfortunately for the legal profession, it has long been known that the level of intoxication of an individual (in terms of their BAC) cannot be directly related to their level of impairment (for example, see Drew, Colquhoun and Long, 1959). Factors such as tolerance to the effects of alcohol developed as a result of frequent drinking (Goldberg, 1951) or being young (Collins and Mertens, 1988) can both contribute to superior performance being observed in some participants with exactly the same BAC as other, more impaired participants. The BAC achieved by the ingestion of a specific amount of alcohol will also vary with respect to such factors as sex; lean body mass; metabolic rate; the presence and type of food in the stomach; gastric motility and the concentration of the alcoholic beverage being consumed (Stein, 1986; Sturtivant and Sturtivant, 1979). Even in carefully controlled experimental conditions using weight-adjusted doses of alcohol, peak BACs have been observed to vary between participants by 200-300% (Duboski, 1985).

As a result of everyday factors such as those described in the previous paragraph, it is almost impossible for a pilot to determine what their level of BAC will be at any point in time after having ingested alcohol. To help avoid flying with a BAC over the prescribed limit specified in the legislative mandates of the FAA and JAA, the UK Civil Aviation Authority (CAA) in Aviation Information Circular 16/1993 (pink 73 paragraph 13) provides pilots with guidance on the elimination rates of alcohol from the body and suggests that 'it would be prudent for a pilot to abstain from alcohol for at least 24 hours before flying'. For several years many airlines have also supplemented the regulations with standing orders and advice for their aircrew. Several airlines require pilots to abstain from drinking alcohol for up to 24 hours before reporting duty. Other operators require flying staff not to consume any alcohol at all for eight hours before reporting for a rostered service or standby duty, and to consume not more than five units of alcohol (approximately 58g) in the 16 hours preceding the eight hour prohibited period (see also Cook, 1997c for more details from a survey of the drug and alcohol policies operated by airlines). While this advice is welcome, as discussed earlier, it will not necessarily prevent flying with a BAC higher than that allowed by legislation. The root of the drink-flying problems are many-fold.

Promulgation of information

In a survey to evaluate the effectiveness of the FAA's 40mg/dl rule (Ross and Ross, 1990), it was found that despite the 40mg/dl rule having been in place for five years, only 37% of pilots were actually aware of its existence. Rules that pilots are unaware of are ineffective.

Stressors

Even if pilots are aware of the existence of regulations that prohibit drinking and flying, this is not to say that they will adhere to them. In a further report evaluating the effectiveness of the FAA's 40mg/dl rule, Ross and Ross (1992) concluded that one of the fundamental reasons for drinking and flying was an inability of some individuals to control their use of alcohol. The initial roots of any problem drinking, though, may again stem from one or more of many sources. Stress may only be one of them, but is perhaps the one most frequently cited (in an occupational context). However, stressors may either be of a personal nature or be a product of work-related pressures. Sloane and Cooper (1984) reported that approximately 12% of professional pilots drank alcohol as a means of coping with stressful situations. Canada Market Research (1990), Ross and Ross (1995) and Maxwell and Harris (1997) also all reported that that job-related stresses were frequently cited as a common cause of heavy drinking in professional pilots. These stressors included being away from home, job-related fatigue, long hours and boredom.

Socialisation

Long-haul flight crewmembers commonly report drinking socially with other crewmembers after flights and, as alluded to at the end of the previous section, also as a means of helping them to relax, especially after crossing several time zones (Sloane and Cooper, 1984). Other authors have suggested that pilots, and in particular military pilots, are from what may be characterised as a 'drinking culture', where great store is placed upon factors such as camaraderie and 'team spirit', much of which is facilitated by social gathering (e.g. Anthony, 1988; Cuthbert, 1997). It is unlikely that a drink-flying event would immediately follow such a social gathering, however, it is more likely that after a heavy drinking session a pilot may fly the following day with an unacceptably high BAC (in addition to a hangover)! This was certainly the case in the instances reported at the beginning of this paper.

Lack of knowledge

In the survey described earlier undertaken by Ross and Ross (1990) it was also suggested that a further factor underlying the drinking and flying problem was a fundamental lack of knowledge about the rate at which BAC declines as a function of time and the amount of alcohol consumed. It was also reported that over 50% of their sample over-estimated the number of drinks it would take to reach a target BAC of 40mg/dl.

A study of car drivers undertaken by Bierness (1987) described three different types of drinkers with regard to the pattern of errors that they made when they were asked to estimate their BAC during and after drinking alcohol. There were chronic over-estimators (estimations of BAC were in excess of actual BAC at all points during the absorption and elimination phases); chronic under-estimators (the exact opposite); and mixed-pattern estimators. The latter tended to over-estimate BAC during the absorption phase and under-estimate it during elimination. Under-estimators were generally found to be heavier drinkers. Mixed-pattern drinkers were, in the context of their study, regarded as potentially being the most 'at risk' group. They were not likely to drink and drive during the absorption phase but may be inclined to do so in the elimination phase. This latter finding has implications for guidelines such as the eight-hour 'bottle to throttle' guidelines that are still often used by many pilots in the absence of any other information. After a moderately heavy drinking session, and assuming an elimination rate of alcohol from the body of 15 mg/dl/ hour (a typical figure used by many researchers, e.g. Balfour, 1988; Mertens, Ross and Mundt, 1988) a pilot may still be over the FAA prescribed 40mg/dl limit eight hours after having consumed six pints (568ml glasses) of normal strength beer. This pilot may therefore be in danger of inadvertently infringing the drinking and flying regulations, especially in Europe where the prescribed BAC is only half of that in the United States. However, Cook (1997b) also observes that the elimination rate of alcohol from the body may, in certain circumstances, be as low as 8mg/dl/ hour, which would almost double the time required before the pilot would be legal to fly.

The problem of accidentally transgressing the drinking and flying regulations in Europe was exactly what was found by Widders and Harris (1997). Widders and Harris identified two potential groups of drinking and flying pilots, one of which was labelled 'inadvertent drink-flyers', who may be prone to drinking and flying as a result of a lack of knowledge about the rate at which alcohol is eliminated from the body (the other group was described as, 'non-believers' and is described later). In this study it was found that up to 24% of UK pilots licence holders could not determine when their BAC was likely to fall below 20mg/dl after drinking and may therefore be in danger of inadvertently infringing the regulation. This finding supports the speculation of Modell and Mountz (1990) who felt that the compliance with drinking and flying regulations was likely to decrease with an increase in the abstinence period required. In this case, though, the potential breaches of the regulations would be non-deliberate, hence the term 'inadvertent drink-flyers'.

Attitudes, beliefs and opinions

Attitudes, beliefs and opinions toward the use of alcohol will all effect the likelihood of drinking and flying in many different ways. Attitudes, beliefs and opinions may all be modified or changed (either to the benefit or detriment of aviation safety) once they have been uncovered and described.

The type of alcohol consumed effects behaviour, even though the final BAC produced as a product of drinking may be the same. Ross and Ross (1990) found that self-reported drinking behaviour was much more conservative when consuming whisky compared to wine or beer. Damkot and Osga (1978) observed a similar pattern of results in an earlier study of American pilots' attitudes toward drinking and flying. In this study respondents reported that they perceived 'hard' liqueur to be more dangerous when consumed prior to flying than either wine or beer.

On a different note, in a survey of US professional pilots conducted by Ross and Ross (1992) most respondents' opinions were that the use of alcohol was a more serious problem in general aviation than in commercial aviation. Widders and Harris (1997) however, in a study of self-reported drinking and flying behaviour in UK pilots identified two potential groups of drinking and flying pilots (as alluded to earlier). To re-iterate slightly these were the 'inadvertent drink-flyers' and the 'non-believers' in the regulation. The latter felt that they were safe to fly before their BAC had dropped below the 20mg/dl limit. Members of the 'non-believers' group of pilots tended to be older, but most surprisingly and in direct contradiction to Ross and Ross's (1992) results, it was found that possessors of an Air Transport Pilot's Licence (ATPL) were over-represented in this category.

The identification of 'at risk' groups of pilot

It was previously stated that there is no simple 'one size fits all' remedy to the prevention of drinking and flying. Effective remedial actions depend upon the correct diagnosis of the causative factors underlying the behaviour. Some potential remedial approaches are described in the following section, however, these need to be appropriately targeted. To target these actions the various categories of drinking and flying pilot need to be identified and described with regard to their fundamental characteristics. Several different approaches have been used with respect to pursuing this goal.

An early approach to define groups 'at risk' of contravening the drinking and flying regulations was largely unsuccessful. On the basis of attitudinal measures, Damkot and Osga (1978) attempted to discriminate between pilots who had admitted to drinking and flying and those who had not, however only 12 pilots out of a sample of 341 actually reported having flown after having consumed alcohol.

Ross and Ross (1992) observed that in general pilots felt that alcohol was a more serious problem in non-commercial aviation than in commercial aviation. Widders and Harris (1997) identified two potential groups of drinking and flying pilots: 'inadvertent drink-flyers' and 'non-believers'. These studies have all been described in some detail in the earlier sections of this paper.

Studies of pilots' drinking and flying behaviour are relatively sparse compared to the wealth of literature available from the study of drinking and driving. Although the motivations underlying a pilot's decision to fly (or not) after having consumed alcohol may be totally different to those of a car driver, a great deal may be learned by the aerospace community from the methodologies employed by researchers into drink and driving. One of the most promising approaches used by drink-driving researchers has been an interactionist approach using structural equation modelling. Albery and Guppy (1995) argued that a great deal of research has been unsuccessful in identifying at-risk offender groups as it has examined simple cause-effect relationships and has dissociated personal from situational factors. It was argued that to produce effective countermeasures, drinking and driving needed to be viewed as a complex system integrating these factors. For example, personal factors (such as a moral attachment to the law) may be mediated by situational factors (e.g. peer group pressure or a lack of readily available public transport) that may result in a person with a basically high regard for the law committing a drink-driving offence. Simple cause-effect regression-based analyses cannot cope with these complex interactions between variables. Structural models of drinking and driving employing such a methodology have been relatively successful in describing the predictors and motivations underlying drinking and driving behaviour (e.g. Albery and Guppy, 1995; Nörstrom, 1978; Nörstrom, 1981; Berger and Snortum, 1986).

Maxwell and Harris (1999), using the same methodology as Albery and Guppy (1995), used a structural equation modelling approach to predict drink-flying offending behaviour. As in the study of drinking and driving, offending behaviour was best described as a combination of personal factors and situational factors. The personal factors identified included the sex of the respondent (male pilots were more likely to offend), the pilot's licence category (professional pilots were more likely to drink and fly) and their experience (more experienced pilots were more likely to offend). The benefit of using a structural equation modelling approach becomes apparent, though, as the results also clearly showed that possessing a professional pilot's licence gives the pilot more opportunity to contravene the drinking and flying regulations partly as a result of simply flying more often. The situational factors in the model also showed the contribution of occupational stressors. These included increasing worries about company stability; a large numbers of last minute schedule changes being forced on the pilots and an increased use of alcohol to relax after a flight. However, not surprisingly, these situational factors only really applied to the professional pilots in the sample. To reiterate slightly, being a professional pilot only partially explains the increased likelihood of people in this category to drink and fly. Part of the reasons why professional pilots drink and fly is attributable to occupational stressors and an increased opportunity to offend. This approach, by considering all aspects of the drinking and flying problem allows far better targeting of effective remedial actions rather than simply attempting to identify 'at risk' groups. In short, it begins to identify the causes, not the symptoms.

Development of effective drinking and flying countermeasures

The study of drinking and driving has a great deal to offer in the development of effective measures to deter drinking and flying, however, very little of this material has been used in this context. A simple, three-level model of deterrence of drinking and driving behaviour was offered by Vingilis and Salutin (1980). This approach can equally as well be applied in the control of drinking and flying. The model suggested remedial actions at three levels.

- *Primary level* interventions are essentially concerned with educating drivers about the effects of alcohol on performance.
- *Secondary level* countermeasures are concerned with enforcement of the regulations (i.e. increasing the likelihood, or *perceived* likelihood of apprehension of offenders).
- *Tertiary level* interventions in the model are aimed to reduce the chances of recidivism through either punitive sanctions (aimed at suppressing offending behaviour) or through counselling and rehabilitation (targeted at eliminating the root cause of offending behaviour).

As an illustration of the operation of countermeasures at these three levels it can be suggested that educating pilots about BAC decay rates would only be an effective drink-flying countermeasure for those pilots falling into the 'inadvertent drink-flyer' group, as identified by Widders and Harris (1997). However, it should also be noted that this group comprised only 16% of offenders. The majority of potential infringers of the 20mg/dl rule identified in this survey were in the 'non-believers' category. In the drinking and driving literature several authors (Nörstrom, 1978; Nörstrom, 1981; Berger and Snortum, 1986; and Albery and Guppy, 1995) have all identified a lack of a moral attachment to the law as a key determinant of drink-driving behaviour. Thus, effective countermeasures for 'non-believers' are likely to be different to those of the 'inadvertent drink-flyer' group as the root cause of the drink-flying offending behaviour is totally different. Effective remedial actions can only be specified with regard to the cause of the offending behaviour, not the behaviour itself. Thus, for 'non-believers' the emphasis in any intervention strategies should be placed on the latter two aspects of the tripartite model (e.g. increasing the perceived likelihood of apprehension to deter the behaviour or, if caught, applying punitive sanctions) whereas 'inadvertent drink-flyers' should respond best to primary level interventions.

The effect of enforcement on suppressing drink-driving behaviour, (a secondary level intervention in Vingilis and Salutin's model) is very well understood in the scientific community (but often seem to be less well understood by politicians)! Increasing the *perceived* likelihood of arrest acts as an effective deterrent (Guppy, 1988). However increasing the *actual* likelihood of arrest when drink-driving also suppresses this behaviour, although this is often less effective. Nevertheless, the introduction of large-scale random breath testing (RBT) in Finland and Australia led to beneficial effects on the suppression offending behaviour (see Dunbar, Penttila and Pikkarainen, 1987; Homel, Carseldine and Kearns, 1988). In Finland a 58% reduction in the level of drinking and driving was observed after the introduction of RBT. An analysis of Australian data showed a 42% reduction in the number of alcohol related road traffic accidents.

As described in the first section of this review, the FAA currently also uses a form of random alcohol testing in an attempt to suppress the incidence of drinking and flying. The effects of this programme seem to be somewhat mixed. McFadden (1997) analysed two approaches used by the FAA aimed at reducing alcohol-related aviation accidents. These were conducting background checks on pilots to check for driving-while-intoxicated (DWI) convictions, and the random pre-flight alcohol testing of airline pilots. Data from over 70,000 US pilots were used. DWI convictions were associated with a significantly greater risk of a pilot-error accident, however, no evidence was found to suggest that random testing for alcohol could have actually prevented any accident. On a more positive note, Lindseth, Vacek and Lindseth (2001) examined pilots' attitudes and opinions over a 10 year period regarding the effectiveness, adequacy and fairness of random drug and alcohol testing as a deterrent for substance abuse. The results showed that respondents believed that alcohol use by pilots had decreased since testing was mandated and that alcohol and drug testing was now more generally accepted by pilots than when it was first introduced.

To be effective, regulations need to be complimented with propaganda if they are to have a deterrent effect. This was patently not the case when the FAA introduced its drinking and flying regulations. Cousins (1980) found that a propaganda campaign aimed at increasing the *subjective* probability of arrest had a beneficial effect when it was undertaken concurrently with the introduction of new sanctions for drink-drivers. This would suggest that anti-drink flying propaganda placing emphasis on the sanctions that offenders could face and emphasising high-profile measures that could be taken to enforce these regulations, would be an effective strategy to employ. The initial introduction of the drinking and flying regulations in the USA, however, was certainly not accompanied by a successful propaganda campaign.

Vingilis and Salutin (1980) argued tertiary level interventions were essentially designed to prevent recidivism not to deter offending behaviour. To progress to the tertiary stage the offender must have passed through all the previous stages. Classical deterrence theory, however, would suggest that sanctions could

211

potentially operate at all stages in the tripartite model. *General* deterrence acts on all members of the population and should deter potential offenders from committing the illegal act; *specific* deterrence is concerned with the effect of punitive sanctions on offenders to reduce the likelihood of recidivism (see Ross, 1984).

With the exception of random breath testing, the effectiveness of *general* deterrence as a drinking and driving countermeasure has been difficult to establish. Mäkinen (1988) reported that from a review of over 200 enforcement studies, the use of severe punishment as a deterrent had no demonstrable effect on improving drivers' behaviour. Ross (1988) supported this finding, suggesting that increasing the likelihood of apprehension on a drink-driving occasion was a more effective deterrent. However, later research has suggested that widely advertised punitive sanctions could also act as a deterrent to initial offending (Kinkade and Leone, 1992). The implementation of severe sanctions for drink-driving in California reduced the arrest rate by approximately 12%. The effectiveness of punitive sanctions as a specific deterrent (i.e. when applied to offenders to deter re-offending) would also seem to be limited. Wheeler and Hissong (1988) observed no difference on the likelihood recidivism with respect to the severity of the sanction imposed (probation, fine or imprisonment). No such evaluation of the actual deterrence value of punitive enforcement sanctions for drinking and flying behaviour has been conducted (to date). This is perhaps for a number of reasons. The population of pilots is much smaller than that of drivers; educated estimates of the size of the drinking and flying problem suggest that it is much, much smaller (in relative terms) than that of drinking and driving; finally, the general emphasis on the eradication of drink-flying has been aimed more toward education rather than enforcement. Particularly in commercial aviation, the inappropriate use of alcohol has mostly been treated as a problem in occupational stress rather than a problem in malicious offending behaviour.

The results of a meta-analysis of 215 studies evaluating rehabilitation programmes for drinking and driving offenders (an alternative approach to sanctions at the tertiary level of the tripartite model), by Wells-Parker, Bangert-Drowns, McMillen and Williams (1995) found that this type of remedial action resulted in a 7-9% reduction in re-offending behaviour. Other reviews of research comparing the effect of sanctions and rehabilitation programmes also concluded that the longer-term benefit of alcohol rehabilitation programmes was greater than the punitive suspension of drivers' licences (McKnight and Voas, 1991; Peck, 1991). The results of an opinion survey of US professional pilots undertaken by Ross and Ross (1995) suggested that the provision of employee assistance programmes would be the most effective approach to reducing the likelihood of drinking and flying. This was followed by (in decreasing order of effectiveness) education of pilots on the effects of alcohol and strengthening sanctions. Harris and Maxwell (2000), elicited opinions from 472 private and professional pilots concerning the effectiveness of various countermeasures to reduce the likelihood of drinking and flying. Overall, punitive sanctions and tougher enforcement of the regulations were regarded as the most effective countermeasures, although self-reported offenders and professional pilots thought these actions less effective than private pilots and non-offenders. The professional pilots in this study tended to regard counselling and rehabilitation more favourably than enforcement, which probably reflected the underlying reasons why some respondents in this section of the sample consumed alcohol. In the US the results of rehabilitation programmes for pilots with alcohol problems have shown considerable success with positive results in up to 85% of cases (see Russel and Davis, 1995 and Flynn, Sturges, Swarsen and Kohn, 1993). The finding from McFadden (1997) that DWI convictions were a significant indicator of alcohol-related pilot error also suggests that alcohol use by pilots may be symptomatic of other stresses and problems.

Conclusions

In summary, there is a growing body of experimental evidence that any amount of alcohol in the bloodstream is detrimental to flight performance. The FAA's prescribed limit of 40mg/dl would certainly seem too high to ensure flight safety. All evidence suggests that the psychomotor aspects of human performance are most resistant to the effects of alcohol and that it is the higher cognitive functions that suffer most. These are certainly impaired well below the 40mg/dl level. As flying a modern, highly-automated airliner is now more a cognitive task than a psychomotor task, the reported comments of the pilot at the beginning of this paper would seem to be misguided. If anything, the cognitively demanding task of managing and monitoring a modern aircraft is more likely to suffer from the effects of alcohol (or a hangover) than is flying it manually. These may also be true even if the pilot is technically fit to fly.

Comments such as that made by the media at the beginning of this paper, that parts of the aviation industry had 'an endemic drinking culture' are sensationalist and naïve and do little to tackle the basic problem. Symptoms should not be confused with diseases. Not all pilots drink alcohol for the same reason and not all pilots who drink alcohol have a problem. Far from it. It can certainly be stated that not all pilots who consume alcohol are likely to breach the flight safety regulations. Interventions aimed at reducing organisational pressures, which *may* cause stress and which *may* subsequently lead to some form of heavier than normal drinking will have little effect on reducing inappropriate social drinking (however, this approach will be effective in helping some pilots suffering from occupational stress). Higher levels of enforcement may deter inappropriate social drinking prior to flying but will have little ultimate deterrent effect on pilots with alcohol-related problems. With no enforcement strategy, though, pilots who are of the opinion that the drinking and flying regulations are inappropriate are also unlikely to adhere to them. This, however, leads to a classical 'Catch-22' situation. The more onerous the drinking and flying regulations become in terms of the effort required to comply with them, the less likely they are to be complied with, however the more likely they are to enhance flight safety. The easier the regulations are to adhere to, the more likely they are to be (willingly) complied with, however they will be less effective in promoting flight safety.

To promote safe alcohol use in the aviation environment countermeasures need to be appropriately targeted in respect of the group that the message is aimed at and the level of intervention (education, enforcement or sanctions and/or counselling and rehabilitation). However, first of all, the piloting population needs to be aware that there is a regulation stipulating a BAC above which it is illegal to take charge of an aeroplane. Supporting propaganda material also needs to be promulgated to express in practical terms what a specified peak BAC means in terms of the number and type of alcoholic drinks consumed and the amount of time required for the alcohol to be eliminated from the body. Furthermore, there is little point in having a regulation to enforce a specified upper BAC if there is no complimentary enforcement effort, as is the case with the JAA regulation. Simply relying on actions taken at one level of intervention will be ineffective.

In a perverse way, documentary programmes bringing the issue of drinking and flying to the attention of the general public illustrate two important points. Firstly, as such an issue is regarded as being newsworthy, it only serves to illustrate how rare the incidence of drinking and flying is. This is also borne out by the accident statistics. Nevertheless, to promote safety it must remain a rare event. Secondly, despite their 'shock-horror' emphasis, such programmes provide better awareness of the regulations than any material distributed by the airworthiness authorities, so despite their sensationalistic bias, and although it is painful to suggest it, they may actually perform a valuable flight safety function.

References

Albery, I.P. and Guppy, A. (1995). The interactionist nature of drinking and driving: a structural model. *Ergonomics, 38*, 1805-1818.

Anthony, E. (1988). Psychiatry. In, J. Ernsting and P. King (Eds.) *Aviation Medicine (2nd Edition)*. London: Butterworths, pp. 619-643.

Balfour, A.C.J. (1988). Aviation pathology. In J. Ernsting and P. King (eds), *Aviation medicine (2nd edition)*. London: Butterworths, 703-709.

Bates, J.E.W. (2002). An examination of hangover effects on pilot performance. *Dissertation Abstracts International: Section B: The Sciences and Engineering, 62(9-B)*, 4257.

Berger, D.E. and Snortum, J.R. (1986). A structural model of drinking and driving: Alcohol consumption, social norms and moral commitments. *Criminology, 24*, 139-153.

Bierness, D.J. (1987). Self-estimates of blood alcohol concentration in a drinking-driving context. *Drug and Alcohol Dependence, 19*, 79-90.

Billings, C.E., Demosthenes, T., White, T.R. and O'Hara, D.B. (1991). Effects of alcohol on pilot performance in simulated flight. *Aviation, Space and Environmental Medicine, 62*, 233-235.

Billings, C.E., Wick, R.L., Gerke, R.J. and Chase, R.C. (1973). Effects of ethyl alcohol on pilot performance. *Aviation Medicine, 44*, 379-382.

Canada Market Research (1990). *Substance Use and Transportation Safety: Aviation Mode.* Toronto: Canada Market Research.

Canfield, D.V., Hordinsky, J., Millett, D.P., Endecott, B. and Smith, D. (2000). *Prevelance of drugs and alcohol in fatal civil aviation accidents between 1994 and 1998 (DOT/FAA/AM-00/21).* Washington DC: US Department of Transportation.

Canfield, D.V., Kuipec, T. and Huffine, E. (1993). Postmortem alcohol production in fatal aircraft accidents. *Journal of Forensic Sciences, 38*, 914-917.

Channel 4 (2000). *Dispatches.* Broadcast, 12 October, 2000.

Code of Federal Regulations. *Title 14: Aeronautics and Space Part 121-Operating Requirements: Domestic, Flag, And Supplemental Operations.* Washington DC: United States Government Printing Office.

Collins, W.E. and Chiles, W.D. (1979). Laboratory performance during acute intoxication and hangover. *FAA Office of Aviation Medicine Report No 79-7.* Oklahoma City, OK: FAA Civil Aeromedical Institute.

Collins, W.E. and Mertens, H.W. (1988). Age, alcohol and simulated altitude: effects on performance and breathalyser scores. *Aviation, Space and Environmental Medicine, 59*, 1026-1033.

Cook, C.C.H. (1997a). Alcohol and aviation. *Addiction, 92*, 539-555.

Cook, C.C.H. (1997b). Alcohol policy and aviation safety. *Addiction, 92*, 793-804.

Cook, C.C.H. (1997c). Aircrew alcohol and drug policies: A survey of commercial airlines. *International Journal of Drug Policy 8*, 153-160.

Cousins, L.S. (1980). The effects of public education on the subjective probability of arrest for impaired driving: A field study. *Accident Analysis and Prevention, 12*, 131-141.

Cuthbert, J.W. (1997). Alcoholism in the aviation industry. *Proceedings of the Royal Society of Medicine, 70*, 116-118.

Damkot, D.K. and Osga, G.A. (1978). Survey of pilots' attitudes and opinions about drinking and flying. *Aviation, Space and Environmental Medicine, 49*, 390-394.

Davenport, M.D. and Harris, D. (1992). The Effect of Low Blood Alcohol Levels on Pilot Performance in a Series of Simulated Approach and Landing Trials. *International Journal of Aviation Psychology, 2*, 271-280.

Department of Transport (1995). *The Air Navigation (No. 2) Order.* London: Her Majesties Stationary Office.

Drew, G.C., Colquhoun, W.P. and Long, H.A. (1959). *Effects of small doses of alcohol on a skill resembling driving.* Medical Research Council Memorandum No. 38, London: HMSO.

Duboski, K.M. (1985). Absorption, distribution and elimination of alcohol: highway safety aspects. *Journal of Studies on Alcohol, 10*, 98-108.

Dunbar, J.A., Penttila, A. and Pikkarainen, J. (1987). Drinking and driving: Success of random breath testing in Finland. *British Medical Journal, 295*, 101-103.

Flynn, C.F., Sturges, M.S., Swarsen, R.J. and Kohn, G.M. (1993). Alcoholism and treatment in airline aviators: One company's results. *Aviation, Space and Environmental Medicine, 72*, 314-318.

Gibbons, H.L. and Plechus, J.L. (1988). Analysis of medical factors in fatal aircraft accidents, in Gibbons, H.L. Alcohol, aviation and safety revisited; a historical review and a suggestion. *Aviation, Space and Environmental Medicine, 59*, 657-660.

Goldberg L. (1951). Tolerance to alcohol in moderate and heavy drinkers and its significance to alcohol and traffic. *Proceedings of the First International Conference on Alcohol and Traffic.* Kugelberg; Stockholm.

Guppy, A. (1988). Factors associated with drink-driving in a sample of English males. In, J.A. Rothengatter and R.A. de Bruin (Eds.) *Road user behavior: Theory and research.* Assen, The Netherlands: Van Gorcum, 375-380.

Harper, C.R. and Albers, W.R. (1964). Alcohol and general aviation accidents. *Aerospace Medicine, 35*, 462-464.

Hashtroudi, S., Parker, E.S., DeLisi, L.E. and Wyatt, R.J. (1983). On elaboration and alcohol. *Journal of Verbal Learning and Verbal Behaviour, 22*, 164-173.

Henry, P.H., Davis, T.Q., Engelken, E.J., Triebwasser, J.H and Lancaster, M.C. (1974). Alcohol-induced performance decrements assessed by two Link Trainer tasks using experienced pilots. *Aerospace Medicine, 45*, 180-189.

Hindmarsh, I., Kerr, J.S. and Sherwood, N. (1991). The effects of alcohol and other drugs on psychomotor performance and cognitive function. *Alcohol and Alcoholism, 26*, 71-79.

Homel, R., Carseldine, D. and Kearns, I. (1988). Drink-driving countermeasures in Australia. *Alcohol, Drugs and Driving, 4*, 113-144.

Joint Airworthiness Authorities. *JAR-OPS Part 1: Commercial Air Transportation (Aeroplanes).* Hoofdorp; Author.

Kinkade, P.T. and Leone, L.M.C. (1992). The effects of 'tough' drunk-driving laws on policing: A case study. *Crime and Delinquency, 38*, 239-257.

Lacefield, D.J., Roberts, P.A. and Blossom, C.W. (1975). Toxicological findings in fatal civil aviation accidents, fiscal years 1968-1974. *Aviation, Space and Environmental Medicine, 46*, 1030-1032.

Levine, J.M., Kramer, G.G., and Levine, E.N. (1975). Effects of alcohol on human performance: An integration of research findings based on an abilities classification. *Journal of Applied Psychology, 60*, 285-293.

Lindseth, P.D., Vacek,, J.L. and Lindseth, G.N. (2001). Urinalysis drug testing within a civilian pilot training program: Did attitudes change during the 1990's? *Aviation, Space and Environmental Medicine, 72,* 647-651.

Mäkinen, T. (1988). Enforcement studies in Finland. In, J.A. Rothengatter and R.A. de Bruin (Eds.) *Road user behavior: Theory and research.* Assen, The Netherlands: Van Gorcum, 584-588.

Maxwell, E. and Harris, D. (1999). Drinking and flying: A structural model. *Aviation, Space and Environmental Medicine 70,* 117-123.

McFadden, K.L. (1997). Policy improvements for prevention of alcohol misuse by airline pilots. *Human Factors, 39,* 1-8.

McKnight, A.J. and Voas, R.B. (1991). The effect of license suspension upon DWI recidivism. *Alcohol, Drugs and Driving, 7,* 43-54.

Mertens, C.H., Ross, L.E. and Mundt, J.C. (1991). Young drivers' evaluation of driving impairment due to alcohol. *Accident Analysis and Prevention, 23,* 67-76.

Modell, J.G. and Mountz, J.M. (1990). Drinking and flying – the problem of alcohol use by pilots. *New England Journal of Medicine, 323,* 455-461.

Morrow, D., Leiber, Von O and Yesavage, J. (1990). The influence of alcohol and aging on radio communication during flight. *Aviation, Space and Environmental Medicine, 61,* 12-20.

Moskowitz, H. and DePry, D. (1968). Differential Effect Of Alcohol On Auditory Vigilance And Divided-Attention Tasks. *Quarterly Journal of Studies on Alcohol, 29(1-A),* 54-63.

Moskowitz, H. and Fiorentino, D. (2000). *A review of the literature on the effects of low doses of alcohol on driving related skills* (DOT/HS/809/028). US Department of Transportation. Washington DC: US Department of Transportation.

Moskowitz, H., Marcelline, J., Burns, M.M. and Williams, A.F. (1985). Skills performance at low blood alcohol levels, *Journal of Studies on Alcohol, 46,* 482-485.

Moskowitz, H. and Murray, J.T. (1976). Alcohol and backward masking of visual information. *Journal of Studies on Alcohol, 37,* 40-45.

Norström, T. (1978). Drunken driving: a tentative causal model. *Scandinavian Studies in Criminology, 6,* 252-283.

Norström, T. (1981). Drunken driving: a causal model. In, L. Goldberg (Ed). *Alcohol, drugs and traffic safety: proceedings of the 8ᵗʰ International Conference on Alcohol, Drugs and Traffic Safety,* Stockholm: Almqvist and Wiksel, 1215-1229.

Parker, E.S., Alkana, R.L., Birnbaum, I.M., Hartley, J.T. and Nobel, E.P. (1974). Alcohol and the description of cognitive processes. *Archives of General Psychology, 31,* 824-828.

Peck, R.C. (1991). The general and specific deterrent effects of DUI sanctions: A review of California's experience. *Alcohol, drugs and driving, 7,* 13-42.

217

Ross, H.L. (1984). *Deterring the drinking driver: Legal policy and social control.* Lexington, MA: D.C. Heath and Co.

Ross, H.L. (1988). Deterrence-based policies in Britain, Canada and Australia. In, M.D. Lawrence J.R. Snortum and F.E. Zimring (Eds.) *Social control of the drinking driver.* Chicago IL: University of Chicago Press, 64-78.

Ross, L.R. and Ross, S.M. (1988). Pilot's attitudes towards alcohol and flying. *Aviation, Space and Environmental Medicine, 59,* 913-919.

Ross, L.R. and Ross, S.M. (1992). Professional pilots' evaluation of the extent causes and reduction of alcohol use in aviation. *Aviation, Space and Environmental Medicine, 63,* 805-808.

Ross, L.R., and Ross, S.M. (1990). Pilots' knowledge of blood alcohol levels and the 0.04% blood alcohol concentration rule. *Aviation, Space and Environmental Medicine, 62,* 412-417.

Ross, S.M. and Ross, L.R. (1995). Professional pilots. views of alcohol use in aviation and the effectiveness of employee assistance programs. *International Journal of Aviation Psychology, 5,* 199-213.

Russel, J.C. and Davis, A.W. (1995). *Alcohol rehabilitation of airline pilots* (FAA/DOT Report no. DOT/FAA-AM-85-12). Washington, DC: Federal Aviation Administration.

Ryan, L.C. and Mohler, S.R. (1972). Intoxicating liquor and the general aviation pilot. *Aerospace Medicine, 43,* 1024-1026.

Sloane, H.R. and Cooper, C.L. (1984). Health-related lifestyle habits in commercial airline pilots. *British Journal of Aviation Medicine, 2,* 32-41.

Smith, F.J. and Harris, D. (1994). The Effects of Low Blood Alcohol Levels on Pilots' Prioritisation of Tasks During a Radio Navigation Task. *International Journal of Aviation Psychology, 4,* 349-358.

Snortum, J.R. and Berger, D.E. (1989). Drink-driving compliance in the United States: perceptions and behavior in 1983 and 1986. *Journal of Studies on Alcohol, 50,* 306-319.

Stein, A.C. (1986). Factors affecting blood alcohol concentrations in humans. *Proceedings of the American Association for Automotive Medicine, 30,* 15-31.

Stein, A.C. and Allen, R.W. (1986). The effects of alcohol on driver decision-making and risk-taking. *Proceedings of the American Association for Automotive Medicine, 30,* 59-73.

Sturtivant, F.M. and Sturtivant, R.P. (1979). Chronopharmacokinetics of ethanol. In, E. Majchroviez and E.P. Noble (Eds), *Biochemistry and Pharmacology of Ethanol (volume 1),* New York: Plenum Press.

Tharp, V.K., Rundell, O.H., Lester, B.K. and Williams, H.L. (1974). Alcohol and information processing. *Psychopharmacologia, 40,* 33-52.

Vingilis, E.R. and Salutin, L. (1980). A prevention programme for drinking and driving. *Accident Analysis and Prevention, 12,* 267-274.

Wells-Parker, E., Bangert-Drowns, R., McMillen, R. and Williams, M. (1995). Final results from a meta-analysis of remedial actions with drink-driving offenders. *Addiction, 9*, 907-926.

Wheeler, G.R. and Hissong, R.V. (1988). Effects of criminal sanctions on drunk drivers: Beyond incarceration. *Crime and Delinquency, 34*, 29-42.

Widders, R. (1994). *Pilots' knowledge of the relationship between alcohol consumption and levels of blood alcohol concentration.* MSc Thesis, Cranfield University. Department of Applied Psychology.

Widders, R. and Harris, D. (1997). Pilots' knowledge of the relationship between alcohol consumption and levels of blood alcohol concentration. *Aviation, Space and Environmental Medicine, 68*, 531-537.

Yesavage, J.A. and Leirer, Von O. (1986). Hangover effects on aircraft pilots 14 hours after alcohol ingestion: A preliminary report. *American Journal of Psychiatry, 143*, 1546-1550.

Section Three
Air Traffic Management

11 Controller workload, airspace capacity and future systems

Peter Brooker

Everything is what it is, and not another thing – Joseph Butler

Introduction

Orville never complained to Wilbur about the workload at Kitty Hawk. 'Workload' is a fairly recently invented word. It seems to have originated in the 1940s as 'work load', allied to teaching load and case load. After a few years with a hyphen, it took its present form. In the dictionary, work means 'physical or mental effort directed towards achieving something', and workload now means 'the amount of work assigned to an individual for completion within a certain time'.

In air traffic control (ATC), controller workload – or controller mental workload – is an extremely important topic. There have been many research studies, reports and reviews on workload (as it will be referred to here). Indeed, the joke is that researchers will produce 'reviews of reviews' (Stein, 1998). The present document necessarily has something of that flavour, and does review many of the 'breakthrough' research results, but there is a concentration on some specific questions about workload.

The aim here is to explore how the understanding of workload feeds into the measurement of ATC airspace sector capacity, and how predictive workload and sector capacity techniques need to be available to estimate the traffic handling capacity of future ATC systems. These future systems could be ones in which controllers use computer assistance tools, or where some controller tasks are delegated to pilots, or where some control tasks are automated, or where all control tasks are transferred to pilots ... The central point is that control

This paper was first published in Human Factors and Aerospace Safety 3(1), 2003, pp. 1-23

workload is a core determinant of future ATC system capacity, whatever the system might be, *and* that the benefits (and costs) of new control arrangements will need to be well understood before investments will take place.

A subtext in this exploration is an examination the role that applied psychology should play to be most useful. What kinds of problems should applied psychologists attack? In the present context, much of the work on sector capacity has in fact been carried out by systems engineers and operational researchers. This paper is written by an operational researcher who recognises the great value that applied psychology can offer – but not all researchers, operational staff or aviation managers share such a positive view. Applied psychologists have often found their role to be that of marginal improvers of operational systems (or worse, carrying remedial work on defective systems) rather than being a trusted part of the research or design teams producing new ATC systems.

An aviation psychology pioneer working on workload precursors serves to illustrate the roles that applied psychologists could play. Three pieces of work by Kenneth Craik serve to substantiate an assertion that he was an originator of workload research, with results are still relevant today. Craik developed the modern formulation of the concept of a mental model (Craik, 1943). He argued that human beings translate external events into internal models and then reason by manipulating these symbolic representations, so a mental model is in essence a dynamic representation or simulation of the world. Craik's work on flight simulators is recognised by the UK's Royal Aeronautical Society (Rolfe, 2002) – his objective was the measurement of the onset of fatigue.

Craik also put forward the important 'single-channel hypothesis'. This holds that an individual cannot normally carry out two distinct tasks (i.e. not ones with close mappings between stimulus and response) completely independently when each of them requires a choice of response (Craik, 1947 and 1948). When this is attempted, substantial delays occur in one or both tasks, even for 'trivial' tasks. Welford (1967) was the first to assert that the brain is subject to a single-channel bottleneck arising in the selection of responses. More recent work (Ruthruff et al, 2001) shows that this bottleneck is structural, i.e. it is a basic limitation of the cognitive/neural architecture.

Operational design and project staff – customers in modern jargon – valued Craik's work and guidance, because he tackled big practical problems and supplied normative answers. It was successful *applied* psychology – 'useful' in the best sense of the word – underpinned by a sound philosophical approach.

The following section lists some useful papers in the published literature. The sections after that are labelled Control Workload, Airspace Capacity, and Future Systems respectively, but these titles just indicate the main topics in each section – the text is essentially continuous. The final section is 'Good Predictive Models', and attempts to set out some lessons about the kinds of problems applied psychologists should be addressing.

The literature

The research and technical literature on workload and airspace capacity is enormous. Perhaps the earliest published work is that by Arad and his colleagues (Arad, 1964); and possibly the earliest critical review article is by Ratcliffe (1969) – who managed to anticipate many of the principal research themes. The concentration here is on techniques used in the UK by National Air traffic Services (NATS), with which the author has been involved, but some of the general references used also need to be acknowledged.

There are several good recent reviews of workload assessment. Stein's 1998 paper has already been noted. Chapter 11 of the book by Wickens and Hollands (2000) titled 'Attention, Time-Sharing, and Workload', analyses the fundamental issues. Kirwan et al. (1998) is written very much from the point of view of the practical applied psychologist.

There are rather fewer references on the topic of sector capacity in the open literature: government research establishments and ATC service providers tend to produce internal reports, so researchers in different countries have often been unaware of existing work. More recently, industrial relations, commercial confidentiality and the use of contractors are increasingly important. One useful survey of sector capacity techniques is that from the INTEGRA project (Eurocontrol, 2000).

A related relevant report is Eurocontrol (1997), a report on the development of a Cognitive Model for ATC (contracted out to the 'Institute of Evaluation Research'). It is intended to provide a basic understanding of the cognitive components and processes in ATC – modelled as an information processing activity governed by rules, plans and the controller's acquired knowledge. Hendy et al .(1997) is not primarily a review paper, but presents 'top-down' examination and critique of information processing and time pressure in relation to workload.

A further Eurocontrol report (2002) examines Human Performance Metrics in ATC. It provides an extensive bibliography and compares the characteristics of different approaches to workload and also:

- Situation awareness
- System monitoring and error detection
- Teamwork
- Trust
- Usability and user acceptance
- Human error.

The need to consider these other metrics serves as a caution that workload is not the only human performance factor that must be investigated when developing future systems.

Peter Brooker

Control workload

One way of dividing the workload literature into categories is to ask if the author(s) propose a definition of workload. Definitions are sometimes suggestive of calculation methods. One appealing definition is from Stein (1998):

> ...the amount of effort, both physical and psychological, expended in response to system demands (taskload) and also in accordance with the operator's internal standard of performance.

This has the advantage of introducing the concepts of taskload (= system demands) and internal (*sic*) standard of performance. Taskload and workload are analogous to physical stress and strain, the latter being the consequence of the former. A second definition is from Kirwan et al. (1998), quoting one of the authors (Megaw):

> ...the more difficult the task is, then the more complex the mental operations are, the more mental processing power and capacity is used, and the more human physiological variables (e.g. heart rate) are affected, and the more the subject 'feels' a higher degree of workload.

This introduces elements such as mental processing, physiological variables and the subject's feelings (although why did Megaw use quotes?). Thus, workload is a multi-dimensional concept encompassing both the difficulty of tasks and the effort – physical and mental – that has to be brought to bear, plus a personal dimension.

The two definitions overlap to a degree but are noticeably different – and seasoned professionals produced them both. Is an agreed definition of workload ever possible? Workload is a construct or concept. Its definition is surely largely a narrative instructing the reader about its relationships to a neighbouring family of concepts. An analogy is a philosopher saying that it is only possible to understand a concept such as 'responsibility' by considering the causes underlying particular actions and then their consequences, including the blame for particular decisions.

Figure 1 shows some of the activities and concepts associated with workload: the figure maps onto to both of the definitions above. Given this complexity, how could there be an objective 'scientific' definition of workload? To be scientific one would have to be able to prove that it had been achieved. Where is the 'gold standard' – an absolute measuring scale – against which it could be compared?

Workload cannot be an 'objectively scientific' concept because it includes subjective elements – 'internal performance standards' and 'feels' are subjective words used in the two definitions, and indeed in most people's understanding about what workload represents. Thus, workload cannot entirely be represented

226

by brain or physiological functions: it necessarily involves consciousness and mental states that are perceived and assessed subjectively.

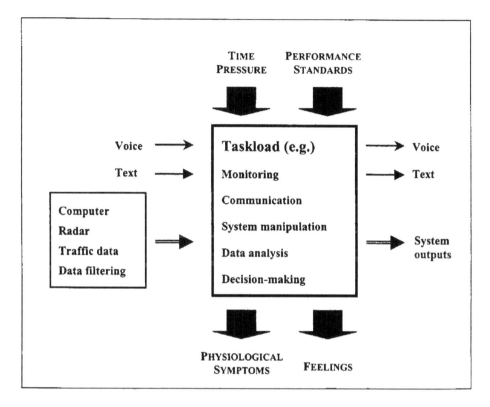

Figure 1 Some aspects of workload

Although the word psychology is derived from the Greek for 'mind', applied psychologists tend to avoid analysis of the mind or consciousness; e.g. Wickens and Hollands (2000) book does not include the words 'mind', 'feelings', 'subjective' or 'consciousness' in its index.   In psychology, definitions of 'cognition' note human thought processes and their components – perception, memory, decision-making, etc. An individual tends to be modelled in information processing terms, with physiological components, such as stress, changing the individual's performance. Psychology is viewed as a science, so the inclination is to use mathematically based techniques, e.g. information theory, and experimentally orientated methods, e.g. physiological indicators, rather than delve into the realms of philosophy. Unfortunately, philosophical methods do not test hypotheses of approximations to the truth – and hence are seldom of practical use to a team trying to design a better ATC system.

The fact that scientific methods operate by trying to eliminate personal subjective prejudices is often somehow equated with the idea that all subjective elements are 'bad' and can/should be eliminated. Nagel (1995) and Searle (1999) provide some arguments to demonstrate that this is a confusion. For present purposes, the assertion is that statements about workload are, in the last resort, subjective ones, albeit overlaying objective data on taskload, time pressure, etc. If there is to be a 'gold standard' for workload comparisons then it has to be the product of subjective assessments. Can such a standard be constructed with 'reasonable accuracy'? To try to answer this question, it is necessary to examine the training, management and culture of controllers.

Controllers are selected to have good intelligence and stable personalities – depressive and introspective tendencies would obviously not be helpful characteristics – and extensively trained over several years. There are usually two phases: classroom and simulator training over about 18 months to earn a 'rating', and then around the same amount of time of OJT (On–the–Job–Training) to earn 'validations' to operate on one or two real sectors. Classroom training takes place in only a few colleges in any one country, e.g. the UK has one college for area ATC. College instructors need to have been operational controllers; in most cases, they would have trained originally at the same college. The time involved for OJT varies between individuals, until they achieve a specified performance. Much of OJT involves sitting with experienced controllers and being mentored about the right techniques to use to move traffic safely and expeditiously in the sector. Controllers work on shifts, and people on the same shift pattern tend to work together for long periods of their career.

Selection and training therefore exhibits considerable consistency of instruction, correction and reinforcement, and this is further conditioned through 'controller culture'. Controllers are trained in standardised ways to learn correct judgements, and to recognise and tackle typical problems, e.g. climbing an aircraft through another's flight level, in a particular way; i.e. sets of heuristics will tend to be adopted by trainees. A standard language – a very restricted subset of English – is used for communication between controllers and pilots. Data entry to computer or paper record uses *pro formas* rather than free formats. Trainee validation on specific sectors – with largely stable routeings and traffic patterns – means that the same common kinds of ATC problems have to be encountered and resolved many times. Controller operational performance is monitored throughout an individual's career. The controller community discusses thoughtfully what is 'best practice' through its professional journals (e.g. Transmit, published by the UK Guild of Air Traffic Control Officers), and studies and debates incident and Airprox reports. There is thus a considerable commonality of experience.

It is therefore argued that experienced controllers are able to assess 'externally' the workload that an operational sector controller is experiencing – 'over-the-shoulder' rating. Workload experience may be mental 'private property' to the controller, but such observers understand the thought processes and pressures for that person. They can comprehend the issues raised by the data flows, the information on the radar screen and in communication messages. They know what the experience being undergone is like for the sector controller. These are reasonable inductive arguments, but are in no sense a formal 'proof' that:

Average external controller assessments ⇔ workload

But how could a proof be constructed for any other technique that one might propose for workload? Subjective assessments bring into play all the elements of figure 1, so they have 'face validity' (an irritating phrase to non-psychologists, as it gives a cryptic hint about some much better technique known only to the cognoscenti). If a new technique did not match controller assessments then why would one believe that would be an adequate workload measure? On what rational basis could a novel technique be shown to be 'better'? How, indeed, could external subjective assessments be falsified – the 'acid test' of a scientific hypothesis (Popper, 1959)?

An example of external controller assessment is the DORA method, developed in the UK in the early 1970s (Smith and Stamp, 1973). The expert observer assesses the workload by noting mentally such things as the activities of the controller on the R/T and marking strips, the verbal liaison with colleagues, the nature of the radar picture, etc. An important element is that of ensuring consistency in ratings between the different controller assessors. (NB: With modern data processing and video facilities, the controller's performance can be replayed and discussed by assessors.) Every two minutes the assessor rates the controller workload, these ratings later being matched against the levels of traffic on the controller's frequency at the same time. The ranking scale is given in table 1 (NB: various labels were used).

Table 1   Controller workload ranking scale

Workload Category	Interpretation
I	Fully loaded – 'could not handle another aircraft'
II	Very busy, but with some spare capacity
III	Busy, but without special difficulties
IV	Workload below III

When the two-minute workload ratings are matched against traffic flow the resulting picture of workload versus hourly traffic produces figure 2 – the actual workload for the period would weight the responses here by the number of aircraft

229

under control. Note that this figure is constructed for particular equipment and particular procedures for this particular sector. As expected, the proportions of time spent in the heavier workload categories increase with the traffic flow, but there is not a sharp cut-off at any sort of critical hourly throughput – so there is no 'inherent' sector capacity figure where 'one more aircraft is too many'. What this means in terms of sector capacity is discussed in the next section.

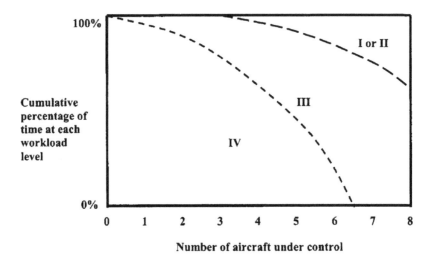

Number of aircraft under control

Figure 2 Illustrative relationship between workload and number of aircraft controlled (adapted from figures and measurements in Smith and Stamp, 1973)

An important factor, which can affect workload dramatically, is the *pattern* of flow through the hour. The highest workload levels (I and II) most generally arise from short-term peaks in traffic, when taskload is highest. If the flow of aircraft is regulated in some way, e.g. by controlling airport departure times, thus preventing strong traffic troughs and peaks, then the frequency of these high taskload periods can be markedly reduced. Very tight and effective flow regulation produces a shift upward in the curves of figure 2.

Other methods for assessing workload

Dozens, perhaps hundreds, of ways have been put forward for measuring workload. Many of these calculation methods are properly called 'metrics' – proxies for workload – as a person's performance of numerical tests is a metric for intelligence but not a complete picture of his or her abilities. Taskload-based and predictive metrics are examined in the next section. The rest of the workload measurement techniques can be categorised as physiological, operator subjective, or performance: Stein (1998), Kirwan et al. (1998) and Eurocontrol (2002) give a very full account – the superficial comments here are just intended to illustrate the possible kinds of metric.

Physiological metrics

Physiological measures assume that changes in workload cause measurable differences in certain physiological processes, generally involuntarily. Some physiological indicators are available even in the absence of overt behaviour. They include Galvanic skin response, heart rate and similar from the electrocardiograph readings, and ocular (eye) responses.

Operator-subjective metrics

Operator-subjective workload assessment methods use the operator's self-reported effort in carrying out some task(s). They are cheap and easy to use and analyse, and acceptable to operational staff. However, there can be significant individual biases – why should individuals' self-perceptions be consistent? As discussed further in the next section, there are very wide variations in people's judgement about workload, memory limitations, and their mental models for different tasks. However, these metrics often have an important 'marketing' role in helping controllers faced with new equipment and/or procedures to 'accept' their operational introduction. The Instantaneous Self Assessment (ISA) technique, developed by the UK NATS, is a '1 to 5 rating' method that is now used by the Eurocontrol Agency: it allows for online registration of controller ratings at intervals down to two minutes or so. Other examples (see Eurocontrol, 2002 for references) include the Subjective Workload Assessment Technique (SWAT), the NASA Task Load Index (TLX), and the Air Traffic Workload Input Technique (ATWIT). The key question is the extent to which these metrics are benchmarked – and then calibrated – against 'external subjective' workload

Performance metrics

Performance metrics estimate workload through direct measurement of task performance. There are essentially two types of methods: *primary (or direct) task* and *secondary task* measures, but both rely on measuring the influence of increasing task load on the performance of a particular task(s). The primary task technique typically involves varying some primary task parameter (e.g., tracking complexity) that will affect task demands to the point that performance falls below some criterion, thereby providing a measure of residual capacity at resource allocations below criterion performance. Thus, primary task measures can directly relate workload to system performance. Performance metrics have shortcomings, e.g. performance dependent on strategic priorities shifts between tasks, and can often be intrusive and artificial. Secondary task performance add in a secondary task and then the analyst examines how its performance deteriorates with increased traffic through the sector, e.g. simple digit reading, repetition of words presented to controller. One variant is the inclusion of realistic 'embedded tasks' – tasks that provide proxy measures of workload, while appearing 'normal' to the controller.

Sector capacity

Sector capacity is more than the application of workload measurement to airspace sectors. Sector capacity can be defined as that sustainable flow of traffic generating maximum acceptable (sic) controller workload. But ATC is a complex 'socio-technical system': people and machines are linked together through structures and processes. Controllers are employed by an organisation that has to operate within an evolving industrial relations framework. The introduction of system changes has to be negotiated rather than imposed. One of the common words that controllers use about themselves is 'professionalism': this is often seen as being at odds with anything reminiscent of F. W. Taylor's 'scientific management'.

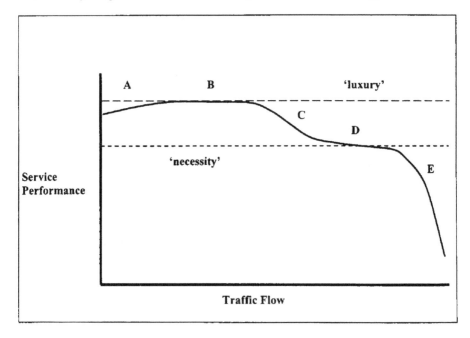

Figure 3   Postulated average service performance by controller on sector for different traffic flows

ATC delivers a *service performance* product to its customers – safe and expeditious flight through airspace. By expeditious is meant the 'economic quality' of the flightpath, with a perfect quality flightpath presumably being one adopted if there were no other aircraft anywhere in the vicinity. How does performance vary with workload?

Consider a single controller handling a specific sector at different levels of traffic flow (measured as flights per hour) – the words 'single' and 'specific' are important. The traffic routeings and patterns through the sector are assumed constant, i.e. increased traffic flow produces 'more of the same'. Figure 3 illustrates what average (sic) service performance by that controller on that sector for the different levels of traffic flow. Performance here is an (undefined) appropriate combination of safety and expedition: a hazardous incident occurring at an unacceptable frequency over time would obviously count as a very low performance component and an economical flightpath as a high performance component.

The general shape of the curve in figure 3 can be supported by results in the research literature (in particular, Sperandio, 1978), noted that controllers handle increasing traffic by adopting successively more economical strategies in operating methods to defer the onset of 'overload' conditions). At very low flow rates (A in diagram) there would be a concern that the controller 'underload' would be reflected in boredom and 'coping behaviours' that might result in increased hazardous error rates (Hopkin, 1988, quoted in Stein, 1998). When there are a few aircraft on the controller's frequency he/she can provide a 'luxury' service to the aircraft and provide the best flight path for each, e.g. provide expeditious routeing and better climb/descent profiles (B). For higher flows, more stereotyped flight paths have to become the norm, although speeds and tracks can still be tailored on some occasions (C) – this explains the non-linearity in figure 3. When the controller has to handle many aircraft, the only feasible control method is to concentrate on keeping the flow of aircraft moving through the sector safely (D): individual operating characteristics are now low priority and ATC instructions have to concentrate on 'necessary' elements. For very high flow rates, operational safety/economy errors would be frequent, and hence general performance is very poor (E).

The most important point, echoing the previous section's comments about workload, is that there is no evidence to suggest that, except at very high flow rates, there is anything but steady changes in the curve in figure 3, i.e. no reason to suppose that any dramatic changes occur at some 'crucial' traffic flow(s).

The natural variations between individuals also have to be addressed by ATC planners and managers. There are well-known differences between the performances of individual controllers on identical tasks. An individual's performance with the same traffic can also vary considerably: on some days the controller might just be a better performer; there might be different kinds of background distractions in the control room; slight changes in communications might affect how the traffic pattern develops. Tattersall (1998) explores these and other kinds of differences: relevant factors include age, experience, gender,

233

personality, cognitive style, time-sharing ability. Stein (1998) identified variations in the mental models used by controllers.

The statistical distribution of controller service performance on a particular sector for a particular flow rate probably looks something like figure 4 – there would be a family of curves for different flow rates. Some individuals at some times perform very well, most produce good service performance, and on a few occasions the performance by some controllers is poor. This is no more than a vaguely Gaussian distribution plus some assumed 'censoring' at the low performance end: chronically poor performers would not have been validated on the sector; others would be removed from their posts if they showed deterioration; those showing short-term degradation of performance would strive to achieve safety; etc.

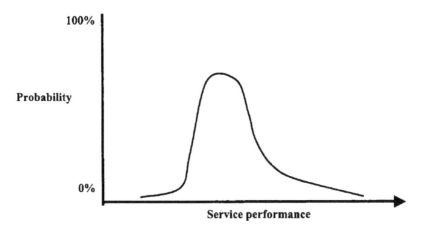

Figure 4 Speculative probability distribution of controller service performance for a particular sector and flow rate

So, given the curves in figures 2, 3 and 4, the word 'acceptable' in the definition of sector capacity, and the comments about variations between controllers, how is sector capacity to be determined? For a given ATC system, there are two crucial points:

- The setting of 'acceptable' workload is an industrial relations issue.
- The only control variable available to ATC planners is traffic flow.

Thus, in practice:

'Acceptable' workload corresponds to a planned (sic) service performance at about the region C in figure 2. Were it to be set at a point where all the aircraft under control would be receiving the 'luxury' service' (i.e. at B) then the hourly throughput would be probably be too low in terms of airlines' commercial needs.

A workload level at D would be too risky – the odd 'unplannable' peak in traffic could put the workload into the unacceptable E region.

This workload would correspond to an individual level of service performance at about the kink in the lower end of the performance distribution in figure 4. This would represent a 'standard validated competent controller', as judged by the managers and negotiated with operational controllers en bloc.

In practice, ATC planners are interested only in those workload levels that are 'just acceptable'. ATC has to control the levels of workload by controlling the levels of taskload. They need to be able to estimate how taskload changes with traffic flows, which *inter alia* will generally produce changes in spatial and time patterns for conflicts. *They therefore want a taskload measure that consistently provides the best match to 'just acceptable' workload.* The desired measure must accurately predict when workload would be at the planned performance level, immaterial of the nature and magnitude of workload components/traffic flows/patterns.

Sector capacity might thus correspond to a set of conditions such as 'no more than 50% of the controller's time at ratings I and II' – 'a good day's work' for a controller and low risks of fatigue.

The significant point here is that it is taskload which the 'instrumental variable'. Taskload measures are traditionally important sources of workload-related data. They can be divided into those that concentrate on some particular aspect of the job, e.g. number of aircraft under control, radio communication bandwidth and duration, and number of flight transitions, and those involving a summation of (most of?) the tasks carried out – i.e. where the processing of information and execution of tasks are of central importance.

An example of the former is some strong current work by the FAA (e.g. Manning et al, 2002), recently examining the addition of communication events – transmissions between pilot/controller and controller/controller – to activity variable taskload factors. The declared aim of the work is 'to develop objective taskload measures that could replace subjective workload measures': ATWIT is used as the (active controller's) subjective workload rating. One notable feature of the work is the depth of statistical analysis employed – mainly principal component analysis and multiple regression. The software used – POWER (Performance and Objective Workload Evaluation Research) includes 20+ variables of aircraft and controller activity. One of the problems about these kinds of performance metrics is the extent to which their predictions can be extrapolated – is the correlation with workload maintained?

Taskload summation metrics were developed from the very outset – Arad (1964) and Ratcliffe (1969). Significant steps forward were made by Schmidt (1976), who stated the main assumptions very succinctly:

'Work load (sic) ... is related to the frequency of occurrence of events which require decisions to be made and actions to be taken by the control team, and to the time required to accomplish the tasks associated with these events ... With proper calibration, the model may be used to assess the impact on work load and sector capacity of future automation features.'

A well-used taskload and simple information processing/action model for workload is DORATASK. This is an analytical model supported by a fast-time simulation model (Phillips (1995) is a general review; Richmond (1989) gives clear examples of the calculation logic). The taskload is calculated by summing the time taken by a controller to carry out all the necessary tasks, both observable and non-observable, associated with the flow of traffic. Sector capacity is then set by total taskload plus a parameter indicating the proportion of time necessary for controller recuperation, i.e. this parameter ensures a march to acceptable workload.

Observable tasks are 'routine' and 'conflict resolution' tasks. A routine task is one that a controller must carry out for all aircraft regardless of whether he has any other aircraft under his control, for example the issuing of standard RT instructions. Conflict resolution tasks are additional tasks that must be performed if any aircraft are in potential conflict. Non-observable tasks are planning tasks carried out by a controller, and mental tasks involved in conflict prediction and detection. The time to carry out observable tasks may be measured directly.

Planning work is not directly observable. DORATASK therefore includes algorithms to estimate workload representing the amount of time a controller spends on planning tasks. Richmond (1989) explains the thinking and gives some examples. In the case of terminal areas, there are two non-observable tasks, initial processing and radar monitoring. Radar monitoring is modelled by the number of visual checks of the radar screen, the time per radar check, and the combination of aircraft pairs that have to be checked. The two non-observable tasks are linear and quadratic in the number of aircraft, each being multiplied by an unknown parameter (compare Arad, 1964!). These parameters have to be estimated by benchmarking against sectors of known capacity. Thus, the DORATASK estimate depends on three parameters.

Future systems

There is considerable interest and debate about future ATC systems, e.g. see Brooker (2002) and Eurocontrol (1998). Workload is a vital element in such studies, where the goals are to handle increased traffic safely and cost-effectively. There are many different possibilities and combinations: controllers may get automation tools to help in their tasks, some control tasks may be passed to pilots, control tasks may be automated in some way, airspace sectors can be completely restructured, etc. Possible roles for the controller and pilot are explored (from very different viewpoints) in Kirwan (2001) and Brooker (2003). New systems must be designed to ensure the required capacity. It is not sufficient to rely upon the results of expensive real-time simulations of possible candidate systems.

A simple diagram may help to illustrate the workload issues. The basis is a geometrical construction used in applications from metallurgy to relativity.

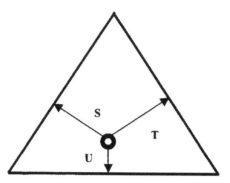

Figure 5   Perpendiculars in an equilateral triangle

Figure 5 shows an equilateral triangle, i.e. with the sides the same length and the angles between them at 60 degrees. From a point O inside the triangle, three lines are drawn so that they are perpendicular to the triangles' sides. It can be proved that the sum of the lengths S, T and U, of these lines is constant, no matter where O is located within the triangle. This enables the possible values of an equation:

S + T + U = Constant,

to be explored within the triangle.

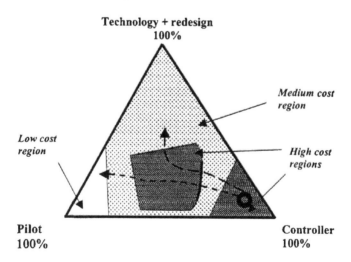

Figure 6   Possible migration paths in the STU triangle with (notional) isocost contours for safe optimised systems (see text)

237

Figure 6 uses figure 5 for control workload in a particular volume of airspace (which may be one or several sectors). The three variables are:

S = Controller workload
T = Pilot workload
U = Technology/redesign workload equivalent

The second and third of these need some explanation. The second is the control workload component of pilot's total workload. The third is essentially a residual after pilot and controller workload have been counted. It consists of the 'workload equivalent' of those tasks that have been allocated to 'the computer', in the widest sense. However, it also includes the equivalent for those tasks that have been eliminated, e.g. if all control functions were to pass to the pilot then there would obviously be no controller/pilot communication tasks.

The present system is shown by the O label in figure 6 – almost entirely controller workload but some tasks have had some degree of computer assistance, e.g. Short Term Conflict Alert systems supplement controller scanning of the screen for conflicts. Two possible migration paths are shown. The lower one moves from the present system to one in which pilots carry out most of the control functions and there is increased automation. The upper one moves to a system in which there is much more 'automation' and in which pilots and controllers share tasks in some way. The first would be termed full delegation and the latter shared responsibility. Which precise tasks might pass from one actor to another is not the question here: it is assumed that the system represented by each point is the *best* that can be achieved with such an STU combination, i.e. it is safe and with minimum full running cost (i.e. operating cost plus capital investment, equipment maintenance, etc).

This cost dimension could be displayed by creating a three dimensional diagram. For present purposes, it is sufficient to add in some (purely illustrative) 'isocost' contours in the triangle: the darker the shading the higher the cost. The lower path finishes up with a lower cost endpoint than the upper one. This now shows the difficulty involved in both the migration paths. The first part of the migration looks appealing because there is an improvement in the cost function for comparatively small changes in operational concept. Then both paths move into an extensive higher cost region, i.e. the benefits of marginal changes are not apparent. The thickened boundary for the high cost region shows what is effectively a barrier for the next phase of changes – what decision-maker would want to incur higher costs? The answer is a decision-maker who could be convinced by workload research results, which predict accurately that the end of the migration path delivers substantial cost effectiveness improvements. This is the challenge for workload research on future systems: considerable faith would be needed to act on the advice of a psychologist to take such a course – when all you can see is an expanse of desert, you have to have a great deal of trust in a guide who says that beyond the desert is the promised land.

Figure 6 is a considerable simplification. There is a time/traffic dimension – increased total workload would correspond to a larger triangle. Moreover, he nature of the isocost contours will change for higher traffic levels. Some STU combinations, e.g. continuing with existing control concept, could become infeasible, so their costs would be very much higher – they would have to include the economic opportunity cost of the flights that could not operate. There may well be areas within the triangle that are not feasible in safety terms, i.e. such STU combinations would not achieve the necessary safety targets: these would effectively have infinite cost.

Real-time simulations are only suitable for evaluating system s at a very late design stage. Designers need workload measure for prediction of new concepts of operation, interfaces and tools early in the development cycle to enable early concentration on the most promising potential systems. Workload models for future systems have to be developed from taskload models plus some new ideas about how task timings will change with different data flows, computer assistance/automation. It is essential that task load is modelled in such a way that it correlates well with acceptable workload over the whole region of interest in the triangle. Research tends to concentrate on information processing, multiple specific resources and time pressures.

Different points in the STU triangle correspond to changes in the nature of workload tasks. This leads to the need for task analysis – breaking down new tasks into constituent 'well-understood' basic-task elements, which may overlap or interfere with each other to produce higher control loading.

The 'secret' is to measure the mental effort that is expended on basic-task mental resources. Mental resources have a variety of limits. Different types of resource are available to deal with different types of mental processing (e.g. visual versus auditory). A mental 'channel' is defined as a distinct information processing capability in the brain; different channels represent loadings on different processing centres.

Two examples are TLAP (Timelines Analysis and Prediction) and VACP (Visual, Auditory Cognitive Psychomotor) – see Kirwan et al. (1998) for descriptions. Wickens Multiple Resource Pool theory – W/INDEX is similar in broad principle to these and has been used in the ATC area. Wickens' (see Wickens and Hollands, 2000, for references) Model of Multiple Resources assumes that the workload experienced by a controller performing an action can be split between a number of different 'channels'. These channels are representative of different functions within the brain, such as talking, thinking, listening, moving. For each action a weighting is assigned to each channel representing the effort required of that channel by that action. This allows the resulting workload to be predicted.

W/INDEX uses six channels – visual, auditory, spatial cognition, verbal cognition, manual response and voce response. Tasks load the channels and produce interference between them, e.g. it is difficult to listen and speak, so a task requiring simultaneous verbal and monitoring is dual processing and weights the channel loading. The demand for each resource are summed and weighted and then summed to produce task workload. Concurrent tasks are likely to interfere in ATC. It should be noted that Wickens' work was based on pilot workload, there do not appear to be any reported validations of his methods for ATC systems.

PUMA (Day et al, 1993, Kilner et al, 1998, Householder and Owens, 1995, Kirwan, 1998) uses W/INDEX. The PUMA toolset is used to explore different future ATC concepts and system designs. However, validity is not assured since it is based on W/INDEX. Observational task analysis must capture not only visual and communication tasks but also cognitive tasks – future ATC systems are likely to have very different cognitive tasks – as evidenced by the large changes in the STU diagram. PUMA hinges on the weighting values used the conflict matrix, which quantify the extent of channel interference. Householder and Owens (1995) note that 'the values of the weightings are obtained from the subjective judgement of human factors experts in the ATC environment' – but how can these people make a subjective judgement on something that they are not directly experiencing? Validation of the weightings through objective experiments involving controllers is therefore a prerequisite. Moreover, validation against (e.g.) DORATASK for some of the different kinds of future systems is essential.

There have been few research studies that attempt to model workload in the STU triangle, i.e. for a wide variety of future concepts. A notable one is by Hudgell and Gingell (2001), arising out of the INTEGRA project. This models the components of the ATC system purely through an examination of information processing load (IPL) – which is stated to be a 'surrogate measure' for capacity in each part of the system. The IPL is calculated for each 'actor' – controllers, pilots, computer tools, communications – in the system.

Hudgell and Gingell identify seven 'causes' of information processing, including 'flight arrival' (into the list of flights relevant to the actor), monitoring and resolution planning. The amount of processing p for actor i on cause α is time dependent. Flight arrival is simple: p is equal to a weighting factor times the number of flights 'arriving in the lists' in each unit time. The weighting factor λ is initially taken as 1 for actors processing that piece of information. Each cause has a different λ.

More complex causes produce more complex expressions. Resolution planning is the task of planning a resolution for each forecast interaction (ie when trajectories breach pre-set separation criteria). An additional weighting factor w is required, to express the difficulty of resolution – the number of constraints present in the interaction. The amount of processing is equal to the product of the λ and w weighting factors times the forecast number of interactions in each unit time.

The IPL for each actor is found by adding the seven IPL contributions. For a current controller, who undertakes all the control tasks, the IPL thus has seven terms, hence seven λ weighting factors plus two additional 'difficulty' weightings for resolution planning and monitoring causes. The authors state:

'The experimental analyst needs to assess the 'cut-off' for each actor – the maximum information the actor can process in unit time ... For pilots and controllers the cut-off can be assessed by calibration simulations in which the actor is known ... to be at capacity ... It is not a simple cut-off ... the actor can accept an overload of information for a short period ...'

The authors stress that the IPL methodology provides a framework (sic) for capacity assessment – with the detailed assumptions about weightings being supplied by the user. But a framework is just part of what is required – a random person with a violin is usually some way short of producing a credible musical performance. Given the kinds of analytical problems noted in the earlier text here, this is obviously an important – and very large – problem: there are potentially many weightings to validate in what is recognised as a model with non-linear components. The extent of the calibration measurements and statistical analyses required to estimate the weighting factors with any confidence is extremely large. The second problem is that IPL appears to take little account of the channel interference aspects explored by Wickens in W/INDEX and used in PUMA. The third problem is that IPL needs to be validated and benchmarked against established 'real world' methods such as DORATASK – asserting that something is a surrogate measure does not make it a reliable or unbiased one.

Hendy et al's (1997) work is relevant to the Hudgell and Gingell approach. (NB: This paper was not picked up in the INTEGRA literature search.) Hendy et al. note that 'while many models of workload exist, few appear to be well founded in theory or to provide a satisfactory basis for a quantitative representation of operator load'. They argue that a workload construct requires three components: a time-based factor (time pressure), a factor due to the intensity of demand for attentional resources (the amount of information to be processed = task difficulty/task complexity) and a catch-all factor attributed to the operator's psychological/physiological state (anxiety, arousal, motivation, fatigue, etc). Hendy et al .construct and test model in an ATC simulation environment explicitly investigating the relationship between a time based-factor and an intensity-based factor, within a simulated air traffic control environment. They model the load on the human information processing system from the ratio of the time necessary to process the required information, to the time allowable for making a decision. This ratio – 'time pressure' – is found to determine both subjective estimates of workload as well as operator performance.

Good predictive models

Customers for applied psychology are generally project or design staff working to tight timescales and budgets. They will ask: 'What will your techniques and models accomplish for me?' Their focus is on usefulness and practical benefit: it is very unlikely that they would value debates on cultural relativism. What kinds of models of ATC (socio-technical) systems should applied psychologists therefore aim to produce?

Social scientists know very well that their models are not 'absolute', as evidenced by the kinds of definitions used, e.g. (Chorley and Haggett, 1968):

> *Model*: A simplified structuring of reality which presents supposedly significant relationships in a generalised form ... (models) are valuable in obscuring incidental detail and in allowing fundamental aspects of reality to appear.

In other words, a good model is one that illuminates what are the 'key factors' at any point in the topic's development, and presumably provide help to the customer in seeing the way forward.

The previous text has demonstrated the importance of control workload: it is a crucial factor in developing future ATC systems. These must produce – in effect – reduced total workload costs per aircraft. Figure 6 demonstrates that a 'marginal analysis'; of workload effects may not be sufficient – or is a local optimum an acceptable objective? Taskload models based on information processing and the summation of the effort required for individual tasks appear to be the way forward, but they need to incorporate channel interference and time pressure aspects. Predictive taskload models, particularly when they direct attention to areas of the figure 6 'STU diagram' well away from present operational practices, need validation against the subjective workload benchmark. However, this kind of activity requires significant resources.

As evidenced by recent work on Human Performance Metrics (Eurocontrol, 2002), these aspects of future ATC systems fall methodologically into the 'very tough' category. This is just one of the challenges for applied psychology in producing useful models to help their ATC designer and planner customers. Human factors research outputs are usually well thought through and intellectually persuasive, but they are not always immediately applicable, as some kind of 'tool kit' or as an integral part of systems design. The debate about 'Human-centred automation' (Billings, 1997) serves as an example. The phrase can be construed in several ways – Sheridan (2000) offers ten alternative meanings, some of which would certainly rather more useful to system designers than others. To an outsider, rather a lot of the applied psychology literature seems to consist of demonstrations that someone else's work or hypotheses are flawed.

The prime objective for applied psychologists is surely to produce fruitful and illuminating models that stand generic validation against the experimental data. This is obviously easier to say than to accomplish. Nevertheless, it is crucial. Systems design customers want guidance beyond the level of 'you can make a small extrapolation but we will need to validate the results through simulations'.

The studies reported in the previous section did not solve all the problems posed, but they are bold and potentially fruitful steps forward. However, without further progress, applied psychologists might well see other disciples – operational research and systems engineering occupy vacant professional territory.

An analogy can be made with the history of chemistry. The atomic theory and knowledge of the relative weights of elements enabled some progress to be made in the early 19th century, but the development of the concept of valency – the number of other atoms with which an atom can combine – was a major step forward in 1852. Valency only really made complete sense to chemists in the early 20th century, when electron orbitals in atoms begin to be understood. The limits and approximations of the valency concept then became clear, but from the start valency was an extremely fruitful hypothesis, both for theory and for practical implementation. Control workload does not yet have a theory to match something like valency. Perhaps information processing, time pressure and channel models are edging towards a new phase?

References

Arad, B.A. (1964). The Control Load and Sector Design. *Journal of Air Traffic Control 12 (60)*, 12–31.

Billings, C.E. (1997). *Aviation Automation: the search for a Human-Centred Approach.* New Jersey, NJ: Lawrence Erlbaum Associates.

Brooker, P. (2002). Future Air Traffic Management – Passing the Key Tests. *The Aeronautical Journal, 106 (1058)*, 211–215.

Brooker, P. (2003). Future Air Traffic Management: Strategy and Control Philosophy. *The Aeronautical Journal, 107, (1076)*, 589-598.

Chorley, R.J. and Haggett, P. (Eds). (1968). *Socio-Economic Models in Geography.* London: Methuen and Co. Ltd.

Craik, K. (1943). *The Nature of Explanation.* Cambridge: Cambridge University Press.

Craik, K. (1947). Theory of the human operator in control systems: The operator as an engineering system. *British Journal of Psychology, Part I, 38*, 56-61.

Craik, K. (1948). Theory of the human operator in control systems: Man as an element in a control system. *British Journal of Psychology, Part II 38*, 142-148.

Day, P.O., Hook, M.K., Warren, C. and Kelly, C.J. (1993). The modelling of air traffic controller workload. In, *Proceedings on Workload Assessment and Aviation Safety.* London: Royal Aeronautical Society.

Eurocontrol. (1997). *Model of the Cognitive Aspects of Air Traffic Control.* Report reference HUM.ET1.ST01.1000–REP–02, Eurocontrol, Brussels. http://www.eurocontrol.int/humanfactors/docs/HF7–HUM.ET1.ST01.1000–REP–02.pdf.

Eurocontrol (1998). Air Traffic Management Strategy for 2000+ Volume 2.

Eurocontrol (2000). *INTEGRA Capacity Metrics: Literature Survey.* Eurocontrol, Brussels. http://www.eurocontrol.int/care/integra/documents/capacity_report1.pdf.

Eurocontrol (2002). *Eurocontrol CARE/ASAS Activity 2: Human Performance Metrics.* Report Reference: CARE/ASAS/NLR/02–034. 034http://www.eurocontrol.int/care/asas/documentation/care–asas–a2–02–34.pdf.

Hendy, K.C., Liao, K., and Milgram, P. (1997). Combining Time and Intensity Effects in Assessing Operator Information-Processing Load. *Human Factors, 39*, 30-47.

Householder, P. and Owens, S. (1995). *An initial assessment of the effects of a number of computer assistance tools upon controller workload: summary report.* CS Report 9503. London: Civil Aviation Authority.

Hudgell, A.J. and Gingell, R.M. (2001). *Assessing the Capacity of Novel ATM Systems.* 4th USA/Europe Air Traffic Management RandD Seminar. http://atm2001.eurocontrol.fr/finalpapers/pap171.pdf.

Kilner, A., Hook, M., Fearnside, P., and Nicholson P. (1998). Developing a predictive model of controller workload in air traffic management. In, E. Hanson, E.J. Lovesey and S.L. Robertson (Eds.). *Contemporary Ergonomics 1998.* London: Taylor and Francis.

Kirwan, B. (2001). The role of the controller in the accelerating industry of air traffic management. *Safety Science, 37(2-3)*, 151-185.

Kirwan, B.I., Kilner, A.R. and Megaw, E.D. (1998). Mental workload measurement Techniques: A Review. R and D Report 9874, National Air Traffic Services Ltd, London.

Manning, C.A., Mills, S.H., Fox, C.M., Pfleiderer, E.M., Mogilka, H.J. (2002). *Using Air Traffic Control Taskload Measures and Communication Events to Predict Subjective Workload.* DOT/FAA/AM–02/4. Office of Civil Aerospace Medical FAA, Washington, USA.

Nagel, T. (1995). *Other Minds: Critical Essays 1969-1994.* Oxford: Oxford University Press.

Phillips, R.M. (1995). *A Guide to DORATASK procedure for sector capacity estimation.* CS Report 9506. London: Civil Aviation Authority.

Popper, K.R. (1959). *The Logic of Scientific Discovery.* London: Hutchinson.

Ratcliffe, S. (1969). *Mathematical Models for the Prediction of Air Traffic Controller Workloads.* RRE Memorandum No. 2532. Malvern, UK: Royal Radar Establishment, Ministry of Technology.

Richmond, G.C. (1989). *The DORATASK methodology of Sector capacity Assessment: an interim description of its adaptation to Terminal Control (TMA) Sectors.* DORA Report 8916. London: Civil Aviation Authority.

Rolfe, J. (2002). History of Flight Simulation (the Cambridge Cockpit). London: The Royal Aeronautical Society. http://www.raes.org.uk/fl-sim/FSG%20Cambridge%20Cockpit.htm.

Ruthruff, E., Pashler, H.E. and Klaassen, A. (2001). Processing bottlenecks in dual-task performance: structural limitation or strategic postponement. *Psychonomic Bulletin and Review 8*, 73-80.

Schmidt, D.K. (1976). On modelling ATC workload and sector capacity. *Journal of Aircraft 13*, 531-537.

Searle, J. (1999). *Mind, Language and Society.* London: Weidenfeld and Nicolson.

Sheridan, T.B. (2000). Function allocation: algorithm, alchemy or apostasy? *International Journal of Human-Computer Studies. 52*, 203-216.

Smith, A.D.N. and Stamp, R.A. (1973). *A method for estimating the capacity of air traffic sectors – An interim report.* CAA DORA Research Paper 7301. London: CAA.

Sperandio, J.-C. (1978). The regulation of working methods as a function of workload among air traffic controllers. *Ergonomics, 21*, 195-202.

Stein, E.J. (1998). *Human Operator Workload in Air Traffic Control.* In, *Human Factors in Air Traffic Control.* San Diego, CA: Academic Press.

Tattersall, A.J. (1998). Individual Differences in Performance. In, *Human Factors in Air Traffic Control.* San Diego, CA: Academic Press.

Welford, A.T. (1967). Single-channel operation in the brain. *Acta Psychologica, 27*, 5-22.

Wickens, C. D. and Hollands, J. (2000). *Engineering Psychology and Human Performance.* New York, NY: Addison Wesley.

Acknowledgements

I would like to acknowledge support from the Civil Aviation Authority's Safety Regulation Group (SRG). Thanks are due to Dr Don Harris for discussions and his comments on an earlier draft.

12 Developing human informed automation in air traffic management

Barry Kirwan

Abstract

Human Centred Automation (HCA) is a design and development concept that has evolved out of necessity in the field of computer-supported (advanced) aviation. However, the advent of so-called 'glass cockpits' (computerised flight decks) saw a series of incidents and accidents, many of which related to a fundamental mismatch between the computer system (the automation) and the mental models of the pilots, often resulting in tragedy. HCA embodies a set of principles through which such mismatches and their consequences can be avoided, or at the least minimised.

HCA is relevant to Air Traffic Management (ATM) system development because many ATM agencies are currently moving towards more computerised support for the controllers, in order to achieve desired increases in capacity levels safely. ATM therefore needs a means of ensuring that the controllers can not only avoid misunderstandings associated with the computerised support they will receive over the next decade, but also that they can maximise the operational effectiveness of the system. The experience from aviation suggests that this will only be achieved through developing the computerised tools around the controllers and their mental models.

The paper firstly presents a vision of possible future ATM automation in European airspace, in order to show the context in which Human Centred Automation must fit and work. Next, it presents an extraction of the HCA design principles that have evolved within aviation, and also other high-technology-high-risk fields (e.g. nuclear power). A number of prototype future ATM system development projects are then considered in order to consider the utility and practicality of implementing such HCA design principles, in particular focusing on a tool to aid controllers in their most critical task of aircraft conflict resolution.

This paper was first published in Human Factors and Aerospace Safety 2(2), 2002, pp. 105-146

This leads to the conclusion that an HCA approach can in fact be incorporated into ATM design and development strategies, and that the approach would benefit ATM, helping to protect it from 'automation-assisted failures' whilst it evolves over the next 10–15 years. However, some elaboration of the HCA concept is called for, to create a more balanced philosophy with system optimisation as the overall goal.

Introduction

The need for automation

With traffic levels projected to increase significantly over the next ten years and beyond, it will become harder for controllers, unaided, to manage traffic safely and efficiently in the future. In particular, as traffic levels increase, there tends to be a significant increase in aircraft conflicts that will arise (i.e. where there is a danger of losing required separation between two aircraft). Although new airspace concepts such as 'free routing' (Europe) or 'free- flight' [4] (US) in theory could lead to fewer conflicts (as there would theoretically be less aircraft on the same routes), there is possibly a trade-off between such a decrease, and the loss of predictability of where conflicts will arise. This is because currently traffic follows relatively fixed routing structures, so controllers know where most conflicts will typically occur. Therefore conflicts in the future could be more frequent, less predictable, and in some cases with less associated room to manoeuvre than at present due to increased levels of traffic. The net result is likely to be a more complex traffic picture facing the controller.

Additionally, as traffic levels rise, the 'throughput' at airports becomes a critical limiting, or enabling factor. It is essential to be efficient at airports, maximising runway usage, handling taxiing traffic efficiently, and managing and matching the inflow from arrivals and the outflow from departures.

At a more strategic level, it becomes more important to look ahead further, in order to optimise traffic flow and efficiency. Problems that can occur in a later airspace sector, leading to major deviations for aircraft, and excess workload for controllers, could often be avoided completely by minor changes in an earlier sector, or even a slight change to take-off time. In effect, for example in Europe, there is currently something of a gap between the Central Flow Management Unit's look-ahead time of two hours, and the more usual Air Traffic Control Centre's operational planning window of 15 minutes. Ideally there would be tools able to help controllers see into this gap, and make use of such information. This ability to

---

[4] Both these concepts will allow pilots to fly more directly, abandoning many of the current and traditional route structures they must currently follow.

see ahead and predict, and then to collaborate effectively to capitalise on such predictions, is perhaps one of the major keys to future safe and expeditious traffic.

The above reasons, and others (see figure 1), have led to the development of a strategic approach to increasing the ability of Air Traffic Management (ATM) to support the role of the controller in handling extra traffic safely. This approach is one of providing extra automation via a set of tools for the controllers in the different (airport) 'Gate-to-Gate' phases of air traffic management. Some of these tools are intended to be used directly by the controller, whereas others will work 'underneath' the interface, although the controller will see their output (and be able to modify it if desired). However, none of the tools are intended to replace the controller, rather they are there to support the controller, and indeed still require significant controller input, judgement and decision-making. The controller will still be 'in charge'.

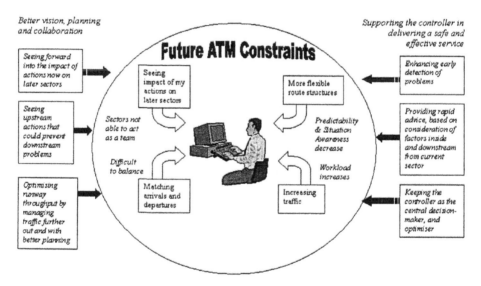

Figure 1   Problems in future ATM, and potential 'keys' to solve them

In Europe, a general picture of the types of developments that are likely to happen can be gained from the Eurocontrol ATM 2000+ Strategy (Eurocontrol, 2000), and in particular the Automation Support to ATM tool-set (called the ASA tool-set). Within this strategy, a number of tools and airspace concepts are proposed, of which some are already developed and being introduced into certain operational air traffic control centres (ATCCs). These are outlined shortly, but first it is worth describing the 'design philosophy' under-pinning the development of the tools, as any Human-Centred Automation approach, in order to work successfully, must be compatible with the overall design philosophy.

Guiding principles for the ASA tool-set

There are a number of 'guiding principles' that are characteristic of the overall automation strategy and the individual tools themselves. The guiding principles are at three 'levels': a strategic level in terms of air traffic services, i.e. what the tools aim to deliver; a functional level, i.e. how the tools aim to achieve that delivery; and an operational level, i.e. how the tools aim to work with the controller. The principles are outlined below.

Strategic principles

- *Safety* – safety should not be degraded, and preferably should be improved by the tools. This principle applies obviously to the tools aimed at supporting conflict detection and reduction[5], but also to the other tools aimed at promoting efficiency. Even these latter tools will be the subject of a safety case to ensure that they are not in any direct or indirect way adding risk to the air traffic system.
- *Optimisation* – the tools together should be able to lead to increased (ATS) system optimisation in terms of more flights handled per controller, less delays, less extra 'track miles', etc. The key aspect here is that the tools must work together, via the controllers in different roles and different sectors. This also requires an element of collaborative decision-making (CDM).
- *Gate-to-gate support* – following on from the principle of optimisation and CDM, the tools should be supporting controllers from departure planning to arrival management, in all types of civil airspace.

Functional principles

- *Layered planning* – there should be more advanced planning, to anticipate and avoid problems, or at least to deal with the problems at an earlier stage to reduce their impact on the optimisation aim. This means more consideration of dynamic traffic flows and airport throughput, and more reliable prediction of potential problems and their resolution. In practice it may mean some new roles or functions for controllers, e.g. a traffic manager role, wherein a controller is able to stand back and predict traffic bunching and determine how to prevent it.
- *Increased look ahead time* – it is essential for optimisation and better planning that the look-ahead 'horizon' is increased. This gives more time to act in ways that will lead to real optimisation for the whole gate-to-gate cycle, rather than short-term solutions that might favour one sector but penalise a

---

[5] It has been estimated that conflict detection and resolution tools could increase safety levels by more than 70%

later one. The tools aim to give this increased look ahead time, via better predictions and thorough but fast analysis of options. In particular the latter will save the controller time. The controller must also be able to see the impact of his or her actions on later downstream sectors, to ensure that problems are not simply being passed 'down the line'. Increased look-ahead time therefore refers both to upstream and downstream vision.

- *Reducing complexity and uncertainty* – Being able to look ahead is no good unless the picture is clear – otherwise, it may be better to do nothing rather than acting needlessly or actually complicating matters. The tools therefore need to help to reduce the complexity of the situation for the controller, or at least enable the controller to manage the complexity more effectively. Such tools must provide not only more information, but also the fast interpretation of that information and presentation to the controller in useful formats, to allow the controller to make good decisions. The tools also need to predict accurately, and to make the controllers aware of any uncertainty involved, so that they can make a judgement about what to do.

Operational principles

- *Human decision-making* – The aim is to keep the controller as the decision-maker in the system. The various tools that are being developed will therefore advise the controller, but the controller will decide which option to evaluate, or may implement his or her own solution. It is also important that the controller does not become complacent about the advice of the tools, i.e. always accepting such advice without evaluating it. The goal is to enhance the controller's performance, and indeed the performance of the system. This requires the controller and the tools working together as a team, with the controller clearly leading that 'team'.
- *Enabling better workload management* - the aim is to support the controller, particularly when workload increases. The tools will work very fast, so that the advice will be available both early and quickly. The controller will then be able to evaluate rapidly the advice and implement it if it is agreeable, or consider an alternative. Additionally, during the later development phases for these tools, considerable efforts will be undertaken to consider the optimum working arrangements between tactical and planner controllers, for example, as well as potentially new roles for traffic management, or new functions in the tower. This focus on making workload more manageable should enable the controller team to remain proactive, and to forestall overload situations. It should also enable controllers to keep their own skills 'fresh', by not having to rely all the time on the tool-set (e.g. for conflict detection and resolution).
- *Maintaining situation awareness* - because the tools are aimed at supporting certain controller functions, rather than replacing them, the controller should remain aware of the traffic characteristics. The planner will probably have a

broader situation awareness than at present, i.e. further upstream and downstream, and certainly a traffic manager will have a very broad situation awareness, if not particularly deep. There should be a net gain in terms of situation awareness with the ASA tool-set, because there will be broader shared awareness across sectors and centres, and also tools for conflict detection will support the early identification of problems. Harnessing this gain in situation awareness to ensure safety and optimisation will however rely on adequate workload management and collaboration between the various controllers and other parties in the ATM system.

- *Enhancing collaboration across airspace sectors and centres* – the aim of the ASA programme is to optimise traffic more widely, both within and across sectors. If optimisation in one sector causes significant workload for the next sector, then clearly the net result for improved traffic flows and capacity will be limited. It is better if different sectors and centres can work together as a 'team'. This is only possible if planning can occur across sectors and centres. This is one of the aims of the tool-set, allowing multi-sector planning and enhanced arrival management, for example. This aim results effectively in more Collaborative decision-making (CDM), and will require and lead to a better 'shared understanding' by controllers of adjacent and up/down-stream sectors and centres, and their respective needs and constraints. Another aspect of CDM relates to airport operations, wherein the tools will also lead to more communication and collaboration between controllers and airlines. It is here in particular that optimisation relies on the understanding of factors that are highly dynamic, somewhat local, and fluctuate on a daily basis. The tools being developed will enable airlines to make their needs clearer, and have some impact on aircraft arrival and departure sequencing, whilst at the same time making clearer to airlines the operational ATC constraints.

The above are the main principles underlying the philosophy for the ASA tool-set. The ASA tool-set which aims to fulfil this philosophy comprises three types of tools:

- *Optimising traffic flow* – e.g. DMAN; AMAN; MSP; EMAN
- *Managing conflicts* – e.g. MTCD; CORA1; CORA2
- *Support tools* – e.g. TP; MONA; SNET; SYSCO; and Data-Link. Such tools enable an environment in which the other higher-level tools can work.

The ASA tool-set helps to optimise traffic flow via the following tools:

- *DMAN* – Departure Manager – optimises take-off sequences and runway efficiency, and integrates departures into the overall traffic scheme
- *AMAN* – Arrival Manager – organises the spacing and sequencing of inbound aircraft, optimising runway efficiency and achieving the most efficient flight path for inbound aircraft, also leading to more accurate Estimated Times of Arrival (ETAs). AMAN will also identify the optimal landing runway for aircraft at multiple runway airports.
- *MSP* – Multi-Sector Planning - will allow analysis of future traffic over several sectors, and produce indications of when and where conditions are

likely to become excessively difficult for sector-level controllers. Having identified potential problems, the 'Traffic and Complexity Manager' component of MSP can then be used to reduce or eliminate such problems early on.

- *EMAN* – En Route Manager - EMAN acts as an integrator for the other tools. In particular it aims to manage the different requests that will arise (including those that may conflict) from the various ASA tools in the gate-to-gate flight process. EMAN will not usually be 'seen' by the controller, but will work 'behind the scenes'. Nevertheless it has a critical role of harmonising the outputs of the other tools.

Some of the above tools can also make use of *SYSCO*, which aids co-ordination between sectors, and data-link, enhancing communications between controller and aircraft.

Two tools support managing conflicts:

- *MTCD* – Medium Term Conflict Detection – predicts where conflicts will occur, and gives the controller an accurate look-ahead, enabling earlier detection and resolution of conflicts. More generally it aims to reduce the controller workload associated with routine monitoring and conflict detection, and to serve as an enabler for the application of free routes.
- *CORA 2* – Conflict Resolution Assistant (level 2) suggests conflict resolutions, providing en-route Air Traffic Controllers with ranked conflict free resolution advice. CORA will address both conflicts between aircraft and conflicts between aircraft and restricted airspace, and will give required clearances direct to the tactical (or 'executive') controller.

These tools in turn rely on or make use of several support tools. *TP* (Trajectory Predictor) predicts where aircraft will be in the future, and so is used by MTCD and CORA1 (and also hence CORA2). *MONA* (Monitoring Aids) assists MTCD and CORA in three main ways. The first involves warning the controller if and deviates from an agreed trajectory (e.g. say, after a resolution). The second involves giving reminders to controllers for certain actions to be carried out in the future. The third way MONA helps MTCD and CORA is by triggering automatic re-calculation of trajectories. *SYSCO* (System Co-ordination) enhances the co-ordination between different sector controllers, and facilitates co-ordination of resolutions that may affect other sectors. Data-link will enhance communications with the aircraft involved in the situation. *SNET* (Safety Net) is not used by the tools as such, but sits there as an independent short-term collision alert system in case a conflict is missed by the controller-tool combination, or in case one suddenly develops in a very short time-frame. Safety net systems, such as Short Term Conflict Alert (STCA), have been implemented successfully in many European ATCCs, and controllers generally value their presence – although some would complain about occasional false alarms, very few controllers used to STCA would give it up as a tool.

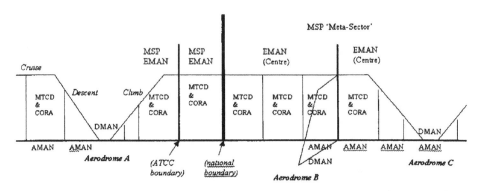

Figure 2 **ASA Tool-set in the gate-to-gate Flight Process. This figure aims
to represent where the tools will be used in the gate-to-gate flight
process. It illustrates the cruise, descent and landing phase of an
aircraft (on the left), landing at an aerodrome (A), taking off and
reaching cruise (central part of the diagram), and then landing at
another aerodrome (C: right hand part of the diagram). The
figure is divided by vertical lines representing different air traffic
airspace 'sectors', each of which would be controlled by one or
two controllers (usually a planner and an executive or tactical
controller). Aerodrome C is displayed merely to remind the
reader that the figure largely shows a single 'slice' of the air
traffic picture, i.e. a single route between two airports. In reality
of course there are many intersecting routes and many airports.
The tools DMAN and AMAN reside mainly at the aerodromes
themselves, and MTCD and CORA are (currently) mainly
intended for the cruise phases of flight. EMAN and MSP can,
however, work 'across' several sectors controlled by a single
ATCC (whose domain is indicated by medium bold lines), or even
possibly across several ATCCs in a single country for example (a
so-called 'meta-sector)**

The ASA tool-set is aimed at supporting controllers throughout the entire
gate-to-gate flight process (see figure 2), from preparations for take-off, to
arrival and disembarkation of passengers. It shows that the amount of change
anticipated for the controller is significant, though the tools are clearly aimed at
supporting rather than replacing the controller. The description above also
shows the context in which Human Factors and Human Centred Automation
must work, if they wish to influence real developments in European ATM.
Fortunately, it is already clear from the description of the underlying principles,

that the philosophy has been written with consideration of the human element as a central key to future ATM effectiveness and safety.

Having defined a possible automation context for future ATM, the next section considers Human Centred Automation in more detail, before returning to one particular project (CORA) to illustrate how HCA is being implemented within this project.

Human centred automation

The field of aviation well over a decade ago embarked on a programme of computerisation of flight decks for large passenger aircraft (e.g. see Billings, 1997; Wiener and Nagel, 1988; Parasuraman and Mouloua, 1996). Most notably the two largest aircraft developers, Boeing and Airbus, opted for 'glass cockpit' design, replacing the conventional dials and switches with cathode ray tube (CRT) technology. The intention was to improve performance and efficiency. However, the introduction of such technology saw a number of incidents occurring that began to produce a familiar pattern: due to a misunderstanding of what the computer was doing, air crashes were occurring (e.g. Woods, 1996; Billings, op cit). This led to the term *'automation-assisted accident'*, on the basis that if the aircraft had been equipped with conventional technology and instrumentation, the crash probably would not have occurred. Furthermore, for a number of times when emergency events occurred, the computers appeared to behave in a confusing way, such that in the height of an emergency, the pilot was being forced to diagnose what the computer was doing and why. This led to another term, namely 'clumsy *automation'*.

This state of affairs identified the need to develop better understanding of how automation can fit the pilot's *mental model* (i.e. the pilot's understanding of the system), and the concept of Human Centred Automation (HCA) was established (Billings, op cit). Currently considerable effort is put into understanding what assistance the pilots need, and to inform the optimum means of presentation of that information. Glass cockpits remain, but they are significantly less 'clumsy' or 'opaque'.

Since NATS is about to embark on a course of increasing the level of automation in its systems, it is appropriate to review what can be learned from aviation's experiences. Although there will be differences in the types and even perhaps the degrees of automation between ATM and aviation (the latter hereafter referring largely to aircraft cockpits and their design and functionality), there are likely to be generic but useful lessons. Such lessons, or guiding design and implementation principles, could help ATM avoid automation-assisted incidents and clumsy automation (e.g. see Wickens et al, 1997; 1998; Smolensky and Stein, 1998; Scerbo and Mouloua, 1999).

Since ATM is embarking on a course of significant levels of computerised support (automation) for the controller, it is useful to adapt HCA lessons learned from the cockpit, to the air traffic controller context. To do this, a more structured breakdown of the specific mismatches and generic problems that can occur in a partially-automated ATM system (i.e. one where the human co-exists with automation, so that operational tasks are 'shared' by the human and the computer) is developed. These generic problems are then related to a set of HCA principles for ATM system designers and developers. Then, to see whether these are really practical, examples of a number of future system development projects are reviewed. This enables conclusions to be drawn on the overall utility of HCA principles for ATM.

Key potential automation-related problem areas for ATM

Based on a review of relevant literature and associated incidents, the key automation impacts on human performance have been identified. These are outlined below. However, to make them more understandable, they have been cast in a simple framework of human performance in ATM. This framework represents the ATM system at three levels: the mental functioning of the controller; the interface (computer software and workstation); and the ATM team or crew organisational environment. This structure is in a sense hierarchical, with the first level 'inside' the human (pilot or controller), relating to the human's mental functioning (Wickens, 1992), situation awareness (Endsley and Smolensky, 1998), the controller's mental 'picture' (MacKendrick et al, 1998; Kirwan et al, 1998a), and decision-making etc. The next level concerns the human's interaction with 'the machine', and relates to the interface and the computer software and functionality. The third level concerns the broader picture, for example how the automation affects teamwork, but also other aspects such as legalistic implications of automation.

Figure 3 shows this three-level framework. Level 1 (mental functions: see Wickens, 1992) comprises the following basic (controller) human functions:

- *Perception* – principally visual and auditory modes.
- *Thinking* – comprising *executive control*, where planning, assessment, judgement and decision-making takes place, and which operates based on the *working memory* – this is where situation awareness or the controller's 'picture' resides.
- *Long term memory* – including knowledge of facts, opinions, past judgements based on experience, and skills.
- *Attentional resources* – mental capacity constraints, which are susceptible to overload or underload, and vigilance constraints.
- *Response* – output modes, usually manual (e.g. activating something using a mouse or keyboard) or vocal.

256

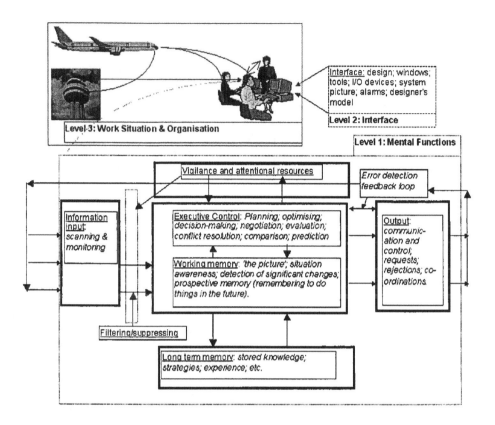

Figure 3   Human performance framework for ATM

Level 2 represents the interface and software design aspects that can lead to problems – they affect (via level 1) the previous functions, but it is useful to focus on the system design aspects themselves.   Level 3 represents the controller's job and work situation, including how controllers work together and interface with other human information sources, and the pilot/aircraft, etc. Automation can clearly change the controllers' roles and responsibilities, and can affect ways of working within the controller team (planner and executive controllers, for example).

The following problem areas have therefore been identified relating to automation impacts on controller (and hence system) performance.

Level 1 – Mental functions

Perception

i   *Visual 'channel' over-load*
    Too much information may be presented visually, rather than using auditory processing as well.   There are limits to how much information can be processed visually.   Currently both pilots and controllers use a mixture of visual and auditory information (the latter mainly radio-telephony or RT), but this is likely to change in favour of mainly visual information once data-link becomes operational (although co-ordination discussions with other sector controllers may actually increase).   In workload theory terms (e.g. Wickens, 1992 – the multiple resource theory of workload) this may appear to yield the same amount of information to process, but because it is shifting more to a single channel, the workload experienced may well rise, possibly leading to performance decrement.

Thinking

ii   *Lack of situation awareness*
     This can arise for a number of reasons - delegation of monitoring and information acquisition skills to the computer; the computer not notifying the pilot of changes in sub-system availabilities; a mistake over information (especially graphical) that relates to the future rather than the present, or vice versa (*information 'currency' confusion*); becoming engrossed in aspects of the system and losing awareness of the big picture (so-called '*tunnelling*'), e.g. during system fault diagnosis.

iii   *Lack of mode awareness*
      A number of incidents and accidents have involved the pilots believing the computer was in one mode when it was actually in another. This will only affect controllers if *proposed* automation is 'modal' in nature.

iv   *Lack of trust in the system*
     This can be caused by problems already mentioned, or by random failures or poor reliability of a system. For example, some ground-sensing systems are prone to spurious alarms, resulting in pilots ignoring them. Additionally automation can naturally be seen as a threat (automation often precedes manpower reductions). Failure to be sensitive to this human trait can result in a distrust of the system from the outset. It should be noted that trust, once lost, is very hard to recover, and such recovery takes a much longer time than to build trust in the first place (Lee and Moray, 1992). Trust is a highly relevant concept for ATM because of the increasing necessary reliance on

computer systems, but the controller will still be accountable if anything goes wrong (i.e. if an incident occurs).

v   *Complacency*

This is the reverse of a lack of trust, and refers to over-trust or over-reliance in the system. This has two problems associated with it. The first is that there will be a delay in response when the system goes wrong, and this delay will be exacerbated by the belief that the system cannot go wrong. The second is that there will be an atrophying of the skills needed to recover, since the controllers will tend to assume that those skills will no longer be needed. A further and important consideration is that humans naturally tend to trust something that appears to benefit them, even if it is not that reliable. This can lead to over-reliance on a system that is not actually always accurate. People therefore need to be made aware of the true limitations of automated systems and tools.

The complacency or *over-trust p*henomenon should not be under-estimated. Humans have a habit of trusting computers more than they should, once some basic benefits of the computer systems are shown. Moreover, other (non automation related) information may be seen as less credible, even if stated by another person (Mosier and Skitka, 1996). There are two basic biases here. The first is where contradictory data from other sources is re-interpreted by the human operator to actually agree with the computer output (called the *'assimilation bias'*); and the second is looking only for confirmatory rather than contradictory evidence (called *'confirmation bias'*). Such biases are dangerous when the computer is either malfunctioning or, more likely, it is forming conclusions based on data which are inappropriate for the situation at hand. Once again this indicates that the human operator, whether pilot or controller, must therefore be aware of the limitations of the computer system.

vi   *False positives and misses*

Automation tends to produce false alarms, and may lead the human pilot or controller to take unnecessary avoidance action (known as 'false positives'). This has been seen in a study of automated checklists at NASA (Mosier and Skitka, op cit), in which operators trusted the automation aid too much and shut down the wrong engine. This type of problem is highly relevant to 'safety net' systems such as TCAS (Traffic Collision Avoidance System) and STCA, where there is very little time to verify the validity of a signal or alarm. Alternatively, where the false alarm rate is too high, this can lead to a 'cry wolf' syndrome in which case real (i.e. valid) alarms can be ignored by the pilot or controller (misses). Achieving a high rate of 'hits' whilst minimising the number of 'false alarms' is not easy with any system, but clearly the system must be optimised in this respect, to gain satisfactory user uptake.

Long term memory

vii   *Knowledge-based rather than skill-based or rule-based tasks*
Originally, flying an aircraft was more of a skill, relying on a set of procedures (rules) for certain eventualities. ATM is similarly (today) largely skill and rule-based: it rarely requires sitting back and thinking from first principles of how to resolve a scenario (as is more common in process control industries such as nuclear power, for example). However, as automation enters a field, there tends to be a shift towards more 'knowledge-based' (Rasmussen et al, 1981) thinking being required, partly because the operations achievable with an automated system are more complex or sophisticated, and partly because the pilot (or controller) knows that the information is being mediated through a level of automation and sometimes must be re-interpreted in this light. This can lead to a less rapid response (there is more to consider before acting) and error (it is easier to forget an aspect in a more complex decision-making situation), and generally will require more varied training to achieve satisfactory performance and knowledge of the various elements and interactions with the automation.

viii   *Insufficient knowledge of automation limitations*
Because of trust in automation and the tendency to delegate monitoring of certain functions to automation, already alluded to above, the human in the system actually needs a fairly deep knowledge of the system's limitations. In particular, humans are good at dealing with novel situations and unusual events - whereas computers are not - such events tend to be outside the automation's design database. Therefore, a degree of depth of knowledge of the automation characteristics will be required in order for the human can detect when the system is unlikely to give reliable advice, and when the system is actually in error. This will allow mutual checking. The computer can check the human's input errors, and support the human in vigilance and complex predictions, and enhance the human's 'big picture'. Correspondingly, the human can also check the computerised guidance that is being given, recover from system failure, and deal with difficult and novel scenarios. Such an approach to system design or allocation of function is *complementary* and *co-operative*, rather than 'competitive'. This represents a 'Team Resource Management' (TRM: Isaac and Ruitenberg, 1999) approach, with the automation being part of the team. One residual difficulty with this 'idealised' scenario, however, is that the controller's workload may increase. This means that the workload reductions gained from automated assistance may in practice not be quite as large as expected.

ix   Skill degradation and immature skills

As reliance on computerised support continues, old skills will be used less frequently, and they will decay. This means that should they suddenly be required (e.g. due to a system problem), then performance of those skills will no longer be fluent and may be error-prone, or performance may have even decayed to the point that the skill has been lost. Additionally, new controllers might never develop some skills that older controllers possess. With such controllers, the first time they have to use such immature skills is likely to be when it really matters.

x   Increased training requirements

Training becomes more important with automated systems, since there will be more tasks and aspects of the automated system that are in less frequent use, hence requiring more basic training and refresher training. Furthermore, as evidenced in the Kegworth air disaster (AAIB, 1990), there is a need for simulator training to show the computerised system in abnormal and emergency mode, otherwise the first time the pilots see it in such a mode is when it is for real.

This aspect of increased training needs is usually a surprise to companies, since an assumption is that automation may actually require less experienced operatives. However, aviation and other industry experience has shown that, perhaps with the exception of the manufacturing industry, the idea that the combination of automation and an inexperienced operator leads to expert performance, is a myth, and a dangerous one (Mosier and Skitka, op cit). The human must still be able to integrate information, interpret inconsistent information, and deal with the unexpected, all products and hallmarks of good training and experience.

Attentional resources

xi   Workload problems

Automation can lead to underload, i.e. not enough to do, resulting in a lack of vigilance and skill and motivation degradation (Parasuraman and Mouloua, 1996). There may also be overload - too much to do - most serious if during an emergency, e.g. if having to navigate through many unfamiliar computer windows when trying to resolve an engine abnormality (*clumsy automation*).

xii   Automation bias

There is a natural human tendency towards 'satisficing' behaviour, i.e. doing just enough work to make reasonably acceptable decisions (Mosier and Skitka, op cit). This is a resource management strategy. What it means with automated decision aids is that the human will tend to come to rely on automated decision/action cues, rather than vigilantly and proactively

261

searching for such information. This has two impacts. The first is that the human will tend to fail to notice when something has been missed by the computer. This can delay and reduce the effectiveness of recovery from system failures or problems, or else the controller can fail to notice difficulties the computer may have in a particular novel or unusual situation. The second is that these proactive skills will atrophy, and this is likely to be a relatively permanent loss of skills if it occurs over an extended period of time.

Response (output)

xiii   *Less active (involved) output*
With automated systems, the human tends to make fewer outputs, or less involved outputs, e.g. rather than orally transmitting a message and interacting with another person, they will simply read a computer-generated message and acknowledge it with the click of a button. This is undoubtedly quicker in many cases, and pertinent for trivial and highly routine tasks. However, because the human is less involved, there will be less 'memory' of having executed (i.e. approved/acknowledged) the action (e.g. similar to watching someone else perform an action versus doing it yourself). This in turn can lead to a lack of situation awareness, such that the controller is then not sure if an action has in fact been executed or not. This can lead directly to two forms of error - repeating an action, and omitting an action.

Level 2 – Interface

xiv   *Lack of understanding of what the computer has done and/or why*
This 'opaqueness' or 'lack of transparency' has occurred in a number of incidents, where the pilots have been surprised and confused by what the system has done, or simply fail to understand its reasoning. Essentially the designers' 'mental model' in such cases does not concord with that of the users, or the designers have failed to anticipate how the system will react in a particular scenario. This leads to error (misinterpretation of the machine's intentions), a lack of trust in the system, and inadequate usage of the system.

xv   *Impact on decision-making*
Automation should enhance rapid and accurate decision-making. This relies on the development of interfaces that are easy to use and concord with the pilot's mental model(s). Some early interfaces failed to provide rapidly 'assimilable' and integrated information. Instead, they transmitted to the pilot large amounts of data, which the pilots then had to integrate and interpret in real time, sometimes during an emergency event. Therefore, the interface must not overwhelm the human with data and information (*information flooding*) particularly during unusual events. This means that

for ATM, the computer [via the system designer] must have some idea of the controller's *intent* and *ways of working*, and their *'mental model'*, to be really helpful. This is not an easy task. It requires a model of the user's goals, their priorities according to different conditions, their strategies, and their information needs. Such information can be collected via task analysis methods and user groups.

xvi   Interface complexity and usability (ergonomics)
At a more specific level, the interface needs to be ergonomically designed to be user-friendly, and error tolerant. For example, there should not be complex interface structures to enter or retrieve information, the human users should not have to hold more than a few necessary pieces of information in their heads whilst working with the system; and any entry should be recoverable should the controller make an error. Some computerised systems onboard aircraft also can occasionally be difficult to see depending on the attitude of the aircraft and direct sunlight, for example. The corresponding environmental ergonomics (e.g. lighting) in an operational ATM control centre, in theory, should be easier to achieve to a good standard.

xvii   Indirect information
If the pilot sends a command and the computer system returns a message that the command has been implemented, the pilot will assume that the action has been executed. The return message to the pilot should therefore be true, and based on direct rather than indirect information. The Paris air crash (see Kirwan, 1994, Appendix 1), in which the cargo door blew open shortly after take-off, leading to loss of the aircraft and all passengers/crew, although not a glass cockpit, showed the dangers of indirect information. The pilot received a signal saying the cargo door was locked - in fact this was not the case, the return signal did not come from a proximity sensor in the hull of the aircraft to tell if the locking bolt from the door was engaged. Rather, it instead simply showed that the door locking mechanism had been activated (the bolt, however, buckled and never entered the hull of the aircraft). The Three Mile Island nuclear power plant accident (Kirwan, 1994) was also at least partly due to indirect information (namely no direct information of water level in the reactor vessel). It is not clear whether the problem of indirect information relates to ATM, but given the magnitude of its effect in other industries and aviation, it is worth bearing in mind when designing future systems. One potentially relevant aspect of ATM is the radar screen itself – currently most radar screens offer relatively direct information (what you see is what you get). However, newer concepts offer effectively large VDU screens where the radar data has been substantially processed before graphical presentation. This can lead to a better picture, and more useful

and flexible functionality for the controller, but there is potentially a risk if the software fails in some way to lead to missing or wrong information on the screen.

xviii   Intolerance and magnification of skill-based errors
Automation systems can allow simple errors (such as typing errors, or inadvertent menu selections, for example) to have gross system impacts. Many of these system vulnerabilities to human error can be avoided by a high level of usability and Human Machine Interface (HMI) design (e.g. radar screens and VDUs; telecommunications; etc. - there are many guidelines on design of such interface aspects (e.g. Cardosi and Murphy, 1995; MacKendrick, 1998). Some errors are more difficult to predict, however, and so other tools must be developed to find these and eradicate them (e.g. using predictive human error analysis - see Shorrock and Kirwan, 1998; Shorrock et al, 2001; Evans et al, 1999).

Level 3 – Work situation and Organisation

xix   Responsibility and legal considerations - 'Who's in charge?'
There can be problems relating to who (or what) has the ultimate responsibility for the safety of the aircraft, the pilot or the machine. Problems may manifest themselves as over-reliance or complacency by the pilot, as well as skill degradation. There will also be problems if the pilot is ultimately responsible for the safety of an aircraft, yet is highly reliant on the Flight Management System (FMS) automation. This aspect may have more relevance for controllers, since the danger, in the case of the automation being 'responsible', is that the controller defers to the automation in a decision-making situation when the computer is actually wrong. This would be a possibility if the controller were not given ultimate responsibility for aircraft under air traffic control. However, it would also be inappropriate, not to say unfair, to leave the controller with the ultimate responsibility and at the same time make control totally reliant on a difficult and error-prone automated system.

Over-reliance on automated decision aids is critically influenced by the degree to which the organisation encourages usage of such systems, and the degree to which usage in certain circumstances is mandated (e.g. as in the pilot's use of TCAS). Therefore, the degree to which such tools are to be encouraged or even mandatory in certain circumstances must be carefully considered.

xx   Job design and the human role in the system
One of the frequent comments about glass cockpits is that pilots who fly them *'used to be pilots but are now system managers'*: they spend a significant amount of time monitoring the computerised system itself, and

less time monitoring the status of the aircraft (more 'head-down' time). Such changes in role of the pilot can have a significant impact upon motivation, and hence on self-monitoring of performance, and on teamwork and recovery from errors or system problems. This may be particularly relevant to ATM since most controllers today are highly motivated and proactive in their ATC roles. A switch to a more automated system may conflict with such proactive styles, forcing the controller into a more *reactive* mode. This may impact on their motivation and ability to perform effectively, particularly with respect to the controller being able to hold 'the picture'. Current high performance, error detection and correction, and teamwork, may therefore be dependent on the high degree of involvement in the task - if this involvement changes dramatically, the 'baby may be thrown out with the bathwater' – i.e. overall performance may suffer.

xxi   Secondary tasks and time management
Automation in aviation has led to the creation of a number of secondary and sometimes administrative tasks. This extra burden may affect workload. In fact, a number of automation interventions have resulted not in workload decreasing, but simply the nature of the work changing, and workload remaining the same or actually increasing. This can again affect motivation and skill degradation, since the pilots (or controllers) are working as hard as before, but with less rewarding tasks.

xxii   Task-paced versus self-paced work, and time management
Most people like to be flexible about the pace of their work. Both pilots and controllers tend to organise tasks to occur in a cluster, for example, saving up and then dealing with a set of related tasks all at once, rather than dealing with everything reactively as it arises. Automation can however rule out such a 'self-paced' approach, leading the pilot or controller into a forced 'task-paced' or 'machine-paced' mode of operation. This tends to have the further effect of smoothing out operations, so that rather than having peaks and troughs of workload, there is a consistent (and typically high) level of workload. It is not clear that this is preferable for humans. First, people get fatigued at different rates on different days, and with 'machine-paced' work there is little flexibility to work around human performance 'dips' (Wickens et al, 1997). Second, there will inevitably be interruptions and distractions the pilot or controller must attend to, which will lead to them falling behind significantly in a machine-paced work situation.

xxiii Recovery from system failure
As already noted, recovery from system failure becomes of increasing concern as humans become reliant on the computerised support system and its tools (Wickens et al, 1998). Furthermore, the difficulty relates not merely

to the recovery but also the detection of system failure, particularly if there is only partial failure. A 'minor' software aberration, for example, that led to a single erroneous output (e.g. a flight level) could be hard to detect.

xxiv   Crew resource management (CRM) issues

The automation, capable of carrying out some tasks on its own, is really part of the team that fly an aircraft. This raises the questions firstly of how such 'autonomy' affects the existing pilot and co-pilot relationship, and other crew members, and secondly, of how proper compliance with the automation, and questioning of unusual automation behaviour is achieved. These are classic CRM (Crew [or Cockpit] Resources Management) issues (Team Resource Management in the ATM domain), although CRM usually refers only to people (e.g. see Helmreich and Merritt, 1998; Isaac and Ruitenberg, op cit). In the future ATM environment automation could also affect the workload or job of one part of the ATM team (e.g. the planner could be far busier than the tactical controller) more than the other. This could lead to TRM-related problems arising (e.g. tactical controller boredom or planner resentment, with a concomitant breakdown of good team-working relations; or joint [i.e. tactical and planner] frustration with the automation).

xxv   Transition

Clearly a difficult time for aviation was when glass cockpits were first introduced to pilots. Similarly with controllers, a difficult time will be the so-called *'transition period'*, when automation is first introduced and subsequently added to the existing system, and gradually evolves over a period of time until it reaches a period of operational stability. Controllers in the early stages of the transition period will have to 'unlearn' certain ways of working and replace them with new ways. Such transition periods inevitably can suffer from initial problems, when errors due to the novelty of the system, and the impossibility of predicting every eventuality, are likely to occur. Such phases of un-learning and re-learning will continue throughout the transition period, and carry with them an increased likelihood of a range of errors. Interfaces must therefore be well-designed to a high ergonomics standard, and they must be intuitive, and forgiving. Training, re-training, and refresher training must also be effective, to minimise the impacts of such errors.

The aviation industry's response

Whilst there are clear benefits of automation in aviation, the major aircraft manufacturers seem more willing nowadays to concede that there is no perfect automated system – instead, there will inevitably be trade-offs between the skills of the pilot and the benefits of the automation. However, because aviation has gone so far down the road of automation, it is unlikely that functions in the cockpit will ever be 'un-automated'. The only route for optimisation of aviation systems has therefore been Human Centred Automation. An example of the commitment to this approach has come from Boeing, for example, who designed the Boeing 777 around the crew-centred design and automation (HCA) principles shown in table 1 (Kelly et al, 1992).

Table 1   Boeing's Human Centred Automation Design Principles (Kelly et al, 1992)

Pilot's role and responsibility
• The pilot is the final authority for the operation of the airplane
• Both crew members are ultimately responsible for the safe conduct of the flight
• Decision making on the flight deck is based on a goal hierarchy

Pilot's limitations
• Expected pilot performance must recognise fundamental human performance limitations
• Individual differences in pilot performance capabilities must be accommodated
• Flight deck design must apply error tolerance and avoidance techniques to enhance safety
• Flight decks should be designed for crew operations and training based on past practices and intuitive operations
• Workload should be balanced appropriately to avoid overload and underload

Pilot's needs
• When used, automation should aid the pilot
• Flight deck automation should be managed to support the pilots' goal hierarchy
• There needs to be a comfortable working environment

Having explored the potential impacts of automation on human performance, the next section defines in more detail what HCA actually means in practice, by developing a set of HCA design principles, for ATM.

Human centred automation – principles for ATM

The following HCA principles have been derived from the available literature and from a consideration of the key problem areas as stated in the previous sections above. Billings (1997) proposed a HCA 'philosophy', which was as follows: 'automation designed to work co-operatively with human operators in the pursuit of stated objectives'.

- The human operator must be in command.
- To command effectively, the human operator must be involved.
- To be involved, the human operator must be informed.
- The human operator must be able to monitor the automated systems.
- Automated systems must be predictable.
- The automated systems must also be able to monitor the human operator.
- Each element of the system must have knowledge of the other's intent.

This HCA philosophy underpins a number of the following principles derived in this current study. The principles themselves are organised into six areas:

- The role of automation – the relationship between human and machine.
- Automation (computerised support system) functional design – what the system aims to do and how it does it.
- Interface design – usability and error tolerant aspects of the interface.
- Implementation and training support aspects – achieving and maintaining good implementation and acceptance.
- Team and organisational issues – fitting computerised support into the ATM team infrastructure.
- Risk and reliability issues – minimising negative safety impacts.

Each of the principles themselves is at a relatively high level. Making such principles operational, i.e. making them 'happen' in real design projects, will require adaptation by the project design teams and operational customers to the context of future automation projects. The principles themselves represent guidance, and there are likely to be occasional exceptions to their application. Nevertheless, the principles below should generally help ATM avoid 'automation-assisted failures'. The following principles are a subset (approximately two thirds) of a more extensive set developed in Kirwan and Cox, 1999.

The role of automation

i   Automation should *support* the controller:
  - With 'housekeeping' and 'nuisance' tasks.
  - By enabling more rapid and accurate task execution.
  - Enabling more complex tasks to be achieved, thus delivering a better service.
  - By enhancing flexibility of operations.
  - Supporting with prediction and interpolation tasks.
  - Supporting the building and maintenance of an appropriate picture.

ii   Automation should *help* guard against human limitations:
  - Helping avoid 'tunnel vision'.

- Helping avoid vigilance decrements.
- Supporting fault/problem detection.
- Helping with integration of multiple diverse inputs.
- Supporting via provision of advice under stressful circumstances.

iii   The controller should be able to over-ride the automation.

iv   Automation should enhance situation awareness, ensuring the controller is aware of whatever needs that awareness. This recognises the fact that the controller, given projected increases in traffic, cannot remain aware of everything. Also, the system should draw the controller into thinking more about the traffic than the automation itself.

v   The automation should not replace the controller. The controller should remain significantly involved in the task of Air Traffic Control, in order to maximise the effectiveness of the system.

Automation functional design

vi   Automation and computerised tools should not be in conflict with controller mental models, goal hierarchies, or strategies, and preferably should build upon them. This requires working with users and, preferably, the application of task analysis (including cognitive task analysis approaches where practicable), prior to any detailed system design.

vii   Automation must not remove all decision-making from the controller.

viii   In order to help the controller maintain the picture, displays must still present the basic information currently used (e.g. location; identity; vector; temporal characteristics, etc.).

ix   Automation should not increase workload. This needs to be tested via predictive methods and via prototyping and real-time simulations, where the secondary tasks are present as well as the primary ones.

x   Automation should be capable of recognising simple (but potentially gross) input errors and reflecting these back to the controller for (rapid) verification. Avoidance of such input errors in the first place can be achieved by offering first to the controller the default (i.e. expected) values, e.g. on a small menu.

xi   There are currently few 'alarms' in ATM. If automation develops to utilise such a function more frequently, an alarm philosophy must be developed for ATM, covering such aspects as prioritisation, coding, and use of audible as well as visual channels.

xii   Information given to the controller should be as direct as possible, rather than indirect (see point *xvii* earlier).

xiii   Automation must not over-load any single information-processing channel (e.g. the visual system).

Interface design

xiv   Interfaces incorporating automation need to have a high standard of usability. Interfaces should aim to be 'intuitive' (i.e. for the controller, not just the designer). Relevant Human Factors guidelines should be applied, as well as utilising user-centred (though not necessarily user-driven) design approaches.

xv   Interfaces should not be cluttered – only display information necessary to maintain situation awareness or to inform a decision.

xvi   An 'are you sure' (i.e. 'confirm') option may need to be present for certain decisions (e.g. destructive commands).

xvii   There should be feedback when automation is operating, so that the user always knows 'who is in control', and when it has finished a task.

xviii   Usage of different 'modes' for automation support should be minimised. If different modes are used, it must be compellingly clear which mode the system is in.

xix   System actions should be transparent to the controller (this transparency should be tested during prototype testing and development with a range of diverse users). Automation should not 'surprise' the controller.

xx   The way in which actions are acknowledged and executed should leave a sufficient 'memory trace' so the controller does not forget what has and has not been done or accepted.

xxi   System faults should be made immediately clear to the controller, with meaningful messages that make sense (to the controller, rather than the system or software designer) in the context in which they occur. The extent of the failure's consequences needs to be understood rapidly.

xxii   System actions should be transparent to the controller – the system should not 'surprise' the controller.

xxiii   The system must not 'flood' the controller with information, particularly when busy or dealing with failure-related events.

Implementation and training support aspects

xxiv   Trust in tools needs to be addressed when designing, developing and introducing them. This will require early involvement of prospective users, and diverse user groups throughout the system development life cycle.

xxv   The controller's training should encompass how the automation works (not merely how to work the automation), and its limitations (i.e. when it won't work), what system failures will look like, and how to compensate for them.

xxvi   Necessary skills in the case of automation failure must be practised and tested regularly.

xxvii   Since transition to new systems tends to lead to a high initial error rate, which in turn leads to a decrease in trust and usage of the system, training prior to operational uptake will need to be more extensive than for other more conventional upgrades or, e.g. re-sectorisation changes. Controllers should have a high degree of confidence in the system, and should be familiar with its strengths and limitations, before it goes operational. This needs a training facility (a simulator or simulation of the system).

xxviii   User groups used to help make the system more user-centred or focused, should comprise a reasonable cross-section of the intended controller population. A small unchanging group of excellent controllers capable of adapting to any interface, will not be the best approach. A minimum recommended user-reference group is six persons, and the personnel on the group should change periodically throughout the design process (as they will become less independent from the design over time).

Team and organisational issues

xxix   The role of automation and the controller needs clear demarcation.

xxx   Controllers in a team may need to be aware of each others' interactions with automation – the need for such awareness will be context dependent and therefore needs to be assessed during task analytical studies.

xxxi Consideration needs to be given as to what back-up skills new controllers will need (i.e. for controllers who will only know the automated environment).

xxxii Special handover procedures should be developed where the automation is functioning (or has recently been functioning) at handover, i.e. so that one controller can accurately hand over what the automation has been doing or is (silently) in the process of doing.

xxxiii Team Resource Management training should include the automation, in terms of when to rely on it and when to over-ride it, and how to judge its performance.

xxxiv Inter-relationships between the controller and the software engineer need to be clearly defined, e.g. what aspects can a controller 'customise' or change, and what events require intervention by an engineer, etc.

Risk and reliability

xxxv Automation should be designed to minimise the occurrence of unrevealed (i.e. not immediately obvious or detectable) system failures.

xxxvi Contingencies must be made for revealed and unrevealed automation failures, including partial and complete failures associated with hardware and software systems. This may include training, procedural, teamwork, and back-up display facilities development.

xxxvii A human error analysis should be carried out in the design phase to check for errors which could lead to safety problems, and to enhance design to achieve better error avoidance, tolerance, and recovery properties.

Feasibility of application of HCA principles

The previously described HCA principles may sound useful, but the real test is whether they can be used in practical design environments. This section therefore firstly gives two short examples[6] of the utilisation of some of the principles for real future ATM design projects, focusing on computerised support tools (automation) for controllers, and based on UK projects. It then gives a more extensive account of a study using a 'deeper' HCA approach to develop a conflict resolution tool for controllers.

---

[6] Thanks to Martin Cox for these two examples.

Application to future trajectory prediction and medium term conflict detection tools for En Route airspace.

The operational concept for these tools, under development (Whysall, 1998), is to 'provide genuine support to the current controller roles, rather than to change those roles significantly'. This indicates that the tool-set is designed around the way controllers currently work and will work in the future. The tools do not change the way controllers operate, but provide additional facilities to allow them to do what they currently do, more easily. From an HCA viewpoint, the tools have been designed to allow controllers to continue their decision-making activities, but to do so more efficiently. For example, a Co-ordination List tool would help the Planner to decide when to co-ordinate aircraft into or out of the sector. This supports the Planner's time management.

When the controllers have decided to perform a co-ordination, lateral and vertical risk tools allow them to judge better what other aircraft are likely to interact with the aircraft at or beyond the sector boundary. Such tools present a graphical representation of the projected positions of both the subject aircraft and those in the vicinity. The controllers currently use their mental picture to mentally gauge the position of aircraft. The fact that this is based on the controller's judgement means that it is influenced by factors such as experience. Consequently, controllers will report that they sub-consciously accompany each mental projection with an idea of uncertainty (usually described as a 'gut feeling'). The tools being designed calculate the uncertainty within future projections and graphically indicate this to the controller, helping them to 'distinguish between acceptable, uncertain and unacceptable situations'. This is therefore an example of where the tools are built around the controller's mental models for controlling traffic.

Electronic strips

In a number of ATM organisations there is a trend towards electronic strips, rather than paper flight strips as are currently used (see also Hopkin, 1995). When designing for electronic strip systems in the UK, it was considered that flight strips are a common thread between the activities of the Planner and Tactical controllers. They are said to 'provide an element of 'team' focus for the controllers' (Goodship and Pember, 1998). This important benefit is one of the key principles that electronic strips seek to maintain. Furthermore, it seeks to perpetuate other human-centred principles:

- The design of the flight strips and the strip boards will be flexible enough 'to allow controllers to use the information presented to assimilate the airspace picture to their individual preference'. The system will permit controllers to organise their strips in a way that continues to support the mental representation of the picture.

- Recording information on electronic strips necessarily moves away from pen on paper but aims to be 'simple and quick'. The designers recognise that 'the entry of flight data becomes second nature and does not distract the controller from the primary task of traffic separation'. This has been achieved by minimal keyboard use and easily accessed strip fields, and using user interface support aspects such as 'implicit focus'.
- The electronic strips do not appear to increase the controllers' workload, either in terms of ascertaining flight data or manipulating (changing) it. The system has been designed so that the strip information has been divided into three types. Thus, information controllers need all the time is always available; the information they need some of the time (but when they do they need permanently displayed for an aircraft) is instantly accessible; the information controllers need only occasionally can be revealed easily and then removed automatically to reduce clutter.
- The controllers are supported in their conflict detection by electronic strips, as it has a facility to highlight aircraft likely to come into conflict in the near future, based on the same flight plan information that controllers normally use.
- The electronic strip concept provides a useful link that did not exist before, between the strips and the radar display. When the controller selects an electronic strip, the track data block for that aircraft is also highlighted on the radar. This is likely to help controllers to integrate their information and highlight errors.
- The prototype system has recently been analysed for human error potential using a human Hazard and Operability approach (Kennedy et al, 2000). This study identified errors via a group error identification approach, considered their consequences, and determined design changes that would prevent the errors or facilitate their detection and recovery.
- The system, and the previous toolset in (i) above, as they develop, are being analysed in prototyping and real-time simulations, and workload is being evaluated throughout its development cycle using a range of workload assessment tools (Atkinson et al, 1997; Kirwan et al, 1998b).

The tools reviewed briefly above are still under development, and so a comprehensive comparison against the principles in this report is neither appropriate nor possible at this stage. Nevertheless, there is clearly already some serious uptake of HCA within the community designing prototype ATM systems and tools. The progressive adoption, adaptation and application of the HCA principles contained in this paper should further ensure that the automation complements, rather than competes, with the controller, and that the required safe increase in capacity is achieved. The example below shows a more formal and analytical approach to the development of a tool that will match the controller's mental model of a critical task in ATM, namely aircraft conflict resolution.

CORA – human centred automation in the development of a conflict resolution assistant (CORA) system

A European study related to Human Centred Automation called the RHEA project (Role of the Human in the Evolution of ATM: Nijhuis, 2000) considered future automation prospects and their likely impact on the controller. The study tried to determine what level of automation would result in best performance. Different levels were considered, from full automation to fully manual, but with many levels in between, such as computer-generated advice, with the controller making the decision, to the computer implementing its own decision unless the controller vetoed it. There were also some flexible levels of automation (e.g. the automation taking over when the controller's workload became too high, or when the controller requested it). These different levels were evaluated qualitatively, and also a predictive error analysis was carried out to try to determine the best level of automation (Kirwan, 2001). The results were that the best levels involved the computer or machine giving advice, and then the controller deciding to accept or reject it. Furthermore, one condition favoured particularly well at this level of automation, was called *'cognitive tools'*. The concept of a cognitive tool is that the tool itself, which gives advice to the controller, is derived around the controller's own mental model of how the situation should be resolved, as opposed to being derived from purely mathematical models etc. Such an approach can be seen as a specific form of 'Human Centred Automation' (Billings, op cit). The Eurocontrol Conflict Resolution Assistant (CORA) Project aims therefore to produce a controller-centred approach to conflict resolution, using the 'Cognitive Tools' concept.

Currently, controllers are masters at real-time conflict detection and resolution, and this expertise in these particular system functions is the result of rigorous selection and intensive training in air traffic control over a prolonged period. Conflict detection and resolution are indeed seen as core functions of the controller today, i.e. controllers, when asked to define their job simply, often say 'separating aircraft'. Any tools that therefore purport to support such functions have two main obstacles to overcome. The first is the development and provision of a viable alternative that is at least as good as controller expertise (and preferably better). The second is ensuring that such tools will be used by controllers, when those very tools can be seen as a threat to those same controllers. This latter aspect is poignant, since conflict resolution is seen as a core task and skill of the controller, especially given their responsibility and culpability should separation be lost.

Today, assistance with conflict detection exists in many places via various forms of short term conflict alert, which warn of impending loss of separation (e.g. a minute or so) and in several air traffic centres, medium term conflict detection is now being piloted and implemented (4 – 15 minutes warning). Therefore, assuming medium term conflict detection systems are at least moderately successful (i.e. they enhance air traffic management and are used effectively by the controllers), the next step to consider is conflict resolution. A conflict resolution tool would be able to advise the controller in terms of which way to turn conflicting aircraft, or whether to climb or descend one or both aircraft, etc. Furthermore, such resolution advice could be based not only on safety parameters, but operational ones also, e.g. turning one aircraft out of a conflict, but giving it a turn which takes it the least distance away from its optimal route. This is effectively what controllers do now, and they do it well. However, in the future with more traffic and more varied traffic patterns, a support tool could improve matters and help maintain safety and quality of service to the airlines and passengers.

There is therefore a need for a tool to help conflict resolution. Conflict resolution is in fact a difficult area. There are many potential approaches to conflict resolution (e.g. see Kuchar and Young, 1999; Mendoza, 1999; Kirwan, 2002a), many of which can work in theory. However, none have been proven in practice, although one is nearing completion (Kirk et al, 2000). Several of the models are mathematical in nature. Such models consider the conflict geometry and the surrounding airspace and simply plot a way out that maintains minimum separation. However, such 'clinically correct' resolutions may be highly inefficient for the aircraft involved. The controller, in contrast, is able to resolve the conflict in a way that minimises penalties to aircraft, and exhibits a certain degree of 'fairness' to the aircraft involved. This is appreciated by the airlines. This ability to optimise according to a range of parameters, in situations that are almost infinite in their variety, is something humans are surprisingly good at, due to their ability to make trade-offs and their pattern recognition faculties.

The area of conflict resolution is therefore complex. A large part of this complexity is due to the multi-dimensionality of the area, in that it is not simply about aircraft conflict geometry, but also about optimisation according to a range of criteria, in a fairly open system environment subject to significant traffic variations (e.g. peaks and troughs), weather effects, etc. Given that the controller currently does this job well, and that automation tools are as yet unproven, it would seem wise to start with a tool that can assist the controller. In fact, what is needed is some automation to help the controller, but the controller must remain in charge, and must be able to decide if the advice the tool is giving is reasonable and can be accepted as it is, or if it needs to be adapted due to some local circumstances. This requirement indeed sounds like a request for Human Centred Automation.

A merging of human and machine models

The main issue is the need for the tool and the human to have a degree of rapport, if they are to work effectively together. This means that the tool will suggest options to the controller that are seen by controllers as being 'smart'. It is perhaps easier to define what the options should not be. They should not be:

- *Unsafe* – e.g. providing a resolution that in fact does not resolve the conflict, or causes a secondary conflict.
- *Ill-advised* - e.g. assuming that nothing can go wrong (e.g. wind changes; below average aircraft performance; etc.).
- *Inefficient* – e.g. sending aircraft away from their destination, or asking them to climb when they are nearing the airport, etc.
- *Naïve* – e.g. assuming perfect aircraft and pilot performance.
- *Unfair* – e.g. penalising aircraft that have already had many alterations to their flight programme.
- *Bad practice* – e.g. climbing through a descending aircraft's level.
- *Complex* – e.g. requiring many multiple movements and commands for involved aircraft.

The way to avoid the above problems is for the automation tool to be 'informed' of, or sensitive to, the same types of parameters and factors that the controllers are considering when carrying out conflict resolution. This requires an analysis of the controllers' expertise in conflict resolution.

A major problem here is that such expertise is not well documented, and in fact it is often said that individual controllers differ greatly in their conflict resolution strategies. Such variation poses significant problems if it is true, since a computerised tool trying to emulate human thought processes will be hard to develop, if those thought processes are in essence 'unstable' or inconsistent. In order to ascertain the stability of the expertise base of controllers in the area of conflict resolution, a study was undertaken, some of the results of which are detailed below (see Kirwan and Flynn, 2001; Kirwan 2002b).

Eliciting expertise

Forty-five air traffic controllers from seven European countries were interviewed individual, and in groups, with the same standardised set of 14 aircraft conflict scenarios. Each scenario contained at least two aircraft in conflict, in a static representation of a generic sector of airspace (see figure 4).

Each controller was asked how (s)he would resolve the scenario. The answer, due to the minimal amount of information in the scenario representation was often 'that depends...'. The controller would then ask questions or make assumptions, until he or she was happy enough to state the principal resolution he or she would propose. The interviewer would note the order of questions/assumptions and list these as 'factors' affecting the determination of the resolution advisory.

Controllers were also asked if there were any potential resolutions (i.e. theoretically possible) that would be considered poor practice, and should therefore definitely *not* be recommended. Such potential resolution advisories (called *No-no's* in the study) might appear reasonable to a non-controller and might even appear mathematically optimal, but would be seen as incorrect by a controller, and would be rejected immediately by real controllers and could cause loss of trust in the tool.

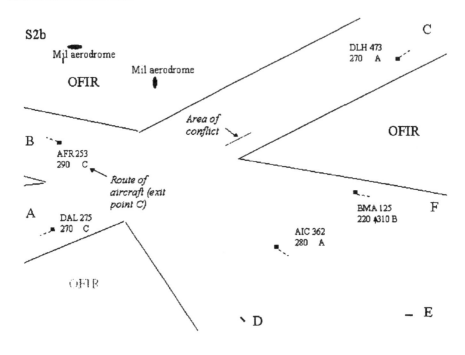

S2b

Mil aerodrome

OFIR

Mil aerodrome

C

DLH 473
270   A

Area of
conflict

OFIR

B

AFR 253
290   C

Route of
aircraft (exit
point C)

A   DAL 275
270   C

BMA 125
220 ₄310 B   F

AIC 362
280   A

OFIR

D

_ E

Figure 4   Example of Scenario 2b

The study, which took place over a six month period, resulted in significant amounts of information on controller expertise in conflict resolution. It identified all the formal rules controllers use in the seven different countries, and the factors and principles controllers consider in a variety of conflict scenarios, and also what controllers would *not* do. Examples of some of the principles controllers apply in various scenarios are given in table 2, and the factors that controllers considered important are highlighted in figure 5[7].

Overall, the study showed more convergence of opinions than was initially hoped for. In practice, this means that a resolution advisory system can offer a relatively small number of suggestions (e.g. 4) and satisfy most controllers. This is indeed a positive result, and suggests that this critical component of the HCA

---

[7] The detailed analyses are not presented here, as the intent in this paper is to show only the general approach and type of information that was gained, to develop a controller-model-based system.

philosophy, i.e. that the machine and human can have a degree of understanding and rapport, is achievable in this area.

The next phase of the work is to 'inform' the computerised tool with the information gained in this study. This will be carried out under another contract, and so it cannot be stated at this point exactly how this will be achieved, but one suggestion is illustrated in figure 6.

Table 2   Extract of principles and strategies used by controllers

Category	Ref.	Principle
		Crossing conflicts
	S1	Turn slower a/c behind (in order to minimise extra distance flown)
	S2	Stabilise until after crossing points
		Converging/Head-on
	S3	When there are few a/c, a temporary ODL is acceptable
	S4	Ask the pilot whether (s)he prefers a level change or a vector
Scenario	S5	Normally if vectoring, vector both a/c
-based	S6	In turbulence, not always good to have level solutions, since they may not maintain their levels
	S8	Solve the head-on first
	S9	Turn faster one direct to route so leaves sector before slower one on same route
	S10	Safe if locked on headings
	S11	Sometimes not changing levels on a/c means you don't have to worry about them
	S12	Give a short-cut which can end the conflict
	S13	Better to put a/c behind than trying to go through the middle

Figure 6 is based on an 'informing' philosophy. The computerised tool will contain an algorithm that calculates all the different ways to resolve the conflict, and there could easily be 10-30 such theoretical resolutions for a conflict scenario. The controller expertise data can then be used as an 'expert system filter' to reduce the resolution set (called the solution space) to an acceptable set of prioritised resolutions, which are optimal for the controller and the aircraft. An example of the synthesis of the expertise is shown in figure 7, which is an algorithmic expression for a particular scenario (wherein one aircraft is directly approaching the other, known as a 'head-on' scenario). This figure is only a prototype, but shows how the various factors etc. can be stated as rules that a conflict resolution algorithm could utilise.

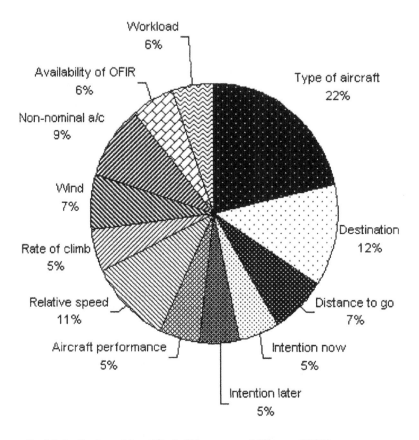

Figure 5   Main factors identified (Kirwan and Flynn, 2001)

This is still theory – there is much work still to take place in developing the support tool:

- Developing the algorithm.
- Using the expertise data to reduce the solution space.
- Determining how to present the data.
- Determining working arrangements between controllers and the tool.
- Testing the system (against operational and safety parameters).
- Training the controllers.
- Developing contingency measures in case of tool failure.
- Implementing the system.

The system development process is now moving into the first four stages outlined above. This will result in a prototype tool.

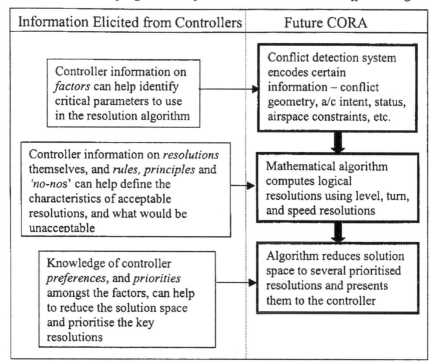

Information Elicited from Controllers	Future CORA
Controller information on *factors* can help identify critical parameters to use in the resolution algorithm	Conflict detection system encodes certain information – conflict geometry, a/c intent, status, airspace constraints, etc.
Controller information on *resolutions* themselves, and *rules, principles* and *'no-nos'* can help define the characteristics of acceptable resolutions, and what would be unacceptable	Mathematical algorithm computes logical resolutions using level, turn, and speed resolutions
Knowledge of controller *preferences*, and *priorities* amongst the factors, can help to reduce the solution space and prioritise the key resolutions	Algorithm reduces solution space to several prioritised resolutions and presents them to the controller

Figure 6   How controller information informs a computerised tool

IF <conflict> is <pair-only> AND <category Head-On> AND <T =10+ mins>
THEN IF <air traffic control centre> is <level-favoured> AND <no turbulence
at level> AND <levels above available> THEN [OPERATION: Determine
Opposite Direction Level {ODL} a/c = A] THEN IF <A not recently taken
off> AND <a/c performance category = ok/Flight Level> THEN
CLIMB A 1000 feet

ELSE IF <A recently taken off> OR <A performance inadequate> OR
<turbulence> OR <no levels available above> AND <levels available below>
THEN
DESCEND A 1000 feet

ELSE IF <B far from destination> AND <B climb performance ok?FL> AND
<levels available above> AND <no turbulence> THEN
CLIMB B 1000 feet

ELSE IF <no OFIR boundaries nearby> AND <no context a/c left/right> AND
<wind = negligible> THEN
[OPERATION: Determine non-   ODL's destination short-cut = Right} THEN
TURN BOTH A/C RIGHT 10 DEGREES

Figure 7   Encoding expertise for 'head-on' scenario

This short case study has aimed to show the following:

- An area which needs automation support.
- A specific need for Human Centred Automation.
- An approach for developing a HCA-based tool.
- The types of expertise required to input into the tool (merging of human and computer models) that allows 'rapport' between human and machine.
- The way forward with this tool.

Discussion of the HCA approach

Human Centred Automation is seen as a useful approach to help ensure safety and performance during the coming 'upgrade' of many air traffic management systems, tools and centres. The controller's job is likely to change significantly over the next decade, and will not be achievable without computerised assistance of some sort, but this assistance must be compatible with the controller's skills, mental models and aptitudes. HCA can help ensure that this occurs.

The HCA approach has been adapted in this paper from its aviation origins towards ATM. The likely aspects of human performance that will be affected by the proposed changes to ATM have been identified, thus prioritising where HCA, and more generally Human Factors, need to focus. A set of guiding principles have been distilled, that have been found to be useful and practicable by designers involved in a small number of controller tool development projects. Such projects show that such principles, if adopted, can help avoid some of the typical problems that can arise with the introduction of additional technology into an already highly-skilled area.

The CORA study goes into more depth, however, showing what can be done at a more fundamental level, by trying to harmonise the tool and the controller, via the study of controller mental strategies, and factors affecting those strategies. Such an approach is only viable if there is a real commitment towards a human centred approach. HCA is, in effect, a design philosophy, and orientation of the designers, supported by human factors specialists, towards achieving a truly human-compatible system, where the human is still 'in charge'. Underlying the approach is the implicit high value placed on the human component of the system (in this case the controller), and a design aim to provide automation that supports, rather than replaces the controller. This needs to be something that is truly accepted by the designers, and then human factors needs to supply the tools and guidance to enable designers to reach such a goal.

Such an approach or philosophy, on a real project where the aim (and need) is system performance improvement, will lead inexorably to debates about whether an automated system would outperform a controller-aided one. The real 'added value' of the human element will be questioned. In a case such as ATM, there are ample defences, since no automated system has been proven, and the controller currently does a good job. Furthermore, ATM is an 'open system', prone to many disturbances that are both variable and stochastic in nature (e.g. weather patterns and storms; aircraft problems; communication problems; traffic blockages; temporary airport shutdowns; etc.), such that the controller's flexibility, awareness, and skills are difficult to emulate and replace reliably. For the medium term future, therefore, it seems that the human must remain firmly in the loop.

But the human has limits and does not always perform optimally, and in some local situations, a machine might perform better. For example in the CORA project, there were certain 'no-no's identified, which are in fact optimal from a global traffic management perspective, and sometimes the computer algorithm is likely to come up with more efficient solutions. Ideally therefore, the 'joint cognitive system' is more of a 'joint collaborative system', i.e. one that can learn. It may be that initially controllers find some of the computer-suggested resolutions not to their preference, but training media could show the controllers that these are in fact better resolutions. This suggests that a period of training and adaptation is needed for such a system to function at peak performance. The end goal is a system that is better than its component parts – better than the controller alone, and better than automation alone. This latter proposition, however, immediately draws into question the term 'Human Centred Automation', which seems too biased towards the human component in the system equation. The term still contains an echo of the 'Human-versus-Machine' paradigm most clearly represented by Fitts List, some forty years ago when Ergonomics and Human Factors were still growing. It has the feel of placing human aspects above system performance aspects. This is no doubt a reaction against the blind ignorance towards human factors over a period of many years, in the context of an attempt to place automation at the top of the 'work chain', with sometimes disastrous and fatal results. But perhaps the time has come for a more balanced perspective, one that reflects a philosophy of co-operation and collaboration, rather than competition between system elements.

In this respect, it is useful to consider when HCA is needed. Effectively, the type of HCA being suggested here is a team approach, the team comprising the human and the automation. Although the question of what each of these team 'members' is bringing to the task is usually asked, the next question of whether the *blend* of these attributes and skills is a sensible blend likely to improve performance, is usually not detailed. In effect, HCA makes generic assumptions about human and machine compatibility that in practice need to be 'unpacked' and explored in more detail if applying HCA to a practical context. In the conflict resolution context, the relative strengths of the human and machine do in fact seem to complement each other (see table 3).

The above discussion suggests the need to elaborate the HCA philosophy and approach. The approach should be driven by the need to improve system performance. However, the human contribution needs to be fully understood before any level of automation is considered, and the search should be for a compatible blend of computer and human attributes. Such a system should be able to 'earn over time, and actually improve in terms of system performance, as the human and the computer system (the latter via upgrades) continue to adapt to each other.

Table 3   Allocation of function (in a ATM conflict resolution context)

Human strengths in conflict resolution	Machine strengths in conflict resolution
Ability to recognise and categorise problems and infinite scenario permutations	Very fast and reliable processing
Ability to make decisions under uncertainty and stress	Ability to predict and project with more accuracy and range
Ability to make judgements that will satisfy most parties	Ability to optimise according to many criteria (where these can be 'parameterised')
Ability to address temporary local or special conditions	Not bound by biases, personal experience, or memory or processing limitations

'Human-centred' design is perhaps too strong and unbalanced a term. A better term might be 'Human-informed', implying that the system is based on a clear understanding and mapping of the human expertise in the task, but is not necessarily a direct replica of that expertise structure. Instead, it aims to provide a system that is cognisant of that structure, and one which will be complementary to it, but will also enhance system performance. To achieve acceptance by the users, training and validation (proof) of the system's capabilities will have to be provided.

HCA (or 'HIA') at this level is therefore not trivial, and not just about interface design. It is about understanding, about communication between human and machine, between psychologist, domain expert, and designer and software engineer. A team process, and a team culture are needed. This team needs to have a (preferably written[8]) philosophy that will make the best utilisation of human capabilities, via an optimised partnership between human and machine.

---

[8] If written into the design philosophy, it is less likely to be sacrificed at the first significant obstacle.

Conclusions

Automation or computerised support for the controller will become a reality within the next decade, in order to realise predicted capacity demands safely. The aviation cockpit system design experience has shown that there are downsides to such automation, and that the solution is to adopt a Human Centred Automation (HCA) approach.

This paper has reviewed the key lessons from aviation, and has distilled a set of guiding principles of HCA for ATM. A number of these principles are already being adopted within ATM future systems design and development programmes. It is therefore recommended that such practices continue, and that the principles and methods in this paper and elsewhere are considered and developed further for all future automation or computerised support-tool projects. A key insight from one of the studies in this paper is that the HCA approach may need to be more 'co-operative' in spirit. The term Human-Informed Automation has been suggested as capturing the cognitive aspect required to achieve human-automation partnerships, and also placing system performance as the ultimate goal, whilst recognising the criticality of the human element and perspective in the system performance equation.

References

AAIB (1990). *Report on the accident to Boeing 737-400 G-OBME near Kegworth, Leics., 8/1/89.* Air Accidents Investigation Board, Air Accident Report 4/90. London: HMSO.

Atkinson, T., Donohoe, L., Evans, A., Gorst, A., Kilner, A., Kirwan, B., Lamoureux, T., and MacKendrick, H. (1997). *Human Factors Guidelines for Air Traffic Management Systems.* NATS RandD Report 9739, ATMDC, August.

Billings C.E. (1997). *Aviation Automation: The Search for a Human-Centred Approach.* Mahwah: Lawrence Erlbaum.

Cardosi, K., and Murphy, E.D. (1995). *Human factors checklist for the design and evaluation of ATC systems – Volpe Centre ATC Human Factors Program.* US Dept. of Transportation, Research and Special Programs Administration, FAA.

Endsley, M.R. and Smolensky, M.W. (1998). Situation awareness in air traffic control: the picture. In, Smolensky, M.W., and Stein, E.S. (Eds.) *Human Factors in Air Traffic Control.* London: Academic Press, pp. 115-154.

Eurocontrol (2000). *ATM 2000+ Strategy.* Eurocontrol Headquarters, 96 Rue de la Fusee, Brussels.

Evans, A., Slamen, A., and Shorrock, S. (1999). *Use of human factors guidelines and human error identification in the design lifecycle of NATS future systems.*

Paper presented at FAA/Eurocontrol Technical Interchange, Toulouse, 27-29 April.

Goodship, T. and Pember, S. (1998). *EPS Concept of Operation.* DASR\EPS\RPT\001. ATMDC, Bournemouth Airport.

Graeber, R.C. and Mumaw, R.J. (1999). Realising the benefits of cognitive engineering in commercial aviation. In, D. Harris (Ed.) *Engineering Psychology and Cognitive Ergonomics, Volume 3.* Ashgate Publishing: Aldershot, pp. 3-26.

Helmreich, R.L. and Merritt, A. (1998). *Culture at work in aviation and medicine.* Aldershot, Ashgate.

Hopkin, V.D. (1995). *Human Factors in Air Traffic Control.* London: Taylor and Francis.

Isaac, A.R. and Ruitenberg, B. (1999). *Air traffic control: human performance factors.* Ashgate Publishing: Aldershot, UK.

Kelly, B.D., Graeber, R.C. and Fadden, D.M. (1992). Applying crew-centred concepts to flight deck technology: The Boeing 777. *Proceedings of The Flight Safety Foundation 45th International Air Safety Seminar.* Long Beach, CA.

Kennedy, R., Jones, H., Shorrock, S., and Kirwan, B. (2000). Use of Hazard and Operability study in Air Traffic Control Interface Design. In, P, T. McCabe, M. A. Hanson and S. A. Robertson (Eds.) *Contemporary Ergonomics 2000.* London: Taylor and Francis.

Kirk, D.B., Heagy, W.S. and Yablonski, M.J. (2000b). *Problem Resolution Support for Free Flight Operations.* MITRE, Center for Advanced Aviation System Development, McLean, Virginia.

Kirwan, B. (1994). *A Practical Guide to Human Reliability Assessment.* London: Taylor and Francis.

Kirwan, B. (1998b). Human Factors techniques in the NATS ATM System Development Process. *Paper presented at the Eurocontrol Workshop on the Integration of Human Factors into the System Design Life Cycle.* Luxembourg, October 7-9.

Kirwan, B. (2001). The Role of the Controller in the Accelerating Industry of Air Traffic management. *Safety Science, 37,* 151-185.

Kirwan, B. (2002a). *Towards a controller-based conflict resolution tool – a literature review.* Eurocontrol Experimental Centre, BP15, F-91222, Bretigny sur Orges, CEDEX, France.

Kirwan, B. (2002b). *Investigating controller air traffic resolution strategies.* Eurocontrol Experimental Centre, BP15, F-91222, Bretigny sur Orges, CEDEX, France.

Kirwan, B. and Cox, M. (1999). *Human Centred Automation.* NATS RandD Report 9913. ATMDC, Bournemouth Airport.

Kirwan, B., and Flynn, M. (2001). Identification of Air Traffic Controller Conflict Resolution Strategies for the CORA (Conflict Resolution Assistant) Project. *Paper presented at the ATM 2001 Conference.* Santa Fe, December 3-7.

Kirwan, B., Donohoe, L., Atkinson, T., Lamoureux, T., MacKendrick, H., and Phillips, A. (1998a) Getting The Picture: - Investigating The Mental Picture Of The Air Traffic Controller. In, S. A. Robertson (Ed.) *Contemporary Ergonomics 1998*. London: Taylor and Francis.

Kuchar, J.K. and Yang, L.C. (1999). *Survey of Conflict Detection and Resolution Modelling Methods*. Department of Aeronautics and Astronautics, Massachusetts Institute of Technology, Cambridge, MA.

Lee, J.D. and Moray, N. (1992). Trust, control strategies and allocation of function in human-machine systems. *Ergonomics, 35*, 1243-1270.

MacKendrick, H., Kirwan, B. and Atkinson, T. (1998). Understanding the Controller's Picture in ATM. In, D. Harris (Ed.) *Engineering Psychology and Cognitive Ergonomics, Volume 3*. Ashgate Publishing: Aldershot, pp. 145-154.

MacKendrick, H.M. (1998). Development of a Human Machine Interface Guidelines Database for Air Traffic Control Centres. NATS RandD Report 9822, ATMDC, April.

Maurino, D., Reason, J., Johnston, N. and Lee, R. (1995). *Beyond Aviation Human Factors*. Aldershot: Avebury Aviation.

Mendoza, M. (1999). *Current State of ATC Conflict Resolution. European Organisation for the Safety of Air Navigation*. EuroControl Experimental Centre, B.P. 15, F-91222 Bretigny-sur-Orge, CEDEX, France.

Mosier, K. and Skitka, L.J. (1996). Human decision-makers and automated decision aids: made for each other? In, Parasuraman, R. and Mouloua, M. (Eds): *Automation and Human Performance: Theory and Applications*. Mahwah: Lawrence Elbaum Associates.

Nijhuis, H. (2000). *Role of the Human in the Evolution of ATM (RHEA): Final Report*. Amsterdam: NLR.

Parasuraman, R. and Mouloua, M. (Eds) (1996). *Automation and Human Performance: Theory and Applications*. Mahwah: Lawrence Elbaum Associates.

Rasmussen, J., Pedersen, O.M., Carnino, A., Griffon, M., Mancini, C., and Gagnolet, P. (1981). *Classification system for reporting events involving human malfunctions*. RISO-M-2240. Riso National Laboratories, Roskilde, Denmark.

Scerbo, M.W. and Mouloua, M. (Eds.) (1999). *Automation technology and human performance*. Lawrence Erlbaum Associates, New Jersey.

Sheridan, T.B. (1980). Computer control and human alienation. *Technology review, 10*, 61-73.

Shorrock, S. and Kirwan, B. (1999). The development of TRACEr: a technique for the retrospective analysis of cognitive errors in ATM. In, D. Harris (Ed.) *Engineering Psychology and Cognitive Ergonomics, Volume 3*. Ashgate Publishing: Aldershot, pp. 163-172.

Shorrock, S., Kirwan, B., MacKendrick, H., and Kennedy, R. (2001). Assessing human error in Air Traffic Management systems design: Methodological issues. *Le Travail Humain, 64*, 269-289.

Smolensky, M.W., and Stein, E.S. (Eds.) (1998). *Human Factors in Air Traffic Control*. London: Academic Press.

Whysall, P. (1998). Future Area Control Tools Support (FACTS). In, *Proceedings of the 2nd USA/Europe Air Traffic Management RandD Seminar.* Orlando: December.

Wickens, C.D. (1992). *Engineering psychology and human performance*. New York: Harper-Collins.

Wickens, C.D. (1999). Automation in air traffic control: the human performance issues. In, M.W. Scerbo and M. Mouloua (Eds.) *Automation technology and human performance*. Lawrence Erlbaum Associates, New Jersey, pp. 2-10.

Wickens, C.D. Mavor, A.S. and McGee, J.P. (Eds) (1997). *Flight to the future: Human factors in air traffic control*. Washington DC: National Academy Press.

Wickens, C.D., Mavor, A.S., Parasuraman, R., and McGee, J.P. (Eds.) (1998). *The future of air traffic control: human operators and automation*. Washington DC: National Academy Press.

Wiener, E.L. and Nagel, D.C. (Eds.) (1988). *Human Factors in Aviation*. San Diego: Academic Press.

Woods, D.D. (1996). Decomposing automation: apparent simplicity, real complexity. In R. Parasuraman and M. Mouloua (Eds). *Automation and Human Performance: Theory and Applications*. Mahwah, New Jersey: Lawrence Elbaum Associates, pp. 3-18.

Disclaimer

The opinions expressed in this paper are those of the author and do not necessarily represent those of the parent organisation(s) concerned.

Acknowledgements

The author would like to thank in particular Martin Cox of UK CAA, and at the Department of ATM Systems Research, NATS, Peter Whysall, Andy Price, Tony Goodship, Andy Webb, Steve Pember, and Alyson Evans, and at Eurocontrol, Seppo Kauppinen, Mary Flynn, Geraldine Flynn, Rod McGregor, and Colin Prescott, and all the controllers who participated in the CORA study.

13 Spinning paper into glass: transforming flight progress strips

Francis T. Durso and Carol A. Manning

Overview

The purpose of this paper is to describe how flight progress strips are currently used in United States (US) en route air traffic control (ATC) and to discuss the Federal Aviation Administration's (FAA's) objective of eliminating them. The paper will begin by briefly describing the US ATC system, in particular the en route environment, then will describe how flight strips are used. Issues surrounding the replacement of flight strips will be discussed, along with the role of various methods of inquiry in answering questions about appropriate strip replacements. We provide several reasons for taking the position that flight progress strips can be eliminated, but argue that for a variety of reasons a transitional system will be valuable for moving the current, strip-dependent workforce away from paper.

US en route Air Traffic Control

To accomplish its primary purpose 'to prevent a collision between aircraft operating in the system and to organise and expedite the flow of traffic' (Federal Aviation Administration, 2001; Section 2-1-1), the ATC system employs four types of facilities to provide ATC services. These are flight service stations (FSS), ATC towers, terminal radar approach control (TRACON) facilities, and air route traffic control centres (ARTCCs, also called 'en route facilities' or 'centres'). Employees of each type of facility provide a different type of ATC service. En route controllers, the focus of this article, work in centres using radar or non-radar procedures to authorise the movement of aircraft operating between

This paper was first published in Human Factors and Aerospace Safety 2(1), 2002, pp. 1-31

terminal areas. A centre may also provide limited approach control services for aircraft landing at airports that do not provide these services.

The men and women in the towers, terminals, and centres around the US excel at accomplishing their primary goal of aviation safety. Although the events of September 11th 2001 have increased the concern of the flying public, taking a commercial flight in the industrialised world remains one of the safest forms of transportation. If we focus on the mishaps caused by the air traffic control system, the safety performance is remarkable. For example, since 1983, the National Traffic Safety Board (NTSB) identified en route ATC as a contributory factor in only two accidents, one landing and one terrain (en route ATC was never a primary factor). If we hold ATC to an even higher standard of 'near misses' that is, operational errors, the level of safety achieved remains superlative. In the US en route environment, an operational error occurs when aircraft violate separation standards; for example, in high altitude en route environments (29,000 feet or above), the standard is 5 nm lateral separation or 2000 ft vertical separation. The percentage of flight legs that result in an operational error is well less than 1% (see, for example, Durso, Truitt, Hackworth, Crutchfield and Manning, 1998; Rodgers and Nye, 1993).

The airspace assigned to a centre is divided into smaller segments called areas of specialisation, which are further divided into even smaller, interrelated airspace segments called sectors. Sectors are classified as Radar, Non-Radar, or Oceanic and are sub-classified by their altitude strata (high, low, super-high, or super-low). Fully certified en route controllers, called Certified Professional Controllers (CPCs), control traffic at all sectors grouped within one area of specialisation and do not control traffic at sectors in any other areas.

One, two, or more controllers can staff a sector depending on the overall level of activity. The ATC tasks to be completed remain the same regardless of the staffing. When one controller is present, he or she must perform all the duties associated with controlling traffic at that sector. However, when more than one controller is present, there is not a universal approach to how the responsibilities are divided (Federal Aviation Administration, 2001; Section 2-10-1). In general, the Radar (R) controller ensures separation, issues control instructions to pilots, operates the radios, accepts and initiates transfer of radar identification for an aircraft from one controller to another (i.e., makes and takes handoffs), coordinates with the Radar Associate (RA) controller, scans the radar display, ensures that clearances issued or received are recorded properly, and ensures the R-side equipment can be used by all members of the sector team. The Radar Associate (RA) controller, also referred to as 'D-Side' or 'Manual Controller,' assists the R controller. The RA controller helps ensure separation, initiates control instructions, communicates with controllers at the same or other facilities, accepts and initiates automated or non-automated handoffs, ensures that the R controller is made aware of any action taken, conducts coordination, monitors radio communications, scans flight progress data, manages data recorded on flight progress strips, ensures that clearances issued or received are accurately recorded, and ensures the RA equipment can be used by all members of the sector team. However, there is considerable variability across centres with respect to the division of responsibilities for the R and RA controllers. Teams staffing a sector can be, on occasion, larger than two. For example, 'trackers' assist at a busy sector, offloading some of the radar controller's duties.

Equipment and information used in en route ATC

En route radar controllers use secondary surveillance radar to identify aircraft operating under instrument flight rules (IFR). The radar system interrogates a transponder on an aircraft, which generates a reply. Computer processing of the information provided by the transponder allows display of information about the altitude and location of the aircraft. The radar information is correlated with flight data processed in parallel, which allows the computer to match the aircraft's identity with its position.

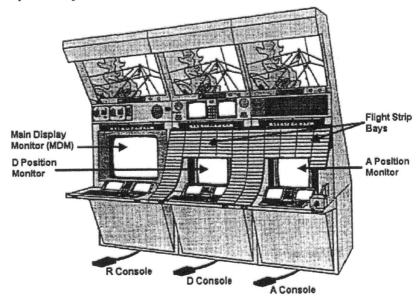

Figure 1   Drawing of the display system replacement (DSR)

In the display system replacement (DSR) work environment (see figure 1) radar controllers view the combination of aircraft position and identity information on a situation display (SD, also called a plan view logical display), a window generated on a 20' x 20' main display monitor. Each radar-tracked aircraft on the display is

291

accompanied by a 'data block.' A data block consists of a position symbol (indicating the type of tracking employed), and up to (as of this writing) three lines of alphanumeric data concerning the flight, a line connecting the position symbol with the alphanumeric data, and a line predicting the aircraft's future position, based on flight plan data.

Controllers use a keyboard, keypad, and a trackball to enter and retrieve information about an aircraft's flight plan. Messages are displayed on several 'views' (windows) located on the R controller's or on auxiliary displays located at the RA controller's workstation. Controllers use a variety of communication devices, including telephone landlines and radio frequencies that allow them to contact pilots, other facilities, and other sector workstations within the ARTCC.

En route controllers also use small pieces of paper called flight progress strips (FPSs, also known as 'flight strips' or just 'strips') on which are printed all the information about a flight that is included in the filed flight plan. The en route flight strip is a $1\,^7/_{16}$' x 6 $^7/_{16}$' (36.6mm x 164.6mm) piece of stiff paper containing 31 blocks or fields that can contain flight plan information (see figure 2).

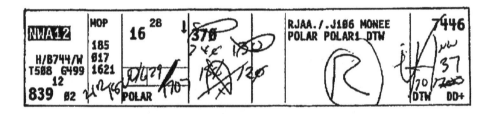

Figure 2 **Example of a flight progress strip currently used in ARTCC facilities. It shows both printed information and the controller's handwritten markings**

Before radar was available, controllers used flight strips to sequence and separate all aircraft. Strips are still used to separate aircraft in environments where radar is not available. When only primary radar (which showed only aircraft positions, but did not include associated flight plan data) was used, controllers studied strips extensively to maintain situation awareness about the identities and characteristics of aircraft moving through the sector and identify potential conflicts. Even when secondary radar was developed, flight strips retained their utility because they provided controllers with access to flight plan data that are not displayed in the data block (such as aircraft type, which indicates the aircraft's performance characteristics). Controllers developed additional uses for strips by moving or offsetting them to indicate that an aircraft was particularly noteworthy, or writing information on them about control actions that are not updated in the flight plan or plans for future activities. Finally, strips are the only backup in case of system failure – if the power goes off, a controller can look at these pieces of paper to identify aircraft that are flying through the sector.

General flight strip uses

Flight strips are used in three different ways. First, strips can be used as an easy reference to a complete set of information about an aircraft's flight plan. Although a considerable amount of important flight plan information is included in the data block (e.g. aircraft ID, assigned and reported altitudes, computer ID, ground speed, handoff indicator), not all flight plan information is displayed there (notably the aircraft type and route/destination). A controller needs to know the aircraft type for each aircraft under control in order to determine its performance characteristics. Such information is useful if, for example, the controller needs to decide which aircraft should go first in a sequence. Because the aircraft type is not shown in the data block, the controller must instead refer to some auxiliary source of information. The controller can make a computer entry that will display an aircraft's flight plan on the computer readout device (CRD) view or can glance at the flight strips. Controllers also need to know the route of flight and destination for each aircraft. If an aircraft will land in the controlling sector or an adjacent sector, the controller needs to know the destination in order to plan its descent. If an aircraft needs to divert around weather, knowledge about its route and destination could influence whether the controller clears the pilot to deviate to the left or right. Some facilities use an automation patch that displays an aircraft's destination in the data block, but no single destination patch is universally employed and some facilities do not use a destination patch at all. Controllers who cannot see the destination in the data block or need more information about an aircraft's route of flight can either refer to the strips or make a computer entry to bring up the flight plan on the CRD view (although if the route is too long, not all of it will be displayed).

A second use for flight strips involves annotating activity concerning an aircraft's flight plan that has either already been completed or needs to be completed in the future. To do this, controllers can either write information on strips or take some action using them. Writing on strips can provide a record of activities that occurred within the sector regarding a particular flight (e.g. issued clearance), can indicate that a controller has coordinated with another controller about a clearance (e.g. coordinated clearance), or can be a reminder that some action needs to be taken in the future (e.g. planned clearance). Some of the information written on strips can also be entered into the computer to update the flight plan (e.g. an altitude clearance) but other information cannot (e.g. heading, speed, holding instructions). Clearances that are issued, planned, or coordinated can be recorded on strips using distinctive annotations, such as writing planned clearances in red or circling information to indicate that coordination has occurred. Other kinds of information not specifically related to clearances, such as pointouts, or releasing/receiving control of an aircraft to another controller are

293

also recorded, as are unusual events, such as issuing infrequently used radio frequencies, comments, pilot information, and so on.

A third use for flight strips is to organise or highlight information. Strips may be re-sorted or moved when an event occurs, such as when an aircraft takes off from an airport or enters from another sector. Strips may also be offset to indicate, for example, that the R controller needs to take an action (or pay special attention to an aircraft) or to communicate to the RA controller that something needs to be done. In addition, the R controller may point to information written on the strip for the benefit of the RA controller when he/she is busy talking with another pilot.

Current use of flight strips

If strips are used as prescribed by regulations, interacting with strips and managing them are important parts of the controller's job. We (Vortac, Edwards, Jones, Manning and Rotter, 1993; Vortac, Edwards and Manning, 1994) observed ATC instructors while they controlled simulated air traffic either individually or as an R/RA sector team. We used Pathfinder network analysis to produce a graph of the activities normally used in ATC. Figure 3 shows an illustrative network from that analysis, specifically from individual controllers working the high-complexity scenarios. In this graph, and in all the other graphs of high or low complexity, individual or team staffing, writing on the strips (WRITE) was a central (in a graph-theoretic sense) component of the networks. In addition, the connection between writing on the strips and manipulating them (WRITE → MANIP) occurred frequently and appeared in all the graphs.

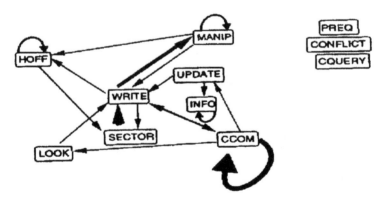

Figure 3 Pathfinder graphs showing interconnections among some major ATC functions.   From Vortac, Edwards and Manning (1994). CCOM = Controller command; PREQ = Pilot Request; CQUERY = Controller query

The graphs also suggested that there was a 'board management' module, bursts of activity during which the controller would manage the strips. The triggers for writing on a strip were quite predictable (Edwards, Fuller, Vortac and Manning, 1995). Writing at time, t, depended on whether an aircraft entered the sector, whether the controller issued a command, and, consistent with the idea of bursts of board management, whether the controller had just written on a strip. Overall, these data indicated that board management was a frequent and central part of the controller's behaviours, but one that occurred as bursts of distinct activity, what Vortac (1993) referred to as a behavioural module. However, these data alone only indicate that changing interactions with the strips will have a large impact on the controller, not whether the change would be negative or positive. Although behavioural modules are possible targets for successful automation (Vortac, 1993), their existence does not suggest that they should be automated. These data also do not indicate the reason for strip activity. Because strip activities are typically mandated and because current day controllers have been interacting with strips in this way for years, board management may be central to ATC.

MacKay (1999) described how a team of controllers at the Athis Mons centre near Paris used paper flight strips. Controllers annotated strips to note an agreement between the controller and pilot regarding changes to an aircraft's assigned route or flight level. Controller scanning patterns started with an overall view of the traffic using the radar display and then focused on detailed information about specific aircraft using the strips. MacKay proposed that flight strips allow controllers to offload mental effort because they record important information on the strips and sort or offset them to better organise or highlight information. While indicating that annotations are important, MacKay (1999) observed that 'a few senior controllers write very little, usually annotating strips quickly just before a new team arrives.' Another important function of the flight strip is to promote communications between members of the controller team. Movement of a strip into a controller's peripheral or focal vision is one method to communicate the urgency with which some action needs to be taken with a specific flight.

Although MacKay (1999) provided an interesting perspective on the use of strips in several types of air traffic facilities, she did not provide any information about the relative frequency with which individual controllers used particular strategies for dealing with strips. Until recently, no frequency data were available to describe how US en route controllers used strips when controlling live traffic. However, in 2001, Durso, Batsakes, Crutchfield, Braden and Manning (under review) conducted an extensive observational study that examined operational flight strip usage at five en route facilities (Kansas City, Chicago, Atlanta, Cleveland and Washington centres) scheduled to receive a decision aid that is intended to replace most paper flight strips. The purpose of the study was to determine how flight strips are actually used so that operational needs might be otherwise accommodated if paper flight strips were eliminated.

In the first part of the study, trained CPCs observed flight strip usage by R controllers, RA controllers, and other controllers at different types of sectors preselected randomly. The observers recorded each time a controller made a strip marking or action during 10-minute observation periods. Approximately 34,000 strip markings and actions were recorded using this methodology. About 2.6 marks, on the average, were made during every minute.

The frequency data derived from the observational study were then matched with a set of importance ratings provided by a group of controllers involved in the development of the en route decision aid for each strip marking and action. For the most part, marks and actions categorised as high frequency and high importance reflected issued clearances. Marks and actions categorised as high importance but low frequency consisted of coordinated clearances. Marks and actions categorised as low in both frequency and importance consisted of planned clearances. Finally, several other markings and actions, including those that constituted four of the five most frequent observations at every facility, fell in the high frequency but low importance category (e.g. incoming and outgoing radar and communications).

The results suggest that strip marking occurs frequently in the en route environment. Observing strip marking for eight hours at one sector alone would witness 1,250 interactions with the strips. Controllers often perform certain actions using the strips and make certain marks frequently. However, frequent marks were not always important, and important marks were not always frequent. Thus, frequency of usage should not be the only thing considered when trying to prioritise automation of flight strip functions.

In the second part of the study, controllers were interviewed to determine why they made certain strip markings and actions. About 84% of the controllers interviewed felt that the marks they discussed were beneficial for what were categorised as memory, communication, organisation, and workload reduction. Perceived value depended on the strip activity. For example, marks related to issued clearances were thought to have primarily communication but also some memorial value. Recording planned clearances also has benefits, but only for controllers working alone and not as part of a team. Non-marking actions involving strips primarily benefit members of the controller team and are seen as helping to organise flight information.

Thus, controllers see the strips and their interactions with them as beneficial in particular ways. Some are thought to aid memory, some workload, some organisation, and many aid communication. Perhaps most critical, those marks that were both frequent and important are seen as communication and memory aids.

Automation of flight progress data

The FAA's planning documents describe an ATC system that is based on an expanded version of electronic flight data that will eventually eliminate the use of

296

paper flight strips (Federal Aviation Administration, 1999). According to the FAA's NAS Architecture V4.0 (1999) new applications software will have the following capabilities:

- New and improved controller decision support tools.
- Utilisation of advanced surveillance and communication information methods.
- Integration with NAS-wide information service to facilitate data sharing.

Tools to be introduced in the first phase of en route automation (called Free Flight Phase 1) include a decision aid that predicts conflicts up to 20 minutes in advance, called the user request evaluation tool (URET) core capabilities limited deployment (CCLD). The traffic management advisor – single center (TMA SC) is another Free Flight Phase 1 tool that can be used by en route controllers for arrival sequencing. These tools are envisioned to provide a variety of benefits, such as user flexibility in selecting flight paths, efficient use of airspace, improved traffic flow, and increased safety through improved conflict prediction and avoidance capabilities.

Modern programming procedures take seriously the notion of data structure, and thus future enhancements to en route automation will depend on the implementation of a data structure called the 'flight object' (Federal Aviation Administration, 1999). The flight object will contain all the information about a flight, starting with the filed flight plan, but will update automatically as the flight progresses. The flight object will then be retained as the record of each flight as it actually occurred. The use of the flight object will allow more accurate flight data to be shared across ATC facilities and with other NAS users.

Is technological change inevitable?

It is easy to believe that once a more modern technology exists, its use is inevitable, and discussions such as the one represented here are not relevant or are merely an academic exercise. There certainly are hints of inevitability in some discussions of the automation of flight progress strips. The silicon snowball rolling down the hills in business and industry has indeed been a formidable force, although as Landauer (1995) pointed out, not necessarily a productive one. Genetically engineered and irradiated foods, despite opposition, are other examples. It is, in fact, often the case that we will use a technology merely because we can; the operators adapt to the instrumentality, rather than the reverse. Human factors professionals understand the difficulty of trying to have an impact on products scheduled to be shipped tomorrow. However, historically, the technological tide has been stemmed on occasion. Recently, nuclear power was seriously curtailed by public opinion associated with accidents at Chernobyl and Three Mile Island. Major disasters are not, however, the only way to slow technology.

Historical incidents of new technology being resisted, sometimes successfully, have parallels in the ATC debate over flight progress strips. In the early 19th century, violent uprisings were held in England to protest the introduction of steam-powered weaving equipment, which was used to produce cloth that replaced hand-woven goods (Englander and Downing, 1988). The craftsmen, who had held a monopoly on their products, were replaced by equipment that could be operated by unskilled labourers to produce (what were considered by the craftsmen to be 'inferior') goods in a significantly shorter period. Thus, the skilled craftsmen, formerly independent contractors, were forced to become factory workers who earned much lower wages than they did previously. Some of the craftsmen rebelled, destroying the new equipment and burning the factor owners' homes. These 'Luddites,' named after Ned Ludd, a craftsman who was blamed for breaking some factory equipment, were arrested and many were convicted and either imprisoned or executed by the British government. Thus, although common use of the term Luddite connotes an unreasonable fear of technology, the historical facts suggest that a more complex debate about responsibility, quality, and livelihood existed.

Noel Perrin (1979) details in *Giving Up the Gun* how the Japanese adopted and then abandoned the gun, while Europeans rapidly replaced the sword. The reasons that the Japanese (but not the Europeans) reverted to the sword may have lessons relevant to the current flight strip debate. Added to the sword's (the strip's) ability to do the job of protecting islands (separating aircraft) there was a lack of universal support by the Samurai (controller) workforce and a general reaction against change initiated from the foreign, West (FAA). Most interesting is Perrin's argument that the new weapon did not fit in any aesthetic sense: the motions associated with a sword fit with the Japanese's sense of motion, but using a gun violated that sense. This is a similar analogy to the position held by some controllers and researchers: The strip fits seamlessly into the ATC environment–the computerised alternative may not.

To spin or not to spin? The flight strip conundrum

There is an inconsistency in the FAA's philosophy about the use of paper flight progress strips. On the one hand, there is a belief that flight progress data must be automated in order to increase NAS efficiency. On the other hand, there is another belief that retention of paper flight progress strips is necessary to ensure NAS safety. The FAA's recognition of both sides of the issue reflects the debate taking place throughout the US and in global ATC communities.

The focus of some research and more speculation has been on the consequences of removing the paper flight strip from the controller's arsenal. The issue has proven to be quite controversial for a number of reasons. The discussion has been on occasion contentious. Some view the issue as union versus management, as controller versus FAA. Some see it as an argument of those wanting to add technology simply because we can, against those concerned with safety; or as those stuck in the technological past against visionaries looking toward the future.

Because air traffic control is a high-risk, safety-critical industrial task, and because in its current state the level of safety is incredibly high, some stakeholders are naturally reluctant to 'fix something that isn't broken.' The controller, with the added issues of being the individual who must pay the legal – and psychological – debt should a catastrophe occur, is often an adamant proponent of the status quo.

The argument is sometimes made that using paper flight strips, especially in today's environment, is necessary to ensure the safety of the NAS. Presently, strips provide the only way to separate aircraft in US non-radar and oceanic environments. Even today, some sectors have no radar coverage while others have only partial radar coverage. No one disagrees that currently strips must be used to control traffic in non-radar environments. However, in the future, the use of global positioning system (GPS) satellites and automatic dependent surveillance – broadcast (ADS-B) may allow using a graphic display of non-radar information that supports more effective conduct of ATC, perhaps even involving a reduction in separation standards. Nevertheless, for the purposes of the current paper we restrict our arguments to the most immediate concern – can strips be eliminated in radar environments?

How do we decide?

The question of what information should enter the decision process is obviously an important one. Depending on to whom one listens, strips can either be an indispensable resource or an historical leftover. Thus, our consideration of different sources of information is more than an academic exercise because the ultimate fate of the paper flight progress strip varies depending on the sources of information given the most weight.

Ask the engineer?

How should we decide whether or not to replace paper flight progress strips? One possibility is to allow the software engineer to decide, who, after all, will be responsible for the coding of the final interface. However, the perspective of the engineer makes it difficult to discriminate possible use from valuable use. In addition, it is well understood by software engineers with a concern for their clients that this perspective requires testing with human users. In fact, the field of human-computer interaction exists because of the engineer's inability to understand the user.

Ask the controller?

One might think, and several have argued, that a good start is to consider the opinion of the expert user, in this case the ATC specialist. Who better, one might argue, to decide whether strips are needed? Although certainly a place to start, such surveys should not be a solution for a number of reasons. First, it is often difficult to reflect on devices used every day; a concern that would apply to the routine use of the strip by today's controllers. Just as engineers are thought to have trouble discriminating possible use from valuable use, controllers understandably seem to have difficulty discriminating required use from valuable use (e.g. Durso et al., under review). Second, people, have only inferential, not privileged, access to their thought processes; controllers would not necessarily be able to tell why they made a particular decision (e.g. Nisbett and Wilson, 1977). A compelling illustration comes from K. Patricia Cross (1992) who suggested that if we asked users of iceboxes in the early part of the last century to indicate what they needed or the improvements they would like, the answer would have been more ice, more often – not chemical refrigeration. In Durso et al. (under review), responses to interview questions seeking alternatives to particular strip markings was uninformative. For example, between 15% and 50% of the controllers, when asked what they could do rather than make their strip mark, believed there was no feasible alternative to making the specific mark or suggested making another strip mark. Third, users do not always agree on the value of a device. For strips, despite hyperbole in the literature to the contrary that 'controllers like strips,' (MacKay, 1999), we have found no unanimity of opinion, at least not in the United States. We have spoken with controllers who passionately cling to their strips, as well as those who blithely dismiss their value altogether. In fact, in Albright, Truitt, Barile, Vortac and Manning (1995), only one of 20 field controllers thought the strip could not be eliminated. Finally, controllers are no more likely to understand the scientific principles of control, generalisation, and causality than would any other person without training in scientific methods.

Nevertheless, input from expert users is a good start; an essential first step. This is true, not only because they understand their jobs better than anyone else, but also because some form of controller participation is needed to secure acceptance of the new system (Wickens, Mavor, Parasuraman and McGee, 1988). The FAA has, in fact, sponsored a number of workgroups on which controllers, supervisors, and researchers participate to identify specifications for new technologies. Unfortunately, turnover is sometimes rapid and because different controllers have different opinions, the development of specifications is sometimes slowed by changes.

Might the notion that controllers should decide be carried further, beyond workgroups and advisory panels? Perhaps controllers in the field could decide, on a strip-by-strip basis, whether or not to post a particular strip and whether or not to mark one that is posted. Truitt, Durso, Crutchfield, Moertl and Manning (2000) tested just such a procedure. Field controllers from Cleveland and Jacksonville ARTCCs controlled high-fidelity simulations either as they normally did or using an optional posting/marking procedure. Controllers posted and marked fewer strips in the optional condition as would be expected. Nevertheless, there were no detrimental effects in performance, workload, or team communication; and controllers preferred the optional posting procedure. Unfortunately, such optional procedures are inherently problematic because a controller who prefers using strips may relieve one who does not use strips at all. Preparing the sector for relief in such a situation would be, under the optional posting system, problematic. This is illustrative of a more general problem: Without regulations, communication breaks down.

Ask the anthropologist?

One problem with relying entirely on controllers is that they are not researchers. Perhaps one solution would be to have researchers become intimately familiar with the ATC situation. This is what anthropological approaches attempt to do.

To put our comments in context, we agree that the anthropological view has merit, especially in the willingness of researchers to learn the intimate details of the system – the environment, tasks, and operators – they are investigating. Consideration at this depth can certainly help frame research questions appropriately and prevent wasted time and effort.

Several researchers have taken an ethnographic perspective in an attempt to understand air traffic control (e.g. Berndtsson and Normark, 1999; Hughes, Randall and Shapiro, 1992; MacKay, 1999). Work by MacKay and by Berndtsson and Normark are perhaps some of the best and most recent investigations of air traffic control that take an anthropological approach. The two studies differ in interesting ways, including their apparent goals. Berndtsson and Normark do a solid job of describing what it is like to be a Copenhagen controller. The report has tremendous value to anyone interested in conducting research in that domain and to researchers conducting ATC research in general. The work is almost exclusively descriptive and shows uncharacteristic restraint in keeping conclusions from going beyond those which the anthropological methods and data allow.

MacKay (1999) also used ethnographic procedures and focused more exclusively on flight progress strips than did Berndtsson and Normark. The MacKay (1999) report also does a good job of description, but her attempts to go beyond this level of analysis are often problematic. Statements such as 'Air traffic controllers like paper flight strips' (p. 315), 'controllers subconsciously prepare for the arrival of new aircraft when they hear the sound of the strip printer,' (p. 326), 'paper strips ... take advantage of tactile memory' (p. 322) are non sequiturs and although some of the statements may be true, the casual use of words like *subconsciously* make it difficult to treat such statements as testable hypotheses. Such anthropological investigations, partly because little quantitative information is provided, make it difficult to separate the data from the researcher's interpretation. So when MacKay (1999) states that '(Maastricht) controllers were surprised at the complexity of the situation in Paris' (p. 334) and then in the same sentence adds that 'we had the sense that those (Maastricht) controllers were working harder' is a good example of how it is difficult to determine where data end and interpretation begins.

Certainly a researcher who enters an unfamiliar environment will bring a different perspective than the operators, in our case the controllers, who work in it. The anthropologist can, for example, help discriminate valuable use from either required use or possible use. By making explicit the implicit, this different, but informed, perspective can lead to insights and solutions not considered by those who have developed a functional fixedness or cognitive set about their workplace. Of course, if the anthropologist becomes too much like a controller in thinking, then he or she may also come to believe that the only way to improve the system is to get 'more ice.'

As the anthropologists become more familiar with the environment, they become more like the controllers in their understanding of the situation. Why prefer their opinion over the controller's? Ideally, the anthropologist will be an objective observer who has developed some of the knowledge of the operator without being biased by the experience. Unfortunately, in our opinion, this ideal situation rarely manifests. More traditional anthropological work (e.g. Mead, 1928) has been criticised (e.g. Freeman, 1999) for reaching inappropriate conclusions, over-interpreting ambiguous data by relying on predispositions, and relying heavily on one or two confederates. Presumably, such criticism may apply to human factors use of the anthropological approach as well. The perspective acquired by the anthropologist is usually not some average controller's perspective, but the perspective of a confederate who has for some reason agreed to serve in that role or who has been assigned, by union or management, to serve in that role. In addition, the confederate may be especially eager to please, providing the anthropologist with evidence that he or she divines would please the investigator.

We have asserted that consulting the controller is a good first step. We also believe that a good second step is to understand the system as deeply as does a good anthropologist. However, we believe that there are other steps on this peripatetic research journey. The other steps take a more traditional scientific perspective, including quantitative tools and experimental methods.

Ask the scientist?

Although much applied research has begun to embrace qualitative methods familiar to the anthropologist (see Durso, Nickerson, Schvaneveldt, Dumais, Lindsay and Chi, 1999, for a variety of applied methods), quantitative scientific methods should also be an integral part of resolving the flight progress strip conundrum. The discipline of psychology has adopted the scientific method, complete with quantitative measurement, statistical analysis, and rigorous control, as its epistemological engine. Like its qualitative sister disciplines in the social sciences, the quantitative methods of applied psychology can supply an informed, but objective, viewpoint different from the controller's. In our view, a good scientific field study would not neglect the opinions of the controller or the rigorous study of the anthropologists. Instead, it would build on this foundation by testing, empirically, the hypotheses that emerge from the ethnographic analysis.

The scientific method is not restricted to laboratory experiments, although it is generally accepted that attempts to prove that a variable (e.g. paper versus glass) *causes* changes in behaviour or cognition requires the kind of control one expects in an experiment. Scientific methods allow for naturalistic observations, surveys, and field experiments. However, understanding what is necessary to show causation is a valuable context in which to view these less controlled methods. These other scientific methods, however, typically have more external validity and ecological validity than do laboratory experiments.

Finally, quantitative measurement and statistical procedures are fundamental to scientific psychology. The precision offered by operational definitions and quantitative measurement helps make it clear when a procedure applies and when it does not, when a finding replicates and when it does not, and when something is data and when it is not. Well-trained scientists are also attuned to the need to distinguish empirical data from hypothetical constructs. Although qualitative researchers have argued that scientists also have their pre-theoretical biases (we agree), the problem is greatly magnified in anthropological procedures. We also agree that statistical methods do not guarantee that a conclusion is correct. In fact, it guarantees that there is some probability that it is not. However, statistical methods help to quantify the chances of error: There is a .05 chance that the difference we are reporting is not present in the general population.

Obviously, we suggest asking the scientist about whether or not to replace paper flight progress strips. However, we hope to have made it clear that scientists should begin in consultation with the operator, in our case the controller. They should then study the domain with the rigor of a good anthropologist. However, this study should end in well-reasoned hypotheses – and alternative hypotheses – that are subject to scientific test.

We do not mean to present science as a panacea. For example, science is a slow process. Efforts to generalise findings from one situation to another require several studies. Findings from US en route centres may or may not generalise to US towers or to en route ATC as it is conducted in Europe. In addition, there are situations that do not lend themselves to traditional scientific approaches. For example, the nature of rare events, such as operational errors, makes it difficult to apply quantitative methods. Moreover, while science is exquisite at evaluating different designs, and offers a huge literature on human strengths and weaknesses that one could use to guide design, standard scientific procedures have played less of a role in the actual design process.

Although we believe strongly that multiple methods are valuable, we are not merely advocating an all-inclusive position. We argue that different methodologies and approaches are valuable for different goals. To know the domain you are studying is a valuable lesson and one that is likely to save the efforts of a scientific study that in hindsight yields 'obvious' results. Scientific and anthropological methods provide valuable descriptive tools, but any attempt to go past a descriptive goal is best supported by scientific methods. Here, the question is whether paper flight progress strips are causally necessary to air traffic safety and performance.

Reasons to switch

Although the current system is incredibly safe, the safety levels enjoyed today are undoubtedly under pressure by the increasing numbers of flights evidenced over the past years and the continuing increases in flights anticipated in the future. Proponents of change argue that the procedures and technology in place today will be inadequate to alleviate the pressures placed on the air traffic system by greater traffic density, the airlines' hub systems, and the flying public's appetite for cheap, frequent flights. The airlines claim to have the technology necessary to make flying more efficient, but that ATC's outdated equipment cannot accommodate the new technologies. The inconvenience of delays witnessed by travellers and covered extensively by the media are the tip of an iceberg that–if nothing changes other than the number of flights–will ultimately compromise efficiency, and perhaps even safety, of air travel. Although terrorists' attacks have temporarily slowed the rise in demand for air travel, the pressures have been mitigated, not eliminated. For example, David Plavin, North American president of Airports Council International, said that airports should continue expansion projects (Fiorino, 2001).

From our review of the evidence, we believe that there are good reasons to switch from the paper flight progress strip to some electronic representation of flight data. People on both sides of the debate seem to acknowledge that the future will bring increasing pressure on the ATC system. Therefore, they agree, something should change. We argue here that changing the paper flight progress strip and its accompanying procedures is the part of the system to change. This is not to say that all automation works the way it was intended; new automation can, in fact, create potential for human error that was not anticipated before the technology was introduced (Billings, 1997). Thus, we argue not for a particular technology, but merely that the target for the new technology should be the paper flight progress strip.

Below, we make six arguments to support our assertion. First, paper strips are a roadblock to future improvements. Second, a modern technology substitute for the paper flight progress strip can make the controller's job easier. Third, the argument that controllers 'like strips' is simply not universally true, although there are clear pressures on controllers, and particularly facility managers, to continue to use strips. Fourth, many reasons for having paper flight progress strips are no longer relevant, even in the current system. Fifth, strips will not supply the functional fit in future environments that they arguably do today. Sixth, we address arguments that paper is inherently superior, that the strip has evolved into an artefact that has attributes other than those for which it was designed, and that strips are indispensable as a redundant backup system. Each of these points will be discussed in more detail over.

Roadblock to future automation

If change is required, why focus on the flight progress strip? Currently, not all flight plan information that controllers write on flight strips is entered into the host computer. While controllers enter altitude and route changes into the computer, they do not enter heading and speed changes, nor do they enter minor route deviations (for example, to avoid weather) that would put the aircraft back on the original route before it leaves the sector. However, in order for en route decision aiding tools and communications to have accurate information, the flight data entered into the host computer must be complete, accurate, and up-to-date. If controllers are required to enter accurate flight plan changes and keep up with strip marking, the increased workload of maintaining two data sources will likely introduce errors in one or the other. Thus, retaining paper strips prohibits not merely their automation, but also prevents the introduction of virtually all other intelligent automation aids.

Reduced workload

The second reason that paper must be automated is that maintaining two sets of records (by both making strip markings and entering information required by the ATC automation) is a monumental task that could easily overload the controller and reduce the effectiveness of new en route decision aids. The human factors plan for URET CCLD (Crown Communications, Inc., 1999) confirms this assertion. The plan said that controllers at facilities using the test version of URET learned the lesson that trying to use URET while simultaneously maintaining flight strips is not feasible; if controllers are required to maintain paper strips, they do not have the time to use the trial planning capability necessary to achieve FAA's expected efficiency and safety goals. Furthermore, electronic and handwritten flight data may contain different information because one is updated more rapidly than the other, potentially resulting in errors, confusion, and increased workload.

Electronic representation of flight data can reduce, in principle, the controllers' workload considerably. Strip marking requires effort that is often used in record keeping, but that could more profitably be used in separating airplanes and ensuring that flights are more efficient. For example, Albright, Truitt, Barile, Vortac, and Manning (1995) showed that field controllers using the ARTCC's dynamic simulator (DYSIM) who did not have access to flight progress strips spent more time looking at the radar than they did when strips were present. Because most electronic flight data can update automatically, just as information on the radar updates, the controller's workload, at least in some situations, will be reduced.

With modern technology, there are few pieces of information that cannot electronically be gathered, displayed, and transferred to other controllers. The situations that do not lend themselves to such automation (assuming no improvements in voice recognition), such as noting pilot requests that cannot yet be accommodated or indicating clearances that have been issued but not yet responded to, may be addressed in other ways in future automation, or even with a notepad. MacKay (1999) disparages the use of notepads, thinking of them as a backhanded admission that paper strips should be retained. However, there is a difference between noting all possible control actions for all flights and noting the few instances that require a memory aid.

We (e.g. Vortac et al., 1994) have shown that a very large number of the controller's activities are involved in board management responsibilities. If the time and workload saved by eliminating record keeping compensates for any perceived benefits obtained from strips, then removal of the responsibility for marking strips would be reasonable *even if* there were some advantages of paper flight progress strips. Consider, for example, the fact that 'moving' flight progress strips was the most frequent activity in Durso et al. (under review), occurring about seven times a minute. Controllers judged movement as having a benefit. However, controller-judges rated movement as low importance, and in controlled studies discussed later we note that eliminating movement did not influence performance. So, why do controllers move strips? We believe it is because it is an important part of managing the strips themselves. Thus, like a bureaucracy, flight strip management spawns its own infrastructure.

So how can we assume that a perceived benefit is not a real one? The techniques and results discussed thus far, whether qualitative or quantitative, cannot resolve that question. For example, observing that controllers mark on strips cannot reveal the value of marking. Asking controllers why they make a mark tells us what the controller perceives as a benefit, not what benefits are actually observed. The answers to such questions require comparisons against control conditions that differ only along the dimension of interest.

Vortac, Edwards, Fuller, and Manning (1993) presented controllers with simulations of air traffic using high-fidelity en route simulators at the US FAA's ATC training facility in Oklahoma City. The researchers prevented controllers from writing on or manipulating strips by gluing the strip holders together and removing their pencils. Results showed no deficits, and in fact some benefits, in the restricted strip condition. Controllers were able to grant more pilot requests and to grant them sooner, presumably because elimination of strip marking requirements freed time to act on these requests.

Of course, in the Vortac et al. (1993) study, the information on the strips was still visible. Perhaps the lack of impact on performance suggests that strip marking was unnecessary, not that the strips and their data were unnecessary. However, Albright, et al. (1995) removed the strips entirely. The controllers did compensate for the lack of strips by requesting more flight plan readouts from the CRD, but these requests did not hurt performance. Interesting, although some controllers complained that asking for flight plans caused them to pay less attention to the PVD, in fact, controllers spent more time looking at the scope, not less; with strips, 57% of the time controllers watched the radar display compared with 76% when they had no strips.

Finally, Vortac, Barile, Albright, Truitt, Manning and Bain (1996) gave controllers a one-line electronic strip that contained only some of the information normally present on the paper strip. Again, any writing or movement of the strip was eliminated or mediated through the system's input devices. No deficits were observed compared with a condition where traffic was controlled normally. Thus, in controlled experiments, the controllers easily compensated for the lack of strips and did so in such a way as to – if anything – improve performance as measured by indices like granting pilot requests and time-on-scope.

Controllers like strips?

It is obvious that most ATC facility managers believe that paper flight strip usage is essential in all sectors in today's environment because most continue to require controllers to perform full strip marking even though optional strip marking is allowed (Federal Aviation Administration, 2000; Section 6-1-6). One reason that ATC managers may continue to emphasise strip usage, even at sectors with full radar coverage, is that many learned to control traffic using only strips (or the combination of strips and primary radar) and so believe that using paper strips is an essential part of ATC. Many controllers and most managers believe that strips should always be consulted to correlate radar data with flight data and predict potential conflicts before an aircraft enters a sector, while many other controllers prefer to identify aircraft by looking at the data block and predict conflicts by examining the targets on the radar display.

Some controllers prefer to access flight plan information using the computer while others instead prefer to read paper strips. Most of the aircraft information available in the flight plan is also available from the host computer without having to use the strip. For example, controllers may enter a flight plan readout command to view text included in an aircraft's flight plan on the DSR CRD view

307

(window). Another command, the route display, shows a line on the situation display that follows an aircraft's route through the sector.

Whether a controller prefers to use the computer or flight strips to accomplish different activities is a matter of preference (Manning, 2000). Some controllers feel they do not need to use strips, even in today's environment, or feel they do not need to look at them again after an initial examination just before an aircraft enters the sector. Other controllers prefer to glance at the strips to obtain flight plan information rather than make the computer entries required to access the information. Manning (2000) found that two styles described the methods most controllers used to interact with strips – when using one style, controllers de-emphasised marking but looked at the strips occasionally, whereas when using the other style, controllers emphasised the traditional role of strips (marking fully and using them to obtain all flight plan information).

Finally, even controllers who would like to eliminate strips have over-learned and extensively practiced flight strip marking behaviours. Controllers are taught and encouraged to use strips throughout their Academy and field training (Federal Aviation Administration, 1998; Appendix 4; Stein, 1994) and part of their OJT instruction/evaluation is based on how well they use flight progress strips (Federal Aviation Administration, 1998; Appendix 2). Accuracy of strip marking is reviewed during periodic over-the-shoulder evaluations, and investigations of operational errors always check on whether flight strips were marked properly. Thus, flight strip usage is required, trained, and emphasised extensively in en route ATC.

Obsolete uses

It is also important to realise that the strip, virtually unchanged for years, does not serve all the same purposes now that it once did. In the past, because of the quality and availability of radar coverage, controllers would often control traffic manually, that is by using crossing-fixes and estimated times of arrival at those fixes. Today, except in a few parts of the US (e.g. over the Rockies, and in small areas without full radar coverage), controllers rarely control traffic without radar, and thus rarely use some of the information printed on the strip.

The paper flight progress strips also served originally as a legal record should an investigation prove necessary. In fact, in the US most en route centres still follow this directive and require controllers to mark strips: 'to post current data on air traffic and clearances required for control and other air traffic control services' (Federal Aviation Administration, 2001; Section 2-3-1). However, today, most air traffic activity is automatically recorded. For example, system analysis recordings (SAR) record all aircraft movements and host data entries, and audio recordings are made of all pilot/controller communications, communications between controllers working at different sectors, and transfers of position responsibility. The data block contains some information about flight plan updates, such as the

308

assigned altitude. In addition, the identity of the sector that has control of the aircraft is displayed in the data block. Thus, most of the information marked on strips is redundant with other recorded ATC data.

As we mentioned, optional strip marking may be authorised at certain sectors for aircraft that meet certain requirements (Federal Aviation Administration, 2000; Section 6-1-6); however, managers at facilities not currently using URET have chosen not to adopt that option. Instead, most en route facilities maintain extensive localised strip marking orders that specify facility-specific procedures for making strip markings and continue to emphasise the use of flight strips. In part, this is because managers believe that controllers will remember important information about a flight if they write that information on a paper strip.

Some controllers have developed other methods for remembering that they have accomplished certain tasks that do not require writing on strips. For example, the length of the leader line can be reduced to zero after communications for an aircraft are transferred to another sector. In addition, the position of the data block in relation to the position symbol can be changed to indicate that transfer of communications has occurred. If a controller always accomplishes certain tasks immediately (such as coordinating a speed change with the next sector) he or she may not feel it necessary to write down the fact that the coordination has been accomplished. In fact, changes are being made to the host system to increase the amount of flight plan information shown on the situation display. For example, an extra line is being added to the data block that will allow the controller to record issued speeds and headings. When this is accomplished, requiring the controller to write this information on the flight strip as well as enter it into the computer will unnecessarily increase the workload.

Anachronistic strips

The introduction of some technology into a work environment, such as a new radar system, often has consequences on other technologies, such as the paper flight progress strip. For example, the DSR workstation recently introduced in the US en route centres to replace aging equipment reduced the amount of space available to post flight progress strips because the 20' by 20' (508mm x 508mm) display is so much larger than the PVD used previously and the RA monitor is much larger than the CRD used previously. The new flight progress strips for the en route DSR are in fact smaller, reduced from the original 8' x $1^3/_8$' (203mm x 35mm) to $6^3/_8$' x $1^3/_8$' (162mm x 35mm). FAA-sponsored research to investigate whether an even smaller strip could be used (Durso, Truitt, Hackworth, Albright, Bleckley and Manning, 1998), but it was found to be too small for many en route applications. So, the debate about the value of paper flight progress strips was suspended temporarily as stakeholders tried to determine how to change the size of the strip to compensate for the reduced space available while not entirely eliminating the strips or their functionality. If planned procedural changes are implemented, the value of the strip's information will become even less. For example, the US is considering 'free flight,' (RTCA, 1995) a change in procedures that will allow pilots to fly direct routes, and in later phases, may allow pilots to vector (e.g. around weather) when necessary without being told to do so by a controller, in fact without necessarily notifying the controller. In such an environment, information on a paper flight strip will become increasingly useless as the control of air traffic becomes more tactical and less strategic. Although there is some evidence that situation awareness will be compromised in free flight (Willems and Truitt, 1999), there is no evidence about the role of strips.

Problems with arguments to keep paper

Arguments to keep paper are of three kinds. One argument is that paper has inherent advantages to glass. A second argument is that the paper flight progress strip has evolved and acquired functionality not anticipated by the original design. These functions are typically thought to be ancillary cognitive functions. The third argument views paper strips as an irreplaceable backup should the electronic system fail.

Inherent advantages   Researchers have pointed out the disadvantages of screen presentation compared with paper in general (Luff, Heth and Greatbach, 1992). Luff et al. argued that there are five disadvantages of screen presentation compared to paper: 1) Keyboard entries are more difficult, 2) the range of entries is restricted, 3) computer entries restrict the sequence of input, 4) glass representations restrict the mobility of the information through the workplace, and 5) screen displays offer fewer ways of differentiating a document.

Luff et al. have done a nice job articulating problems with glass, but for our purposes, the question is the extent to which these issues apply to ATC and, if they do apply, the extent to which concomitant benefits outweigh the disadvantages. Point 1 applies only to the entries that must be made. In ATC, many entries made today are unnecessary for operational purposes. Most entries that are required to be made for operational purposes are already made by keyboard entry; often the strip marking is made in addition to entries via keyboard. Entries studied in controlled research settings (e.g. Albright et al., 1995) that are made only by pen for ancillary purposes may not, in reality, be necessary at all. Thus, although Luff et al.'s first point is well taken, in ATC it is not clear how many additional keyboard entries will be necessary.

In ATC, there are sometimes advantages to restricting the range of entries (point 2); this need for restricted range of entries manifests even with paper strips: Many facilities have their own strip-marking guides to help standardise marking. What seems critical from point 2 is not that entries will be restricted with glass, but that they will be restricted inappropriately. It is important that entries be developed to take into account the important functions needed in flight data representations.

Point 3 would be highly dependent on the particular software implementation. If, and it is a big if, all of the electronic representations can be presented on one screen, problems with paging and sequential entries can be eliminated. In ATC, although the tasks are performed in the order the controller prefers, evidence exists that interacting with the paper flight progress strips is already treated as a separate 'board management module' (Vortac, 1993); Vortac and colleagues showed that controllers waited until the activity slowed down to update the strips, and then did so in a burst of strip activity.

Moving information around the workplace (point 4) is actually quite difficult now with paper strips. The mission-critical nature of ATC minimises occasions when information on the strip can be passed hand-to-hand. Once information is represented electronically, this concern should be reduced. At one level, point 5, differentiating aircraft, can be argued to be of little concern given that the radar display distinguishes aircraft spatially. Overall, applying general concerns about paper to the ATC domain suggests that the abstract limitations of glass will not apply.

Evolution of strips Arguments that are more particularly addressed at flight progress strips exist in the literature. Many of these arguments derive from the suspicion that the flight progress strip evolved over the years to meet demands of the ATC task that may not have been part of the original design. There is some evidence to warrant such a concern. Research has shown that designers of a high-tech, electronic device intended to replace a low-tech device that has evolved over many years of use, can miss the nuances provided by the older device. For example, the speed bugs associated with the airspeed indicator of the MD-80 have been used in ways never intended in the initial design process. Redesigning an indicator that did not realise these other uses would prove problematic and inferior to the device it replaced (see Hutchins, 1995).

Opinions of controllers often fuel this concern. Even in our data (Durso et al., under review) the comments made by controllers suggest particular benefits. Although controlled laboratory work that we have discussed indicates that some of these opinions about the beneficial functions of strips do not seem to have an impact on performance. As an example, while controllers who did not have access to strips (Albright et al., 1995) thought they were important, their performance suggested otherwise. Thus, while the possibility exists that an artefact could have evolved ancillary cognitive value that aids performance, there is no evidence that flight progress strips are that type of artefact.

MacKay (1999) notes that when she visited a facility that had eliminated strips, paper was nevertheless used throughout the facility. When we visited a facility in the US that was using a decision aid that provided electronic flight data representations, there was no apparent use of paper. However, our visit over a two-day period was not to assess the use of paper, and so we too have no quantitative data.

Finally, the Vortac, Edwards, Fuller and Manning (1993) study mentioned earlier employed several cognitive measures to test directly the speculation that controllers who could not interact with strips would suffer performance deficits because of underlying cognitive deficits. It has been proposed that potential deficits in cognitive processing could occur as a result of automating flight progress strips (Hopkin, 1991; Isaac and Guselli, 1996). For example, Isaac and Guselli (1996) suggested that writing information on a flight progress strip (and recognising that they have written something) reinforces controllers' working memory. Moreover, physically manipulating strips should facilitate both memory for and understanding of the information contained there. And physically interacting with strips should improve prospective memory, which is remembering that something needs to be done in the future.

Not only did Vortac, Edwards, Fuller and Manning (1993) find no performance decrement, but neither were cognitive measures of attentional engagement, visual search, radar recall, flight progress strip recall, and planning affected. The only cognitive measure affected was one of prospective memory, and that one was facilitated when the controller did not have to interact with the strips.

Backup issue Strips provide a hard copy backup in case of a system failure at the facility level; a failure so severe that the first-line backup system, DARC, is also knocked out. The notion that the paper flight progress strip is the last barrier to disaster after a power failure may be overstated. One controller, when asked about the strips as a backup for outages, replied that there would be chaos with the strips as well. In some power failures, neighbouring centres have expanded their coverage to handle the affected area. During some types of failures, communications are terminated so it would not matter whether or not strips were available. In addition, the main reason for needing strips during a system failure is simply to be able to identify the aircraft under control of a sector, and *not* to provide extensive ATC services. An electronic system that represents the last known state of the airspace could be maintained on the display by an alternative battery backup. Thus, we see the backup issue as one that can be easily solved once a decision is made about the future of the flight progress strip, yet it may be this backup issue that drives the decision about the future of the flight progress strip.

Making the transition

It might be argued not only that the switch to electronic representation of flight data is prudent, but also that it should happen sooner, rather than later. First, it seems only reasonable to take advantage of the advances in information technology when old machines (and software) are replaced with new ones. Second, some groups encourage the reduction of paper flight strip usage now, in anticipation of new technologies. Indeed, if reliance on flight strips is reduced now, it might be easier for controllers to adopt new habits regarding the use of electronic flight data in the future. Finally, we note that in the US, the controllers hired in 1981 after the President's dismissal of the Professional Air Traffic Controllers Organization (PATCO) controllers who went on strike are reaching eligible retirement ages and many will be eligible to retire within a decade.

From this perspective, the question is not whether flight progress strips will be replaced but rather how can those who are resistant to change among the US controller workforce be persuaded to accept the change? Outside the US, change may be even more contentious. MacKay (1999) relates the fact that French controllers demanded and received a bonus for using a keyboard to enter modifications in flight plans. She relates (from a dissertation by Poirot-Delpech, 1991) that one controller put it this way: 'If we had not received something interesting in exchange, we never would have done it.'

Of course, a critical part of the transition will be the development of a system that effectively supplies the controller with the information needed. The new representation of flight data may, but need not, look like a glass version of the paper strip. It might range from a copy of today's flight progress strip, to a one-line flight plan entry, to a time-accelerated projection of aircraft positions on the radar screen, to representations that have yet to be imagined. Input into the new system may range from standard keyboard/trackball entry to provocative ideas like MacKay's (1999) idea to use paper-like input to entry methods that resemble controllers' physical movements (e.g. Mertz, Chatty, and Vinot's, 2000, Digistrips interface) to voice recognition. We turn now to characteristics that are likely to be part of the replacement.

SPIN

We are developing a theoretical abstraction of the flight progress strip replacement system that we have named SPIN. The Shift from Paper Information envisioned to be necessary over the next decade must take place in an informed and cooperative environment. The motivation behind SPIN is not to replace paper flight data representations in the far future, but merely to aid in the design of a transition system, one explicitly designed to allow the socio-cultural transition to proceed. Although we do not have the complete picture, we do have pieces to the puzzle. We know what, technically, the capabilities are of present day computational systems. We also know, based on the results of scientific research, the important actions, the ones that are taken frequently, the operational value of those actions, and their cognitive/behavioural benefits as perceived by today's field controller. If it is premature to rip strips from the controller's hand, then the decision makers should take these pieces of the puzzle into account and build a transitional electronic flight data system.

SPIN assumes that transition may be slow, primarily because of the current workforce's history with paper strips. Transition should take place in phases, eliminating those aspects of flight progress strip use that are redundant or anachronistic based on available research. Thus, consideration of prior studies, temporal patterns of marking, and controller comments all lead SPIN to suggest that a reduction in strip marking should precede a reduction in strip availability. SPIN has many other specific components that derive directly from the scientific work. As examples, if automation is applied to the strip markings/actions believed to be important during the strip observation study (Durso et al., under review), then four categories of markings (issued clearances, coordinated clearances, non-clearance co-ordinations, including pointouts, and information updates) should be addressed first. One strategy for automating these markings is to determine how best to accommodate their perceived benefits, regardless of whether or not these perceptions are accurate.

For instance, if a mark is perceived to benefit memory, then it is necessary to display updated flight plan information as changes occur so the controller can examine the information as needed and not have to remember it. To determine whether flight plan information is accurate and ascertain how the flight plan has evolved, it may be necessary to view a history of clearance changes. This history does not need to be displayed all the time but should be available to observe only when needed. As another example, electronic representations that benefit communications must emphasise information that a team member can detect easily, without requiring much interpretation. SPIN suggests that the automation replacement be placed at the workstation between the R and RA controllers, allowing the communication benefits of the flight data representation to manifest most directly, thus improving communication and reducing workload.

Reducing workload further can occur with a reduced number of message entry methods. Both team members should be able to update the information to support different strip marking procedures used at different facilities. Specifically, at some facilities the R controller marks the clearances that he/she issued, while at others the RA controller marks the clearances that the R controller issued. Because these facility differences are real in the transition workforce, SPIN emphasises that a strip replacement should be flexible enough to accommodate both methods of recording issued clearances rather than requiring controllers at one facility to change the way they do business at the same time that they have to change the way they record strip markings.

Combining electronic methods that support specific strip markings having multiple perceived benefits will be more complicated. For example, in the strip observation study, markings concerning issued clearances were perceived to benefit memory, communications, organisation, and reduced workload. To support all these benefits, an electronic representation should be visible to all team members, display current flight plan information, have an available history that can be examined if necessary, be easy to enter, and support modification by all team members.

At the same time, a paper backup, such as a notepad can be used to write down specific information that is inconvenient to record electronically and can be used to highlight information that needs to be emphasised to the other team member.

SPIN requires that some flight data representation survive a power failure, suggesting the need for automation with battery backup for a last-position display.

Conclusions

This paper has considered research and opinions concerning both the need to eliminate paper flight strips and the need to retain them. If ATC automation enhancements are to be realised in the future, it will be necessary to supply them with increasingly specific and accurate data regarding an aircraft's position and any clearances that have been issued. Although aircraft positional data can be provided by surveillance methods (radar, ADS-B), clearance information must be provided by the controller. If controllers are required to maintain two data sources by entering clearance information into the computer and maintaining the same information on paper flight strips, the result will be increased workload and increased likelihood of error (in one source or the other). Thus, we must get rid of paper because writing on strips will not support the goal of maintaining an accurate database for the automation's use.

However, today, many controllers, especially those in management, strongly believe that it is necessary to retain flight strips. At present, there is no universally accepted method for performing the same functions supported by strip marking without the use of paper strips. Consequently, some controllers have developed short-cuts (such as accessing the aircraft type using the flight plan readout function of the current computer system) or cues (such as setting the length of the leader line to 0 after transferring communications for a flight to the next sector) that they believe sufficiently replace important functions of strips. However, other functions, such as making a check mark next to the altitude when a pilot checks on a frequency, or circling a clearance when it has been coordinated, cannot be duplicated using the DSR system and, thus, a controller who does not mark strips must somehow remember that he/she has accomplished these tasks. Some controllers and managers believe it is always necessary to record this information on strips, whereas other controllers feel confident in their ability to remember all the relevant information.

Another concern regarding the elimination of paper strips is what happens when the system goes down or the power goes out? Although backup systems significantly reduce the likelihood of a failure that would result in a facility-wide blackout of radar displays while leaving communication capabilities intact, the possibility of such a failure remains, and such failures have occurred occasionally.

So, should flight progress data be spun from paper into glass? Most of the research indicates that no performance impairments would occur and some performance improvements would be realised. In addition to laboratory work, operational use of URET has resulted in general acceptance of the tool as a strip replacement. It might be argued that the research is based on laboratory studies having limited generalisability, and the operational use occurred at centres that may have different types of operations than some other centres in the US. Certainly, additional testing in specific environments would be prudent (sectors having partial radar coverage, providing approach control services, or where extensive holding occurs). For example, in Durso et al. (under review), weather happened not to be a factor during the observations, raising the concern that holding, which accounted for less than 2% of the marks, was underrepresented. It would also be reasonable to place controllers in different situations under controlled conditions. For example, in Albright et al. (1995) controllers were not required to pass information (i.e. headings and speed) to another sector. Therefore, this communicative function of strips may not have been stressed. Additional research addressing issues such as the appropriate location of displayed information (on the situation display as opposed to an auxiliary display) would also be of value. Currently, however, there is no scientific or operational evidence that suggests that automation of flight data will have negative consequences.

The immediate issue, however, is not whether glass will ultimately replace paper, but how the transition necessitated by socio-cultural factors should proceed. While some feel it is desirable to reduce or eliminate the use of flight strips in anticipation of new technologies (in order to break the habit before controllers are introduced to a new tool), others, including most managers and some controllers, are reluctant to reduce their usage before an electronic flight strip replacement becomes available. As a result, not all strip replacements will be found to be acceptable. Moreover, of course, the issue of what to do when the power goes off is still under discussion. Well-motivated changes in procedures as well as an electronic strip replacement that incorporates the important functionality of strips will be important parts of a transitional environment for the current workforce.

It is clear the implementation of advanced tools, technology, and associated procedures necessary to replace paper flight strips is a complicated and important issue. It is also clear, however, that viable solutions will require the subject matter knowledge of the expert controller and the scientific knowledge of the aviation researcher.

References

Albright, C.A., Truitt, T.R., Barile, A.L., Vortac, O.U. and Manning, C.A. (1995). Controlling traffic without flight progress strips: Compensation, workload, performance, and opinion. *Air Traffic Control Quarterly, 2*, 229-248.

Berndtsson, J. and Normark, M. (1999). The coordinative functions of flight strips. *Proceedings of the international ACM Siggroup conference on supporting group work*, New York: ACM Press, 101-110.

Billings, C.E. (1997). *Aviation automation: The search for a human-centered approach.* Mahwah, NJ: Lawrence Erlbaum Associates, Inc.

Cross, K.P. (1992). *Adults as Learners: Increasing Participation and Facilitating Learning.* Jossey-Bass Publishing.

Crown Communications, Inc. (1999, August). *User Request Evaluation Tool (URET) Core Capabilities Limited Deployment (CCLD) Human Factors Plan.* (Document No. G004-001-01). Washington, DC: Author.

Durso, F.T., Batsakes, P.J., Crutchfield, J.M., Braden, J.B. and Manning, C.A. (Under review). Flight Progress Strips while Working Live Traffic: Frequencies, Importance, and Perceived Benefits.

Durso, F.T., Hackworth, C.A., Truitt, T.R., Crutchfield, J., Nikolic, D. and Manning, C.A. (1997). Situation awareness as a predictor of performance for en route air traffic controllers. *Air Traffic Control Quarterly, 6*, 1-20.

Durso, F.T., Nickerson, R., Schvaneveldt, R.W., Dumais, S., Lindsay, D.S. and Chi, M.T.H. (1999). *Handbook of Applied Cognition,* Wiley: Chicester.

Durso, F.T., Truitt, T.R., Hackworth, C.A., Albright, C.A., Bleckley, M.K. and Manning, C.A. (1998). *Reduced Flight Progress Strips in En Route ATC Mixed Environments.* (Report No. DOT/FAA/AM-98/26). Washington, DC: Office of Aviation Medicine.

Durso, F.T., Truitt, T.R., Hackworth, C.A., Crutchfield, J.M. and Manning, C.A. (1998). En Route Operational Errors and Situation Awareness. *International Journal of Aviation Psychology, 8*, 177-192.

Edwards, M.B., Fuller, D.K., Vortac, O.U. and Manning, C.A. (1995). The role of flight progress strips in en route air traffic control: A time series analysis. *International Journal of Human-Computer Studies, 43*, 1-13.

Englander, D. and Downing, T. (1988). The Mystery of Luddism. *History Today, 38*, 18.

Federal Aviation Administration (1998, July). *Air Traffic Technical Training.* (FAA Order 3120.4J). Washington, DC: Author.

Federal Aviation Administration. (1999, January). En Route/Oceanic. In, *Blueprint for Modernization: An Overview of the National Airspace System Architecture, Version 4.0.* [Online]. Available: http://www.faa.gov/nasarchitecture/blueprnt/oceanic.htm.

Federal Aviation Administration (2000, February). *Facility Operation and Administration.* (FAA Order 7210.3R). Washington, DC: Author.

Federal Aviation Administration (2001, July). *Air Traffic Control.* (FAA Order 7110.65M, Change 3). Washington, DC: Author.

Fiorino, F. (2001, Ed.), ACI urges airport expansion. *Aviation Week and Space Technology, 155*, p. 17.

Freeman, D. (1999). *The Fateful Hoaxing of Margaret Mead: A Historical Analysis of Her Samoan Research.* Westview Press.

Hopkin, V.D. (1991). Automated flight strip usage: Lessons from the functions of paper strips. In, *Proceedings of the AIAA/NASA/FAA/HFS Symposium on Challenges in Aviation Human Factors: The National Plan*, Tyson's Corner, VA, 62-64.

Hughes, J.A., Randall, D. and Shapiro, D. (1992). Faltering from ethnography to design. In, Turner and Kraut (eds.), *CSCW '92, Proceedings of the Conference on Computer-Supported Cooperative Work,* Toronto, Canada, New York: ACM Press, 115-122.

Hutchins, E. (1995). How a cockpit remembers its speeds. *Cognitive Science, 19,* 265-288.

Isaac, A. and Guselli, J. (1996). Technology and the air traffic controller: Performance panacea or human hindrance? In, B.J. Hayward and A.R. Lowe (Eds.) Applied *Aviation Psychology: Achievement, change, and challenge* (Proceedings of the Third Australian Aviation Psychology Symposium). Aldershot: Ashgate Publishing Limited.

Landauer, T.K. (1995). *The Trouble with Computers.* Cambridge: MIT Press.

Luff, P., Heath, C. and Greatbach, D. 1992. Tasks-in-interaction: Paper and screen based documentation in collaborative activity. In, *Proceedings of CSCW '92.* ACM Press, New York, 163-170.

MacKay, W.E. (1999). Is paper safer? The role of paper flight strips in air traffic control. *ACM Transactions on Computer-Human Interaction, 6,* 311-340.

Manning, C.A. (2000). Controller opinions of flight progress strip usage in today's en route environment. In, R.S. Jensen and J. Callister (Eds.) *Proceedings of the Tenth International Symposium on Aviation Psychology.* Columbus, OH: Ohio State University.

Mead, M. (1928). *Coming of Age in Samoa.* New York: William Morrow.

Mertz, C., Chatty, S. and Vinot, J. (2000, June). Pushing the limits of ATC user interface design beyond SandM interaction: the DigiStrips experience. In, *Proceedings of 3rd USA/Europe Air Traffic Management RandD Seminar,* Napoli, Italy.

Nisbett, R.E. and Wilson, T.D. (1977). Telling more than we can know: Verbal reports on mental processes. *Psychological Review, 84,* 231-259.

Perrin, N. (1979). *Giving Up the Gun: Japan's Reversion to the Sword.* Boston: David R. Godine.

Rodgers, M.D. and Nye, L. (1993, December). Factors associated with the severity of operational errors at en route air traffic control centers. In, M.D. Rodgers (Ed.) *An examination of the operational error data base for en route air traffic control centers.* (Report No. DOT/FAA/AM-93/22). Washington, DC: Office of Aviation Medicine, 11-26.

RTCA (1995). *Final Report of RTCA Task Force 3: Free Flight Implementation.* Washington, DC: RTCA, Inc.

Stein, E. (1994). *The controller memory guide: Concepts from the field.* (Report No. DOT/FAA/CT-TN94/28). Atlantic City, NJ: Federal Aviation Administration.

Truitt, T.R., Durso, F.T., Crutchfield, J.M., Moertl, P.M. and Manning, C.A. (2000). Test of an optional strip posting and marking procedure. *Air Traffic Control Quarterly, 8,* 131-154.

Vortac, O.U. (1993). Should Hal open the pod bay doors? An argument for modular automation. In, D.J. Garland and J.A. Wise (1993), *Human Factors and Advanced Aviation Technologies*, Embry-Riddle, 159-163.

Vortac, O.U., Barile, A.B., Albright, C.A., Truitt, T.R., Manning, C.A. and Bain, D. (1996). Automation of flight data in air traffic control. In, D. Hermann, C. McEvoy, C. Hertzog, P. Hertel and M.K. Johnson, (Eds.) *Basic and Applied Memory Research*, Volume 2. Mahwah, NJ: Lawrence Erlbaum Associates.

Vortac, O.U., Edwards, M.B., Fuller, D.K. and Manning, C.A. (1993). Automation and cognition in air traffic control: An empirical investigation. *Applied Cognitive Psychology, 7*, 631-651.

Vortac, O.U., Edwards, M.B., Jones, J.P., Manning, C.A. and Rotter, A.J. (1993). En route air traffic controllers' use of flight progress strips: A graph-theoretic analysis. *International Journal of Aviation Psychology, 3*, 324-343.

Vortac, O.U., Edwards, M.B. and Manning, C.A. (1994). Sequences of actions for individual and teams of air traffic controllers. *Human-Computer Interaction, 9*, 319-343.

Vortac, O.U., Edwards, M.B. and Manning, C.A. (1995). Functions of external cues in prospective memory. *Memory, 3*, 201-219.

Wickens, C.D., Mavor, A., Parasuraman, R and McGee, B. (1998). *The future of Air Traffic Control*. Washington DC: National Academy of Sciences.

Willems, B. and Truitt, T.R. (1999). *Implications of reduced involvement in en route air traffic control*. (Report No. DOT/FAA/CT-TN99/22). Atlantic City, NJ: Federal Aviation Administration.

Acknowledgements

Thanks to Paul Krois, Larry Bailey, and Henry Mogilka for comments on an earlier version of this manuscript.

Index